BOWLING, BEATNIKS, AND BELL-BOTTOMS

Pop Culture of 20th- and 21st-Century America

BOWLING, BEATNIKS, AND BELL-BOTTOMS

Pop Culture of 20th- and 21st-Century America

VOLUME 3: 1940s–1950s

Cynthia Johnson, Editor
Lawrence W. Baker, Project Editor

U·X·L
A part of Gale, Cengage Learning

GALE
CENGAGE Learning·

Detroit • New York • San Francisco • New Haven, Conn • Waterville, Maine • London

GALE
CENGAGE Learning

Bowling, Beatniks, and Bell-Bottoms: Pop Culture of 20th- and 21st-Century America, 2nd ed.

Cynthia Johnson, Editor

Project Editor: Lawrence W. Baker

Rights Acquisition and Management: Robyn Young

Composition: Evi Abou-El-Seoud

Manufacturing: Wendy Blurton

Imaging: John Watkins

Product Design: Kristine Julien

© 2012 Gale, Cengage Learning

For product information and technology assistance, contact us at
Gale Customer Support, 1-800-877-4253.
For permission to use material from this text or product, submit all requests online at **www.cengage.com/permissions.**
Further permissions questions can be emailed to **permissionrequest@cengage.com**

Front cover photographs: (Left to right) The Game of Life, © CameraShots-Concept/Alamy; Radio City Music Hall, © Sam Dao/Alamy; Slinky, © Garry Gay/Workbook Stock/Getty Images; Hollywood sign, © Gavin Hellier/Alamy. Back cover photographs: (Top to bottom) Nickelodeon, © Lewis Hine/Historical/Corbis; Bobbysoxers, © Bettmann/Corbis; Man bowling, © H. Armstrong Roberts/ClassicStock/Alamy.

LIBRARY OF CONGRESS CATALOGING-IN-PUBLICATION DATA

Bowling, beatniks, and bell-bottoms : pop culture of 20th- and 21st-century America / Cynthia Johnson, editor ; Lawrence W. Baker, project editor. —2nd ed.
    v. cm. —
    Contents: v. 1. 1900s-1910s — v. 2. 1920s-1930s — v. 3. 1940s-1950s — v. 4. 1960s-1970s — v. 5. 1980s-1990s — v. 6. 2000-2009.
    ISBN-13: 978-1-4144-1165-1 (set : alk. paper)
    ISBN-10: 1-4144-1165-0 (set : alk. paper)
    ISBN-13: 978-1-4144-1166-8 (v. 1 : alk. paper)
    ISBN-10: 1-4144-1166-9 (v. 1 : alk. paper)
    [etc.]
    1. United States—Civilization—20th century—Miscellanea—Juvenile literature. 2. United States—Civilization—21st century—Miscellanea—Juvenile literature. 3. Popular culture—United States—History—20th century—Miscellanea—Juvenile literature. 4. Popular culture—United States—History—21st century—Miscellanea—Juvenile literature. I. Johnson, Cynthia, 1969- II. Baker, Lawrence W.
    E169.1.B7825 2012
    306.097309'04—dc23   2012002579

Gale
27500 Drake Rd.
Farmington Hills, MI, 48331-3535

978-1-4144-1165-1 (set)
978-1-4144-1166-8 (vol. 1)
978-1-4144-1167-5 (vol. 2)
978-1-4144-1168-2 (vol. 3)
978-1-4144-1169-9 (vol. 4)
978-1-4144-1170-5 (vol. 5)
978-1-4144-1171-2 (vol. 6)

1-4144-1165-0 (set)
1-4144-1166-9 (vol. 1)
1-4144-1167-7 (vol. 2)
1-4144-1168-5 (vol. 3)
1-4144-1169-3 (vol. 4)
1-4144-1170-7 (vol. 5)
1-4144-1171-5 (vol. 6)

This title is also available as an e-book.
ISBN-13: 978-1-4144-1181-1   ISBN-10: 1-4144-1181-2
Contact your Gale, a part of Cengage Learning sales representative for ordering information

.d in China
1 2 3 4 5 6 7 16 15 14 13 12

Contents

1910s

Commerce

Fashion

Film and Theater

Film and Theater

Food and Drink

Music

Print Culture

VOLUME 3
1940s

Commerce

Fashion

Film and Theater

The Way We Lived

Entries by Alphabetical Order

l

Entries by Topic Category

Food and Drink

Music

Sports and Games

TV and Radio

First-edition Contributors

Timothy Berg. Visiting assistant professor, Western Michigan University. Ph.D., History, Purdue University, 1999.

Charles Coletta, Ph.D. Instructor, Department of Popular Culture, Bowling Green State University. Contributing writer, *St. James Encyclopedia of Popular Culture* (2000).

Rob Edelman. Instructor, State University of New York at Albany. Author, *Baseball on the Web* (1997) and *The Great Baseball Films* (1994). Co-author, *Matthau: A Life* (2002); *Meet the Mertzes* (1999); and *Angela Lansbury: A Life on Stage and Screen* (1996). Contributing editor, *Leonard Maltin's Movie & Video Guide, Leonard Maltin's Movie Encyclopedia,* and *Leonard Maltin's Family Viewing Guide.* Contributing writer, *International Dictionary of Films and Filmmakers* (2000); *St. James Encyclopedia of Popular Culture* (2000); *Women Film-makers & Their Films* (1998); *The Political Companion to American Film* (1994); and *Total Baseball* (1989). Film commentator, WAMC (Northeast) Public Radio.

Tina Gianoulis. Freelance writer. Contributing writer, *World War I Reference Library* (2001–2); *Constitutional Amendments: From Freedom of Speech to Flag Burning* (2001); *International Dictionary of Films and Filmmakers* (2000); *St. James Encyclopedia of Popular Culture* (2000); and mystories.com, a daytime drama Web site (1997–98).

Sheldon Goldfarb. Archivist, Alma Mater Society of the University of British Columbia. Ph.D., English, University of British Columbia. Author, *William Makepeace Thackeray: An Annotated Bibliography, 1976–1987* (1989). Editor, *Catherine,* by William Makepeace Thackeray (1999).

Jill Gregg Clever, A.A., B.A., M.L.I.S. Graduate of Michigan State University, Thomas Edison State College, and Wayne State University. Business-technology specialist, Toledo–Lucas County Public Library.

Justin Gustainis. Professor of communication, State University of New York at Plattsburgh. Author, *American Rhetoric and the Vietnam War* (1993).

Audrey Kupferberg. Film consultant and archivist. Instructor, State University of New York at Albany. Co-author, *Matthau: A Life* (2002); *Meet the Mertzes* (1999); and *Angela Lansbury: A Life on Stage and Screen* (1996). Contributing editor, *Leonard Maltin's Family Viewing Guide*. Contributing writer, *St. James Encyclopedia of Popular Culture* (2000); *Women Filmmakers & Their Films* (1998); and *The American Film Institute Catalog of Feature Films*.

Edward Moran. Writer of American culture, music, and literature. Associate editor, *World Musicians* (1999); *World Authors* (1996); and *Random House Dictionary of the English Language* (1987; 1991). Contributing writer, *St. James Encyclopedia of Popular Culture* (2000). Editor, *Rhythm,* a magazine of world music and global culture (2001).

Sara Pendergast. President, Full Circle Editorial. Vice president, Group 3 Editorial. Co-editor, *St. James Encyclopedia of Popular Culture* (2000). Co-author, *World War I Reference Library* (2001), among other publications.

Tom Pendergast. Editorial director, Full Circle Editorial. Ph.D., American studies, Purdue University. Author, *Creating the Modern Man: American Magazines and Consumer Culture* (2000). Co-editor, *St. James Encyclopedia of Popular Culture* (2000).

Karl Rahder. M.A., University of Chicago Committee on International Relations. Author, several articles on international history and politics.

Chris Routledge. Freelance writer and editor. Ph.D., American literature, University of Newcastle upon Tyne (UK). Author, "The Chevalier and the Priest: Deductive Method in Poe, Chesterton, and Borges," in *Clues: A Journal of Detection* (2001). Editor, *Mystery in Children's Literature: From the Rational to the Supernatural* (2001).

Robert E. Schnakenberg. Senior writer, History Book Club. Author, *The Encyclopedia Shatnerica* (1998).

Steven Schneider. Ph.D. candidate, philosophy, Harvard University; Ph.D. candidate, cinema studies, New York University. Author, *An Auteur on Elm Street: The Cinema of Wes Craven* (forthcoming). Co-editor, *Horror International* (forthcoming) and *Dark Thoughts: Philosophic Reflections on Cinematic Horror* (forthcoming). Contributing writer, *British Horror Cinema* (2002); *Car Crash Culture* (2001); and numerous film journals.

Robert C. Sickels. Assistant professor of American film and popular culture, Whitman College. Ph.D., English, University of Nevada. Author, "A Politically Correct Ethan Edwards: Clint Eastwood's The Outlaw Josey Wales" in *Journal of Popular Film & Television* (forthcoming); "'70s Disco Daze: Paul Thomas Anderson's Boogie Nights and the Last Golden Age of Irresponsibility" in *Journal of Popular Culture* (forthcoming). Contributor, *St. James Encyclopedia of Popular Culture* (2000).

Reader's Guide

Popular culture—as we know it—was born in America, though historians disagree as to exactly when. Was it in 1893, when magazine publishers used new technologies to cut the costs of their magazines to a dime and sell hundreds of thousands of copies? Or was it in 1905, when the invention of the nickelodeon brought low-cost films to people all across the nation? Or was it back in 1886, when Richard Sears and Alvah Roebuck sent out their first catalog, which allowed people from all over to choose from among hundreds and then thousands of the same goods?

No matter the exact date, by the turn of the twentieth century, American magazine publishers, retailers, moviemakers, and other entertainers were bringing their goods before larger numbers of Americans than ever before. These magazines, movies, advertisements, shopping experiences, sports teams, and more were what we know as "popular culture," because they could be enjoyed firsthand by masses of Americans.

The story of America as revealed by its popular culture is complex and fascinating. Readers of *Bowling, Beatniks, and Bell-Bottoms: Pop Culture of 20th- and 21st-Century America* will discover, for example, that the comedic forms first developed by vaudeville comedians at the turn of the twentieth century lived on in film, radio, and finally television. They will learn that black musicians created the musical forms that are most distinctly American: blues and jazz. And they will realize that popular culture reacted to things like war and economic depressions in ways that were surprising and unexpected. The study of popular culture has a great deal to teach the student who is interested in how people use entertainment and consumption to make sense of their lives and shape their experience.

Bowling, Beatniks, and Bell-Bottoms gathers together essays that reflect the variety, diversity, and excitement of American popular culture of the twentieth and twenty-first centuries. This collection focuses more on events, fads, programs, performances, and products than on biographies of people, which are well documented in other sources. Even so, brief biographies of notables are sprinkled throughout. With approximately 850 essays on individual topics and dozens of overviews of pop culture trends, *Bowling, Beatniks, and Bell-Bottoms* covers a great deal of American popular culture, though not nearly enough. There are hundreds more people, bands, TV programs, films, and products that were worthy of mention but were left out due to space consideration. Our advisory board of media specialists, however, helped assure that the most prominent and studied subjects were included.

Have you ever wondered how the Slinky was invented, what Velveeta cheese is made of, or what people danced to before rock and roll? Those answers are in *Bowling, Beatniks, and Bell-Bottoms,* along with many others. It is our hope that this collection will bring both information and pleasure to all students of American culture.

Organization

Bowling, Beatniks, and Bell-Bottoms is arranged chronologically by decade over six volumes (two decades per volume for the twentieth century, and one volume covering the first decade of the twenty-first century). The approximately 850 entries are grouped into nine topic sections: Commerce, Fashion, Film and Theater, Food and Drink, Music, Print Culture, Sports and Games, TV and Radio, and The Way We Lived (though not all topics appear in every decade). Many subjects can easily appear in several different decades, so those essays are placed in either the decade in which the product was invented or the fad initiated, or in the decade in which the subject was most prominent or popular. In addition, several of the essays could have appeared under different topics (such as a book that was made into a movie), so those essays appear under the topic where it was best known. Users should make frequent use of the index or the two additional tables of contents (arranged alphabetically by entry name and by topic category) to locate an entry.

Essays range in length from 150 to 1000 words, with the majority averaging less than 500 words. Every essay aims to describe the topic and analyze the topic's contribution to popular culture. Each essay lists additional sources on the topic, including books, magazine or journal articles, and Web sites. Whenever possible, references to books are geared to younger readers. The editor and writers have personally visited every Web site mentioned and believe that these sites contain content that will assist the reader in understanding the subject. Due to the nature of the World Wide Web, it is possible that not all Web links will still function at the time of publication.

Bowling, Beatniks, and Bell-Bottoms also provides these features:

- A timeline that highlights key historic and pop culture events of the twentieth and twenty-first centuries
- A general overview of each decade
- A multipaged "At a Glance" box that breaks down "What We Said," "What We Read," "What We Watched," "What We Listened To," and "Who We Knew"
- An overview of each topic section in each decade
- Approximately 450 photos and illustrations
- Extensive use of cross references (pointing to decade, topic, and volume)

Acknowledgments

A thank-you encore goes to the advisors of this publication (their professional affiliation at the time of the publication of the first edition is noted): Catherine Bond, Department Chair, Library and Media Services, Conestoga High School, Berwyn, Pennsylvania; Cathy Chauvette, Assistant Regional Branch Manager, Fairfax County Public Library, Fairfax County, Virginia; Nancy Schlosser Garabed, Library Media Specialist, Council Rock High School, Newtown, Pennsylvania; Ann West LaPrise, Junior High/Elementary Media Specialist, Huron School District, New Boston, Michigan; and Nina Levine, Library Media Specialist, Blue Mountain Middle School, Cortlandt Manor, New York. Their input during the preparation of the first edition remains valuable.

The contributions of the writers from the first edition are noted on the contributors page (which reprints their background at the time of the first edition). For this second edition, much gratitude is given to writers David Larkins, Annette Petrusso, Maureen Reed, Patrick Walsh, and Greg Wilson.

Much appreciation goes to copyeditor Maxwell Valentine, proofreader Rebecca Valentine, indexer Theresa Murray, and typesetter

PreMediaGlobal. Additional thanks to Scott Rosen at the Bill Smith Group for permissions and imaging selection and Barry Puckett for image processing assistance.

Comments and Suggestions

We welcome your comments on *Bowling, Beatniks, and Bell-Bottoms.* Please send correspondence to: Editors, *Bowling, Beatniks, and Bell-Bottoms,* U•X•L, 27500 Drake Rd., Farmington Hills, MI 48331-3535; call toll-free: 800-877-4253; fax to 248-414-5043; or send e-mail via www.cengage.com.

Cynthia Johnson, Editor

Timeline

1900 On January 29, Ban Johnson forms the American League to compete against baseball's National League.

1900 In February, Eastman Kodak introduces the Brownie Camera.

1900 In March, the Good Roads Campaign tries to build support for better roads. At the time, there are only ten miles of paved roads in the nation.

1900 On March 31, the first ad for an automobile appears in the *Saturday Evening Post.*

1900 On April 23, Buffalo Bill Cody's *Wild West Show* opens at Madison Square Garden in New York City.

1900 On November 6, Republican William McKinley is reelected U.S. president, with New York governor Theodore Roosevelt as his vice president.

1900 On November 12, *Floradora,* one of the most popular theatrical musicals of the decade, premieres in New York. It runs for more than five hundred performances.

1901 On February 25, U.S. Steel is formed out of ten companies and becomes the world's largest industrial corporation.

1901 On March 13, steel tycoon Andrew Carnegie donates $2.2 million to fund a New York public library system.

1901 On September 6, President William McKinley is shot by an assassin in Buffalo, New York, and dies eight days later from complications from gangrene due to improperly dressed wounds. Theodore Roosevelt becomes president.

1901 On October 16, President Theodore Roosevelt starts a national controversy when he dines with black leader Booker T. Washington in the White House.

1902 The Teddy Bear is introduced, named after President Theodore Roosevelt.

1902 On January 1, in the first Rose Bowl football game, the University of Michigan defeats Stanford 49–0.

1902 On March 18, Italian opera singer Enrico Caruso produces his first phonographic recording.

1902 On April 16, Tally's Electric Theater, the first theater solely devoted to presenting motion pictures, opens in Los Angeles, California.

1902 On December 21, Guglielmo Marconi transmits the first wireless signals across the Atlantic Ocean.

1903 *Redbook* magazine is founded.

1903 The Portage Lakers of Houghton, Michigan—the first professional hockey team from the United States—win the International Hockey League championship.

1903 On January 22, the United States signs a 99-year lease on what will become the Panama Canal Zone, where it will build a canal that connects the Caribbean Sea to the Pacific Ocean.

1903 In February, the *Ladies' Home Journal* becomes the first American magazine to reach one million paid subscriptions.

1903 On May 23, two men make the first transcontinental automobile trip from San Francisco to New York in sixty-four days. Upon returning home, one driver is ticketed for exceeding the speed limit of six miles per hour.

1903 On August 14, Jim Jeffries defeats James J. "Gentleman Jim" Corbett to retain the world heavyweight boxing title.

1903 On September 12, Scott Joplin's ragtime opera *A Guest of Honor* begins a midwest tour.

1903 In October, the Boston Pilgrims defeat the Pittsburgh Pirates in the first World Series to pit an American League team against a National League team.

1903 On December 1, Edwin S. Porter's film *The Great Train Robbery* is considered the first Western and the first American film with a plot.

1903 On December 17, Wilbur and Orville Wright make the first sustained flight at Kitty Hawk, North Carolina.

1904 The Ford Motor Company sells fourteen hundred of its Model A cars.

1904 On April 20, the World's Fair opens in St. Louis, Missouri.

1904 On May 5, Cy Young pitches baseball's first perfect game.

1904 On November 8, Theodore Roosevelt is reelected president.

1905 The German navy launches the first submarine.

1905 African American leader W. E. B. Du Bois helps found the Niagara Movement, an organization to advance African American issues.

1905 On May 5, the *Chicago Defender,* the first major black newspaper, begins publication.

1905 In June, the era of the nickelodeon begins when Harry Davis's Pittsburgh, Pennsylvania, movie theater offers continuous movie showings. By the end of the decade, more than eight thousand nickel-admission movie theaters are in operation.

1905 On June 18, the Twentieth Century Limited begins train service between Chicago, Illinois, and New York City and boasts a travel time of only eighteen hours.

1906 Kellogg's Corn Flakes breakfast cereal is introduced.

1906 In February, Upton Sinclair publishes *The Jungle,* a novel depicting the horrible conditions in the meat-packing industry. The work prompts the passage of the Meat Inspection Act.

1906 On April 14, President Theodore Roosevelt coins the term "muckraking" when he criticizes journalists who expose abuses and corruption and miss the larger social picture.

1906 On April 18, a major earthquake and fire destroy much of San Francisco, California.

1906 On May 3, the First Annual Advertising Show in New York City heralds the beginning of an important American industry.

1906 On November 21, the first voice radio transmission travels eleven miles from Plymouth to Brant Rock, Massachusetts.

1907 Work begins on the Panama Canal.

1907 On January 23, in what newspapers call the "trial of the century," millionaire Harry K. Thaw is tried for the murder of world-famous architect Stanford White over the honor of Thaw's wife, showgirl Evelyn Nesbit.

1907 On June 10, French motion picture pioneers Auguste and Louis Lumière announce they have developed a method for producing color film.

1907 On July 8, Florenz Ziegfeld's musical revue, the *Ziegfeld Follies,* opens in New York.

1907 On December 3, actress Mary Pickford makes her stage debut in *The Warrens of Virginia.*

1908 The world's first skyscraper, the forty-seven-story Singer Building, is completed in New York City.

1908 The General Motors Corporation is formed and soon becomes the biggest competitor of the Ford Motor Company.

1908 In March, the Original Independent Show, organized in New York, includes works by American painters Edward Hopper, George Bellows, and Rockwell Kent.

1908 On September 6, Israel Zangwill's play *The Melting Pot* opens in New York City; the title becomes an internationally recognized description of the United States.

1908 On October 1, the Ford Motor Company unveils its Model T with a price tag of $825. It soon becomes the best-selling automobile of its time.

1908 On November 3, former U.S. secretary of war William Howard Taft is elected president.

1908 On December 26, Jack Johnson defeats Tommy Burns to become the first black world heavyweight boxing champion. His victory is considered an outrage by white racists.

1909 The fifty-story Metropolitan Life Insurance Tower in New York City becomes the world's tallest building.

1909 The Ford Motor Company manufactures nineteen thousand Model T cars.

1909 On March 16, the Federal Bureau of Investigation is created as a federal law enforcement agency.

1909 On March 23, former president Theodore Roosevelt leaves for a safari in Africa. He is paid $50,000 by *Scribner's Magazine* for his account of the trip.

1909 On April 6, U.S. Navy commander Robert Peary reaches the North Pole.

1909 On May 3, the first wireless press message is sent from New York City to Chicago, Illinois.

1909 On July 12, the U.S. Congress asks the states to authorize a national income tax.

1910 Western novelist Zane Grey's book *Heritage of the Desert* becomes a huge commercial success, starting his career of bringing the American West to the reading world.

1910 Levi Strauss and Company begins making casual play clothes for children.

1910 The Boy Scouts of America are founded in Chicago, Illinois.

1910 On February 28, Russian ballerina Anna Pavlova makes her American debut at the Metropolitan Opera House in New York City.

1910 On March 28, the first one-man show by artist Pablo Picasso opens at photographer and editor Alfred Stieglitz's 291 Gallery in New York City.

1910 In November, the National Association for the Advancement of Colored People (NAACP) publishes the first issue of the *Crisis* magazine, edited by W. E. B. Du Bois.

1910 On November 3, the Chicago Grand Opera opens with a production of *Aida,* by Giuseppe Verdi.

1911 Irving Berlin composes "Alexander's Ragtime Band," the song that popularized ragtime music.

1911 Air conditioning is invented.

1911 *Photoplay,* the first movie fan magazine, is published.

1911 On March 25, in New York City, 146 female workers are killed in the Triangle Shirtwaist Factory fire, alerting Americans to the dangers women face in industrial labor.

1911 On May 23, President William Howard Taft dedicates the New York Public Library.

1911 On May 30, the first Indianapolis 500 auto race is won by Ray Harroun with an average speed of 74.59 mph.

1911 On August 8, *Pathe's Weekly,* the first regular newsreel to be produced in the United States, is released to motion picture theaters.

1911 On December 19, the Association of American Painters and Sculptors is founded.

1912 New Mexico and Arizona become the forty-seventh and forty-eighth states.

1912 The Little Theater in Chicago, Illinois, and the Toy Theater in Boston, Massachusetts, the first influential little theaters in the United States, are founded.

1912 Dancers Irene and Vernon Castle start a craze for ballroom dancing.

1912 On April 15, the *Titanic* sinks on its maiden voyage from Ireland to the United States, killing 1,517.

1912 In August, photographer and editor Alfred Stieglitz devotes an entire issue of his periodical *Camera Work* to the modern art movement.

1912 On August 5, former president Theodore Roosevelt is nominated as the presidential candidate of the newly formed Progressive Party.

1912 On October 31, *The Musketeers of Pig Alley,* a film by D. W. Griffith that points out the social evils of poverty and crime on the streets of New York, is released.

1912 On November 5, New Jersey governor Woodrow Wilson is elected president.

1912 On December 10, the Famous Players Film Company registers for copyright of the five-reel feature film *The Count of Monte Cristo,* directed by Edwin S. Porter.

1913 The 792-foot-high Woolworth Building in New York City becomes the world's tallest building, a record it holds until 1930.

1913 The first crossword puzzle is published.

1913 The Jesse Lasky Feature Play Co., which later would become Paramount Pictures, is established in Hollywood, California.

1913 The Panama Canal is completed, and officially opens on August 15, 1914.

1913 On February 17, the International Exhibition of Modern Art, known as the Armory Show, opens in New York City. It is the first opportunity for many Americans to view modern art.

1913 On February 25, the Sixteenth Amendment to the Constitution is approved, authorizing a federal income tax.

1913 On March 24, the million dollar, eighteen-hundred-seat Palace Theatre opens in New York City.

1913 On May 31, the Seventeenth Amendment to the Constitution is approved, providing for the direct election of U.S. senators by citizens, rather than by state legislatures.

1914 On February 13, the American Society of Composers, Authors, and Publishers (ASCAP), an organization that seeks royalty payments for public performances of music, is founded in New York City.

1914 In March, comedian Charles Chaplin begins to evolve the legendary character of the Little Tramp in the film *Mabel's Strange Predicament.*

1914 On July 3, the first telephone line connects New York City and San Francisco, California.

1914 On August 3, World War I starts in Europe when Germany invades Belgium. Soon all of Europe is drawn into the conflict, though the United States remains neutral.

1914 On September 5, a German submarine scores its first kill, sinking the British cruiser *Pathfinder,* as World War I intensifies.

1914 In September, in the World War I Battle of the Marne, Germany's advance into France is halted.

1914 On November 3, the first American exhibition of African sculpture opens at the 291 Gallery in New York City.

1914 On December 3, the Isadorables, six European dancers trained by American dancer Isadora Duncan, perform at Carnegie Hall in New York City after escaping with Duncan from her war-torn Europe.

1915 The first taxicab appears on the streets of New York City.

1915 The first professional football league is formed in Ohio and is called simply the Ohio League.

1915 Modern dancers Ruth St. Denis and Ted Shawn found the Denishawn School of Dancing in Los Angeles, California.

1915 Five hundred U.S. correspondents cover World War I in Europe.

1915 On March 10, the Russian Symphony Orchestra plays the American debut performance of the symphony *Prometheus* by Aleksandr Scriabin at Carnegie Hall in New York City. Color images are projected onto a screen as part of the show.

1915 On December 10, the Ford Motor Company manufactures its one millionth Model T automobile.

1916 The Boeing Aircraft Company produces its first biplane.

1916 Newspaper publisher William Randolph Hearst inaugurates the *City Life* arts section as a supplement to his Sunday newspapers.

1916 In November, inventor and radio pioneer Lee De Forest begins to transmit daily music broadcasts from his home in New York City.

1916 On November 7, Woodrow Wilson is reelected president after campaigning on the pledge to keep the United States out of the war in Europe.

1917 The Russian Revolution brings communism to Russia, setting the stage for nearly a century of intermittent conflict with the United States.

1917 Showman George M. Cohan composes the song that was a musical call-to-arms during World War I: "Over There."

1917 Motion picture pioneer Cecil B. DeMille directs *The Little American,* a patriotic melodrama starring Mary Pickford.

1917 On April 6, the United States declares war on Germany after German submarines continue to attack U.S. merchant ships.

1917 On May 28, Benny Leonard wins the lightweight boxing championship, which he holds until his retirement in 1924 while building a record of 209–5; he makes a comeback in 1931.

1917 On August 19, the managers of the New York Giants and Cincinnati Reds are arrested for playing baseball on Sunday.

1917 On October 27, sixteen-year-old Russian-born violinist Jascha Heifetz makes his debut American performance at Carnegie Hall in New York City.

1918 The annual O. Henry Awards for short fiction are inaugurated in honor of short story writer O. Henry (a pseudonym for William Sydney Porter).

1918 On January 8, President Woodrow Wilson delivers his "Fourteen Points" address before Congress, outlining his plans for the shape of the postwar world.

1918 In March, *The Little Review* begins to serialize the novel *Ulysses,* by James Joyce, which features stream of consciousness techniques and a kind of private language.

1918 On November 11, Germany signs an armistice with the Allies, ending the fighting in World War I.

1918 In December, the Theatre Guild is founded in New York City.

1919 *Maid of Harlem,* an all-black-cast musical starring "Fats" Waller, Mamie Smith, Johnny Dunn, and Perry Bradford, draws enthusiastic crowds at the Lincoln Theatre in New York City.

1919 On January 29, Prohibition begins with the adoption of the Eighteenth Amendment to the Constitution, which bans the manufacture, sale, and transportation of intoxicating liquors.

1919 On February 5, United Artists, an independent film distribution company, is founded by Charles Chaplin, Douglas Fairbanks, D. W. Griffith, and Mary Pickford.

1919 On June 28, the Treaty of Versailles is signed by the Allied powers, officially ending World War I. Germany is forced to pay costly reparations for the damage it caused during the war.

1919 On July 4, Jack Dempsey defeats Jess Willard to win the world heavyweight boxing championship.

1919 On October 31, the Provincetown Players stage *The Dreamy Kid,* by Eugene O'Neill, with an all-black cast.

1919 On December 22, Attorney General A. Mitchell Palmer authorizes government raids on communists, anarchists, and other political radicals. These "Palmer raids" are part of a nationwide "red scare."

1920 Sinclair Lewis publishes the novel *Main Street.*

1920 Douglas Fairbanks stars in the film *The Mark of Zorro.*

1920 On January 5, the Radio Corporation of America (RCA) is founded and becomes a leading radio broadcaster.

1920 On February 12, the National Negro Baseball League is founded.

1920 On August 20, the first radio news bulletins are broadcast by station 8MK in Detroit, Michigan.

1920 On August 26, the Nineteenth Amendment to the Constitution gives women the right to vote.

1920 On September 28, eight Chicago White Sox players are charged with throwing the 1919 World Series in what becomes known as the "Black Sox Scandal." They are eventually banned from the game for life.

1920 On September 29, New York Yankee Babe Ruth breaks his own single-season home run record with 54 home runs.

1920 On November 1, Eugene O'Neill's play *The Emperor Jones* opens in New York City.

1920 On November 6, U.S. senator Warren G. Harding of Ohio is elected president.

1921 The Ford Motor Company announces a plan to produce one million automobiles a year.

1921 The Phillips Gallery in Washington, D.C., becomes the first American museum of modern art.

1921 In this year, 13 percent of Americans own telephones.

1921 On March 10, the first White Castle hamburger chain opens in Wichita, Kansas.

1921 On April 11, radio station KDKA in Pittsburgh, Pennsylvania, broadcasts the first sports event on radio, a boxing match between Johnny Ray and Johnny Dundee. Later that year, the World Series is broadcast.

1921 On May 23, *Shuffle Along* is the first black Broadway musical written and directed by African Americans.

1921 On July 29, Adolf Hitler is elected dictator of the Nazi Party in Munich, Germany.

1921 On September 8, the first Miss America pageant is held in Washington, D.C.

1921 On November 2, Margaret Sanger founds the American Birth Control League in New York City, raising the anger of many religious groups, especially Catholic groups.

1922 Robert Flaherty releases the documentary film *Nanook of the North*.

1922 Irish author James Joyce publishes *Ulysses,* which is banned in some countries for its alleged obscenity.

1922 F. Scott Fitzgerald publishes *Tales of the Jazz Age.*

1922 The American Professional Football Association changes its name to the National Football League (NFL).

1922 *Reader's Digest* magazine is founded.

1922 Al Jolson pens the popular song "Toot Toot Tootsie."

1922 On May 5, Coco Chanel introduces Chanel No. 5, which becomes the world's best-known perfume.

1922 On August 28, the first advertisement is aired on radio station WEAF in New York City.

1922 On December 30, the Union of Soviet Socialist Republics (USSR) is established with Russia at its head.

1923 Cecil B. DeMille directs the epic film *The Ten Commandments.*

1923 Charles Kettering develops a method for bringing colored paint to mass-produced cars.

1923 Bessie Smith's "Down Hearted Blues" is one of the first blues songs to be recorded.

1923 *Time* magazine begins publication.

1923 On April 6, trumpet player Louis Armstrong records his first solo on "Chimes Blues" with King Oliver's Creole Jazz Band.

1923 On August 3, President Warren G. Harding dies and Vice President Calvin Coolidge takes office.

1924 John Ford directs the Western film *The Iron Horse.*

1924 The Metro-Goldwyn-Mayer (MGM) film studio is formed in Hollywood, California.

1924 Evangelist Aimee Semple McPherson begins broadcasting from the first religious radio station, KFSG in Los Angeles, California.

1924 The stock market begins a boom that will last until 1929.

1924 On January 1, there are 2.5 million radios in American homes, up from 2,000 in 1920.

1924 On February 12, the tomb of King Tutankhamen, or King Tut, is opened in Egypt after having been sealed for four thousand years.

1924 On February 24, George Gershwin's *Rhapsody in Blue* is performed by an orchestra in New York City.

1924 On March 10, J. Edgar Hoover is appointed director of the Federal Bureau of Investigation.

1924 In June, the Chrysler Corporation is founded and competes with General Motors and Ford.

1924 On November 4, incumbent Calvin Coolidge is elected president.

1925 In one of the most famous years in American literature, F. Scott Fitzgerald publishes *The Great Gatsby,* Ernest Hemingway publishes *In Our Time,* and Theodore Dreiser publishes *An American Tragedy.*

1925 Lon Chaney stars in the film *The Phantom of the Opera.*

1925 The *WSM Barn Dance* radio program begins broadcasting from Nashville, Tennessee; the name is later changed to *Grand Ole Opry* and it becomes the leading country music program.

1925 The *New Yorker* magazine begins publication and features the prices paid for bootleg liquor.

1925 In February, the Boeing aircraft company builds a plane capable of flying over the Rocky Mountains with a full load of mail.

1925 On May 8, the Brotherhood of Sleeping Car Porters, founded by A. Philip Randolph, is one of the first black labor unions.

1925 In July, in the Scopes "Monkey" trial, a Tennessee teacher is tried and found guilty of teaching evolution in a trial that attracts national attention.

1925 On August 8, forty thousand Ku Klux Klan members march in Washington, D.C., to broaden support for their racist organization.

1926 Latin idol Rudolph Valentino stars in the film *The Son of the Sheik.*

1926 Ernest Hemingway publishes *The Sun Also Rises.*

1926 The Book-of-the-Month Club is launched to offer quality books to subscribers.

1926 On March 7, the first transatlantic radio-telephone conversation links New York City and London, England.

1926 On March 17, *The Girl Friend,* a musical with songs by Richard Rodgers and Lorenz Hart, opens on Broadway.

1926 On April 18, dancer Martha Graham makes her first professional appearance in New York City.

1927 Al Jolson stars in the film *The Jazz Singer,* the first film to have sound. Clara Bow—the "It" girl—stars in *It.*

1927 On January 1, the Rose Bowl football game is broadcast coast-to-coast on the radio.

1927 On April 7, television is first introduced in America, but investors are skeptical.

1927 On May 21, Charles Lindbergh completes his nonstop flight from New York City to Paris, France, and is given a hero's welcome.

1927 On May 25, the Ford Motor Company announces that production of the Model T will be stopped in favor of the modern Model A.

1927 On September 22, the heavyweight championship fight between Jack Dempsey and Gene Tunney becomes the first sports gate to top $2 million.

1927 On December 4, Duke Ellington's orchestra begins a long run at the Cotton Club nightclub in Harlem, New York.

1927 On December 27, the Jerome Kern and Oscar Hammerstein musical *Show Boat* opens on Broadway in New York City.

1928 On April 15, the New York Rangers become the first American team to win the National Hockey League Stanley Cup.

1928 On May 11, WGY in Schenectady, New York, offers the first scheduled television service, though the high price of televisions keeps most people from owning them.

1928 On July 30, the Eastman Kodak company introduces color motion pictures.

1928 On November 6, former U.S. secretary of commerce Herbert Hoover is elected president.

1928 On December 13, George Gershwin's *An American in Paris* opens at Carnegie Hall in New York City.

1928 On December 26, swimmer Johnny Weissmuller retires from competition after setting sixty-seven world records.

1929 Mickey Mouse makes his first appearance in *Steamboat Willie,* an animated film made by Walt Disney.

1929 Commercial airlines carry 180,000 passengers during the year.

1929 Ernest Hemingway publishes *A Farewell to Arms,* a novel set during World War I.

1929 Nick Lucas's "Tiptoe through the Tulips with Me" and Louis Armstrong's "Ain't Misbehavin'" are two of the year's most popular songs.

1929 On February 14, in the Saint Valentine's Day Massacre, gunmen working for Chicago, Illinois, mobster Al Capone gun down seven members of a rival gang.

1929 On October 29, the stock market collapses on a day known as "Black Tuesday," marking the start of what will become the Great Depression.

1930 Grant Wood paints *American Gothic.*

1930 The Continental Baking company introduces Wonder Bread to the nation, the first commercially produced sliced bread.

1930 Unemployment reaches four million as the economy worsens.

1930 On January 14, jazz greats Benny Goodman, Glenn Miller, Jimmy Dorsey, and Jack Teagarden play George and Ira Gershwin's songs, including "I've Got a Crush on You," in the musical *Strike Up the Band* at the Mansfield Theater in New York City.

1930 On March 6, General Foods introduces the nation's first frozen foods.

1930 On May 3, Ogden Nash, a poet who will become famous for his funny, light verse, publishes "Spring Comes to Murray Hill" in the *New Yorker* magazine and soon begins work at the magazine.

1930 On September 8, the comic strip *Blondie* begins.

1930 On October 14, *Girl Crazy,* starring Ethel Merman, opens at New York's Guild Theater. The musical features songs by George Gershwin, Walter Donaldson, and Ira Gershwin, including "I Got Rhythm" and "Embraceable You."

1931 The horror films *Dracula* and *Frankenstein* are both released.

1931 Nevada legalizes gambling in order to bring revenue to the state.

1931 On March 3, "The Star Spangled Banner" becomes the national anthem by congressional vote.

1931 On April 30, the Empire State Building, the tallest building in the world, opens in New York City.

1931 On June 3, brother-and-sister dancers Fred and Adele Astaire perform for the last time together on the first revolving stage.

1931 On July 27, *Earl Carroll's Vanities,* featuring naked chorus girls, opens at the three-thousand-seat Earl Carroll Theater in New York City.

1931 On October 12, the comic strip *Dick Tracy* begins.

1932 Edwin Herbert Land, a Harvard College dropout, invents Polaroid film.

1932 On May 2, *The Jack Benny Show* premieres as a variety show on radio and runs for twenty-three years and then another ten years on television.

1932 On July 30, the Summer Olympic Games open in Los Angeles, California, and feature record-breaking performances by Americans Babe Didrikson and Eddie Tolan.

1932 On July 31, in German parliamentary elections, the Nazi Party receives the most seats but is unable to form a government.

1932 On November 7, the radio adventure *Buck Rogers in the Twenty-Fifth Century* premieres on CBS and runs until 1947.

1932 On November 8, New York governor Franklin D. Roosevelt is elected president, promising to take steps to improve the economy. In his first one hundred days in office, Roosevelt introduces much legislation to use the government to aid those harmed by the Great Depression.

1932 On December 27, Radio City Music Hall opens at the Rockefeller Center in New York City.

1933 President Franklin D. Roosevelt presents the nation with his first radio address, known as a "fireside chat."

1933 Walt Disney releases the feature film *The Three Little Pigs.*

1933 On January 3, *The Lone Ranger* radio drama premieres on WXYZ radio in Detroit, Michigan.

1933 On January 30, Nazi leader Adolf Hitler becomes chancellor of Germany. Hitler soon seizes all power and sets out to attack his party's political enemies.

1933 On May 27, fan dancer Sally Rand attracts thousands with her performance at the Chicago World's Fair that celebrated the Century of Progress.

1933 On September 30, *Ah, Wilderness,* acclaimed American playwright Eugene O'Neill's only comedy, opens at the Guild Theater in New York City.

1933 On December 5, the Twenty-first Amendment to the Constitution puts an end to Prohibition.

1934 The first pipeless organ is patented by Laurens Hammond. The Hammond organ starts a trend toward more electrically amplified instruments.

1934 Dashiell Hammett publishes *The Thin Man,* one of the first hard-boiled detective novels.

1934 The Apollo Theater opens in Harlem, New York, as a showcase for black performers.

1934 German director Fritz Lang flees Nazi Germany to make movies in the United States.

1934 On May 5, bank robbers and murderers Bonnie Parker and Clyde Barrow are killed by lawmen in Louisiana.

1934 On July 1, the Motion Picture Producers and Distributors of America (MPPDA) association creates the Hay's Office to enforce codes that limit the amount and types of sexuality and other immoral behavior in films.

1934 On July 22, "Public Enemy No. 1" John Dillinger is shot and killed outside a Chicago, Illinois, theater by FBI agents and local police.

1934 On August 13, Al Capp's *Li'l Abner* comic strip debuts in eight newspapers.

1934 On August 19, Adolf Hitler is declared president of Germany, though he prefers the title Führer (leader).

1935 One out of four American households receives government relief as the Depression deepens.

1935 Twenty million Monopoly board games are sold in one week.

1935 The first Howard Johnson roadside restaurant opens in Boston, Massachusetts.

1935 The Works Progress Administration Federal Arts Projects, some of President Franklin D. Roosevelt's many New Deal programs, give work to artists painting post offices and other federal buildings.

1935 In April, *Your Hit Parade* is first heard on radio and offers a selection of hit songs.

1935 On April 16, the radio comedy-drama *Fibber McGee and Molly* debuts on NBC and runs until 1952.

1935 On May 24, the first nighttime major league baseball game is played in Cincinnati, Ohio.

1935 On October 10, *Porgy and Bess,* known as the "most American opera of the decade," opens in New York City at the Alvin Theater. The music George Gershwin wrote for the opera combined blues, jazz, and southern folk.

1936 American Airlines introduces transcontinental airline service.

1936 Ten African American athletes, including Jesse Owens, win gold medals in the Summer Olympics held in Berlin, Germany, embarrassing Nazi leader Adolf Hitler, who had declared the inferiority of black athletes.

1936 Dust storms in the Plains states force thousands to flee the region, many to California.

1936 Popular public-speaking teacher Dale Carnegie publishes his book *How to Win Friends and Influence People.*

1936 To increase feelings of nationalism, the Department of the Interior hires folksinger Woody Guthrie to travel throughout the U.S. Southwest performing his patriotic songs such as "Those Oklahoma Hills."

1936 In the Soviet Union, the Communist Party begins its Great Purge, executing anyone who resists the party's social and economic policies. By 1938, it is estimated that ten million people have been killed.

1936 Throughout Europe, countries scramble to form alliances with other countries for what seems to be a likely war. Germany and Italy join together to support the military government of Francisco Franco in Spain, while Great Britain and France sign nonaggression pacts with the Soviet Union.

1936 On July 18, the Spanish Civil War begins when Spanish military officers rise up against the Republican government of Spain.

1936 In October, the New York Yankees win the first of four World Series in a row.

1936 On November 3, Franklin D. Roosevelt is reelected as president of the United States.

1936 On November 23, the first issue of *Life* magazine is published.

1937 Dr. Seuss becomes a popular children's book author with the publication of *And to Think That I Saw It on Mulberry Street.*

1937 The Hormel company introduces Spam, a canned meat.

1937 A poll shows that the average American listens to the radio for 4.5 hours a day.

1937 *Porky's Hare Hunt,* a short animated cartoon by Warner Bros., introduces audiences to the Bugs Bunny character and the talents of Mel Blanc, the voice of both Bugs Bunny and Porky Pig.

1937 The first soap opera, *Guiding Light,* is broadcast. It continues as a radio program until 1956 and moves to television.

1937 British writer J. R. R. Tolkien publishes *The Hobbit.*

1937 On June 22, black boxer Joe Louis knocks out Jim Braddock to win the world heavyweight boxing championship.

1937 On December 21, *Snow White and the Seven Dwarfs,* the first feature-length animated film, is presented by Walt Disney.

1938 Glenn Miller forms his own big band and begins to tour extensively.

1938 On January 17, the first jazz performance at Carnegie Hall in New York City is performed by Benny Goodman and His Orchestra, with Duke Ellington, Count Basie, and others.

1938 In June, the character Superman is introduced in *Action Comics #1.* By 1939, he appears in his own comic book series.

1938 On August 17, Henry Armstrong becomes the first boxer to hold three boxing titles at one time when he defeats Lou Ambers at New York City's Madison Square Garden.

1938 On October 31, Orson Welles's radio broadcast of H. G. Wells's science fiction novel *The War of the Worlds* is believed by many listeners to be a serious announcement of a Martian invasion, resulting in panic spreading throughout the country.

1938 On November 11, singer Kate Smith's performance of "God Bless America" is broadcast over the radio on Armistice Day.

1939 Singer Frank Sinatra joins the Tommy Dorsey band, where he will soon find great success.

1939 Federal spending on the military begins to revive the economy.

1939 Pocket Books, the nation's first modern paperback book company, is founded.

1939 The National Collegiate Athletic Association (NCAA) holds it first Final Four championship basketball series, which is won by the University of Oregon.

1939 *Gone with the Wind,* David O. Selznick's epic film about the Civil War, stars Vivien Leigh and Clark Gable.

1939 *The Wizard of Oz* whisks movie audiences into a fantasyland of magic and wonder. The film stars Judy Garland and includes such popular songs as "Somewhere Over the Rainbow," "Follow the Yellow Brick Road," and "We're Off to See the Wizard."

1939 On May 2, baseball great Lou "The Iron Man" Gehrig ends his consecutive game streak at 2,130 when he removes himself from the lineup.

1939 On September 1, German troops invade Poland, causing Great Britain and France to declare war on Germany and starting World War II. Days later, the Soviet Union invades Poland as well, and soon Germany and the Soviet Union divide Poland.

1940 The radio program *Superman* debuts, introducing the phrases "Up, up, and away!" and "This looks like a job for Superman!"

1940 On February 22, German troops begin construction of a concentration camp in Auschwitz, Poland.

1940 The first issue of the comic book *Batman* is published.

1940 On May 10, German forces invade Belgium and Holland, and later march into France.

1940 On June 10, Italy declares war on Britain and France.

1940 On June 14, the German army enters Paris, France.

1940 On August 24, Germany begins bombing London, England.

1940 On November 5, President Franklin D. Roosevelt is reelected for his third term.

1940 On November 13, the Disney film *Fantasia* opens in New York City.

1941 "Rosie the Riveter" becomes the symbol for the many women who are employed in various defense industries.

1941 *Citizen Kane,* which many consider the greatest movie of all time, is released, directed by and starring Orson Welles.

1941 On January 15, A. Philip Randolph leads the March on Washington to call for an end to racial discrimination in defense-industry employment. President Franklin D. Roosevelt eventually signs an executive order barring such discrimination.

1941 On March 17, the National Gallery of Art opens in Washington, D.C.

1941 On July 1, CBS and NBC begin offering about fifteen hours of commercial television programming each week—but few consumers have enough money to purchase television sets.

1941 On October 19, German troops lay siege to the Russian city of Moscow.

1941 On December 7, Japanese planes launch a surprise attack on the U.S. naval and air bases in Pearl Harbor, Hawaii, and declare war against the United States.

1941 On December 11, the United States declares war on Germany and Italy in response to those countries' declarations of war.

1942 On January 1, the annual Rose Bowl football game is played in Durham, North Carolina, rather than the usual Pasadena, California, location, to avoid the chance of a Japanese bombing attack.

1942 Humphrey Bogart and Ingrid Bergman star in *Casablanca,* set in war-torn Europe.

1942 On February 19, President Franklin D. Roosevelt signs an executive order placing all Japanese Americans on the West Coast in internment camps for the rest of the war.

1942 On May 5, sugar rationing starts in the United States, followed by the rationing of other products.

1942 In June, American troops defeat the Japanese at the Battle of Midway.

1942 On December 25, the comedy team of Abbott and Costello is voted the leading box-office attraction of 1942.

1943 Gary Cooper and Ingrid Bergman star in *For Whom the Bell Tolls,* the film version of the novel by Ernest Hemingway.

1943 On January 25, the Pentagon, the world's largest office complex and the home to the U.S. military, is completed in Arlington, Virginia.

1943 On March 14, composer Aaron Copland's *Fanfare for the Common Man* premieres in Cincinnati, Ohio.

1943 On March 30, the musical *Oklahoma!* opens on Broadway in New York City.

1943 During the summer, race riots break out in Detroit, Michigan, and Harlem, New York.

1943 On September 8, Italy surrenders to the Allies.

1943 On November 9, artist Jackson Pollock has his first solo show in New York City.

1943 On December 30, *Esquire* magazine loses its second-class mailing privileges after it is charged with being "lewd" and "lascivious" by the U.S. Post Office.

1944 *Seventeen* magazine debuts.

1944 *Double Indemnity,* directed by Billy Wilder, becomes one of the first of a new genre of movies known as *film noir.*

1944 On March 4, American planes bomb Berlin, Germany.

1944 On June 6, on "D-Day," Allied forces land in Normandy, France, and begin the liberation of western Europe.

1944 On June 22, the Serviceman's Readjustment Act, signed by President Franklin D. Roosevelt, provides funding for a variety of programs for returning soldiers, including education programs under the G.I. Bill.

1944 On August 25, Allied troops liberate Paris, France.

1944 On November 7, Franklin D. Roosevelt is reelected for an unprecedented fourth term as president.

1945 Chicago publisher John H. Johnson launches *Ebony* magazine.

1945 The radio program *The Adventures of Ozzie and Harriet* debuts.

1945 On January 27, the Soviet Red Army liberates Auschwitz, Poland, revealing the seriousness of German efforts to exterminate Jews.

1945 On April 12, President Franklin D. Roosevelt dies of a cerebral hemorrhage and Vice President Harry S. Truman takes over as president.

1945 On April 21, Soviet troops reach the outskirts of Berlin, the capital of Germany.

1945 On April 30, German leader Adolf Hitler commits suicide in Berlin, Germany, as Allied troops approach the city.

1945 On May 5, American poet Ezra Pound is arrested in Italy on charges of treason.

1945 On May 8, Germany surrenders to the Allies, bringing an end to World War II in Europe.

1945 On August 6, the United States drops the first atomic bomb on the Japanese city of Hiroshima, killing more than fifty thousand people.

1945 On August 9, the United States drops a second atomic bomb on Nagasaki, Japan.

1945 On September 2, Japan offers its unconditional surrender onboard the U.S.S. *Missouri* in Tokyo Bay, bringing an end to World War II.

1946 The Baby Boom begins as the birthrate rises 20 percent over the previous year.

1946 *It's a Wonderful Life,* starring Jimmy Stewart and directed by Frank Capra, becomes one of the most popular Christmas movies of all time.

1946 On January 10, the first General Assembly of the United Nations meets in London, England.

1946 On June 19, Joe Louis retains his title by knocking out Billy Conn in the first heavyweight boxing match ever shown on television.

1946 On December 11, country singer Hank Williams cuts his first single, "Calling You."

1947 On January 29, Arthur Miller's play *All My Sons* opens in New York City.

1947 On March 12, President Harry S. Truman announces his "containment" policy aimed at stopping the spread of communism. It will later become known as the Truman Doctrine.

1947 On March 21, Congress approves the Twenty-second Amendment, which limits the president to two four-year terms in office. The amendment is ratified in 1951.

1947 On April 10, Jackie Robinson breaks the "color barrier" when he signs a contract to play for professional baseball's Brooklyn Dodgers. He is later named Rookie of the Year by the *Sporting News.*

1947 Beginning September 30, the World Series is televised for the first time as fans watch the New York Yankees defeat the Brooklyn Dodgers in seven games.

1947 On October 13, the Hollywood Ten, a group of film directors and writers, appears before the House Un-American Activities Committee (HUAC).

1947 On December 3, Tennessee Williams's *A Streetcar Named Desire* opens on Broadway in New York City.

1948 The Baskin-Robbins ice cream chain opens.

1948 On April 3, Congress approves $6 billion in Marshall Plan aid for rebuilding European countries.

1948 On May 14, the state of Israel is established.

1948 On May 29, the play *Oklahoma!* closes after a record 2,246 performances.

1948 On June 25, heavyweight boxing champion Joe Louis knocks out Joe Walcott for his twenty-fifth title defense; following the fight, he announces his retirement from boxing.

1948 On September 13, Margaret Chase Smith of Maine becomes the first woman elected to the U.S. Senate.

1948 On November 2, incumbent Harry S. Truman is elected president.

1949 Builder Abraham Levitt and his sons begin construction on a Long Island, New York, suburb called Levittown, which will become a symbol for the postwar housing boom.

1949 On February 10, Arthur Miller's *Death of a Salesman* opens on Broadway in New York City.

1949 On April 4, the North Atlantic Treaty Organization (NATO) is formed by the United States and twelve other mainly European countries to provide for mutual defense.

1949 On September 23, American, British, and Canadian officials reveal that the Soviet Union has successfully detonated an atomic bomb.

1949 On October 1, the Communist People's Republic of China is proclaimed.

1950 The first Xerox copy machine is produced.

1950 Miss Clairol hair coloring is introduced, making it easy for women to dye their hair at home.

1950 Desegregation continues when Charles Cooper becomes the first black player in the National Basketball Association and Althea Gibson becomes the first black woman to compete in a national tennis tournament.

1950 In March, the Boston Institute of Contemporary Art and New York's Metropolitan Museum and Whitney Museum release a joint statement on modern art opposing "any attempt to make art or opinion about art conform to a single point of view."

1950 On May 8, President Harry S. Truman sends the first U.S. military mission to Vietnam.

1950 On June 30, U.S. combat troops enter the Korean War.

1950 On October 2, *Peanuts,* the comic strip written and drawn by Charles Schulz, debuts in seven U.S. newspapers.

1951 *The Caine Mutiny,* a war novel by Herman Wouk, is published and soon becomes one of the longest lasting best-sellers of all time, holding its place on the *New York Times* list for forty-eight weeks.

1951 On April 5, Julius and Ethel Rosenberg receive death sentences for allegedly giving secret information to the Soviet Union.

1951 On June 25, CBS offers the first color television broadcast.

1951 On August 5, the soap operas *Search for Tomorrow* and *Love of Life* premiere on CBS.

1951 On October 15, the sitcom *I Love Lucy* premieres on CBS.

1951 On November 18, the news program *See It Now,* hosted by Edward R. Murrow, premieres on CBS.

1952 *Gunsmoke* debuts as a radio drama. In 1955, the Western drama moves to TV where it lasts until 1975. The show, which starred James Arness as Marshal Matt Dillon, becomes the longest running prime-time TV show with continuing characters.

1952 In January, *American Bandstand,* a popular teen-oriented music program, debuts as a local show in Philadelphia, Pennsylvania. Dick Clark, its most famous host, joins the show in 1956.

1952 On January 14, *The Today Show* debuts on NBC.

1952 In September, *The Old Man and the Sea,* a short novel by Ernest Hemingway, is printed in *Life* magazine and is the Book-of-the-Month Club's co-main selection.

1953 On October 5, the New York Yankees become the first team in history to win five consecutive World Series when they defeat the Brooklyn Dodgers.

1952 In November, *Bwana Devil,* the first 3-D movie, is released.

1952 On November 4, World War II general Dwight D. Eisenhower is elected president.

1953 *Playboy* becomes the first mass-market men's magazine and rockets to popularity when it publishes nude pictures of rising movie star Marilyn Monroe.

1953 IBM introduces its first computer, the 701.

1953 On January 1, Hank Williams, the father of contemporary country music, dies at age twenty-nine from a heart disease resulting from excessive drinking.

1953 On April 3, the first national edition of *TV Guide* is published.

1953 On July 27, the Korean War ends.

1953 On September 13, Nikita Khrushchev is named first secretary of the Soviet Union's Communist Party.

1953 In November, an eleven-day photoengravers strike leaves New York City without a daily newspaper for the first time since 1778.

1954 U.S. senator Joseph McCarthy of Wisconsin leads hearings into the presence of communists in the U.S. Army; his actions are later condemned by the Senate.

1954 *Sports Illustrated* becomes the first glossy weekly magazine about sports.

1954 Swanson Foods introduces the first TV dinners.

1954 On April 4, legendary conductor Arturo Toscanini makes his final appearance conducting the NBC Symphony Orchestra. The concert is broadcast on the radio live from New York City's Carnegie Hall.

1954 On April 4, Walt Disney signs a contract with ABC to produce twenty-six television films each year.

1954 On May 14, the Soviet Union joins with seven Eastern European countries to form the Warsaw Pact, a union of nations pledged to mutual defense.

1954 On May 17, with its *Brown v. Board of Education* decision, the U.S. Supreme Court ends segregation in public schools.

1954 In July, the Newport Jazz Festival debuts in Newport, Rhode Island.

1954 On July 19, "That's All Right, Mama" and "Blue Moon of Kentucky," the first professional records made by Elvis Presley, are released on Sun Records.

1954 On September 27, *The Tonight Show* debuts on NBC.

1954 In October and November, Hungary tries to leave the Warsaw Pact but is attacked and reclaimed by the Soviet Union.

1955 Velcro is invented.

1955 *The $64,000 Question* debuts and soon becomes the most popular game show of the 1950s.

1955 In January, Marian Anderson becomes the first black singer to appear at the Metropolitan Opera.

1955 On January 19, President Dwight D. Eisenhower holds the first televised presidential news conference.

1955 In March, *The Blackboard Jungle,* the first feature film to include a rock and roll song on its soundtrack—"Rock Around the Clock," by Bill Haley and The Comets—opens. The song becomes the country's number-one single in July.

1955 On April 12, large-scale vaccinations for polio are administered throughout the United States.

1955 On July 17, the Disneyland amusement park opens in Anaheim, California.

1955 On September 30, actor James Dean dies after his Porsche roadster slams into another car on a California highway.

1955 On October 13, poet Allen Ginsberg gives the first public reading of *Howl,* his controversial poem-in-progress.

1955 On December 5, Rosa Parks refuses to give up her seat to a white man on a bus in Montgomery, Alabama, sparking a bus boycott that will become a key moment in the Civil Rights Movement.

1956 On June 20, Loew's Inc. releases MGM's pre-1949 film library—excluding *Gone with the Wind* (1939)—for television broadcast.

1956 On November 6, President Dwight D. Eisenhower is reelected.

1956 On November 30, videotape is first used commercially on television, during the broadcast of CBS's *Douglas Edwards with the News.*

1957 On September 26, the landmark musical *West Side Story,* a modern-day adaptation of *Romeo and Juliet* by William Shakespeare, opens on Broadway at the Winter Garden Theatre in New York City.

1957 On October 5, the Soviet Union launches the satellite *Sputnik,* the first man-made satellite in space.

1958 On October 2, Leonard Bernstein begins his first season as director of the New York Philharmonic.

1958 On October 16, sponsors drop the NBC quiz show *Twenty-One* after a grand jury investigation determines that contestants were provided with pre-show answers.

1959 On January 2, revolutionary leader Fidel Castro assumes power in Cuba.

1959 On January 3, Alaska becomes the forty-ninth state.

1959 On February 3, rock and roll legends Buddy Holly, Ritchie Valens, and J. P. Richardson (known as "The Big Bopper") die in a plane crash outside Clear Lake, Iowa.

1959 On August 21, Hawaii becomes the fiftieth state.

1959 On October 21, the Solomon R. Guggenheim Museum, designed by architect Frank Lloyd Wright, opens in New York City.

1960 Designer Pierre Cardin introduces his first fashion designs for men.

1960 On January 3, the Moscow State Symphony begins a seven-week tour at New York City's Carnegie Hall, becoming the first Soviet orchestra to perform in the United States.

1960 On February 11, Jack Paar, host of *The Tonight Show,* walks off the show when an NBC censor deletes a joke from his performance without his knowledge.

1960 On February 20, black students in Greensboro, North Carolina, stage sit-ins at local lunch counters to protest discrimination.

1960 In April, the New York state legislature authorizes the City of New York to purchase Carnegie Hall, which was scheduled for demolition.

1960 On April 1, Lucille Ball and Desi Arnaz appear for the last time as Lucy and Ricky Ricardo on *The Lucy-Desi Comedy Hour.*

1960 On May 5, the Soviet Union announces the capture of American pilot Francis Gary Powers, whose U-2 spy plane was shot down over the Soviet Union.

1960 On September 26, U.S. senator John F. Kennedy of Massachusetts and Vice President Richard M. Nixon appear in the first televised presidential debate.

1960 On October 13, jazz trumpeter Louis Armstrong begins a goodwill tour of Africa, partially sponsored by the U.S. State Department.

1960 On November 8, U.S. senator John F. Kennedy of Massachusetts is elected president.

1961 On January 20, Robert Frost reads his poem "The Gift Outright" at the inauguration of President John F. Kennedy.

1961 On January 27, soprano Leontyne Price first performs at New York's Metropolitan Opera.

1961 In April, folk singer Bob Dylan makes his debut at Gerde's Folk City in New York City's Greenwich Village.

1961 On April 12, Soviet cosmonaut Yuri Gagarin becomes the first man to orbit the Earth.

1961 During the summer, Freedom Rides across the South are aimed at desegregating interstate bus travel.

1961 On August 15–17, East Germany constructs the Berlin Wall, separating communist East Berlin from democratic West Berlin.

1961 On October 1, Roger Maris sets a new single-season home run record with 61 homers.

1962 On February 10, Jim Beatty becomes the first person to run a mile in less than four minutes with a time of 3:58.9.

1962 On May 30, jazz clarinetist Benny Goodman begins a six-week, U.S. State Department–arranged tour of Russia.

1962 On July 10, the *Telstar* satellite is launched and soon brings live television pictures to American television viewers.

1962 On August 5, actress Marilyn Monroe dies from an overdose of barbiturates.

1962 On September 25, Philharmonic Hall, the first completed building of New York's Lincoln Center for the Performing Arts, is inaugurated by Leonard Bernstein and the New York Philharmonic.

1962 On September 29, *My Fair Lady* closes on Broadway after 2,717 performances, making it the longest-running show in history.

1962 In October, the United States and the Soviet Union clash over the presence of Soviet missiles in Cuba.

1962 On October 1, James Meredith becomes the first black person to enroll at the University of Mississippi as federal troops battle thousands of protesters.

1963 On January 8, *Mona Lisa,* by Leonardo da Vinci, is shown at Washington's National Gallery, the first time the painting ever has appeared outside the Louvre in Paris, France.

1963 On May 7, the Guthrie Theatre in Minneapolis, Minnesota, the first major regional theater in the Midwest, opens.

1963 On November 22, President John F. Kennedy is assassinated in Dallas, Texas, and Vice President Lyndon B. Johnson assumes the presidency.

1963 On November 24, the murder of alleged presidential assassin Lee Harvey Oswald is broadcast live on television.

1964 Ford introduces its Mustang, a smaller sporty car.

1964 On February 9, the Beatles make their first live appearance on American television, on *The Ed Sullivan Show.*

1964 On February 25, Cassius Clay (who later changes his name to Muhammad Ali) beats Sonny Liston to become the heavyweight boxing champion of the world.

1964 In May, the just-remodeled Museum of Modern Art in New York City reopens with a new gallery, the Steichen Photography Center, named for photographer Edward Steichen.

1964 On July 2, President Lyndon B. Johnson signs the Civil Rights Act of 1964, which bans racial discrimination in public places and in employment.

1964 On August 7, in the Gulf of Tonkin Resolution, Congress gives President Lyndon B. Johnson the power to use military force to protect U.S. interests in Vietnam.

1964 On November 3, incumbent Lyndon B. Johnson is elected president.

1965 In January, Bob Dylan plays an electric guitar on his new single, "Subterranean Homesick Blues."

1965 On February 21, black leader Malcolm X is murdered in Harlem, New York.

1965 On March 8, the first U.S. combat troops are sent to Vietnam.

1965 On April 26, *Symphony No. 4* by Charles Ives is performed in its entirety for the first time by the American Symphony Orchestra, conducted by Leopold Stokowski.

1965 On May 9, piano virtuoso Vladimir Horowitz returns to the Carnegie Hall stage after a twelve-year "retirement."

1965 On June 2, in a letter to President Lyndon B. Johnson, Pulitzer Prize–winning poet Robert Lowell declines an invitation to attend a White House arts festival, citing his "dismay and distrust" of American foreign policy.

1965 In July, Bob Dylan and his electric guitar are booed off the Newport Folk Festival stage.

1965 On September 29, President Lyndon B. Johnson signs into law the Federal Aid to the Arts Bill.

1965 On October 15, demonstrations against the Vietnam War occur in forty U.S. cities.

1965 On December 9, *A Charlie Brown Christmas* becomes the first *Peanuts* special to air on TV.

1966 The National Organization for Women (NOW) is established.

1966 On June 8, the National Football League and the American Football League merge.

1966 On July 12, rioting by blacks breaks out in twenty U.S. cities over racial discrimination.

1966 On August 29, the Beatles play their last live concert.

1966 On December 8, philanthropist, horse breeder, and art collector Paul Mellon donates his collection of British rare books, paintings, drawings, and prints, valued at over $35 million, to Yale University.

1967 On January 15, in the first Super Bowl, the Green Bay Packers defeat the Kansas City Chiefs, 35–10.

1967 On February 18, the National Gallery of Art arranges to purchase Leonardo da Vinci's *Ginevra dei Benci* for between $5 million and $6 million, the highest price paid to date for a single painting.

1967 In June, the Monterey International Pop Festival, an important early rock music event, is held in California.

1967 On June 20, Muhammad Ali is stripped of his boxing titles after being found guilty of tax evasion.

1967 On July 23, federal troops are called in to put a stop to rioting in Detroit, Michigan. Forty-three people are killed in the rioting, which lasts a week.

1967 On November 9, the first issue of *Rolling Stone* magazine is published. On the cover is a portrait of the Beatles' John Lennon.

1967 In December, Universal News, the last of the movie newsreel companies, closes because it is unable to compete with television news.

1968 On January 30, North Vietnam launches the Tet Offensive, escalating the war in Vietnam.

1968 On April 4, civil rights leader Martin Luther King Jr. is murdered in Memphis, Tennessee.

1968 On April 19, *Hair* opens on Broadway, at New York City's Biltmore Theatre.

1968 On June 5, presidential candidate and U.S. senator Robert F. Kennedy of New York is murdered in Los Angeles, California.

1968 On September 16, presidential candidate and former vice president Richard Nixon appears as a guest on TV's *Rowan and Martin's Laugh-In* and delivers one of the show's signature lines: "Sock it to me."

1968 On November 1, the Motion Picture Association of America inaugurates its film ratings system.

1968 On November 5, former vice president Richard Nixon is elected president.

1969 Hot pants make their first appearance.

1969 On July 20, U.S. astronaut Neil Armstrong becomes the first man to walk on the moon when the *Apollo 11* mission succeeds.

1969 On August 15–17, the Woodstock Music and Art Fair is held on a six-hundred-acre hog farm in upstate New York.

1969 On November 15, a quarter million Vietnam War protesters march in Washington, D.C.

1969 On December 6, a fan is murdered during the Altamont Rock Festival in California.

1970 Soviet cosmonauts spend seventeen days in space, setting a new record for space longevity.

1970 Across the nation, protests continue over the ongoing Vietnam War.

1970 Rock stars Jimi Hendrix and Janis Joplin die within three weeks of each other, both as a result of drug overdoses.

1970 In March, three women—Elizabeth Bishop, Lillian Hellman, and Joyce Carol Oates—win National Book Awards.

1970 On May 4, National Guard members shoot antiwar protesters at Kent State University in Ohio, killing four students.

1970 On April 10, the Beatles disband.

1970 On April 30, U.S. and South Vietnamese troops invade Cambodia, which has been sheltering North Vietnamese troops.

1970 On September 6, four airliners bound for New York are hijacked by Palestinian terrorists, but no passengers are harmed.

1970 On September 19, *The Mary Tyler Moore Show* debuts on CBS.

1970 On September 21, *Monday Night Football* debuts on ABC.

1970 On October 2, the Environmental Protection Agency (EPA) is created to regulate environmental issues.

1971 Disney World opens in Orlando, Florida.

1971 Hot pants become a fashion sensation.

1971 On January 2, cigarette advertising is banned from television and radio.

1971 On February 6, British troops are sent to patrol Northern Ireland.

1971 On February 9, the European Economic Community, a precursor to the European Union, is established.

1971 On March 8, Joe Frazier defeats Muhammad Ali to retain the world heavyweight boxing title.

1971 On April 20, the U.S. Supreme Court rules that students can be bused to end racial segregation in schools.

1971 In June, the Twenty-sixth Amendment to the Constitution lowers the legal voting age to eighteen.

1971 On June 13, the *New York Times* publishes the "Pentagon Papers," which reveal Defense Department plans for the Vietnam War.

1971 In September, a prison uprising in Attica, New York, ends with forty-three people killed, including ten hostages.

1971 On October 12, the rock musical *Jesus Christ Superstar* opens on Broadway in New York City.

1971 On October 13, the Pittsburgh Pirates and the Baltimore Orioles play in the first World Series night game.

1971 On December 25, "Christmas bombing" occurs in North Vietnam.

1972 In a sign of the cooling of Cold War tensions, East and West Germany and North and South Korea each enter into negotiations to normalize relations.

1972 *Ms.* magazine begins publication.

1972 *Pong*, the first video game available to play at home, becomes popular, as does the first video game machine, Odyssey, introduced by Magnavox.

1972 On February 14, the musical *Grease* opens on Broadway in New York City.

1972 On February 21, President Richard Nixon begins a seven-day visit to Communist China.

1972 On May 22, President Richard Nixon begins a nine-day visit to the Soviet Union.

1972 On June 17, the Watergate scandal begins with the arrest of five men caught trying to bug the Democratic National Committee headquarters at the Watergate building in Washington, D.C. The investigation soon reveals deep corruption in the Nixon administration.

1972 On July 24, the United Nations asks the United States to end its bombing of North Vietnam.

1972 On August 12, the last American combat troops leave Vietnam.

1972 On November 8, cable TV network HBO premieres in Pennsylvania with 365 subscribers.

1973 Three major American cities—Los Angeles, California; Atlanta, Georgia; and Detroit, Michigan—elect a black mayor for the first time.

1973 Investigations into the Watergate affair capture the public attention and shatter the Nixon administration.

1973 The Sears Tower (now known as the Willis Tower), at the time the world's tallest building, is completed in Chicago, Illinois.

1973 Ralph Lauren designs the costumes for the film *The Great Gatsby*, helping build his reputation.

1973 Fantasy-adventure game Dungeons and Dragons is created by Dave Arneson and Gary Gygax.

1973 The first Internet is set up by the U.S. Department of Defense as a way of connecting all the department's computers.

1973 On January 14, the Miami Dolphins win the Super Bowl and become the first professional football team to finish a season undefeated.

1973 On October 16, the Organization of Petroleum Exporting Countries (OPEC) declares an embargo (ban) on the export of oil to the United States and other Western countries.

1973 On October 23, the House of Representatives begins impeachment proceedings against President Richard Nixon.

1974 The Ramones launch the American punk movement with their performances at the New York City club CBGB.

1974 The streaking fad sweeps the country.

1974 President Richard Nixon tours the Middle East and the Soviet Union.

1974 On January 18, Israel and Egypt sign a peace accord that ends their long armed conflict.

1974 On April 8, Hank Aaron of the Atlanta Braves breaks Babe Ruth's lifetime home run record when he hits his 715th career homer.

1974 In May, screenwriter Dalton Trumbo, who had been blacklisted in the 1950s during the anticommunist crusades of U.S. senator Joseph McCarthy of Wisconsin, receives an Academy Award for the 1957 film *The Brave One.*

1974 On August 8, Richard Nixon announces that he would become the first U.S. president to resign from office, amid evidence of a cover-up of the Watergate affair.

1974 On August 9, Vice President Gerald Ford replaces Richard Nixon as president. Less than a month later, he officially pardons Nixon.

1974 On September 8, motorcycle stunt rider Evel Knievel tries to jump a rocket over the Snake River Canyon in Idaho but falls short.

1974 On October 3, Frank Robinson joins the Cleveland Indians as major league baseball's first black manager.

1974 On October 30, boxer Muhammnad Ali regains his world heavyweight boxing title by defeating George Foreman.

1974 In December, unemployment hits 6.5 percent amid a prolonged economic slump and rises to 8.9 percent by May 1975.

1975 The video cassette recorder (VCR) is invented by Sony Corporation in Japan.

1975 The first personal computer, the Altair 8800, is sold in a kit form.

1975 The cult film *The Rocky Horror Picture Show* is released.

1975 Skateboarding becomes popular, and mood rings and pet rocks are popular fads.

1975 Rock star Bruce Springsteen appears on the cover of both *Time* and *Newsweek* thanks to his popular album *Born to Run*.

1975 The Soviet Union and the United States cooperate in the manned *Apollo-Soyuz* space mission.

1975 On January 5, the all-black musical *The Wiz* opens on Broadway in New York City. It eventually tallies 1,672 performances.

1975 On April 30, Saigon, the capital of South Vietnam, is invaded by the communist North Vietnamese, ending the Vietnam War.

1975 On October 1, the Organization of Petroleum Exporting Countries (OPEC) raises crude oil prices by 10 percent.

1975 On October 11, *Saturday Night Live* debuts on NBC.

1976 The first personal computer, the Apple, is developed by Steve Jobs and Steve Wozniak. The Apple II, introduced a year later, offers color graphics.

1976 Model and actress Farrah Fawcett-Majors sets a trend with her feathered haircut and appears on millions of posters in her tiny red bathing suit.

1976 On July 4, the United States celebrates its bicentennial.

1976 On November 2, former Georgia governor Jimmy Carter is elected president.

1976 On November 6, *Gone with the Wind* is broadcast on TV for the first time.

1977 The film *Saturday Night Fever* helps make disco music popular.

1977 Studio 54 becomes New York City's hottest nightclub featuring disco music.

1977 Egyptian artifacts from the tomb of King Tutankhamen, or King Tut, draw huge audiences across the nation.

1977 Alex Haley's book *Roots* becomes a best-seller after the airing of the TV miniseries based on the book.

1977 On January 21, President Jimmy Carter signs an unconditional pardon for most Vietnam-era draft evaders.

1977 On February 8, *Hustler* magazine publisher Larry Flynt is convicted of obscenity.

1977 In April, the Christian Broadcasting Network (CBN) makes its debut.

1977 On August 16, Elvis Presley, the king of rock and roll, dies at Graceland, his Memphis, Tennessee, mansion.

1978 The Walkman personal cassette player is introduced by Sony.

1978 On July 25, the first human test-tube baby is born in England.

1978 On September 17, U.S. president Jimmy Carter hosts negotiations between Israeli prime minister Menachem Begin and Egyptian president Anwar Sadat at Camp David, Maryland.

1978 On October 13, punk rock musician Sid Vicious of the Sex Pistols is arrested for the stabbing death of his girlfriend.

1978 On November 18, Jim Jones and over nine hundred followers of his People's Temple cult are found dead after a mass suicide in Jonestown, Guyana.

1978 On December 5, the Soviet Union and Afghanistan sign a treaty of friendship, and within a year U.S. support for the Afghan government disappears.

1979 Eleven people are trampled to death at a Who concert in Cincinnati, Ohio.

1979 Jerry Falwell organizes the Moral Majority to lobby politicians regarding the concerns of Christian fundamentalists.

1979 On January 1, the United States and the People's Republic of China establish formal diplomatic relations.

1979 On March 28, a major accident in the nuclear reactor at the Three Mile Island power plant near Harrisburg, Pennsylvania, raises concerns about nuclear power.

1979 On November 4, Iranian militants seize the U.S. embassy in Tehran, Iran, and take fifty-two hostages, whom they will hold for over a year.

1979 On December 27, the Soviet Union invades Afghanistan, beginning more than two decades of war and disruption in that country.

1980 Post-it notes are created by 3M chemist Arthur Fry.

1980 On February 22, the U.S. Olympic ice hockey team wins the gold medal, sparking national celebration.

1980 On April 12, the United States votes to boycott the Summer Olympics in Moscow to protest the Soviet presence in Afghanistan.

1980 On April 21, the Mariel boatlift begins, bringing 125,000 refugees from Cuba to Florida before being halted in September.

1980 In June, the all-news CNN cable TV network debuts.

1980 On August 19, a report issued by the *Los Angeles Times* indicates that 40 to 75 percent of NBA players use cocaine.

1980 On November 4, former California governor Ronald Reagan is elected president.

1980 On November 21, the "Who Shot J.R.?" episode of *Dallas* draws the largest television audience of all time.

1980 On September 4, Iraq begins an eight-year war with Iran.

1980 On October 2, in his last fight, heavyweight boxer Muhammad Ali is defeated by World Boxing Council champion Larry Holmes.

1980 On December 8, former Beatles musician John Lennon is shot and killed in New York City.

1981 Nintendo's *Donkey Kong* is the most popular coin-operated video game.

1981 NASA launches and lands the first reusable spacecraft, the space shuttle.

1981 On January 13, the National Collegiate Athletic Association (NCAA) votes to sponsor women's championships in twelve sports after the 1981–82 season.

1981 On January 20, American hostages held at the U.S. embassy in Tehran, Iran, are released on the day of President Ronald Reagan's inauguration.

1981 On January 23, the United States withdraws support for the Marxist government of Nicaragua and begins to support antigovernment rebels known as Contras.

1981 On March 26, comedian Carol Burnett wins a $1.6 million libel lawsuit against the tabloid *National Enquirer.*

1981 On March 30, President Ronald Reagan and three others are wounded in an assassination attempt in Washington, D.C.

1981 On July 29, Great Britain's Prince Charles marries Lady Diana Spencer in an event televised around the world.

1981 On August 1, the Music Television Network (MTV) starts offering music videos that soon become as important as the actual music.

1981 On September 21, Sandra Day O'Connor is confirmed as the first woman to serve on the U.S. Supreme Court.

1982 The compact disc is introduced.

1982 The popular movie *E.T.: The Extra-Terrestrial* sets box office records.

1982 Michael Jackson's album *Thriller* is the year's most popular recording.

1982 Americans frustrate themselves trying to solve Rubik's Cube, a popular puzzle.

1982 On April 2, Argentina invades the Falkland Islands off its coast, sparking a short war with Great Britain, which claims the islands.

1982 On June 7, Graceland, the late Elvis Presley's Memphis, Tennessee, home, is opened as a tourist attraction.

1982 On July 27, acquired immune deficiency syndrome (AIDS) is officially named.

1982 On September 15, *USA Today* becomes the first national newspaper.

1982 On October 7, *Cats* opens on Broadway in New York City and will become the decade's most popular musical.

1983 First lady Nancy Reagan announces a "War on Drugs."

1983 Sally Ride becomes the first woman astronaut in space when she joins the crew of the space shuttle *Challenger.*

1983 Actor Paul Newman introduces his own line of spaghetti sauces to be sold in grocery stores; he uses the proceeds to benefit charities.

1983 On February 28, the farewell episode of the sitcom *M*A*S*H* is seen by 125 million viewers.

1983 On March 23, President Ronald Reagan proposes a space-based antimissile defense system that is popularly known as "Star Wars."

1983 On April 18, terrorists bomb the U.S. embassy in Beirut, Lebanon, killing sixty-three.

1983 On September 1, the Soviet Union shoots down a Korean Air Lines flight that has strayed into its airspace, killing 269.

1983 On October 25, three thousand U.S. soldiers invade the Caribbean island nation of Grenada to crush a Marxist uprising.

1983 In November, Cabbage Patch Kids dolls, with their soft faces and adoption certificates, become the most popular new doll of the Christmas season.

1984 Trivial Pursuit becomes the nation's most popular board game.

1984 *The Cosby Show* debuts on NBC.

1984 Rap group Run-DMC is the first rap group to have a gold album.

1984 Apple introduces a new personal computer, the Macintosh, with a dramatic advertising campaign.

1984 On November 6, Ronald Reagan is reelected president.

1984 On December 3, a Union Carbide plant in Bhopal, India, leaks poison gas that kills two thousand and injures two hundred thousand.

1985 Nintendo Entertainment System, a home video game system that has brilliant colors, realistic sound effects, and quick action, is introduced to the United States.

1985 On March 16, U.S. journalist Terry Anderson is kidnapped in Lebanon; he will be held until December 4, 1991.

1985 In April, Coca-Cola changes the formula of its popular soft drink and the public reacts with anger and dismay, prompting the company to reissue the old formula as Classic Coke.

1985 On July 13, British rock star Bob Geldof organizes Live Aid, a charity concert and album to aid the victims of African famine.

1985 On October 2, the death of handsome movie star Rock Hudson from AIDS raises awareness about the disease.

1986 Country singer Dolly Parton opens a theme park in Tennessee called Dollywood.

1986 On January 28, the space shuttle *Challenger* explodes upon liftoff, killing the six astronauts and one teacher who were aboard.

1986 On February 26, Robert Penn Warren is named the first poet laureate of the United States.

1986 On April 26, a serious meltdown at the Chernobyl nuclear power plant near Kiev, Ukraine, releases a radioactive cloud into the atmosphere and is considered a major disaster.

1986 On May 1, in South Africa, 1.5 million blacks protest apartheid (the policy of racial segregation). Around the world, foreign governments place sanctions on South Africa.

1986 On June 10, Nancy Lieberman becomes the first woman to play in a men's professional basketball league when she joins the United States Basketball League.

1986 On July 15, the United States sends troops to Bolivia to fight against drug traffickers.

1986 On July 27, Greg LeMond becomes the first American to win France's prestigious Tour de France bicycle race.

1986 In October, it is discovered that members of the Reagan administration have been trading arms for hostages in Iran and illegally channeling funds to Contras in Nicaragua. This Iran-Contra scandal will eventually be investigated by Congress.

1986 On November 22, twenty-one-year-old Mike Tyson becomes the youngest heavyweight boxing champion when he defeats World Boxing Council champ Trevor Berbick.

1987 On March 19, televangelist Jim Bakker resigns after it is revealed that he has been having an adulterous affair with church secretary Jessica Hahn.

1987 On June 25, Soviet leader Mikhail Gorbachev announces *perestroika,* a program of sweeping economic reforms aimed at improving the Soviet economy.

1987 On October 3, Canada and the United States sign a free-trade agreement.

1987 On October 17, the stock market experiences its worst crash in history when it drops 508 points.

1987 On November 11, Vincent van Gogh's painting *Irises* is sold for $53.9 million.

1988 McDonald's opens twenty restaurants in Moscow, Russia.

1988 Singer Sonny Bono is elected mayor of Palm Springs, California.

1988 On February 5, former Panamanian dictator General Manuel Noriega is charged in a U.S. court with accepting bribes from drug traffickers.

1988 On February 14, Ayatollah Khomeini of Iran calls author Salman Rushdie's book *The Satanic Verses* offensive and issues a death sentence on him. The author goes into hiding.

1988 On April 14, Soviet forces withdraw from Afghanistan after ten years of fighting in that country.

1988 On July 3, believing it is under attack, a U.S. warship shoots down an Iran Air passenger liner, killing 290 passengers.

1988 On November 8, Vice President George Herbert Walker Bush is elected president.

1988 On December 21, Pan Am Flight 747 explodes over Lockerbie, Scotland, killing 259 on the flight and 11 on the ground. Middle Eastern terrorists are eventually charged with the crime.

1989 On March 24, the Exxon *Valdez* oil tanker runs aground in Alaska, spilling 240,000 barrels of oil and creating an environmental disaster.

1989 In May, more than one million Chinese demonstrate for democracy in Beijing.

1989 In June, Chinese troops crack down on demonstrators in Tiananmen Square, drawing attention to the repressive government.

1989 On August 9, Colin R. Powell becomes the United States' first black chairman of the Joint Chiefs of Staff.

1989 On August 23, the Soviet states of Lithuania, Latvia, and Estonia demand autonomy from the Soviet Union. Later, across the former Soviet-dominated region, Soviet republics and satellite countries throw off communist control and pursue independence.

1989 On August 24, former baseball star Pete Rose is banned from baseball for life because it is believed that he bet on games in which he was involved.

1989 On October 15, Wayne Gretzky of the Los Angeles Kings becomes the National Hockey League's all-time leading scorer with his 1,850th point.

1989 On October 17, a major earthquake hits the San Francisco, California, area.

1989 On December 16, American troops invade Panama and seize dictator General Manuel Noriega. Noriega will later be convicted in U.S. courts.

1989 On December 22, the Brandenburg Gate in Berlin is officially opened, allowing people from East and West Berlin to mix freely and signaling the end of the Cold War and the reunification of Germany.

1990 The animated sitcom *The Simpsons* debuts on the FOX network.

1990 Ken Burns's documentary *The Civil War* airs on PBS.

1990 British scientist Tim Berners-Lee invents the World Wide Web.

1990 On April 25, the Hubble Space Telescope is deployed in space from the space shuttle *Discovery.*

1990 On July 26, President George Herbert Walker Bush signs the Americans with Disabilities Act, which provides broad protections for those with disabilities.

1990 On August 2, Iraq invades Kuwait, prompting the United States to wage war on Iraq from bases in Saudi Arabia. Much of this conflict, called the Persian Gulf War, is aired live on television and makes CNN famous for its coverage.

1990 On October 3, East and West Germany are reunited.

1991 Mass murderer Jeffrey Dahmer is charged with killing fifteen young men and boys near Milwaukee, Wisconsin.

1991 On March 3, U.S. general Norman Schwarzkopf announces the end of the Persian Gulf War.

1991 In October, confirmation hearings for U.S. Supreme Court justice nominee Clarence Thomas are carried live on television and feature Anita Hill's dramatic accusations of sexual harassment. Despite the charges, Thomas is confirmed.

1991 On November 7, Los Angeles Lakers basketball star Earvin "Magic" Johnson announces that he has contracted the HIV virus.

1991 On December 8, leaders of Russia and several other former Soviet states announce the formation of the Commonwealth of Independent States.

1992 On April 29, riots erupt in Los Angeles, California, following the acquittal of four white police officers in the beating of black motorist Rodney King. The brutal beating had been filmed and shown widely on television.

1992 On May 21, Vice President Dan Quayle criticizes the CBS sitcom *Murphy Brown* for not promoting family values after the main character has a child out of wedlock.

1992 In August, the Mall of America, the nation's largest shopping mall, opens in Bloomington, Minnesota.

1992 On August 24, Hurricane Andrew hits Florida and the Gulf Coast, causing a total of over $15 billion in damage.

1992 On October 24, the Toronto Blue Jays become the first non-U.S. team to win baseball's World Series.

1992 On November 3, Arkansas governor Bill Clinton is elected president, defeating incumbent George Herbert Walker Bush and strong third party candidate H. Ross Perot.

1992 On December 17, the United States, Canada, and Mexico sign the North American Free Trade Agreement (NAFTA).

1993 Jack "Dr. Death" Kevorkian is arrested in Michigan for assisting in the suicide of a terminally ill patient, his nineteenth such action.

1993 On February 26, six people are killed when terrorists plant a bomb in New York City's World Trade Center.

1993 On April 19, more than eighty members of a religious cult called the Branch Davidians are killed in a mass suicide as leaders set fire to their compound in Waco, Texas, following a fifty-one-day siege by federal forces.

1993 In July and August, the Flood of the Century devastates the American Midwest, killing forty-eight.

1994 Tiger Woods becomes the youngest person and the first black to win the U.S. Amateur Golf Championship.

1994 Special prosecutor Ken Starr is appointed to investigate President Bill Clinton's involvement in a financial scandal known as Whitewater. The investigation will ultimately cover several scandals and lead to impeachment proceedings against the president.

1994 In January, ice skater Nancy Kerrigan is attacked by associates of her rival, Tonya Harding, at the U.S. Olympic Trials in Detroit, Michigan.

1994 On May 2, Nelson Mandela is elected president of South Africa. The black activist had been jailed for decades under the old apartheid regime and became the country's first black president.

1994 On August 11, major league baseball players go on strike, forcing the cancellation of the playoffs and World Series.

1994 On November 5, forty-five-year-old boxer George Foreman becomes the oldest heavyweight champion when he defeats Michael Moorer.

1995 On April 19, a car bomb explodes outside the Alfred P. Murrah Federal Office Building in Oklahoma City, Oklahoma, killing 168 people. Following a manhunt, antigovernment zealot Timothy McVeigh is captured, and later he is convicted and executed for the crime.

1995 On September 1, the Rock and Roll Hall of Fame opens in Cleveland, Ohio.

1995 On September 6, Cal Ripken Jr. of the Baltimore Orioles breaks the long-standing record for most consecutive baseball games played with 2,131. The total reaches 2,632 games before Ripken removes himself from the lineup in 1998.

1995 On October 3, former football star O. J. Simpson is found not guilty of the murder of his ex-wife and her friend in what many called the "trial of the century."

1996 Three years after the introduction of H. Ty Warners's Beanie Babies, the first eleven toy styles are retired and quickly become collector's items.

1996 On September 26, American astronaut Shannon Lucid returns to Earth after spending 188 days in space—a record for any astronaut.

1996 On November 5, Bill Clinton is reelected to the presidency.

1997 Researchers in Scotland successfully clone an adult sheep, named Dolly.

1997 The Hale-Bopp comet provides a nightly show as it passes by the Earth.

1997 Actress Ellen DeGeneres becomes the first openly gay lead character in her ABC sitcom *Ellen.*

1997 On January 23, Madeleine Albright becomes the first woman sworn in as U.S. secretary of state.

1997 On March 27, thirty-nine members of the Heavens Gate religious cult are found dead in their California compound.

1997 On April 13, Tiger Woods becomes the youngest person and the first black to win a major golf tournament when he wins the Masters with the lowest score ever.

1997 On June 19, the play *Cats* sets a record for the longest-running Broadway play with its 6,138th performance.

1997 On June 20, four major tobacco companies settle a lawsuit with states that will cost companies nearly $400 billion.

1997 On June 28, boxer Mike Tyson is disqualified when he bites the ear of opponent Evander Holyfield during a heavyweight title fight.

1997 On July 5, the *Pathfinder* spacecraft lands on Mars and sends back images and rock analyses.

1997 On August 31, Britain's Princess Diana is killed in an auto accident in Paris, France.

1998 Mark McGwire of the St. Louis Cardinals sets a single-season home run record with seventy home runs.

1998 The final episode of the popular sitcom *Seinfeld* is watched by an estimated audience of seventy-six million.

1998 On January 22, Unabomber Ted Kaczynski is convicted for a series of mail bombings and sentenced to life in prison.

1998 On March 24, the movie *Titanic* wins eleven Academy Awards, tying the record set by *Ben-Hur* in 1959.

1998 On April 10, a new drug for male impotence known as Viagra hits the market and is a popular sensation.

1998 On August 7, terrorists explode bombs outside the U.S. embassies in Nairobi, Kenya, and Dar es Salaam, Tanzania.

1998 In November, former professional wrestler Jesse "The Body" Ventura is elected governor of Minnesota.

1998 On December 19, the House of Representatives initiates impeachment proceedings against President Bill Clinton, but the U.S. Senate acquits Clinton on two charges in early 1999.

1999 The U.S. women's soccer team wins the World Cup by defeating China.

1999 On March 24, NATO launches a bombing campaign against Serbia to stop its actions in Kosovo.

1999 On March 29, the Dow Jones Industrial Average closes above 10,000 for the first time in history thanks to a booming stock market dominated by high-tech companies.

1999 On April 20, in Littleton, Colorado, two students go on a vicious shooting spree, killing themselves and twelve other students.

1999 On September 24, *IKONOS,* the world's first commercial, high-resolution imaging satellite, is launched into space; it can detect an object on Earth as small as a card table.

2000 The world wakes up on January 1 to find that the so-called "Y2K" computer bug had failed to materialize.

2000 In May, Eminem releases his *Marshall Mathers LP,* which sells 1.76 million copies in its first week, becoming the fastest-selling album by a solo artist of all time.

2000 The fourth Harry Potter book, *Harry Potter and the Goblet of Fire,* is released in July and sets new publishing sales records.

2000 Tiger Woods becomes the youngest golfer to win all four Grand Slam golf tournaments.

2000 The first inhabitants of the International Space Station take up residence in orbit over the Earth.

2000 In November, outgoing First Lady Hillary Rodham Clinton wins a seat in Congress as a senator representing New York state.

2000 On December 12, over a month after Election Day, Texas governor George W. Bush is declared the winner of the presidential race against Vice President Al Gore after contentious vote recounting in Florida is ordered stopped by the Supreme Court. Bush takes Florida by a margin of 527 votes and edges Gore in the Electoral College by only four votes.

2000 On December 28, squeezed by "big box" retailers like Wal-Mart, Montgomery Ward announces it will be closing its doors after 128 years in business.

2001 Wikipedia is launched.

2001 On April 1, a U.S. spy plane collides with a Chinese fighter jet and is forced to land on Chinese soil, causing an international incident.

2001 The first draft of the human genome, a complete sequence of human DNA, is published.

2001 The "dot com bubble" bursts, leading to widespread bankruptcies in the software and Internet industries.

2001 On September 11, nineteen terrorists hijack four planes, flying two into the twin towers of the World Trade Center in New York City and one into the Pentagon in Arlington, Virginia. The fourth plane goes down in a field in Pennsylvania during a fight over the controls and fails to reach its intended target, believed to be the White House.

2001 In October, Afghanistan, accused of harboring terrorist training camps and 9/11 mastermind Osama bin Laden, is invaded by the United States and its allies, initiating the so-called War on Terror.

2002 Europe introduces its first universal currency, the Euro, initially accepted in twelve countries.

2002 The U.S. State Department issues its report on state sponsors of terrorism, singling out seven countries: Cuba, Iran, Iraq, Libya, North Korea, Sudan, and Syria.

2002 The United States begins detaining suspected terrorists without trial at its military base in Guantanamo Bay, Cuba.

2002 Halle Berry wins the Academy Award for best actress, becoming the first African American to win the honor.

2002 Bulgaria, Estonia, Latvia, Lithuania, Romania, Slovakia, and Slovenia, all former Soviet bloc nations, are invited to join the North Atlantic Treaty Organization (NATO).

2003 On February 1, the space shuttle *Columbia* disintegrates during reentry, scattering the craft's debris across the United States and killing all seven astronauts aboard.

2003 SARS, a new respiratory disease, first appears in Hong Kong before spreading around the world.

2003 In the face of mass global protests, the United States invades Iraq on March 19 as part of its continuing war on terror. By April 9, the capital city of Baghdad is taken. The weapons of mass destruction that were reported to be harbored by Iraqi dictator Saddam Hussein and were the publicly stated reason behind the invasion are never found.

2003 On December 13, Saddam Hussein is found hiding in a bolt hole in an Iraqi village.

2004 Online social network Facebook is founded.

2004 On March 11, Madrid, Spain, is the target of the worst terrorist attacks since September 11, 2001; 191 people are killed and 2,050 wounded in a series of coordinated train bombings.

2004 George W. Bush is elected to a second term by a wider margin than in 2000.

2004 On December 26, a tsunami caused by an earthquake measuring 9.3 on the moment magnitude scale in the Indian Ocean kills over three hundred thousand people across eleven countries in Southeast Asia and Sri Lanka.

2005 The video-sharing Web site YouTube is launched.

2005 Prince Charles, the heir to the throne of Great Britain, marries his longtime love, Camilla Parker Bowles.

2005 In June, pop star Michael Jackson is acquitted of child molestation charges.

2005 On July 7, coordinated bombings on three trains and a bus kill fifty-six people in London, England.

2005 On July 26, American cyclist Lance Armstrong wins his record seventh-straight Tour de France.

2005 On August 29, Hurricane Katrina makes landfall on America's Gulf Coast. The resulting destruction, largely centered on New Orleans, Louisiana, after the city's levee system fails, leads to billions of dollars in damage and over eighteen hundred deaths. The federal government is widely criticized for its slow reaction to the disaster, with rapper Kanye West famously declaring on live television, "George Bush doesn't care about black people."

2005 In November, French surgeons perform the world's first face transplant.

2006 The issue of global warming becomes a mainstream subject of discussion with the release of former vice president Al Gore's film *An Inconvenient Truth* and the accompanying book of the same name.

2006 The *Oxford English Dictionary* adds the verb "google" to its pages.

2006 Online social network Twitter is launched.

2006 The United States reaches a population of three hundred million only thirty-two years after hitting the two hundred million mark.

2006 Pluto is downgraded from planetary status, reducing the number of planets in the solar system to eight.

2006 On February 22, the one billionth digital song is downloaded from Apple's iTunes store.

2006 Riding a backlash against the ongoing wars in Iraq and Afghanistan and dissatisfaction with the George W. Bush administration, the Democratic Party wins back majorities in both houses of Congress for the first time in twelve years.

2006 On December 30, Iraqis execute former president Saddam Hussein.

2007 President George W. Bush announces that 21,500 more troops will be sent to Iraq as part of a "surge" to stem the ongoing guerrilla attacks being carried out against U.S. troops and Iraqi civilians by Iraqi dissidents and Arab terrorists.

2007 On the night of February 17, pop star Britney Spears, increasingly under media scrutiny for her erratic behavior, shaves her head and lashes out against paparazzi and reporters who had been tailing her.

2007 Apple introduces the iPhone.

2007 In the wake of Barry Bonds setting a new home run record amongst whispers of his use of performance-enhancing drugs, the Mitchell Report is released, detailing a year-long investigation into the widespread abuse of steroids in major league baseball.

2008 The Iraq troop surge is judged largely a success by July, eighteen months after it was implemented.

2008 On August 17, swimmer Michael Phelps sets a new Olympic record when he wins his eighth gold medal.

2008 With the September 15 collapse of lending firm Lehman Brothers, a major panic sweeps the world financial markets. Along with the collapse of the housing bubble, these are the first clear signals of the onset of the Great Recession, the worst global economic crisis since the Great Depression.

2008 On November 4, U.S. senator Barack Obama of Illinois becomes the first African American elected president of the United States.

2009 Barack Obama's historic inauguration on January 20 draws over one million people to the National Mall in Washington, D.C.

2009 Upon assuming office, President Barack Obama orders the closing of the Guantanamo Bay detention center and passes a $75 billion economic stimulus package.

2009 On April 15 (tax day), protests break out across the country, marking the beginning of the loosely affiliated Tea Party movement. Although lacking a single guiding organization or national leader, the conservative, ostensibly grassroots, movement is united by its concern over certain types of government spending and increasing federal deficit levels.

2009 On June 25, pop star Michael Jackson is found dead of an apparent prescription drug overdose. His passing ignites worldwide mourning and an outpouring of grief from hundreds of millions of fans, despite the singer's legal and personal troubles through the 1990s and the first decade of the 2000s.

2009 On October 31, jobless claims break the 10 percent barrier for the first time since the Great Recession began.

2009 With the situation in Iraq less dire and attacks by the Afghan Taliban on the rise, President Barack Obama announces a surge of thirty thousand more troops in Afghanistan.

BOWLING, BEATNIKS, AND BELL-BOTTOMS

Pop Culture of 20th- and 21st-Century America

1940s

The Pivotal Decade

It is impossible to overstate the importance of World War II (1939–45) in U.S. history. America became involved in the conflict after the December 7, 1941, attack on Pearl Harbor in Hawaii by Japanese aircraft. From that moment, massive changes swept the nation, which would be felt for the rest of the century.

When the decade began, America continued to suffer from the effects of the economic depression (the Great Depression, 1929–41) that had lasted throughout the 1930s. Although the New Deal policies of President Franklin D. Roosevelt (1882–1945) had helped the nation avoid outright economic disaster, many Americans remained unemployed and business activity was stuck in a difficult state. Then, German leader Adolf Hitler (1889–1945) invaded Czechoslovakia and Poland in 1939. Americans looked at the war that was gripping Europe and felt lucky that they were not involved. The overriding attitude toward foreign wars was that America should not get involved. But this non-interventionism, as it was called, did not last long after America was attacked on its own soil.

When President Roosevelt called his nation into war against the Japanese, the Germans, and their allies—a combination known collectively as the Axis forces—he wakened a mighty force. Hundreds of thousands of young men volunteered to fight. American factories mobilized to produce guns, tanks, and airplanes. The entire American

1940s At a Glance

WHAT WE SAID:

Big eyes: A crush, as in "I have big eyes for her!"

Cooling: Unemployed.

Geets: Money.

"Here's looking at you, kid": These famous words, uttered by Humphrey Bogart's Rick Blaine to Ingrid Bergman's Ilsa Lund in the film *Casablanca,* quickly passed into popular usage as a toast.

Hollywood eyes: A description of a pretty girl: "She has Hollywood eyes."

Icky drip: A person whose looks or interests set them apart from the crowd.

"Mash me a fin": "Would you loan me $5?"

"Murder!": "Wow!," an expression of surprise or great excitement.

Nab: A policeman.

Oomph girl or Sweater girl: A term first used by the Hollywood press to describe a full-figured, good-looking girl. Many Hollywood starlets would claim to be the "original" oomph or sweater girl.

Percolator: A car.

Pin-up girl: Attractive women featured on posters during World War II to entertain military men. The most famous pin-up girl was Betty Grable, shown in a bathing suit and high-heeled shoes looking over her shoulder; a pin-up of Rita Hayworth was stuck to the first atomic bomb dropped on Hiroshima.

Roost: A person's home.

WHAT WE READ:

Paperback books: Born in the late 1930s, these tomes, which featured flashy covers, racy stories, and cheap prices, were read by the millions during the 1940s. The first paperback publisher was Pocket Books (1939). Soon publishers Avon Books (1941), Dell Books (1943), Popular Library (1943), Bantam Books (1945), New American Library (1948), and Gold Medal Books (1949) were all enticing readers with paperback editions.

Comic books: Readers could select from among more than 150 different titles. The adventures of superheroes were the most popular, particularly those of Captain Marvel (1940), Wonder Woman (1941), Captain America (1941), and Plastic Man (1941).

***For Whom the Bell Tolls* (1940):** Having already established his international celebrity as a talented writer with the novels *The Sun Also Rises* (1926) and *A Farewell to Arms* (1929), Ernest Hemingway offered years of short fiction and reporting from around the world. *For Whom*

population steeled itself for what soon came to be regarded as a vital mission to defend American freedom. But it was not an easy fight.

Fighting alongside the other Allied forces, including France, Great Britain, and the Soviet Union, American forces waged war for four years. Thousands of young American men died, though their losses remained small compared with the toll that war took on the countries in which it *the Bell Tolls* was a novel that provided an insightful portrayal of humanity during wartime, the Spanish civil war in this case.

The Sun Is My Undoing (1941): This novel by Marguerite Steen was the first in a trilogy including *Twilight on the Floods* (1949) and *Jehovah Blues* (1952), which follow the Floods family through two centuries of their involvement in the slave trade. Steen's dramatic style of writing and action-packed novels won her a large following.

The Robe (1942): Lloyd C. Douglas's novel told of a centurion's quest to learn more about Christ after crucifying him. It remained on the bestseller list for three years and was made into a movie in 1953. Douglas had spent nearly twenty years as a Lutheran minister before becoming a writer.

Yank: This military magazine began publication in 1942 and by the end of the war had more than two million subscribers. The magazine was best known for its two cartoon characters, G.I. Joe and Sad Sack, which helped boost the morale of servicemen in the field.

Forever Amber (1944): Kathleen Winsor's first historical romance novel. Its racy content caused it to be banned in Boston, Massachusetts, but others clamored to read it. The book had eleven printings within a year of its publication. The movie rights to the story were purchased for a higher amount than that paid for Margaret Mitchell's *Gone With the Wind*.

Stars and Stripes: The largest military newspaper, which released almost thirty editions during World War II. The paper carried news of the war, news from the United States, cartoons, and photographs of beautiful women to military servicemen throughout the war.

The Common Sense Book of Baby and Child Care (1946): One of the best-selling books of all time, with over fifty million copies sold by the end of the twentieth century. This work by Dr. Benjamin Spock became the bible of child care for generations of Americans, and was last updated in 1998, the year of Spock's death.

I, the Jury (1947): This hard-boiled story featuring Mickey Spillane's famous detective Mike Hammer proved the importance of paperback books, selling more than two million copies in paperback in 1948 after achieving only moderate success as a hardcover book the previous year.

WHAT WE WATCHED:
Walt Disney animated films: Disney's *Fantasia* (1940), *Pinocchio* (1940), *Bambi* (1942), and *Cinderella* (1949) were among the most popular films of the decade. They captivated audiences with their stunning animated scenes and endearing characters.

was fought. Germany, France, and Great Britain were devastated both physically and financially. Finally, thanks to overwhelming victories in Europe and the dropping of two atomic bombs on Japan, America and its allies were able to claim victory in 1945.

The world looked far different after the war than it had before. For one thing, Americans realized that they could no longer avoid getting

1940s At a Glance (continued)

***Citizen Kane* (1941):** Orson Welles's masterpiece drama about the life of wealthy Charles Foster Kane is considered one of the greatest films ever made.

***Casablanca* (1942):** This drama was the film in which Humphrey Bogart perfected the tough-guy image he had crafted in *The Maltese Falcon* (1941). Co-starring Ingrid Bergman, this drama remained among the top five films throughout the decade.

***Yankee Doodle Dandy* (1942):** James Cagney won an Academy Award for best actor for his role in this musical about the extraordinary life of composer, singer, and dancer George M. Cohan.

***Oklahoma!* (1943):** Without chorus lines or comedic interruptions, this Broadway musical blended a love story with folk music and modern dance to transform the American musical.

***It's a Wonderful Life* (1946):** In this perennial classic, James Stewart, playing George Bailey, found out how his life had positively impacted the lives of those in his community with the help of an angel who distracted him from committing suicide on Christmas Eve.

***Song of the South* (1946):** The tales of Br'er Rabbit were intermixed in this film about life on a southern plantation. The musical included the popular song "Zip-A-Dee-Doo-Dah."

***The Best Years of Our Lives* (1946):** This dramatic film traced the lives of three war veterans as they returned home after the war. One lost his hands, another came home to a larger family than the one he left, and the third returned to a loveless marriage and a dead-end job.

WHAT WE LISTENED TO:

The Ink Spots: Between 1940 and 1949, this African American vocal group had eleven Top Ten hits on the charts, including "Whispering Grass" and "Don't Worry." They were among the first black recording groups to have "crossover" hits that were popular with whites, and laid the foundation for later "doo-wop" groups.

Charlie Parker: The most influential jazz musician of the 1940s. Parker, a saxophonist, led the transformation of jazz to "be-bop," a style of jazz that highlighted complex improvisations and faster beats.

Glenn Miller: Big band trombonist Miller earned the first gold record ever presented to a recording artist for his song "Chattanooga Choo-Choo," which sold over a million copies. He was the most successful recording artist of the decade, hitting the Top Ten thirty-one times in 1940 alone. He dissolved his band to enter the army's air force in 1942. He died in a plane crash in 1944.

---

entangled in foreign conflicts. Now that technological advances allowed war to be waged on countries halfway around the world, mere oceans could not provide protection. America became increasingly involved in foreign affairs. In fact, over the coming decades American forces would be sent all over the globe. Secondly, the war not only lifted America out of its long economic depression but also left the nation with the world's most vibrant

Superman: This radio show premiered in 1940, adding catchphrases such as "Up, up, and away!" and "This looks like a job for Superman!" to everyday language.

"Back in the Saddle Again": The theme song of Gene Autry, the "Singing Cowboy." Originally written in 1938 by Ray Whitley for the film *Border Men,* Autry soon revived it for his own movies and also regularly sang it on his radio and TV shows.

"The Boogie Woogie Bugle Boy" (1941): A hit song by the Andrews Sisters, the top-selling girl group of all time. The song was featured in the Abbott and Costello farce *Buck Privates,* in which the Andrews Sisters played themselves.

Censored news: All reporting of news and war information was censored by the "Code of Wartime Practices for American Broadcasters" starting in 1942.

"White Christmas": Bing Crosby sang this hit song in the 1942 film *Holiday Inn*. The song's longing for a family gathering during the holidays became popular with Americans as they hoped for the best for their soldiers.

"All or Nothing at All": This single by Frank Sinatra sold more than one million copies. It also marked a shift in popular music. The Harry James Orchestra originally recorded the song in 1939 (with Sinatra singing), but Sinatra wanted

to rerecord it in 1943. When a musicians strike prevented that, Sinatra's managers decided to rerelease the earlier song, renaming the single to highlight Sinatra's name. Until this time, bandleaders were the most important musicians to feature on musical covers.

Paul Harvey News: Debuting on the radio in 1944, Paul Harvey's distinctive reporting style kept him on the air into the twenty-first century.

The Adventures of Ozzie and Harriet: This sitcom about America's favorite couple and their sons David and Ricky debuted on the radio in 1944. The show moved to television in 1952 and stayed on the air until 1966.

"I'm Looking Over a Four-Leaf Clover": This song by Art Mooney's orchestra became the #1 single on the Billboard chart in January 1948 and began a revival of "old-time" banjo songs.

"I'm So Lonesome I Could Cry" (1949): One of the last songs by Hank Williams, this ballad became a country music classic.

WHO WE KNEW:

Gutzon Borglum (1867–1941): The Idaho-born sculptor of Mount Rushmore died just months before work was to be completed. He had begun carving four presidents' faces out of a South Dakota mountain in 1927.

economy. Although there were difficulties in the transition to peace, America's economy was the only one in the world that emerged from the war fully functioning.

Victorious in war and with a booming economy, Americans were determined to enjoy the fruits of their labors. Many families who had put off having children during the Depression and the war now regarded

1940s At a Glance (continued)

Bing Crosby (1904–1977): One of the most popular stars of the 1940s. His talent was firmly established in the 1930s when his music was played constantly on the radio, but his acting talent became more recognized in the 1940s, when he gave an Oscar-winning performance in *Going My Way* (1944) and received an Oscar nomination for his part in *The Bells of St. Mary's* (1945).

Charles Richard Drew (1904–1950): This African American physician directed the first American blood bank. A professor and surgeon at Howard University from 1935 to 1936 and again from 1942 to 1950, Drew discovered how to preserve blood plasma for transfusion. From 1940 to 1941, he headed the American program that sent blood to Great Britain and later directed the first American Red Cross Blood Bank from 1941 to 1942. Despite Drew's scientific discovery and leadership of the blood bank, segregation laws prohibited him from donating his own blood.

Anne Frank (1929–1945): After hiding with her family in a secret room in Amsterdam, Holland, from 1942 to 1944, this Jewish teen and her family were discovered by the Nazis and sent to a concentration camp. She died there in 1945, but her diary was discovered and published in 1947 to great international acclaim.

Billy Graham (1918–): One of the best-known American preachers of the twentieth century. Graham's evangelistic crusades have taken him around the world, put him on television and radio, and won him friendships with presidents.

Billie Holiday (1915–1959): The top jazz performer of the decade. Some of her recordings are regarded as the best jazz songs of all time, including "Lover Man" and "Now or Never."

George S. Patton (1885–1945): Nicknamed "Old Blood and Guts," his leadership helped

child-rearing as a primary goal. They helped create a "baby boom," a surge in population growth that made itself felt throughout the decade as these "boomers" came of age. In order to accommodate this growing population, Americans built highways and houses. Looking forward to jobs and careers that would allow them to provide well for their families, thousands of men attended college with the financial assistance of a government program known as the G.I. Bill.

American popular culture during this decade shifted to match the changing tenor of the times. During the war newspapers, magazines, and radio programs devoted themselves to providing Americans with up-to-date information on the war effort. Radio, especially, made the world seem smaller by bringing live news from distant points of the globe into American living rooms. American moviemakers did their part by producing light, entertaining diversions as an alternative to the difficult war news. Sports went on, even though many athletes served overseas.

the Allied victory at the crucial Battle of the Bulge in 1945 and his tactics modernized the U.S. cavalry. Known as a fearless leader, whose desire for victory was infectious to his troops, Patton nevertheless lost his position of command when he declared that the United States should be fighting with Germany against the Russians.

Ernie Pyle (1900–1945): This roving reporter penned stories from the front lines of battles in World War II in Britain, Italy, North Africa, and the Normandy Beach of France. Pyle was on assignment on a Pacific island when he was killed from a shot by a Japanese soldier. Americans dearly missed their link to the warfront, and American soldiers posted a marker at the site of his death, noting that they had lost a "buddy."

Jackie Robinson (1919–1972): The first African American to play baseball in the modern major leagues, Robinson joined the Brooklyn Dodgers in 1947 and played ten years with them, leading the team to six World Series. In 1962, he became the first African American to be inducted into the National Baseball Hall of Fame.

Benjamin "Bugsy" Siegel (1906–1947): Gangster Siegel established the first legal gambling casino in the United States. The Flamingo Hotel in Las Vegas, Nevada, proved enormously successful and became famous across the nation. Siegel's involvement with a large crime syndicate proved to be his undoing. Shortly after a supposed disagreement with the syndicate over the portion of the Flamingo's profits due as payment for help financing the hotel, Siegel was shot three times in the head and died instantly.

Richard Wright (1908–1960): The author of *Native Son* (1940) and his autobiography *Black Boy* (1945) has been referred to as the "father" of a generation of black writers who came after him. He is credited with expressing the black experience in a brand new light.

After the war, however, a new force in American popular culture made itself felt. Although television sets had been available before the war, it was only with renewed postwar prosperity that numbers of Americans were able to purchase the new devices they called "TVs." Soon, television networks were offering a small but growing number of programs to those living in urban areas. By the end of the 1940s it was clear that TV would be the entertainment format of the future. Both during and after the war, music provided a release from daily life, and new forms like rhythm and blues, bebop, and boogie-woogie excited listeners.

Even as Americans recovered from the difficulties of war and began to enjoy their lives again, a dark cloud appeared on the horizon. By the end of the decade, it was becoming clear that America's ideas for the shape of the postwar world were very different than those being advocated by the Soviet Union. The United States, led by President Harry S.

Truman (1884–1972), wanted countries in Africa, Asia, and the Middle East to embrace capitalism. The Russians hoped that the not-yet-aligned countries would embrace their system, communism. Both countries wanted their way, but they did not want to engage in open warfare now that the world had seen the destruction of modern warfare, especially that caused by the atomic bomb. Therefore, the United States and the Soviet Union locked themselves into a "Cold War" (1945–91) in which the two world superpowers engaged in a political stalemate, with both sides using diplomats, spies, and anything short of outright war to get their way. The Cold War would dominate American political life for nearly fifty years, casting shadows over the sunny landscape of postwar American prosperity.

1940s

Commerce

The 1940s were a time of incredible growth for American business. The country had recovered from the Great Depression (1929–41) and the war and government spending helped American businesses become strong, solid, and profitable. The fastest growing parts of the economy involved those involved in the production of consumer goods and military supplies. With such growth in business, unemployment declined and wages rose to an unprecedented level. By the end of the war, America had the strongest economy in the world. The starting of the Cold War (1945–91) at that time ensured the continuing governmental support for military expenditures, which helped keep the economy growing until the early 1990s.

With an excess of disposable income, Americans could buy the new consumer products offered after the war. Kitchens were stocked with electric appliances. Washing machines cleaned clothes. Tupperware preserved food in refrigerators across the country. Wanting more than mere transportation, people bought flashy new sports cars or hardworking Jeeps in addition to the traditional four-door family car. Late in the decade, more Americans than ever were living the "good life."

Best-sellers

Perhaps the most famous of books at the time of their publication, best-sellers win public notice not for their quality, but for their popularity. Since the late nineteenth century, booksellers, book publishers, and book critics have collected and printed lists of best-selling books in order to learn and document which books appeal most to readers at the moment. This information reveals much about American culture. As Michael Korda writes in *Making the List: A Cultural History of the American Bestseller, 1900–1999,* "Like a mirror, [the best-seller list] reflects who we are, what we want, what interests us…." In a circular way, best-seller lists also determine what the public will be reading in the future, since publishers use the lists when deciding which books will be most profitable to publish.

During the 1890s, the publishing industry in the United States was on the rise. Improved public education had produced a population that wanted to read. Advances in printing technology along with an increase in bookstores made books more readily available to the public. It did not take long before those involved in the book industry began to track the popularity of different books. The first list of best-sellers was published by Harry Thurston Peck (1856–1914) in the magazine *The Bookman* in 1895. The top selling novel that year was *Beside the Bonnie Brier Bush* by Ian Maclaren (a name used by John Watson, 1850–1907). In 1912, *Publisher's Weekly* used the term "best-seller" for the first time and began to publish its own list, topped by *The Harvester* by Gene Stratton Porter (c. 1868–1924). That year, *Publisher's Weekly* also added a list of nonfiction best-sellers for the first time, led by *The Promised Land* by Mary Antin (1881–1949). One of the most respected best-seller lists is published in the **New York Times** (see entry under 1900s— Print Culture in volume 1), which began printing its list in 1942, when the top-selling fiction book was *The Robe* by Lloyd Douglas (1877–1951). The nonfiction list that year was headed by *Under Cover* by John Roy Carlson.

By the end of the twentieth century, many newspapers and magazines worldwide published their own best-seller lists, based on their own criteria, such as local sales. In the early twenty-first century, the publishing industry was transformed as the **Internet** (see entry under 1990s—The Way We Lived in volume 5) became a part of everyday life and bookstores competed with online merchants like **Amazon.**

com (see entry under 2000s—Commerce in volume 6). The powerful Amazon published its own best-sellers lists in a number of categories based on its sales. **Oprah's Book Club** (see entry under 2000s—Print Culture in volume 6) boosted lagging sales both at book stores and for online sellers as any choice the popular talk show host made became an instant best-seller. As **e-readers** (see entry under 2000s—Print Culture in volume 6) became more common, best-seller lists were created to reflect what was selling well for those devices.

Many critics dislike the best-seller lists, claiming that, by glorifying only those books that make the most money, they often ignore the best literature. However, best-seller lists continue to abound, giving readers, bookstores, and publishers alike valuable information about the reading tastes of the general public.

Tina Gianoulis

For More Information

"Bestsellers in Books." *Amazon.com.* http://www.amazon.com/gp/bestsellers/books (accessed July 17, 2011).

Bear, John. *The #1 New York Times Bestseller.* Berkeley, CA: Ten Speed Press, 1992.

Goldstein, Bill. "Let Us Now Praise Books Well Sold but Seldom Read." *New York Times* (July 15, 2000): p. B11.

Korda, Michael. *Making the List: A Cultural History of the American Bestseller, 1900–1999.* New York: Barnes and Noble, 2001.

Mott, Frank Luther. *Golden Multitudes: The Story of Best Sellers in the United States.* New York: Macmillan, 1947.

Offman, Craig. "Gray Lady Down: Has the Influence of the New York Times Bestseller List Declined?" *Salon.com.* http://www.salon.com/books/feature/1999/10/14/nytimes (accessed July 17, 2011).

"Oprah's Book Club and Books." *Oprah.com.* http://www.oprah.com/book_club.html (accessed July 17, 2011).

Jeep

Jeeps are four-wheel utility vehicles created for the use of the army in the late 1930s and early 1940s. Tough, rugged, and practically unstoppable, the Jeep is not only the star of hundreds of war and adventure films; it is also the ancestor of the stylish yet rugged **sport-utility vehicles** (SUVs; see entry under 1980s—The Way We Lived in volume 5) now produced by most automobile manufacturers.

Tough and rugged, the Jeep helped the Allies win World War II. © HOLMES GARDEN PHOTOS/ALAMY.

Shortly after World War I (1914–18), the American armed forces recognized a need for a light, tough automobile for use in reconnaissance (survey and exploration of battle areas). By 1940, as another war loomed on the horizon, the American military challenged 135 American automakers to produce such a vehicle. The army gave the car manufacturers a list of specifications. These specifications included four-wheel drive; a pedestal to hold a machine gun; extra ground clearance (space between the bottom of the vehicle and the ground); and an enhanced cooling system to allow the vehicle to drive for extended periods at speeds as low as three miles per hour without overheating. The deadline for submitting a working model of such a car was September 23, 1940, only forty-nine days after the guidelines were issued.

Only one company met the army's deadline, a small auto manufacturer called American Bantam Car Company. Bantam designed a car that suited the army's needs. The company was not in a solid financial state, so the army granted the contract to two other companies, Willys and Ford, using Bantam's design.

There are various explanations of why the small military vehicle was called a Jeep. Such names as Peep, Bug, Puddle Jumper, Leapin' Lena, and Blitz Buggy were sometimes used, but Jeep remained the most popular. Some trace the name back to the army designation, General Purpose Vehicle. Others claim that the name Jeep had been military slang since World War I, when it was used to mean a new, untested vehicle or a new, untested recruit. Still others point to a popular character in the 1930s *Popeye* (see entry under 1920s—Print Culture in volume 2) cartoon strip called Eugene the Jeep. Fans of the strip began calling any good product or upright person a "Jeep."

However it came about, the name Jeep is now associated with rugged four-wheel-drive vehicles. The name has remained, though the manufacturing company has changed several times since the first civilian Jeep was manufactured by Willys in July 1945. In 1953, Kaiser took over Willys and continued to manufacture the Jeep. In 1970, the American Motor Company (AMC) took over Kaiser Jeep, and in 1987 AMC was bought out by Chrysler. In 1998, Chrysler merged with Mercedes Benz to create Daimler Chrysler, which operated until 2007, when the company sold the Chrysler Group to Cerberus Capital Management. Though Chrysler went into bankruptcy under Cerberus and underwent complex financial reorganization, the Chrysler and Jeep brands emerged stronger than ever after Italian automaker Fiat bought into the company and gained controlling interest of the reorganized Chrysler Group in the spring of 2011. Chrysler continues to make all types of Jeeps, from the rugged Wrangler to the luxury Grand Cherokee, which are regularly updated.

Tina Gianoulis

For More Information

Allen, Jim. *Jeep.* Rev. ed. St. Paul, MN: Motorbooks International, 2004.

Allen, Jim. "Will the Real Jeep Please Stand Up?" *Fourwheeler* (March 1995).

Brown, Arch. *Jeep: The Unstoppable Legend.* Lincolnwood, IL: Publications International, 1994.

Foster, Patrick R. *The Story of Jeep.* 2nd ed. Iola, WI: Krause, 1998.

Guttmacher, Peter. *Jeep.* New York: Crestwood House and Maxwell Macmillan, 1994.

"Jeep History: A Heritage of Heroes." *Jeep.* http://www.jeep.com/en/history/ (accessed July 21, 2011).

Morr, Tom. *The Joy of Jeep.* St. Paul, MN: Motorbooks, 2007.

Tupperware

Earl S. Tupper (1907–1983) trademarked his "Poly-T" plastic in 1945. Soon after, he started using it to make plastic kitchen containers. Tupperware has always been far more than just a range of storage boxes, however. Over the next twenty years, it became a suburban obsession. When Americans moved in large numbers to the **suburbs** (see entry under 1950s—The Way We Lived in volume 3) in the 1950s, they bought Tupperware to equip their new kitchens. Through direct selling, Tupperware turned homemakers into entrepreneurs (businesspeople) and became a symbol of the optimism and materialism of the age. Sold in bright, cheerful colors and smooth shapes, Tupperware gave a stylish, modern edge to traditional domestic accessories.

Unlike containers made from metal, glass, or china, Tupperware is light, easy-to-clean, and almost indestructible. It comes in almost any shape, from butter dishes and bowls to ice cube trays and cocktail

With invitations such as this, Tupperware made an entry through direct sales into households across the United States following World War II. © TASSI/ALAMY.

shakers. The merchandise is good, but the early marketing strategy was brilliant. Coordinated from 1951 by Brownie Wise (1914–1992), the Tupperware "party" system helped women to meet and socialize together. Each Tupperware party "hostess" would invite a group of women into her home, where she would display Tupperware products for sale. Hostesses would show their guests how to use each item, including how to "burp" the airtight lids. They would run games and competitions to win Tupperware products. The reward for recruiting new hostesses was yet more Tupperware. In a postwar world in which status was measured by earning ability, Tupperware made running a household into a commercial activity.

By the end of the twentieth century, Tupperware had become one of the world's biggest direct sales companies, with an independent sales force of nearly one million people worldwide. In the 1990s, Tupperware was redesigned in even brighter colors and new shapes. The Tupperware product line included a range of children's toys called "Tupperkids." By the early 2000s, the Tupperware line had been expanded to include cook's tools and cutlery. Worldwide sales reached $2.3 billion in 2010. Still available at parties, Tupperware also could now be purchased online. Company officials claimed that a Tupperware party occurred somewhere in the world every 1.7 seconds, thanks to a direct sales force that had then reached 2.6 million in nearly 100 markets.

Besides keeping food fresh, Tupperware containers have won design awards and appear as exhibits in design museums around the world. When Earl Tupper called his new plastic the "material of the future," he turned out to be right. Fifty years later, Tupperware is so familiar that the word itself is often applied to any brand of plastic container with an airtight lid.

Chris Routledge

For More Information

"Tupperware!" *American Experience.* http://www.pbs.org/wgbh/amex/tupperware/ (accessed July 21, 2011).

"Can a '50s Icon Do It Again? Tupperware Struggles to Reinvigorate its Empire." *Newsweek* (March 20, 2006): 44.

Clarke, Alison J. *Tupperware: The Promise of Plastic in 1950s America.* Washington, DC: Smithsonian Institution Press, 1999.

Italie, Leanne. "Party Like It's 1954: Tupperware Rebounds Years After It First Hit the Market." *Detroit Free Press* (September 8, 2011): 7D.

Kealing, Bob. *Tupperware, Unsealed: Brownie Wise, Earl Tupper, and the Home Party Pioneers.* Gainesville: University Press of Florida, 2008.

"Six Years of Tupperware." *Advertising Age* (June 4, 2007): 19.

"Tupperware." *Good Housekeeping* (February 2011): 124.

Tupperware.com. http://order.tupperware.com/coe/app/home (accessed July 21, 2011).

1940s

Fashion

The rationing that took place during World War II (1939–45) seriously affected fashion in America for the first half of the decade. Even though businesses were prospering and people were finding more jobs and making more money than they had during the Depression of the 1930s, for the most part the country's newfound wealth could not be spent on clothes. Supplies of wool, cotton, linen, rayon, silk, and nylon that would have been used for fashionable attire were diverted to the war effort for the manufacture of uniforms, parachutes, and other supplies. The government even determined the maximum amount of fabric that could be used to make dresses (three-quarters of a yard) and tried to discourage fashion trends from shifting enough to spur interest in buying anything but the necessary attire.

Government restrictions and the limited availability of fabric effectively froze fashion styles for women at 1939 looks. Without silk stockings, women either shaved their legs and drew a "seam" line down the back of their legs or wore bobby socks with their skirts. Padded shoulders were popular in dresses and jackets. With limited selections of jewelry and scarves to accessorize their outfits, women turned to hats, of which many styles could be found. Red lipstick was also a popular adornment to women's outfits during this lean period.

Men's fashions changed from generous three-pieced, double-breasted suits with cuffed and pleated pants to fabric-conserving suits with single-breasted jackets and plain-front, straight-legged pants. Supplies of these new suits were limited and many stores simply had none until after the war.

By the end of the war, men and women alike were ready to spend money on clothes. Among those in African American and Mexican American communities, the sleek zoot suit was popular. In 1947, French designer Christian Dior (1905–1957) introduced his "New Look," resulting in many American designers quickly copying his fashions with tiny waistlines and flowing long skirts. The New Look remained popular until the 1960s. For those who could not afford designer fashions, ready-to-wear clothes from American manufacturers offered similar, less extravagant copies of expensive fashions.

Bobbysoxers

Bobby socks are white, ankle-length socks, most often made from cotton, that have been worn by women, and children—especially teenage girls—since the 1930s. In particular, adolescents wore them with penny-loafers or saddle shoes. However, bobby socks are more than just a type of footwear. In December 1942, **Frank Sinatra** (1915–1998; see entry under 1940s—Music in volume 3), then a skinny, bow-tied young singer from New Jersey, opened at the Paramount Theatre in New York. Those same girls and young women who favored bobby socks came to see him and spontaneously screamed and collapsed as he performed. They danced the jitterbug—the latest craze in **dancing** (see entry under 1900s—The Way We Lived in volume 1)—in the theater aisles. They swooned in their seats and jammed the area surrounding the stage door and demanded his autograph. They flowed out into the streets of midtown Manhattan, tying up traffic. These crazy youngsters were dubbed "bobbysoxers." In fact, one of the more colorfully named of Sinatra's countless fan clubs was "The Bobbysox Swoonerettes."

The media quickly stereotyped bobbysoxers. On the negative side, *Newsweek* magazine portrayed their behavior as a kind of madness, a mass sexual delirium, labeling bobbysoxers immoral female juvenile delinquents. However, the general feeling was that they were nothing more than ridiculous young girls who were unable to control their emotions. When not swooning over their "Frankie," they talked nonstop on the

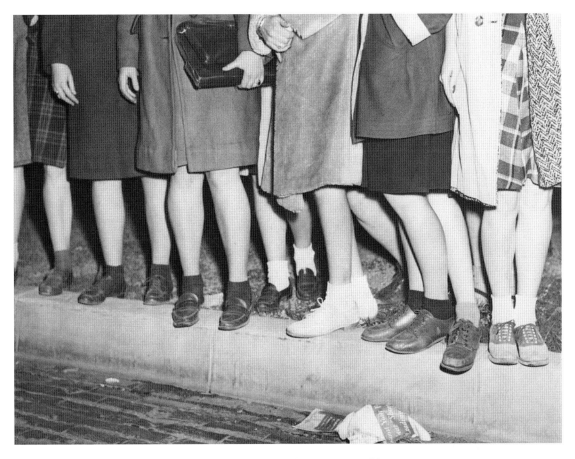

A brigade of bobbysoxers await crooner Frank Sinatra in Los Angeles in January 1944. © BETTMANN/CORBIS.

telephone and obsessed over the latest fads and styles. By the 1950s, the typical fashionable bobbysoxer wore her socks rolled down to her ankles, kept her hair in a ponytail, and wore tight sweaters. She completed her look with a felt poodle skirt that covered layers of petticoats made of a stiff material called crinoline, allowing the skirt to bulge out from her waist and hips. An alternate look was the choice of a straight, hemmed skirt that almost brushed against her bobby socks.

Frank Sinatra was not the only popular singer associated with bobby socks. In 1959, Frankie Avalon (1939–), an idol for a future generation of adolescent girls, had a million-selling hit single titled "Bobby Sox to Stockings." The lyrics point out that when a girl replaces her bobby socks with stockings, she is grown-up enough to fall in love and "give her heart away."

Rob Edelman

For More Information

"Bobby-Soxers' Gallup." *Time.* http://www.time.com/time/magazine/article/0,9171,865481,00.html (accessed July 21, 2011).

"Frank Sinatra and the 'bobby-soxers.'" *Guardian.co.uk.* http://century.guardian.co.uk/1940-1949/Story/0,,127764,00.html (accessed July 21, 2011).

Palladino, Grace. *Teenagers: An American History.* New York: Basic Books, 1996.

Schrum, Kelly. *Some Wore Bobby Sox: The Emergence of Teenage Girls' Culture, 1920–45.* New York: Palgrave Macmillan, 2004.

"Sinatra and the Bobby-Soxers." *The Paley Center for Media.* http://www.paleycenter.org/sinatra-the-bobby-soxers (accessed July 21, 2011).

Zoot Suit

Enormously popular among young African American and Mexican American (Chicano) men in the 1940s, the zoot suit was more than a piece of clothing. Designed sleek enough to be stylish and loose enough for **dancing** (see entry under 1900s—The Way We Lived in volume 1), the zoot suit also represented a culture that belonged to people of color in the United States. It reflected an open pride in nonwhite ethnic roots that was new to American society. Many whites felt threatened by displays of pride and racial identity among people of color. Some even reacted violently to the sight of young men wearing the distinctive zoot suit.

Some say the zoot suit was designed in 1941 by Chicago tailor and band leader Harold C. "Zoot Suit" Fox (1910–1996). Inspired by the styles he saw on poor urban teenagers, who raised the hems of large men's suits to fit their smaller frames, Fox wanted to design a dancing suit with style. Because **jazz** (see entry under 1900s—Music in volume 1) slang labeled everything cool and hip as "the end,"—and the letter z was the end of the alphabet—he called his suit a zoot, and designed it with a "reet pleat, reave sleeve, ripe stripe, and drape shape." In less hip English, the zoot suit had a long jacket with broad padded shoulders and baggy pants with

A man models a zoot suit in 1942. © MARIE HANSEN/TIME LIFE PICTURES/GETTY IMAGES.

narrow cuffs. It was often worn with a flat crowned hat called a pork pie, a long key chain, and shoes with thick soles.

The zoot suit was soon adopted by many hip young blacks and Chicanos. The suit became part of a larger zoot culture that included jazz music, dance, and jive talk. Young Chicano zooters spoke a slang called *Calo* that was a rich mixture of Spanish and English. This zoot suit culture set young African American and Chicano men apart from mainstream white culture, and whites soon began to fear and mistrust the zoot suited **"gangs"** (see entry under 1980s—The Way We Lived in volume 5). The fear erupted more than once into violence, the most famous incident being the "zoot suit riots" in Los Angeles, California. In June 1943, hundreds of uniformed white sailors and marines attacked zoot-suited Mexican Americans and African Americans, beating them severely and tearing their suits off. The riots lasted almost two weeks. Los Angeles police did little to stop the violence, and local newspapers supported the servicemen's actions. Hundreds of Chicanos were injured. The publicity surrounding the incident did serve to educate white Americans about the large Mexican American minority that lived among them.

A musical inspired by the riots appeared on Broadway in 1979. *Zoot Suit* was written by Luis Valdez, but it flopped before being recrafted as a film written and directed by Valdez. A revised version of the stage musical was more successfully staged by the Goodman Theater in Chicago, Illinois, in 2000. The narrator, as well as other characters, wore a zoot suit.

Tina Gianoulis

For More Information

Alvarez, Luis. *The Power of the Zoot: Youth Culture and Resistance during World War II.* Berkeley: University of California Press, 2008.

Behnke, Alison. *The Little Black Dress and Zoot Suits: Depression and Wartime Fashion from the 1930s to 1950s.* Minneapolis: Twenty-First Century Books, 2012.

Daniels, Douglas Henry. "Los Angeles Zoot: Race 'Riot,' the Pachuco, and Black Music Culture." *The Journal of Negro History* (Vol. 82, no. 2, Spring, 1997): pp. 201–21.

Del Castillo, Richard Griswold. "The Los Angeles 'Zoot Suit Riots' Revisited: Mexican and Latin American Perspectives." *Mexican Studies-Estudios Mexicanos* (Vol. 16, iss. 2, Summer 2000): pp. 367–78.

Eig, Jonathan. "'Zoot Suit' Fox Dead at Age 86." *Down Beat* (Vol. 63, no. 11, November 1996): pp. 16–19.

Jones, Chris. "*Zoot Suit* Tailored for Contempo Auds." *Variety* (July 24, 2000): pp. 53.

Peiss, Kathy. *The Zoot Suit: The Enigmatic Career of an Extreme Style.* Philadelphia: University of Pennsylvania Press, 2011.

Thorne, Tony. *Fads, Fashions and Cults: From Acid House to Zoot Suit.* London: Bloomsbury, 1993.

Tyler, Bruce. "Zoot-Suit Culture and the Black Press." *Journal of American Culture* (Vol. 17, no. 2, Summer 1994): pp. 21–35.

White, Shane, and Graham J. White. *Stylin': African American Expressive Culture, from Its Beginnings to the Zoot Suit.* Ithaca, NY: Cornell University Press, 1999.

"Zoot Suit Riots." *American Experience* http://www.pbs.org/wgbh/amex/zoot/ (accessed July 21, 2011).

1940s

Film and Theater

Hollywood's golden age had reached a peak by 1940. The eight largest studios (Warner Brothers, Metro-Goldwyn-Mayer [MGM], RKO Radio, Twentieth Century Fox, United Artists, Paramount, Universal, and Columbia) controlled more than 90 percent of film production and distribution. The big studios were churning out at least one film per week. The Production Code Association (PCA) maintained strict regulations about the topic matter that could be presented in films. The association made sure the good guys always won, sexuality was suggested rather than mentioned openly, and social issues were not debated. The strict censorship in Hollywood was meant to protect the nearly eighty million Americans who went to the movies each week. When regular Americans and those in Hollywood began to wonder what role the United States would play in the war, attitudes about censorship changed. Studios wanted to explore political issues in films, but many feared that ticket sales might be hurt. By 1941, Hollywood had decided to support the war, making training films for the army and releasing *Sergeant York,* the first of many films supporting U.S. engagement in the war.

Although the films that did comment on the war supported U.S. involvement, 95 percent of the films made during the period had nothing to do with war. The majority of the movies released in the 1940s were playful romps, such as *The Philadelphia Story* (1940), starring

Cary Grant (1904–1986), James Stewart (1908–1997), and Katharine Hepburn (1907–); or the comedies of Bud Abbott (1895–1974) and Lou Costello (1906–1959). Walt Disney (1901–1966) also released his animated symphony performance called *Fantasia.* More serious films included *The Grapes of Wrath* (1940), the film based on the Pulitzer Prize–winning novel about the Great Depression (1929–41) by John Steinbeck (1902–1968), and *Citizen Kane* (1941), the first film by Orson Welles (1915–1985). Many consider *Citizen Kane* the greatest film of all time.

After the war, film noir ("dark cinema") became a popular style for movies. These dark, serious films, such as *The Maltese Falcon* (1941) and *The Big Sleep* (1946), gave new life to the detective stories that had been well-liked by readers during the 1920s and 1930s. Some of the most popular detective writers, including Dashiell Hammett (1894–1961), Raymond Chandler (1888–1959), and James M. Cain (1892–1977), adapted their novels and stories into screenplays. Americans were intrigued with these films, especially as fear and apprehension grew with the onset of the Cold War (1945–91). Even with the popularity of a new film style, movie attendance sank after the war, mostly because more Americans stayed home to watch their newly affordable television sets.

Elaborate musicals were enormously popular during the 1940s. Nearly eleven million people attended Broadway extravaganzas in 1943. Most of the shows had upbeat, patriotic themes with casts of singing soldiers or high-kicking women. Popular shows included *This Is the Army* (1942), *Something for the Boys* (1943), and *Winged Victory* (1945). All proceeds from *This Is the Army* and *Winged Victory* (millions of dollars) were contributed to the Army Emergency Relief Fund.

Although Broadway enjoyed great success, dramatic theater suffered during the 1940s. Dramatic theatrical productions had difficulty finding paying audiences. The Federal Theatre Project of the 1930s was discontinued, and dwindling attendance pushed Project-funded plays off Broadway and into smaller theaters. Despite the smaller profits, two of the greatest American playwrights wrote during the 1940s: Tennessee Williams (1914–1983) and Arthur Miller (1915–) wrote dramatic masterpieces. Williams's *The Glass Menagerie* (1945) and Miller's *All My Sons* (1947) introduced audiences to themes of disillusionment and the difficulties of attaining the "American dream" of success and happiness.

Abbott and Costello

Tall, thin man Bud Abbott (1895–1974) and short, fat man Lou Costello (1906–1959) worked together for Universal Pictures between 1939 and 1956 after a career in comic theater and **radio** (see entry under 1920s—TV and Radio in volume 2). Throughout the 1940s, but especially during the years of World War II (1939–45), they were Hollywood's top comedy act. At their peak, the duo released four films a year, specializing in silly voices and overacting. In their best early films, a simple misunderstanding soon leads to hilarious situations.

The most memorable of such misunderstandings is found in the classic "Who's on First" bit, which was first a radio routine, and then a scene from *The Naughty Nineties* (1945). In it, Abbott continuously frustrates Costello by trying to explain to him the odd nicknames of players on a baseball team: "Who's" on first, "What's" on second, and "I Don't Know's" on third. Costello: "Who's on first?" Abbott: "Yes." Costello: "I mean the fellow's name on first base." Abbott: "Who." And on it went.

Abbott and Costello's comedy routine worked well in films for a while, but after the war their movies became more creative. *Abbott and Costello Meet Frankenstein* (1948) is the first of a series of "monster movies" and one of the most cherished spoof horror films of all time. In the 1950s, they made *The Abbott and Costello Show* for **television** (see entry under 1940s—TV and Radio in volume 3), reusing material from their days in theater. The series has regularly been used to fill empty time on TV schedules around the globe ever since. *Abbott & Costello: The Complete Universal Pictures Collection* was released on DVD in 2008, while the complete collection of the duo's television series became available on DVD in 2010.

Chris Routledge

Bud Abbott and Lou Costello, Hollywood's top comedy act during World War II, in a scene from the 1941 film Buck Privates. © EVERETT COLLECTION.

For More Information

"Abbott and Costello." *The Museum of Broadcast Communications.* http://www.museum.tv/rhofsection.php?page=154 (accessed July 21, 2011).

Cox, Stephen, and John Lofflin. *The Official Abbott and Costello Scrapbook.* Chicago: Contemporary Books, 1990.

Cox, Stephen, and John Lofflin. *The Abbott and Costello Story: Sixty Years of "Who's on First?"* Nashville, TN: Cumberland House, 1997.

Nollen, Scott Allen. *Abbott and Costello on the Home Front: A Critical Study of the Wartime Films.* Jefferson, NC: McFarland, 2009.

The Official Abbott & Costello Website. http://www.abbottandcostello.net/ (accessed July 21, 2011).

Casablanca

Casablanca is one of the most famous films of the 1940s. The movie contains some of the most memorable dialogue and images in any **Hollywood** (see entry under 1930s—Film and Theater in volume 2) production. Most of the action takes place in Rick's Café Américain in Casablanca, Morocco, in North Africa, where refugees from a Europe ravaged by World War II (1939–45) gather to wait for their U.S. visas (documentation on a passport giving permission to travel). *Casablanca* has an unoriginal plot and characters made up from a set of stereotypes: a cynical, clever American; a ruthless German; a weak but brave Frenchman; and an untrustworthy Arab. It is surprising then that the film should have captured not only the mood of the time but the imaginations of millions of filmgoers ever since.

Casablanca was a low-budget movie, one of fifty filmed that year by Warner Brothers. The cast consists of the best-known actors of the time, including **Humphrey Bogart** (1899–1957; see entry under 1930s—Film and Theater in volume 2), Ingrid Bergman (1915–1982), Paul Henreid (1908–1992), Peter Lorre (1904–1964), Claude Rains (1889–1967), Sydney Greenstreet (1879–1954), and Conrad Veidt (1893–1943). Even with its star-laden cast, much of the film's early success was due to the date of its release—1942—about the same time as the first Allied landings in North Africa. Nominated in several categories, in 1943 the film won Oscars for Best Picture, Best Direction (Michael Curtiz, 1886–1962), and Best Writing (Julius J. Epstein, 1909–2000, and Philip G. Epstein, 1909–1952). The rendition by Dooley Wilson (1886–1953) of the song "As Time Goes By" and many memorable lines, such as "Here's lookin' at you, kid," have added to *Casablanca*'s enduring appeal. The final foggy scene at the airport is one of the most famous in Hollywood's history.

A still from the final scene of the popular 1942 film Casablanca. *From left to right: Unidentified actor, Claude Rains, Paul Henreid, Humphrey Bogart, and Ingrid Bergman.* © MICHAEL OCHS ARCHIVES/GETTY IMAGES.

As in many other Bogart films of the period, the reluctant heroism of *Casablanca*'s main character reflects the American war effort. The film is also a touching love story told with good humor and a sharp wit. One reason for its popularity is that it boils down the large-scale horrors of the war into a simple human drama. Although it was an accidental classic, *Casablanca* and its stars have become a point of contact between the twenty-first century and the heroic yet dark days of World War II.

Chris Routledge

For More Information

"*Casablanca* (1942)." *TCM.com.* http://www.tcm.com/tcmdb/title/610/ Casablanca/ (accessed July 21, 2011).

Harmetz, Aljean. *The Making of Casablanca: Bogart, Bergman, and World War II.* New York: Hyperion, 2002.

Miller, Frank. *Casablanca: As Time Goes By, 50th Anniversary Commemorative.* Atlanta: Turner Publishing, 1992.

Schwartzbaum, Lisa, and Kate Meyers. "The Beginning of a Beautiful Friendship." *Entertainment Weekly* (March 1994): p. 86.

Siegel, Jeff. *The Casablanca Companion: The Movie and More.* Dallas: Taylor, 1992.

Citizen Kane

Citizen Kane (1941) is acclaimed as one of the greatest sound films in the history of cinema. It was cowritten by Orson Welles (1915–1985) and Herman J. Mankiewicz (1897–1953). Welles also produced and directed the film for RKO Radio Pictures in **Hollywood** (see entry under 1930s—Film and Theater in volume 2). At the time he created *Citizen Kane,* Welles was a twenty-five-year-old theater and **radio** (see entry under 1920s—TV and Radio in volume 2) genius who had not yet made a feature-length film. His youth and inexperience are astounding considering the complexity and accomplishment of the visual and narrative (storytelling) techniques used in the movie. In an unusual move by any Hollywood-based film studio, Welles was given complete artistic control over this production. He was able to have the final decision in every area of production, including elements such as screenplay, camera, lighting, art direction, and music. The music in the film was composed and conducted by Bernard Herrmann (1911–1975).

The story of *Citizen Kane* begins with the death of a wealthy, influential American newspaper publisher named Charles Foster Kane. In six creative narrative sequences—bookended by an introduction and an epilogue—the biography of Kane is related, beginning with a newsreel capsule of the man's life, followed by glimpses of his childhood and adult years. Kane's controversial life unfolds through a clever manipulation of time through editing. Much of the film is constructed from flashbacks, which are sequences that have taken place in the past, before the present time of the motion picture. The details of Kane's life are told through journal entries and interviews with those he knew as a reporter seeks to

Orson Welles portrayed newspaper publisher and gubernatorial candidate Charles Foster Kane in the renowned 1941 film Citizen Kane.
© HULTON ARCHIVE/GETTY IMAGES.

solve the mystery of the significance of the last word that Kane speaks, "Rosebud." As the details of Kane's biography are disclosed, the larger story of a man's quest for "the American dream" also is explored.

The character of Kane, portrayed by Welles himself, is in many ways a thinly cloaked, fictional version of real-life multimillionaire newspaper publisher William Randolph Hearst (1863–1951). Hearst was outraged at the unauthorized and unflattering interpretation of his life story, and he tried to prevent the film from being released. When that attempt failed, Hearst used his many newspapers to prevent the film from becoming popular. He refused to print advertisements for the film and threatened to stop advertising and reviewing RKO films in the future. These actions were effective, and the film performed poorly at the box office. At RKO, angry film executives got even with Welles. They removed his right to make final artistic decisions about future motion picture productions at the studio. As a result, Welles's next few films were badly tampered with by lesser talents. The rest of his film career was characterized by inadequate budgets and production schedules. Welles never again created a motion picture as renowned as his first feature film.

Although *Citizen Kane* had a disappointing initial release, it was rediscovered by film critics and historians twenty years later. Since then, many articles and several books have praised its artistry and intelligence. In university classrooms, in art houses, and at film festivals worldwide, *Citizen Kane* is frequently screened. It is included on almost every significant listing of the world's greatest films, including a 2002 poll featured in the authoritative *Sight and Sound* magazine published by the British Film Institute.

Audrey Kupferberg

For More Information

"The Battle Over *Citizen Kane*." *American Experience.* http://www.pbs.org/wgbh/amex/kane2/ (accessed July 21, 2011).

Carringer, Robert L. *The Making of Citizen Kane.* Rev. ed. Berkeley: University of California Press, 1996.

Higham, Charles. *The Films of Orson Welles.* Berkeley: University of California Press, 1970.

Kemp, Stuart. "*Kane* No. 1 on BFI Polls; Coppola, Hitchcock Lauded." *Hollywood Reporter* (August 9, 2002): p. 12.

Lennon, Thomas, producer. *The Battle Over "Citizen Kane"* (video). Boston: WGBH Boston Video, 1996, 2000.

Walsh, John Evangelist. *Walking Shadows: Orson Welles, William Randolph Hearst, and Citizen Kane.* Madison: University of Wisconsin Press/Popular Press, 2004.

Welles, Orson, and Peter Bogdanovich. *This Is Orson Welles.* New York: HarperCollins, 1992.

Fantasia

The now-classic animated film *Fantasia* opened on November 13, 1940, to lukewarm reviews. However, the **Disney** (see entry under 1920s—Film and Theater in volume 2) film went on to earn acclaim as one of the best animated films of all time and remains unique for its attempt to bring together highbrow and popular culture. Its depiction of animated

Sorcerer's apprentice Mickey Mouse in a scene from the 1941 Disney animated film classic Fantasia. © PHOTOFEST.

characters "acting" to classical music had never been attempted before. The music was performed by the Philadelphia Symphony Orchestra, conducted by the legendary Leopold Stokowski (1882–1977).

Motion-picture executive Walt Disney (1901–1966) had long envisioned a film that would finally bring respect to the art of animation. How better to bring respectability to animation than to match animation with the most respectable of art forms at the time, classical music? He and Stokowski began to work together on the first of the sections, "The Sorcerer's Apprentice," starring Disney's most famous creation, Mickey Mouse. That sequence alone cost $125,000, a huge sum at the time. With classical music and dancing hippos and mushrooms, *Fantasia* seemed to have something for everyone. When it opened in theaters, however, audiences did not know what to make of it. After a dull opening, it was cut from its original length down to eighty minutes. *Fantasia* played on a double bill with a **Western** (see entry under 1930s—Film and Theater in volume 2) and then disappeared.

Fantasia earned back its production costs when it was re-released in 1956. Audiences finally appreciated the film and came by the millions to theaters to see it, most for the first time. *Fantasia* was re-released again in 1969 for a whole new generation to see. This time it truly caught fire, for it seemed to fit the cultural spirit of the late 1960s. Many of the so-called **hippies** (see entry under 1960s—The Way We Lived in volume 4) of the time consumed illegal drugs, such as LSD and **marijuana** (see entry under 1960s—The Way We Lived in volume 4), before seeing the film. They said it gave them a different view of the film.

Since 1969, *Fantasia* has been periodically re-released in movie theaters. It also proved very popular among viewers of all ages when released on videocassette and DVD. The film is now among the two hundred top-grossing (highest earning) motion pictures of all time. In 2000, a new version, *Fantasia 2000,* was shown in giant-screen IMAX theaters to large crowds of people. *Fantasia* also served as the source material for the 2011 live action film *The Sorcerer's Apprentice,* a box office failure.

Jill Gregg Clever

For More Information

Corliss, Richard. "Disney's Fantastic Voyage." *Time* (December 13, 1999): pp. 94–96.

Culhane, John. *Walt Disney's Fantasia.* New York: Harry N. Abrams, 1983.

Nelson, Michael J. "*The Sorcerer's Apprentice*: Like a Magical Sentient Mop, the Story Just Got Away from Them." *Home Theater* (January 2011): pp. 82.

Film Noir

The term *film noir,* meaning "dark cinema," was coined by French film critics to describe the American films that arrived in Europe in the years after World War II (1939–45). Emerging in the 1940s as an alternative to "classical" Hollywood cinema, film noir is a curious blend of violent crime, national identity crisis, and low-budget moviemaking. It takes a bleak view of human nature and American life. Its shadowy photography and troubled characters perfectly represent the turmoil of the postwar years.

Filmed on cheap black-and-white film stock, most film noir movies are low-budget affairs. Their style owes much to the European filmmakers who arrived in Hollywood in the years leading up to the war. German directors such as Fritz Lang (1890–1976) and Robert Siodmak (1900–1973) found expression for their cynical outlook in adapting American "hardboiled" crime novels to film. The characteristic look of film noir is also the result of frugality. Dark, shadowy images were used to cover up for missing sets, so a doorway framed in light might be just that, a doorway with no walls surrounding it. Classic films in the film noir genre (category) include *The Maltese Falcon* (1941), *Mildred Pierce* (1945), *The Big Sleep* (1946), *The Killers* (1946), *Sunset Boulevard* (1950), and *The Night of the Hunter* (1955).

Film noir is more than just a look. It concentrates on the psychology of crime and criminals. The films focus on the clash between morality and desire and deal with the lowest of human instincts. The heroes of film noir are weak, troubled men, and the women are dangerous and threatening. At a time when women were not expected to be independent and self-sufficient, the "femme fatale," as this female character archetype became known, proved very shocking.

Over the years, film noir has been spoofed, revamped, and updated. A comedy by Steve Martin (1945–), *Dead Men Don't Wear Plaid* (1982), satirizes the style. *Blade Runner* (1982)—described as "future noir"— reimagines the style in a science-fiction setting. Thrillers like *Taxi Driver* (1976), *Seven* (1995), *The Black Dahlia* (2006), and *Duplicity* (2009) update the film noir tradition for contemporary audiences. Film noir was created in the 1940s to challenge the morality and values of Hollywood's mainstream. By the twenty-first century, the style's dark images, dangerous characters, and brusque dialogue have come to define that era of America's history and create new images of modern times.

Chris Routledge

For More Information

Crowther, Bruce. *Film Noir: Reflections in a Dark Mirror.* London: Columbus Books, 1988.

"Film Noir." *AMC Filmsite.* http://www.filmsite.org/filmnoir.html (accessed July 21, 2011).

Hannsberry, Karen Burroughs. *Bad Boys: The Actors of Film Noir.* Jefferson, NC: McFarland, 2003.

Hannsberry, Karen Burroughs. *Femme Noir: Bad Girls of Film.* Jefferson, NC: McFarland, 1998.

Hirsch, Foster. *The Dark Side of the Screen: Film Noir.* 2nd ed. Cambridge, MD: Da Capo Press, 2008.

Silver, Alain, Elizabeth Ward, James Ursini, and Robert Porfirio. *Film Noir: The Encyclopedia.* 4th ed. New York: Overlook Press, 2010.

Spicer, Andrew. *Historical Dictionary of Film Noir.* Lanham, MD: Scarecrow, 2010.

Stephens, Michael L. *Film Noir: A Comprehensive, Illustrated Reference to Movies, Terms and Persons.* Jefferson, NC: McFarland, 1995.

It's a Wonderful Life

The film *It's a Wonderful Life* (1946) has become an important part of the Christmas season for millions of Americans. Each year, families gather around the **television** (see entry under 1940s—TV and Radio in volume 3) to watch the story of George Bailey (James Stewart, 1908–1997), a man who grew up yearning for a life of travel and adventure. Personal and national events thwarted George's plans to escape his hometown of Bedford Falls. He grows into one of the community's leading citizens as he runs the local Building and Loan Association and repeatedly tangles with Mr. Potter (Lionel Barrymore, 1878–1954), the town's miserly, mean-spirited millionaire. On Christmas Eve, George is threatened with financial ruin and contemplates suicide. Before committing the desperate act, he is saved by Clarence, an elderly angel (Henry Travers, 1874–1965), who allows George to see how the world would be if he had never been born. George soon discovers how one man's life can touch so many others and learns that no man is a failure if he has friends. The film concludes with all the townspeople George has aided over the years donating all the money they can to rescue George and to defeat Potter.

It's a Wonderful Life originated as a short story by Philip Van Doren (1900–1984) titled "The Greatest Gift," which was published in **Good Housekeeping** see entry under 1900s—Print Culture in volume 1). The rights to the story were bought by acclaimed director Frank Capra (1897–1991), who viewed the tale as an opportunity to express his ideas on the importance of the accomplishments of the ordinary American citizen. In the film, he shows the people of Bedford Falls living with courage and good humor through the 1918 influenza epidemic, the Roaring Twenties, the **Great Depression** (1929–41; see entry under 1930s—The Way We Lived in volume 2), and World War II (1939–45).

The final scene of the beloved 1946 film It's A Wonderful Life *shows Thomas Mitchell (left), Donna Reed, and Jimmy Stewart (center).* © PHOTOFEST.

Capra incorporated sentimentality, **film noir** (a dark, gloomy style of moviemaking; see entry under 1940s—Film and Theater in volume 3), and the supernatural in his film. George's boyhood scenes offer the audience a nostalgic perspective on life in the early decades of the twentieth century. The Pottersville sequence employs the film noir techniques of odd camera angles and deep shadows to highlight George's fear and desperation. Furthermore, the film boasts one of Hollywood's finest ensemble casts: Donna Reed (1921–1986), Thomas Mitchell (1892–1962), Gloria Grahame (1923–1981), Ward Bond (1903–1960), and Beulah Bondi (1889–1981).

It's a Wonderful Life received Academy Award nominations for Best Picture, Best Actor, and Best Director, but failed to win. Its box-office earnings were poor as audiences found the film overly bleak. When the film was sold to television stations, however, it began to gain recognition as Capra's masterpiece. During the 1980s and early 1990s, some cable networks were running the film nearly twenty-four hours a day. Because of copyright issues, NBC became the only American television network licensed to broadcast *It's a Wonderful Life* in 1994 and is allowed to air the film only twice a year. NBC still shows it on Christmas Eve. A number of official DVD editions of *It's a Wonderful Life* have been released since 2001, allowing viewers to continue their holiday viewing tradition.

In the 1990s, the American Film Institute honored *It's a Wonderful Life* as one of cinema's one hundred greatest works. It has now become as much a part of the Christmas holiday as *A Christmas Carol* by Charles Dickens (1812–1870). Frank Capra said *It's a Wonderful Life* was his personal favorite of all his films.

Charles Coletta

For More Information

Basinger, Jeanine, and the Trustees of the Frank Capra Archives. *The "It's a Wonderful Life" Book.* New York: Knopf, 1986.

Capra, Frank. *The Name Above the Title.* New ed. New York: Da Capo Press, 1997.

Carney, Raymond. *American Vision: The Films of Frank Capra.* New York: Cambridge University Press, 1986.

"The Enduring Joys of a *Wonderful Life.*" *Chicago Tribune* (December 8, 2006): p. 8.

Fishgall, Gary. *Pieces of Time: The Life of James Stewart.* New York: Scribner's, 1997.

Hawkins, Jimmy. *It's a Wonderful Life: The Fiftieth Anniversary Scrapbook.* Philadelphia: Courage, 1996.

Willian, Michael. *The Essential It's a Wonderful Life: A Scene-by-Scene Guide to the Classic Film.* 2nd ed. Chicago: Chicago Review Press, 2006.

Lassie

Lassie, America's most popular and successful canine star, has appeared in books, in film, on **radio** (see entry under 1920s—TV and Radio in volume 2), in comics, and on **television** (see entry under 1940s—TV and Radio in volume 3). The brave, intelligent, and ever-loyal collie's adventures often involved finding and rescuing lost people, alerting humans to danger, and comforting those in distress. Lassie first appeared in a ***Saturday Evening Post*** (see entry under 1900s—Print Culture in volume 1) short story in 1938. Author Eric Knight (1897–1943) modeled the character after Toots, his own loyal dog. The public's enthusiastic reaction to Lassie encouraged Knight to expand his tale into a 1939 novella, which was soon optioned for film by **MGM** (see entry under 1920s—Film and Theater in volume 2).

The original Lassie story concerns a poor Yorkshire family that is forced to sell its beloved dog to pay for rent and food. The collie soon escapes her new owner and travels across Scotland and England to return to her young master. The 1943 film *Lassie Come Home* faithfully retold Knight's tale and featured child stars Roddy McDowall (1928–1998) and **Elizabeth Taylor** (1932–2011; see entry under 1940s—Film and Theater in volume 3). The success of the film spawned several sequels, including *Son of Lassie* (1945), *Courage of Lassie* (1946), and *Challenge to Lassie* (1949). Although the Lassie character was female, a male dog named Pal played her.

Beginning in 1954, the TV series *Lassie* debuted on the CBS network. It starred Pal's son, who was named Lassie. The series, which aired with various human cast members until 1974, was an immediate hit. From 1954 until 1957, Lassie was accompanied on her adventures by Jeff Miller (Tommy Rettig, 1941–1996), a young farm boy. In 1957, Timmy (Jon Provost, 1950–) became Lassie's owner. After 1964, Lassie had several other masters and spent many episodes roaming the wilderness without human companionship. The character also appeared in an animated adventure series, *Lassie's Rescue Rangers,* from 1973 to 1975.

In 1973, Lassie became the first inductee of the American Humane Association's Hall of Fame. Lassie was seen by a new generation of fans in a 1994 film and a syndicated TV series (a TV show sold to independent TV stations). A critically acclaimed film version of *Lassie* based on the original novella was released in 2005. The fictional Lassie also lent her name to the Lassie Natural Way line of dog food during this time period. Lassie is the great American icon (symbol) representing humans' special relationship with their canine companions.

Charles Coletta

For More Information

Collins, Ace. *Lassie: A Dog's Life, the First Fifty Years.* New York: Penguin, 1993.
Feldman, Gene, and Suzette Winter. *The Story of Lassie* (video). Harrington Park, NJ: Wombat Productions, 1994.

Felix, Sarah. "Lassie's Back! From a New Movie to Her Own Line of Pet Food, America's Favorite Canine Has Plenty of Reasons to Wag Her Tail." *Good Housekeeping* (September 2006): p. 95.

Lassie: The Official Site of the World's Most Famous Dog. http://www.lassie.com/ (accessed July 21, 2011).

Lassie Network. http://www.lassie.net (accessed July 21, 2011).

Leder, Jane Mersky. *Stunt Dogs.* Mankato, MN: Crestwood House, 1985.

Elizabeth Taylor (1932–2011)

Most child stars enjoy a few brief years in the spotlight, only to fade from public consciousness upon reaching adolescence. Likewise, many adult actors, if they are fortunate, enjoy stardom for a few years before being replaced by a new batch of up-and-comers. Only a handful of cinema greats remain in the spotlight for decades, from youth through middle and old age. Elizabeth Taylor was one such legend. This strikingly beautiful actress enjoyed movie fame—and international celebrity—for most of her life.

Taylor first became a movie name in the mid-1940s, while still a teenager, in such classic children's fare as the **Lassie** (see entry under 1940s—Film and Theater in volume 3) films *Lassie Come Home* (1943) and *Courage of Lassie* (1946). But it was *National Velvet* (1944), in which Taylor plays a horse-loving young girl, that made her a star. She grew into a charming all-American beauty, playing characters who were innocent or calculating in *Father of the Bride* (1950), *A Place in the Sun* (1951), *Giant* (1956), *Cat on a Hot Tin Roof* (1958), and *Suddenly Last Summer* (1959). *A Place in the Sun* stands out as her first mature role; she was cast as a young heiress involved in a doomed love affair. Accepted in her adult roles, she won two Academy Awards, for *Butterfield 8* (1960) and *Who's Afraid of Virginia Woolf?* (1966). Her marriages, romances, battles to control her weight, and numerous life-threatening illnesses kept her in the headlines throughout her life. While filming *Cleopatra* (1963), her very public romance with costar Richard Burton (1925–84) was front-page news. That continued over the years when she married him, divorced him, then remarried him, then redivorced him.

As she grew older, Taylor's film appearances became less frequent, but her stardom never faded. She used her name to successfully market a line of perfumes. Most significantly, she was at the forefront of the effort to raise money for **AIDS** (acquired immunodeficiency syndrome; see entry

under 1980s—The Way We Lived in volume 5) research and to increase AIDS awareness. Suffering ill health in her final years, Taylor died of congestive heart failure on March 23, 2011, at the age of 79.

Rob Edelman

For More Information

Elizabeth Taylor. http://www.reelclassics.com/Actresses/Liz_Taylor/liz.htm (accessed July 21, 2011).
The Elizabeth Taylor AIDS Foundation. http://www.elizabethtayloraidsfoundation. org/ (accessed July 21, 2011).

Guzman, Rafer. "Film Legend Elizabeth Taylor Dead at 79." *Newsday* (March 23, 2011).

Heymann, C. David. *Liz: An Intimate Biography of Elizabeth Taylor*. New York: Carol Publishing, 1995.

Papa, Joseph. *Elizabeth Taylor: A Passion for Life*. New York: Harper Design, 2011.

Puente, Maria. "The Biggest Star Ever?" *USA Today* (March 24, 2011): p. 1A.

Taraborrelli, J. Randy. *Elizabeth*. New York: Warner Books, 2006.

1940s

Food and Drink

The economic boom that World War II (1939–45) started in America offered disposable income to more people than had previously been available. With more people working, wages more than twice the norm of the previous decade, and businesses producing more and more consumer products, Americans began living differently. By the end of the war, instead of laboring over their Depression-era (1929–41) or wartime gardens, families in the newly developed suburbs could afford to buy more processed food and to eat at restaurants more often.

Breakfast or a coffee break could be satisfied at bakeries, including the Dunkin' Donuts franchises. For a quick meal, workers on a lunch break or families tired of doing their own dishes could visit restaurants such as Stuckey's and McDonald's, which were opened in towns across the country. Pizza became an especially popular dish, and mom-and-pop pizzerias with their typical red-and-white-checkered tablecloths soon became familiar in cities and small towns. People wanting to sneak a snack in between meals could pop into their mouths a few M & M's candies, which were first introduced in the 1940s.

Dunkin' Donuts

Dunkin' Donuts is to **coffee** (see entry under 1990s—The Way We Lived in volume 5) and doughnuts what **McDonald's** (see entry under 1940s—Food and Drink in volume 3) is to **hamburgers** (see entry under 1950s—Food and Drink in volume 3) and **French fries** (see entry under 1950s—Food and Drink in volume 3): the shining example of a successful **fast food** (see entry under 1920s—Food and Drink in volume 2) concept. With stores throughout the nation and the world, Dunkin' Donuts is the largest coffee and baked goods chain nationally and globally. Each year, all of its franchises (stores sold to individual business owners around the country) in the United States sell one billion cups of coffee. Dunkin' Donuts franchise owners must agree to sell Dunkin' Donuts products according to the company rules.

The origin of Dunkin' Donuts dates to 1946, when a young businessman named William Rosenberg (1917–) opened Industrial

A popular morning stop in the United States, Dunkin' Donuts now serves customers in China. © RYAN PYLE/CORBIS.

Luncheon Services, which provided food and snacks to Boston-area factory workers. The company's success, plus the realization that 40 percent of its business came from coffee and doughnuts, inspired Rosenberg to open a coffee and doughnut shop in Quincy, Massachusetts, in 1948. He called it the Open Kettle. Two years later, he changed the name to Dunkin' Donuts and eventually opened five additional shops. Rosenberg originally charged five cents for each doughnut and ten cents per cup of coffee.

In 1955, Rosenberg signed his initial franchise agreement, allowing others to operate Dunkin' Donuts stores. The one hundredth such operation opened in 1963. The first overseas store, located in Japan, opened in 1970. Among the other Dunkin' Donut milestones were the one thousandth store opening in the United States (1979); the largest store, with 130 seats, opening in Bangkok, Thailand (1988); the two thousandth U.S. store (1990); the three thousandth U.S. store (1992); and the one thousandth international store (1995). In 1990, Allied Domecq PCL, a British conglomerate, purchased the company from the Rosenberg family. The decade also brought many additions to the Dunkin' Donuts menu, including flavored coffees, bagels, low-fat muffins, and a frozen beverage known as Coolatta.

By 2002, Dunkin' Donuts was offering fifty-two varieties of doughnuts, selling approximately 6.4 million of them each day. Sales came from over five thousand Dunkin' Donuts outlets located in forty countries, making it the largest coffee, doughnut, and bagel franchise in the world. The company became owned by a consortium of investment companies in 2005 after being divested from French beverage conglomerate Pernod Ricard. In 2011 Dunkin' Brands, its parent company, went public. Dunkin' Donuts continued to be innovative in this time period, adding new Coolatta flavors and Frozen Hot Chocolate to its menu, as well as introducing a loyalty rewards program for its customers.

Rob Edelman

For More Information

Dunkin' Donuts. http://www.dunkindonuts.com (accessed July 21, 2011).

"Dunkin' Donuts Goes Public." *Specialty Coffee Retailer* (June 2011): p. 6.

Rosenberg, William, with Jessica Brilliant Keener. *Time to Make the Donuts: The Founder of Dunkin Donuts Shares an American Journey.* New York: Lebhar-Friedman Books, 2001.

Steinberg, Sally Levitt. *The Donut Book: The Whole Story in Words, Pictures, and Outrageous Tales.* North Adams, MA: Storey, 2004.

M & M's

Each day, Mars Inc.'s candy division produces over four hundred million M & M's, the popular chocolate snack with the candy coating that "melts in your mouth, not in your hand." At first a wartime treat for soldiers on the go, the convenient portable sweet has become a part of daily life for candy-crazed kids and busy adults alike.

The name M & M's comes from the first letter of the last names of Forrest Mars (1904–1999) and William Murrie (1873–1950), the founders of the company that produces M & M's to this day. Mars also makes such other well-known candies as Mars Bars, Milky Way, and Skittles. However, M & M's remain its most popular product. M & M's Plain Chocolate Candies were introduced in 1941. They first gained popularity with American military personnel serving in World War II (1939–45), who received the candies in their food rations. Originally, the tiny candies were packaged in paper tubes, making them easy to carry along regardless of climate or conditions. Eventually the packaging changed to the familiar brown plastic pouch (yellow for peanut M & M's).

At first, M & M's came in six colors: red, yellow, green, brown, orange, and violet. In 1949, tan replaced violet. It was the first of many

M&M's have enjoyed immense popularity with candy lovers since 1941. © ENVISION/CORBIS.

changes that have been made to the product over the years. In 1954, for example, Mars introduced a new variety of M & M's with a peanut center. Peanut would be followed in later years by three additional varieties: peanut butter chocolate, almond, and crispy chocolate. In addition, the color blue replaced tan in 1995. In the summer of 2000, the company decided that "plain" was too bland a name for their most important product and changed its name on the package to "M & M's Milk Chocolate Candies." All these changes received extensive news coverage.

Unlike most candies, M & M's has managed to expand its influence from the food industry into the larger popular culture. The 1990s saw the creation of M & M's World, a retail and entertainment complex located in Las Vegas, Nevada. There, fans of the candy-covered chocolates could purchase more than three thousand M & M's brand items, including everything from **T-shirts** (see entry under 1910s—Fashion in volume 1) and caps to calculators and home decor.

In the early 2000s, M & M's continued its innovative ways. Its popular marketing featured cartoon characters shaped like the candies, known as Red, Yellow, Orange, and Ms. Green. M & M's appeared in colors like black and white, at least for limited time periods, and new flavors like coconut and pretzel-filled were also introduced. Through its online My M & M's program, anyone could customize their candies with phrases, pictures, and certain sports team logos.

Robert E. Schnakenberg

For More Information

Brenner, Joel Glenn. *The Emperors of Chocolate: Inside the Secret World of Hershey and Mars.* New York: Broadway Books, 2000.

Jorgensen, Janice. *Encyclopedia of Consumer Brands.* Detroit: St. James Press, 1994.

M & M's. http://www.m-ms.com/us/ (accessed July 21, 2011).

My M & M's. http://www.mymms.com/default.aspx (accessed July 21, 2011).

Olson, Elizabeth. "A Campaign for M&Ms with a Salty Center?" *New York Times* (June 22, 2010): p. B6.

McDonald's

The McDonald's **fast-food** (see entry under 1920s—Food and Drink in volume 2) chain started small but has grown since its founding in 1948 into America's best-known pit stop for **hamburgers** (see entry under 1950s—Food and Drink in volume 3), **French fries** (see entry under 1950s—Food and Drink in volume 3), milkshakes, and a variety of other premade delicacies. In addition, aggressive global marketing has enabled McDonald's to become one of the most recognizable brand names in the world.

Brothers Dick (1909–1998) and Mac (c. 1902–1971) McDonald developed the idea for McDonald's with an eye on the growing popularity of the automobile after World War II (1939–45). The first McDonald's restaurants featured "carhops" who would serve customers food orders in their cars. In time, the brothers abandoned the carhop concept in favor of a standardized self-service system. In this way, customers could have speedier access to nine standard menu items. Most popular among these were hamburgers, cheeseburgers, milkshakes, and French fries. The restaurants grew so popular that they were soon franchised, or sold to individual operators around the country who agreed to abide by

The McDonald's Museum in Des Plaines, Illinois, is a replica of the first McDonald's franchise that opened in 1955. © BETTMANN/ CORBIS.

the McDonald's cooking system. Ray Kroc (1902–1984), a milkshake tycoon, opened the first franchised McDonald's in Des Plaines, Illinois, in 1955. Kroc bought the company from the McDonald brothers for $2.7 million in 1961.

Under Kroc's guidance, McDonald's grew even more popular. The company's iconic "golden arches" logo and its clown mascot Ronald McDonald were marketed all over America, particularly to families with children. A number of new menu items were introduced, including the "Big Mac," the signature McDonald's sandwich, in 1968 and the "Happy Meal," which aimed to attract kids by including a toy with the food, in 1979. In 1973, the restaurant even began serving breakfast. By the 1970s, McDonald's had become a vital part of many Americans' daily lives.

It was no surprise, then, that the company began to expand globally as well. The 1970s saw McDonald's restaurants in Europe, Japan, and South America. With the collapse of communism in Russia and improved American diplomatic relations with China, McDonald's opened its doors there, too. Some citizens in these countries complained that the burger giant was "Americanizing" their culture, but people of all ethnic backgrounds continued to line up for the company's inexpensive, filling food.

McDonald's ever-growing global reach has made it a reliable reference point for popular culture. The 1994 film ***Pulp Fiction*** (see entry under 1990s—Film and Theater in volume 5), for example, included a long, rambling conversation between two hit men about what people call various McDonald's sandwiches in foreign countries.

In the face of criticism about fast food adding to the obesity crisis and increased competition on the quick food industry, McDonald's made some changes to its menu in the early 2000s. The company added fruit smoothies, McCafé coffee drinks, and other items intended to enhance its image worldwide. The coffee drinks proved particularly popular, accounting for five percent of its $23.5 billion in sales in 2008.

Like **Coca-Cola** (see entry under 1900s—Food and Drink in volume 1), **Levi's** (see entry under 1950s—Fashion in volume 3), and **Budweiser** (see entry under 1960s—Commerce in volume 4), McDonald's is one of the all-American brand names that keeps popping up all over the world.

Robert E. Schnakenberg

For More Information

Bell, Jonathan. "Another Huge Market for Coffee: McCafé Is Bringing Coffee to the Masses." *Tea & Coffee Trade Journal* (September 2009): p. 62.

Boas, Max, and Steve Chain. *Big Mac: The Unauthorized Story of McDonald's.* New York: Dutton, 1976.

A Brief History of McDonald's. http://www.mcspotlight.org/company/company_history.html (accessed July 21, 2011).

Kroc, Ray. *Grinding It Out: The Making of McDonald's.* Chicago: Contemporary Books, 1977.

Love, John F. *McDonald's: Behind the Arches.* Rev. ed. New York: Bantam, 1995.

McDonald's. http://www.mcdonalds.com/us/en/home.html (accessed July 21, 2011).

Schlosser, Eric. *Fast Food Nation.* New York: Houghton Mifflin, 2001.

Pizza

Pizza is among the most popular foods in America. By the end of the twentieth century, pizza was a $32 billion industry. Children aged three to eleven ranked pizza as their favorite lunch or dinner meal in 2000.

Pizza consists of flat dough baked with toppings of tomato sauce, cheese, and a varying assortment of vegetables and meats. Pizza has been made in the United States since the early 1900s, when Italian immigrants first came to America. Italian immigrant Gennaro (or Giovanni, depending on the source) Lombardi opened the first pizzeria (pizza restaurant) in 1905 in the portion of New York City known as Little Italy.

Although pizzerias had spread across the country by the 1930s, American soldiers returning from Naples, Italy, at the end of World War II (1939–45) made pizza a true national fad. The soldiers craved the food they had savored in Italy. Pizzerias sprang up across the country to feed their hunger. Pizzerias— often decorated with red-and-white checked tablecloths—offered casual dining. Pizza could be delivered to one's home starting in the 1960s or purchased frozen in the local supermarket.

Americans relished the informality and convenience of pizza. "Pizza parties" were held during casual gatherings in homes and in college dorm rooms. People even began eating pizza slices with their hands in public. **Television** (see entry under 1940s—TV and Radio in volume 3) events also inspired pizza parties; on **Super Bowl** (see entry under 1960s—Sports and Games in volume 4) Sunday, more pizza is eaten than on any other day of the year.

Whether a New York slice or a Chicago pie, pizza's popularity is unquestioned by millions of hungry diners. © SHUTTERSTOCK.COM.

By the late 1990s, pizza had become one of America's favorite foods. Much of the cheese Americans ate came melted on pizzas. The amount of mozzarella cheese Americans ate increased seven times between 1970 and 1996. Seventeen percent of all restaurants were pizzerias. Three pizza restaurants ranked among the top eleven restaurant chains in the United States: Pizza Hut, ranked third; Domino's Pizza, ranked ninth; and Little Caesars Pizza, ranked eleventh.

Americans' love for pizza produced unlikely types of pizza. By 2001, almost anything topped with tomato sauce and mozzarella cheese—bagels, crackers, or hamburgers—could be called "pizza." Pizza-flavored snack foods such as corn chips, crackers, and even cheese could be found lining grocery isles.

In the early 2000s, pizza chains continued to see increasing sales. While pizza-flavored snacks were still available, real pizzas could be expensive gourmet masterpieces or inexpensively priced. In 2003, Little Caesars introduced the $5, ready-made carry-out pizza, and many other chains followed suit with discount pies. As the worldwide economy faltered during a global economic downturn that began in 2008, affordable pizzas from popular companies like Pizza Hut, Domino's, Papa John's, and Little Caesars appealed to consumers on a tight budget.

Sara Pendergast

For More Information

"As American as Apple Pizza Pie." *Smithsonian Magazine* (June 1997). http://www.smithsonianmag.com/people-places/pizza-abstract.html (accessed July 22, 2011).

Buonassisi, Rosario. *Pizza: From Its Italian Origins to the Modern Table.* Willowdale, Ontario: Firefly, 2000.

Helstosky, Carol. *Pizza: A Global History.* London: Reaktion, 2008.

"The History of Pizza." *Homemade Gourmet Pizza.* http://home.comcast.net/~cmptj/pizza/history.htm (accessed July 21, 2011).

"Pizza—History & Legends of Pizza." *What' Cooking America.* http://whatscookingamerica.net/History/Pizza/PizzaHistory.htm (accessed July 21, 2011).

Slomon, Evelyne. *The Pizza Book: Everything There Is to Know About the World's Greatest Pie.* New York: Times Books, 1984.

Strong, Michael. "Hungry for More: Sales Increase for Local Pizza Chains, but Crowded Field Intensifies Battle for Market Share." *Crain's Detroit Business* (September 13, 2004): p. 3.

1940s

Music

The variety of music that was introduced to Americans during the Depression (1929–41) continued to evolve during the 1940s. Blues became electrified and transformed into rhythm and blues (R&B), boogie-woogie, and what became known as "jump blues," laying the foundations for the emergence of rock and roll in the coming decades. Blues music was now easily and cheaply recorded on new magnetic tape recorders. Another new musical style called "bebop" developed in jazz dance clubs in Manhattan and Chicago. Bebop offered talented musicians, such as trumpet players Dizzy Gillespie (1917–1993) and young Miles Davis (1926–1991) and piano player Thelonious Monk (1917–1982) a chance to shine. There was room in bebop for improvisation (spontaneous music-making) in the songs.

As part of the New Deal program to give people work, government researchers paid by the New Deal sought and recorded the folk music of America. This folk and hillbilly (as early country and western music was sometimes known) music was also changing, though. Like blues, country music incorporated elements of other styles, especially swing, and made use of electric and steel guitars, which moved it closer to what would become rock and roll. Country music was especially popular with the large populations of rural people who had moved to cities, although servicemen also loved the music. The Special Services Division of the European

Theater of Operations organized a tour of country bands to the troops fighting in Europe. The *Grand Ole Opry* radio program was one of the most listened-to radio shows during the decade. Roy Acuff (1903–1992) was one of the most popular country singers. Like jazz, country music had an offshoot that valued improvisation. Bluegrass, as this subgenre became known, developed during the 1940s and highlighted banjo and guitar players' skills and featured songs about the "hard life": drunkenness, joblessness, marital troubles, and regrets.

At the beginning of the decade, swing-jazz orchestras played in dance halls, on the radio, on movie soundtracks, and on single and long-playing records. These big bands often featured a popular singer, such as Billie Holiday (1915–1959), Bing Crosby (1904–1977), or Frank Sinatra (1915–1998), who crooned (sang in a smooth voice just right for amplification through a microphone) to audiences. After World War II (1939–45), the dynamic brass sounds of the big bands were replaced by more string instruments to develop a softer style of pop music.

Bluegrass

Since its development in the mid-1940s, bluegrass music has become one of the most distinctive American musical forms, attracting an ardent audience of supporters. A close cousin of **country music** (see entry under 1940s—Music in volume 3), bluegrass is an acoustic musical style that features banjo, mandolin, guitar, double bass, fiddle, and harmony singing. Bluegrass is largely the creation of mandolin player, singer, and songwriter Bill Monroe (1911–1996). Monroe formed a band called the Blue Grass Boys in 1938. The band hired an impressive banjo player named Earl Scruggs (1924–) in 1945. Scruggs's up-tempo banjo-playing combined well with Monroe's distinctive mandolin playing and singing. Together, they created an entirely new sound in American music. Songs such as "I'm Going Back to Old Kentucky" and "Blue Moon of Kentucky" put them on the American musical map. Other musicians who imitated their style later gave that sound the name "bluegrass" in honor of Monroe's band.

The success of Monroe's band attracted other musicians to play bluegrass, including such greats as the Foggy Mountain Boys, the Stanley Brothers, and the Osborne Brothers. Bluegrass was most popular in the late 1940s and early 1950s, but its popularity began to fade slightly by the late 1950s as **rock and roll** (see entry under 1950s—Music in volume 3) gained prominence among young audiences. However, the **folk music** (see entry under 1960s—Music in volume 4) revival of the early 1960s revived interest in the music. Bluegrass was later featured in the theme song for the popular 1960s **television** (see entry under 1940s—TV and Radio in volume 3) show *The Beverly Hillbillies* (see entry under 1960s—TV and Radio in volume 4) and in the 1967 film *Bonnie and Clyde* (see entry under 1930s—The Way We Lived in volume 2). Since the 1970s, bluegrass has continued to develop and attract new audiences. Newer artists such as the New Grass Revival and David Grisman (1945–) took bluegrass in new directions in the 1970s and beyond. This new sound, called "progressive" bluegrass, or "newgrass," incorporated **jazz** (see entry under 1900s—Music in volume 1) music and sometimes electric instruments into its sound, both of which appealed to younger audiences. In the 1990s and early 2000s, artists such as Alison Krauss (1971–), who performed both as a solo artist and with Union Station, Ricky Skaggs (1954–), Nickel Creek, and countless local bluegrass bands continued to bring this music to new listeners.

Although bluegrass music has never been as popular as rock and roll, **pop music** (see entry under 1940s—Music in volume 3), or country music, it has become increasingly popular with thousands of people across the United States and around the world. Bluegrass groups do not fill huge stadiums like many popular rock groups, but bluegrass festivals remain common in rural America. People camp out, enjoy the outdoors, and visit with friends, all while enjoying bluegrass music. Many amateur musicians bring their instruments to these gatherings, and the campsites are always filled with music. The popularity of bluegrass in the 2000s and beyond is a strong indication that the style is alive and well. Its healthy mix of tradition and innovation has made it one of the United States' most unique and enduring musical traditions.

Timothy Berg

For More Information

Bluegrass Country. http://bluegrasscountry.org/ (accessed July 21, 2011).

The Country Music Foundation, eds. *Country: The Music and the Musicians.* New York: Abbeville Press, 1994.

Malone, Bill C. *Country Music U.S.A..* 3rd ed. Austin: University of Texas Press, 2010.

Price, Deborah Evans, and Phyllis Stark. "*O Brother!* Bluegrass Is Blooming: Doors Open for Acoustic Ads as the Industry Guards the Music's Integrity." *Billboard* (July 20, 2002): p. 1.

Rosenberg, Neil V. *Bluegrass: A History.* Rev. ed. Urbana: University of Illinois Press, 2005.

Smith, Richard D. *Bluegrass: An Informal Guide.* Chicago: A Cappella Books, 1995.

Country Music

With its themes of love, loss, hope, and heartbreak, country music speaks to the basic emotions of humans. Because of this appeal, it is one of the most original and persistent of American musical forms. Although its origins are humble, with the style having developed in the poor white communities of the American South, country music has grown throughout the twentieth century into a major musical style with great popular and commercial appeal. It is now an industry all its own. Part of its enduring appeal comes from how it touches people deeply. In addition, its styles are varied enough to attract new listeners continually.

Country music emerged in the American South, particularly along the Appalachian Mountains, in the early twentieth century. Its roots can be found in the songs brought over by early immigrants from England, Scotland, and Ireland. Those songs expressed the hardships of rural life and the deep religious devotion of these immigrants. From these roots, country music developed into a commercial form of music in the 1920s, when the first recordings of it were made. Among the most important early "stars" of country music were the Carter Family, now called the Original Carter Family, consisting of A. P. Carter (1891–1960), Sara Carter (1899–1979), and Maybelle Carter (1909–1978). They were known for their vocal harmonies on such songs as "Keep on the Sunny Side" and "Wildwood Flower." Another important early country music star was **Jimmie Rodgers** (1897–1933; see entry under 1920s—Music in volume 2), known as "the Singing Brakeman"

Country singer and movie star Gene Autry in a still from the 1947 film The Last Round-up. © BETTMANN/CORBIS.

because he worked on the railroads. He was famous for his original songs, especially his "blue yodel" songs, which featured his distinctive yodeling (a form of singing in which the vocalist switches rapidly between a regular and a falsetto—high-pitched—singing voice). These early musicians established strong traditions in country music—good songwriting and top-notch singing and playing.

Country became much more widely known in the 1940s when it was featured on national **radio** (see entry under 1920s— TV and Radio in volume 2) programs such as the ***Grand Ole Opry*** (see entry under 1920s—Music in volume 2) and in movie **Westerns** (see entry under 1930s—Film and Theater in volume 2) that featured singing cowboys like Gene Autry (1907–1998) and Roy Rogers (1911–1998). The *Grand Ole Opry,* with singing star Roy Acuff (1903–1992) as its leader in the 1940s and beyond, was a weekly radio show based in Nashville, Tennessee. The *Grand Ole Opry* featured a wide variety of country music artists. At first the program was only heard in the South, but it was later broadcast nationally and could be heard across the United States. To be on the *Grand Ole Opry* in the 1940s and 1950s was as important for country music stars as it is for modern musicians to be on **MTV** (see entry under 1980s—Music in volume 5). The *Opry* provided a way for people to hear these new stars, and promoted record and concert ticket sales. One of the biggest stars in the early years of the *Grand Ole Opry* was Hank Williams (1923–1953). Williams's hits "Your Cheatin' Heart," "Hey Good Lookin'," and "Jambalaya" became country music standards. Williams's death in 1953 at the age of twenty-nine robbed country music of one of its greatest figures, but his influence lives on in the work of others.

In the 1950s and early 1960s, as country music became more commercially successful, it moved away from its rough country roots towards a more slick and produced sound. The country music recording industry, based in Nashville, sought out talent that could appeal to a wider audience. Potential recording artists had to have a smoother sound more removed from the country tradition. The Nashville Sound, as this new style was called, did produce some big names and big hits in country music. These smoother voices included Eddy Arnold (1918–), who sang "Bouquet of Roses"; Patsy Cline (1932–1963), who had hits with "I Fall to Pieces," "Walking After Midnight," and "Crazy" before she died in a plane crash in 1963; and Jim Reeves (1924–1964), who sang "Welcome to My World" and "He'll Have to Go." With these singers, and others like them, slick arrangements, often with string instruments, provided the musical backdrop.

While the Nashville Sound was making country music in the 1950s and 1960s much more mainstream and commercialized, other emerging stars struck out on their own with unique sounds that remained more in touch with country music's roots. George Jones (1931–) developed a twangy sound in the 1950s that was very in touch with its country origins, especially in songs such as "White Lightning." Also important were Buck Owens (1929–2006) and Merle Haggard (1937–). Significantly, many of these artists came from Bakersfield, California, not Nashville, so they felt free to create their own sound. Owens created a guitar-driven sound with his band the Buckeroos, and they had hits with "Together Again," "Love's Gonna Live Here," and "Act Naturally." Haggard brought his harder-edged sound to country music in such songs as "Tonight the Bottle Let Me Down" and "Okie from Muskogee," which celebrated the hard life Haggard had known. Against the mainstream country music sound, Haggard and Owens established an outsider tradition that lives on in country music.

In the 1970s, 1980s, and 1990s, country music existed on two levels. There was the mainstream country sound, which produced such later stars as Garth Brooks (1962–), Reba McEntire (1955–), Faith Hill (1967–), and Alan Jackson (1958–). They had huge hits on mainstream country radio and sold millions of records. Critics, however, complained that much of this music sounded manufactured, lacking the originality and emotion of "real" country music. The other level was called at first "outlaw" country and later "alternative country." Outlaw country, played by such greats as Willie Nelson (1933–), Johnny Cash (1932–2003), and Waylon Jennings (1937–2002), showcased the great songwriting of these artists and reached its peak in the 1970s.

In the 1990s, **"alternative country music"** (see entry under 1990s—Music in volume 5) arose from the instruments and voices of younger artists who, bored with mainstream country music, turned to older country music styles and mixed them with elements of rock and roll. Musicians such as Steve Earle (1955–), Lucinda Williams (1953–), Lyle Lovett (1957–), and k.d. lang (1961–) all developed their own unique styles that pushed country music in new directions while keeping it in touch with its roots. The growth of alternative country music is proof that country music is an enduring tradition.

Alternative and outlaw country remained influential in the early 2000s, with artists like Josh Turner (1977–) and the regionally popular Texas country music finding an audience. As a whole, however, country music became more mainstream and commercialized.

One reason was the rise of **pop country** (see entry under 2000s—Music in volume 6) stars like the Dixie Chicks, Sugarland, Tim McGraw (1967–), and Taylor Swift (1989–), all of whom crossed over from country to pop music charts. McGraw performed a popular duet called "Cause It's All in My Head" with rap star Nelly (1974–), while the young Swift moved from teen country sensation to full-blown pop star, playing to packed arenas and selling millions of albums. Country music continues to develop in new ways that speak to people of all ages and backgrounds.

Timothy Berg

For More Information

Academy of Country Music. http://www.acmcountry.com/home/index.php (accessed on July 23, 2011).

Collins, Ace. *The Stories Behind Country Music's All-Time Greatest 100 Songs.* New York: Boulevard Books, 1996.

Country Music Hall of Fame and Museum. http://countrymusichalloffame.org/ (accessed on July 23, 2011).

Editors of Country Music Magazine. *The Comprehensive Country Music Encyclopedia.* New York: Times Books, 1994.

Grand Ole Opry. http://www.opry.com/ (accessed on July 23, 2011).

Kingsbury, Paul. *The Encyclopedia of Country Music.* 2nd ed. New York: Oxford University Press, 2012.

Malone, Bill C. *Country Music U.S.A.* 3rd ed. Austin: University of Texas Press, 2010.

Malone, Bill C., and Judith McCulloh. *Stars of Country Music.* Urbana: University of Illinois Press, 1975.

Mansfield, Brian, and Gary Graff, eds. *MusicHound Country: The Essential Album Guide.* Detroit: Visible Ink, 1997.

Richards, Tad, and Melvin B. Shestack. *The New Country Music Encyclopedia.* New York: Simon & Schuster, 1993.

Tosches, Nick. *Country: The Biggest Music in America.* New York: Stein and Day, 1977.

Long-playing Record (LP)

Since the invention of sound-recording technology by Thomas Edison (1847–1931) in the 1800s, people have looked for new and better ways to bring recorded sound to mass audiences. Before cassettes, **compact discs** (also called CDs; see entry under 1980s—Music in volume 5), and MPEG-1 Audio Layer-3 (MP3) files, the long-playing record (LP) was for more than forty years the main way people heard recorded music.

Long-playing records (33⅓ rpms) were superior to old 78 rpms because more music could fit and vinyl discs were less breakable.
© JORG GREUEL/JUPITERIMAGES/GETTY IMAGES.

During the first half of the twentieth century, the 78-rpm record—spinning on a turntable 78 times, or revolutions, per minute—was the major way people heard recorded music. The 78-rpm record had a number of drawbacks, however: It could only hold a few minutes of music on each side, it was heavy, and it broke easily. Peter Goldmark (1906–1977), working for Columbia Records, developed the LP in 1948. He overcame the 78's limitations in two ways. First, he lowered the speed of the recording to 33⅓ revolutions per minute. Second, he squeezed more and smaller grooves onto each side of the record so that more sound could be recorded onto each side of the disc. These grooves would reach almost one half mile if stretched out in a straight line. The LP also required a diamond needle to play the records, which resulted in improved sound. The LP was immediately hailed by classical music lovers because the longer pieces of classical music could now be heard in a mostly uninterrupted format.

By the 1950s, the LP was the dominant form for recorded music, and it changed the face of popular music in many ways. It improved the sound quality of recordings, lasted longer than 78s, was less prone to breaking, and was cheaper to produce. Although 45-rpm singles (developed at the same time as the LP) were preferred for single songs, the LP allowed musicians to experiment with longer works, including related songs on a single disc. By the 1960s, **rock and roll** (see entry under 1950s—Music in volume 3) musicians in particular were using the extended format to produce concept albums, the most famous of which was *Sgt. Pepper's Lonely Hearts Club Band* (1967) by the **Beatles** (see entry under 1960s—Music in volume 4). In the late 1960s, FM **disc jockeys** (see entry under 1950s— Music in volume 3) preferred to play songs from LPs rather than from 45-rpm singles.

Although the arrival of the CD in 1982 and the rise of MP3 player in the early 2000s seemed to spell the end of the LP, some people still listened to their old LPs and the format never really went away. A handful of new recordings continued to be released in LP format, and by 2008, vinyl sales were growing again. Though LPs were only a small part of the music market, more and more albums were released in this format and the sales of turntables on which to play them also increased. Sound quality and the collectability of high-quality vinyl were two reasons cited by collectors for the revival of the LP, a movement embraced by young and older fans alike. The revitalization of LPs was a testament to the enduring appeal of the technology.

Timothy Berg

For More Information

Engelbrekston, Lisa. "Hot Wax: Vinyl Makes a Comeback: Will the LP Outlive the CD?" *Variety* (December 7, 2009): p. 18.

Gillen, Marilyn A. "From the Cylinder to the CD." *Billboard* (November 1, 1994).

Goldmark, Peter. *Maverick Inventor: My Turbulent Years at CBS.* New York: Dutton, 1973.

Millard, Andre. *America on Record: A History of Recorded Sound.* New York: Cambridge University Press, 1995.

Peoples, Glenn. "Back from the Audio Abyss: Youth-Driven Vinyl Sales, Premium Over-the-Ear Headphones, VC Investment in Hardware Companies, More Turntables at Big-Box Stores—10 Signs That Sound Quality Is Making a Comeback." *Billboard* (June 18, 2011): p. 18.

Read, Oliver, and Walter Welch. *From Tin Foil to Stereo: The Evolution of the Phonograph.* Indianapolis: Howard Sams, 1977.

Pop Music

There has always been "popular" music in the United States, and all forms of music are popular with certain audiences. The term "pop music," though, generally refers to styles of music that are nonclassical, mainstream, and intended for very wide audiences. Pop music is often controlled by large music companies. In the early decades of the twentieth century, these large companies were sheet-music publishers. After 1930, the large music companies controlling the release of pop music were the recording companies. Pop music is usually music meant to turn a profit rather than as a platform for innovation or self-expression. That does not mean pop music is not good music, however—throughout the twentieth century and into the twenty-first century, pop music has provided some of the greatest works of all time.

Because pop music is meant to sell records, music companies have constantly been on the lookout for the next marketable performer. Thus, pop music is in many ways a history of one musical trend after another. When a record in a certain style catches on and becomes a hit, other singers, musicians, and record companies often imitate it, attempting to cash in on the trend. In the 1920s, pop music meant mellow "sweet bands" such as Paul Whiteman (1890–1967) and his orchestra, which played soothing melodies, or singers such as Al Jolson (1885–1950) or Rudy Vallee (1901–1986). In the 1930s and early 1940s, the big-band sound of songs from **Broadway** (see entry under 1900s—Film and Theater in volume 1) or **Hollywood** (see entry under 1930s—Film and Theater in volume 2) musicals supplied the pop hits. During the late 1940s and early 1950s, smooth singers, or crooners, such as **Frank Sinatra** (1915–1998; see entry under 1940s—Music in volume 3), Tony Bennett (1926–), and Patti Page (1927–) dominated the pop charts. Crooners sang in a smooth voice just right for amplification through a microphone. They often sang songs written by some of the great composers of American popular music: Cole Porter (1891–1964), Irving Berlin (1888–1989), George Gershwin (1898–1937), Ira Gershwin (1896–1983), and others.

Prior to 1955, pop music was rather unified. One style dominated for a period before giving way to a different but related style. Abrupt changes rarely occurred. Sweet bands gave way to **big bands** (see entry under 1930s—Music in volume 2); big bands to big bands with singers;

bands with singers to solo singing stars. After 1955, however, the pop-music field fragmented, thanks to the rise of **rock and roll** (see entry under 1950s—Music in volume 3). Early rock and roll was often rough, performed by amateurs, and produced by small record companies. Rock and roll took the pop field by surprise, but of course bigger record companies paid attention to its money-making possibilities. Once the big record companies got into the act, they began producing rock and roll that would appeal to a broader audience. That music blurred the lines between rock and pop. For example, **Elvis Presley** (1935–1977; see entry under 1950s—Music in volume 3) was a rock-and-roll pioneer whose early records were rough and full of energy. Once he moved to the big time with RCA Records, his sound softened so he could appeal to a wider audience and sell more records. By the 1970s, Presley was singing some of the same songs Frank Sinatra had recorded, such as "My Way."

After 1955, the histories of pop and rock remained closely tied together. Big record companies were constantly trying to produce pop-rock music that would appeal to many listeners. In the late 1950s, these companies largely succeeded, producing many **teen idols** (see entry under 1940s—The Way We Lived in volume 3) such as Fabian (1943–) and Pat Boone (1934–). While rock fans grooved to African American singer Little Richard (1935–) shouting his song "Tutti Frutti," pop fans heard Boone's less dynamic version. Boone's version was easier to listen to and appealed to largely white audiences, but it lost much of the power and excitement of the original. Pop music was also dominated in this period by professional songwriters. Some great music did come out of this era, but it largely conformed to the demands of commerce. The pop music was unthreatening, easy to listen to, and geared toward mass appeal.

When the **Beatles** (see entry under 1960s—Music in volume 4) arrived on the rock and pop scenes in 1964, they blurred the lines between the two genres even further. They were both great rock and great pop artists. They had a broad appeal, but they also pushed the boundaries of rock music in new directions, changing the musical landscape forever. Following after them were lesser bands who attempted to mimic their style as the large record companies attempted to cash in on the Beatles' sound. After the Beatles, however, it became extremely difficult to define pop music. Pop music in the 1960s was the snarl of the **Rolling Stones** (see entry under 1960s—Music in volume 4) singing "(I Can't Get No) Satisfaction"; the funk of the **rhythm and blues** (see entry under 1940s—Music in volume 3) sound of **Motown** (see entry under

1960s—Music in volume 4) artists, which included many manufactured groups; and the smooth-voiced Dionne Warwick (1940–) singing "Walk On By," which was composed by one of the era's most successful songwriting duos, Burt Bacharach (1929–) and Hal David (1921–). These sounds were commercially successful, and they all could be classified as pop music, but they were quite different musically.

By the late 1960s, the pop and rock fields had begun to move in different directions. There were still artists who crossed over the lines, but rock moved in a harder-edged direction after 1968. Pop music continued to offer softer sounds dominated by the commercial needs of the record companies to sell records. Always searching for the next big trend, record companies in the pop music field tried one style after another. In the late 1960s and 1970s, manufactured groups surfaced with elaborate marketing plans behind them. These included the **Monkees** (see entry under 1960s—Music in volume 4) and the **Partridge Family** (see entry under 1970s—TV and Radio in volume 4). Both groups were created by hiring individuals to form groups to be seen on **television** (see entry under 1940s—TV and Radio in volume 3) shows. The concept worked: Both groups sold lots of records. In the 1970s, trends in pop music included soft rock by songwriters such as Carole King (1942–), John Denver (1943–1997), and James Taylor (1948–). Teen idols such as Leif Garrett (1961–), Shaun Cassidy (1958–), and Andy Gibb (1958–1988) had pop hits, but not much lasting power. Finally **disco** (see entry under 1970s—Music in volume 4), a rhythmic dance music, appeared.

In the 1980s and 1990s, pop music followed a number of similar trends. After disco's dance-oriented pop faded, pop dance music evolved with **Michael Jackson** (1958–2009; see entry under 1980s—Music in volume 4), **Madonna** (1958–; see entry under 1980s—Music in volume 4), and others in the early years of **MTV** (Music Television cable network; see entry under 1980s—Music in volume 5) in the 1980s. British pop groups had a resurgence in the mid-1980s with such collectives as Duran Duran, Wham!, and Culture Club. The vocal tradition revived with stars like Whitney Houston (1963–2012), Mariah Carey (1970–), and Celine Dion (1968–). Pop hits were also heard from teen idols such as Debbie Gibson (1970–) and Tiffany (1971–). New manufactured vocal groups such as Menudo (called MDO thereafter), New Edition, *NSYNC, and the Backstreet Boys had successful pop hits. These record-industry formulas—offering American audiences a British sound; the pop diva, or star vocalist; the heavy promotion of a teen idol; the practice of assembling groups to produce hits rather than constantly being on the lookout for musical groups with the potential for success—had proved popular in the past, and they succeeded again and again in the 1980s and onward. Right alongside these trends in pop music, other forms of rock and roll continued to develop, including **punk** (see entry under 1970s—Music in volume 4), New Wave, **alternative rock** (see entry under 1990s—Music in volume 5), and **rap and hip-hop** (see entry under 1980s—Music in volume 5). All these styles influenced more mainstream pop music, as they would continue to do in the early twenty-first century.

Timothy Berg

For More Information

Breithaupt, Don, with Jeff Breithaupt. *Precious and Few: Pop Music of the Early '70s.* New York: St. Martin's Press, 1996.

Clarke, Donald, ed. *The Penguin Encyclopedia of Popular Music.* 2nd ed. New York: Penguin Books, 1998.

The Encyclopedia of Popular Music. 4th ed. New York: Oxford University Press, 2010.

Gregory, Hugh. *A Century of Pop: A Hundred Years of Music That Changed the World.* New York: Acapella Publishers, 1998.

Langley, Andrew. *Twenty Names in Pop Music.* New York: Marshall Cavendish, 1988.

Miller, Jim, ed. *The Rolling Stone Illustrated History of Rock & Roll.* 3rd ed. New York: Random House, 1992.

The Official American Idol Music Site. http://www.americanidolmusic.com/ (accessed July 24, 2011).

Pop Culture Madness. http://www.popculturemadness.com/Music/ (accessed July 24, 2011).

Shuker, Roy. *Understanding Popular Music.* 2nd ed. New York: Routledge, 2001.

Smith, Joe, ed. *Off the Record: An Oral History of Popular Music.* New York: Warner Books, 1988.

Whitburn, Joel. *Billboard Top 1000 Singles, 1955–2000.* Milwaukee: Hal Leonard Publishing Corp., 2001.

Rhythm and Blues

Without rhythm and blues, or R&B, there would be no such styles of music as **rock and roll** (see entry under 1950s—Music in volume 3) or soul. Emerging after 1945 in African American communities in northern and western cities in the United States, R&B fused elements of **jazz** (see entry under 1900s—Music in volume 1) and **blues** (see entry under 1920s—Music in volume 2) into an entirely new sound based around vocals, piano, saxophone, bass, and drums. Hip, usually danceable, and often funny, R&B most importantly appealed to the tastes of black Americans in urban centers.

Rhythm and blues emerged when it did for a number of reasons. During World War II (1939–45), many African Americans had moved from the rural South to the urban North. The new conditions they found there prompted the need for a new kind of music that seemed up-tempo and more sophisticated than rural country blues. The economic needs brought on by wartime money-saving measures encouraged many small bands to form. The invention of inexpensive tape-recording technology gave rise to many small record companies that recorded these bands. Companies such as Specialty, Modern, and Imperial in Los Angeles, California; Chess in Chicago, Illinois; King in Cincinnati, Ohio; and Atlantic in New York City were all formed to promote and exploit the black public's interest in R&B. To distinguish this music from music listened to by whites, the music publication *Billboard* created the Rhythm and Blues title for its black music chart in 1949.

Among the first of the many important R&B performers was Louis Jordan (1908–1975). Jordan created a small band that combined jumping rhythms propelled by piano, bass, and saxophone with Jordan's comical lyrics. He proved very influential and had a number of hits in the mid-1940s, including *Five Guys Named Moe*. Other important early R&B artists and bands were Joe Liggins (1915–1987) and the Honeydrippers, Charles Brown (1922–1999), Cecil Gant (1913–1951), Roy Milton (1907–1983) and His Solid Senders, Johnny Otis (1921–), Dinah Washington (1924–1963), and Ruth Brown (1928–2006). These artists dominated the R&B charts in the late 1940s and early 1950s.

Rhythm and blues was also largely responsible for the development of rock and roll and of soul music. Rock and roll basically combined elements of black R&B with white **country music** (see entry under 1940s—Music in volume 2), producing a hybrid style that appealed to white teenagers as well as many black listeners. By the mid-to-late 1950s, R&B itself was giving way to a new form of black music: soul. When singer and pianist Ray Charles (1930–2004) began combining elements of R&B with black gospel music, a new form of music was born. Soul music—especially the **Motown** (see entry under 1960s—Music in volume 4) sound, from Detroit, Michigan—dominated the charts well into the 1970s. Soul music left behind the honking saxophones of R&B for a more refined sound that highlighted gospel-style singing. In its primary years, between 1945 and 1955, R&B was one of the most important musical forms in the United States. Its legacy has touched almost all forms of American popular music that came after it, including **rap and hip-hop** (see entry under 1980s—Music in volume 5) in the late twentieth and early twenty-first centuries.

Timothy Berg

For More Information

George, Nelson. *The Death of Rhythm and Blues.* New York: Plume, 1988.

Gillett, Charlie. *The Sound of the City.* 3rd ed. London: Souvenir Press, 1996.

Rhythm & Blues Foundation. http://www.rhythm-n-blues.org/ (accessed July 22, 2011).

Shaw, Arnold. *Honkers and Shouters: The Golden Years of Rhythm and Blues.* New York: Collier, 1978.

Frank Sinatra during an NBC radio broadcast in 1942.
© HULTON ARCHIVE/GETTY IMAGES.

Frank Sinatra (1915–1998)

Frank Sinatra was one of the greatest singers in the history of American popular music. Sinatra first gained fame with Tommy Dorsey (1905–1956) and his band in the late 1930s before becoming a solo star in his own right in 1942. He inspired mass hysteria among his many female fans, known as **bobbysoxers** (see entry under 1940s—Fashion in volume 3). In addition to his many hit songs, he promoted the use of the concept album in the 1950s, assembling a number of songs around a single theme, as he did on such albums as *Only the Lonely* in 1958. Sinatra's hits were incredibly numerous, including "Love and Marriage," "Luck Be a Lady," "My Way," "New York, New York," and "Strangers in the Night."

Sinatra also acted in movie musicals and films, including *Anchors Aweigh* (1944); *From Here to Eternity* (1954), for which he earned an

Oscar; and *The Manchurian Candidate* (1962). Although he was at his musical peak in the 1950s, Sinatra remained in the spotlight until his death in 1998 through his concerts, recordings, films, and his very public, and often controversial, lifestyle.

After his passing, Sinatra's legacy was not forgotten as his music and personality remained popular. In May 2008, he was honored with a stamp from the U.S. Postal Service, and a collection of his remastered classics, *Nothing but the Best,* debuted at number two on the *Billboard* 200 that same month. Also, May 20, 2008, was designated Frank Sinatra Day by the U.S. Congress.

Timothy Berg

For More Information

Frank Sinatra: The Best Is Yet to Come (video). MGM/UA, 1996.

Hamill, Pete. *Why Sinatra Matters.* Boston: Little Brown, 1998.

High, Kamau. "Still the Chairman: Sinatra Compilation Enjoys Huge Debut Week." *Billboard* (May 31, 2008): p. 39.

Kaplan, James. *Frank: The Voice.* New York: Doubleday, 2010.

Lahr, John. *Sinatra: The Artist and the Man.* New York: Random House, 1997.

The Official Frank Sinatra Website. http://www.sinatra.com/ (accessed July 21, 2011).

Sinatra Family. http://sinatrafamily.com (accessed July 21, 2011).

Summers, Anthony, and Robbyn Swan. *Frank: The Life.* New York: Knopf, 2005.

1940s

Print Culture

World War II (1939–45) dominated serious print media from 1939 until most of the last troops returned from Europe in 1946. American newspapers and magazines focused intently on bringing news from the warfront to the doorsteps of almost every American. Stories and photographs of soldiers and battles filled most of the papers' pages. Thirty-seven American reporters and other newspeople died while trying to get their stories during the war.

Even though the news of the war was the most important topic of the decade, the 1940s was also the golden age of the comic book. Comic strips had tickled the funny bones of readers since 1890, and comic books now offered entertainment in their own package. Aimed mostly at young readers, comic books about superheroes like the Green Lantern and Captain America, about detectives, and about just-plain-funny characters such as the kids in the Archie Comics were printed in abundance.

Unlike in other decades, young readers could find many magazines, comic books, and books written specifically for them. Golden Books offered the youngest children colorful picture books. *Highlights* magazine offered educational reading entertainment. *Seventeen* gave advice on teenage life to young women. The Bobbsey Twins and Cherry Ames characters entertained young readers in their series of books.

With the rise of comic books and other reading materials for young people and the increase in paperback books for adults, the pulp magazines that were dominant in the 1920s and 1930s lost their appeal. The pulps lost writers to book publishers and comic books. Sales of racy, longer stories in paperback proved too damaging to many pulps to continue publication. Throughout the decade, fewer and fewer pulps could remain in print. By the 1950s, the pulps had virtually disappeared, with the exception of a small number of detective, science fiction, and fantasy magazines.

Archie Comics

Since 1941, Archie Andrews and his pals from Riverdale have been one of the comics industry's leading non-superhero comic books. With their wholesome plots revolving around the adventures and romantic entanglements of a group of all-American teens, Archie Comics have delighted generations of young readers. Archie debuted as the American public was becoming increasingly aware of the emerging teenage subculture. The strip helped to shape the popular imagination's image of the ideal American teen.

Archie Andrews was created by John Goldwater (1915–1999) of MLJ Comics. Goldwater was inspired by the success of **Andy Hardy** (see entry under 1930s—Film and Theater in volume 2), a teen character who appeared on **radio** (see entry under 1920s—TV and Radio in volume 2) and later in a very popular movie series. Goldwater wanted to feature a "normal" comics character who would stand in contrast to the many superheroes who had come to dominate the marketplace since the arrival of **Superman** (see entry under 1930s—Print Culture in volume 2) in 1938. Archie's creator turned to cartoonist Bob Montana (1920–1975) to expand upon his initial premise and develop a supporting cast of characters. Archie Andrews first appeared in *Pep Comics #22* (December 1941). Several years would pass before the feature evolved into its characteristic format.

The characters of Archie Comics reside in Riverdale, an idealized version of small-town America. Many of the stories focus on the triangular relationship between Archie, Betty Cooper (a prototypical wholesome blonde next door), and Veronica Lodge (a rich brunette). Others who inhabit Riverdale include Jughead (Archie's hamburger-loving best

Archie Andrews, center, and the rest of the gang from Riverdale High School (left to right): Jughead, Veronica Lodge, Betty Cooper, and Reggie. © PHOTOFEST.

friend), Reggie (Archie's rival for Betty and Veronica's affections), and Mr. Weatherbee (Archie's perpetually flustered principal).

Although the feature has existed for decades, it has changed very little since its debut. Archie's teen friends live in an innocent world where romance never leads to sexual thoughts, drugs do not pose a threat, and other major social problems are nonexistent. Archie and his pals are cleaned-up versions of typical modern teens. They serve as an attractive fantasy for the comic's preteen audience. Archie's success inspired many spinoffs, including a cartoon series and a 1960s pop band (who had a big hit with "Sugar, Sugar"). Among the other characters created in the Archie studios were Sabrina the Teenage Witch and Josie and the Pussycats.

In recent years, Archie's writers have been more willing to employ a broader ethnic mix of characters as well as contemporary fashions, props, references, and problems in their stories. As the comic reached its six hundredth issue in 2009, the characters had been allowed to grow up, graduate from college, and reach young adulthood. However, the writers have generally remained true to the upbeat wholesomeness that characterized the feature in the 1940s, whether the reader is consuming the comic in book or digital form.

Charles Coletta

For More Information

Alverson, Brigid. "The New Archie Comics: More Diversity, Graphic Novel Collections, and Digital Delivery." *Publishers Weekly* (February 14, 2011): p. 18.

Archie Comics. http://www.archiecomics.com/index.html (accessed July 22, 2011).

Benton, Mike. *The Comic Book in America.* Dallas: Taylor, 1989.

"Do Blondes Have More Fun?" *National Review* (June 22, 2009): p. 14.

Horn, Maurice, ed. *100 Years of American Newspaper Comics.* New York: Gramercy Press, 1996.

Phillips, Charles. *Archie: His First 50 Years.* New York: Abbeville Press, 1991.

Yoe, Craig. *Archie: A Celebration of America's Favorite Teenagers* San Diego: IDW Publishing, 2011.

The Bobbsey Twins Series

The Bobbsey Twins was the longest-running children's book series in the twentieth century. From 1904 to 1992, over one hundred volumes about the two sets of Bobbsey twins appeared. The series won a large audience among children not quite ready for the **Hardy Boys** (see entry under 1920s—Print Culture in volume 2) or **Nancy Drew** (see entry under 1930s—Print Culture in volume 2) series of adventures.

Beginning with *The Bobbsey Twins; or, Merry Days Indoors and Out* (1904), the series depicted the adventures of two sets of twins: Freddie and Flossie Bobbsey and their older brother and sister, Nan and Bert. Especially in the early volumes, the adventures were fairly tame, usually involving travel to places like the seashore, the mountains, or a big city. The fair-haired Freddie and Flossie were four years old in the early books and then six years old in later books. Sometimes the younger twins got into some real danger. Other times, all that would happen was that someone's doll would go missing or the family cat would get stuck in a tree.

The dark-haired older twins, Nan and Bert, were eight years old in the early books and twelve years old in the later books. The older twins were more obedient and responsible and got into less trouble. Bert sometimes had to fight bullies like Danny Rugg, but everything always ended happily. The overall impression expressed by the books was of an almost perfect world with only very minor and easily solved problems. The twins' well-to-do parents gave them everything they asked for. As Bobbie Ann Mason says in *The Girl Sleuth,* the twins' life was like one long vacation.

The apparent author of the Bobbsey books was Laura Lee Hope, but in fact there was no Laura Lee Hope, just as there was no Franklin W. Dixon writing the *Hardy Boys* books and no Carolyn Keene writing about Nancy Drew. All these authors' names were the invention of Edward Stratemeyer (1862–1930), who set up a syndicate (a group of writers) at the beginning of the twentieth century to produce *The Bobbsey Twins* and dozens of other series.

After 1950, the syndicate began revising some of the early Bobbsey books to update them and remove negative portrayals of minority groups. The syndicate also began issuing new volumes in which the twins solved mysteries and had more exciting adventures. However, sales began to decline, and no further books were issued after 1992. Perhaps *The Bobbsey Twins* books were too much an expression of a more innocent time that had passed away.

Sheldon Goldfarb

For More Information

Billman, Carol. *The Secret of the Stratemeyer Syndicate: Nancy Drew, the Hardy Boys, and the Million Dollar Fiction Factory.* New York: Ungar, 1986.

The Bobbsey Twins' Page. http://pw2.netcom.com/~drmike99/bobbsey.html (accessed July 22, 2011).

"Hope, Laura Lee." In *Something About the Author: Facts and Pictures about Contemporary Authors and Illustrators of Books for Young People.* Vol. 67. Detroit: Gale, 1992.

Johnson, Deidre. *Edward Stratemeyer and the Stratemeyer Syndicate.* New York: Twayne, 1993.

Mason, Bobbie Ann. "Bobbsey Bourgeois." In *The Girl Sleuth: A Feminist Guide.* Old Westbury, NY: Feminist Press, 1975.

Brenda Starr, Reporter

In 1940, newspaper readers were introduced to Brenda Starr, a strikingly beautiful newswoman who traveled the world in search of exciting stories and romance. Created by cartoonist Dalia (Dale) Messick (1906–2005), the *Brenda Starr, Reporter* comic strip depicted an independent career woman at a time when such portrayals were uncommon in American popular culture. The strip's success allowed Messick to be one of the few women of her era to produce her own comic-strip feature.

Both Dale Messick and Brenda Starr were pioneers in the field of comic strips. During the 1930s and 1940s, all the people who created, drew, syndicated, and owned comics were men. After years of struggling to enter the comics profession, the *Chicago Tribune* gave Messick the opportunity to create her own strip. She originally wanted to make Brenda a female bandit but was told the public would find such a figure unacceptable. Instead, she made Brenda a prominent reporter whose assignments constantly took her on thrilling adventures in exotic locales.

Despite Brenda's status as a career woman, her romantic life dominated many of the strip's episodes. Mobsters, industrialists, and various members of royalty constantly pursued her. However, none could compete with the mysterious Basil St. John, a handsome and mysterious millionaire who wore a black patch over one eye. Although their meetings were intense, Basil was often forced to leave Brenda so he could cultivate a rare black orchid that served as the only cure for his "secret disease." The *Brenda Starr* strip was also known for its emphasis on high fashion. Brenda was consistently shown in elegant gowns and with perfectly styled red hair.

Although **soap opera** (see entry under 1930s—TV and Radio in volume 2) conventions dominated much of the strip, Brenda was always seen as a good role model for young girls because of her sense of independence, her take-charge attitude, and her dedication to her profession. Messick retired from the strip in the 1980s, but Brenda's adventures continued with new writers and artists until the strip was retired in January 2011. Author Maurice Horn in *100 Years of American Newspaper Comics* wrote, "*Brenda Starr* remains a rarity among the more aseptic soap-opera strips of the newspaper page."

Charles Coletta

For More Information

"Brenda Starr." *Tribune Media Services.* http://www.tmsfeatures.com/comics/comic-strips/brenda-starr/ (accessed July 22, 2011).

Horn, Maurice, ed. *100 Years of American Newspaper Comics.* New York: Gramercy Books, 1996.

Itzkoff, Dave. "Stop the Presses! Brenda Starr Is Retiring." *New York Times* (December 20, 2010): p. C2.

Messick, Dale. *Red-Headed Bombshell.* Newbury Park, CA: Malibu Graphics, 1989.

Robinson, Jerry. *The Comics: A Illustrated History of Comic Strip Art.* Rev. ed. Milwaukie, OR: Dark Horse Comics, 2011.

Captain America

One of America's best-loved superheroes, Captain America is also one of the longest-running comic-book characters in existence. In the 1940s, he fought the Nazis in World War II (1939–45). In the 1950s, he was enlisted in the **Cold War** (1945–91; see entry under 1940s—The Way We Lived in volume 3) against Russia. Since the 1960s, he has been battling a wide range of evil villains as the star of his own monthly **Marvel Comics** (see entry under 1940s—Print Culture in volume 3) adventure. The star-spangled crusader's ability to adapt to the changing times has made him an enduring symbol of American patriotism.

Captain America was the brainchild of writer Joe Simon (1913–) and artist Jack Kirby (1917–1994), part of the creative team at Marvel Comics in the 1940s. Both men favored U.S. intervention to stop Adolf Hitler (1889–1945) from conquering the nations of Europe. They came up with the Captain America character as a vehicle to draw attention to the threat posed by Nazi Germany. Clad in a red, white, and blue costume and carrying a shield emblazoned with the stars and stripes, Captain America was a "super soldier" who would lead the fight against freedom's enemies abroad. Accompanying him in his adventures was his faithful companion Bucky, a youthful masked sidekick similar to **Batman's** Robin (see entry under 1930s—Print Culture in volume 2). Together they fought off the evil schemes of archenemies like the Red Skull, making *Captain America Comics* one of the most popular comic book series of the 1940s.

When the war ended, however, the public tired of the super-patriotic superhero. Captain America was canceled, only to find himself revived in 1954, this time as a "Commie Smasher," fighting against the communists. The Cold War version of the character did not prove quite as popular. Another revival, this time in 1964 by writer Stan Lee (1922–) and original illustrator Jack Kirby (1917–1994), marked the start of a continuous run that took the character into the next millennium. In a new twist, Captain America began to question some of his country's actions, as issues like the Vietnam War (1954–75), poverty, and the **civil rights movement** (see entry under 1960s—The Way We Lived in volume 4) of the 1960s came to dominate the comic. When the turbulent 1960s and 1970s ended, Captain America returned to his patriotic roots, remaining one of Marvel Comics' most popular characters throughout the late twentieth and early twenty-first centuries until his death by sniper shot in an issue released in 2007. Despite his death, further comics were released featuring Captain America in subsequent years. In 2011, a financially successful film version of the comic was released, *Captain America: The First Avenger.* Along with the Hulk and **Spider-Man** (see entry under 1960s—Print Culture in volume 4), Captain America is one of the most recognizable superheroes that Marvel has ever produced.

Robert E. Schnakenberg

For More Information

Captain America (Steve Rogers). http://marvel.com/characters/bio/1009220/captain_america_steve_rogers (accessed July 22, 2011).

"Captain Dies." *Hollywood Reporter* (March 8, 2007): p. 3.

Jensen, Jeff "Doc." "Captain America Reports for Duty." *Entertainment Weekly* (November 5, 2010): p. 32.

Lee, Stan. *Origins of Marvel Comics.* New York: Simon & Schuster, 1974.

Lee, Stan, et al. *The Essential Captain America.* New York: Marvel Books, 2000.

Simon, Joe, with Jim Simon. *The Comic Book Makers.* Rev. ed. New York: Vanguard Productions, 2003.

The Star-Spangled Site. http://www.medinnus.com/winghead/ (accessed July 22, 2011).

Curious George

Curious George, the mischievous monkey who goes on all sorts of adventures, began delighting children's book readers in 1941. Created by a husband-and-wife team of animal lovers, George was often accompanied on his escapades by his faithful friend, known only as "the man in the yellow hat." His adventures have sold more than twenty million copies worldwide and inspired a line of toys, clothes, and greeting cards.

Hans Augusto (H. A.) Rey (1898–1977) was a talented German illustrator who spent many days visiting the local zoo as a child. His wife Margret (1908–1996), also an animal lover, was a writer. Together they ran a successful advertising business in the 1930s. Hoping to work together on a children's book, the couple created Curious George just as

Curious George, world-famous literary monkey. © UNIVERSAL/THE KOBAL COLLECTION/ART RESOURCE, NY.

World War II (1939–45) was breaking out across Europe. In fact, when Germany invaded France in 1940, the authors reportedly had to flee Paris on bicycles with the manuscripts for the first *Curious George* adventure strapped to their bike racks.

Settling in America, the Reys published their first *Curious George* book in 1941. Six more book-length adventures followed over the course of four decades. The stories included no words but were simple enough to appeal to children everywhere. Usually the book's title explained the entire story. In *Curious George Takes a Job* (1947), the rowdy monkey runs away from the zoo and gets a job as a window washer. In *Curious George Rides a Bike* (1952), he gets into trouble trying to help a young boy with his paper route. Often at the end of the story the man in the yellow hat appears to rescue Curious George from his predicament.

Children related to Curious George, analysts have said, because they saw him as being just like them—curious, mischievous, and prone to getting into trouble. It helped that the stories were fast paced and colorfully drawn as well. The Reys continued producing new *Curious George* adventures until H. A. Rey's death in 1977. In the 1980s, Margret Rey (1906–1996) began writing a new series of *Curious George* books with illustrator Alan J. Shalleck (1929–2006). The Curious George character remains popular with young readers. Merchandise bearing the lovable monkey's image continues to sell briskly. The character was the star of a full-length animated feature, also named *Curious George,* which was released in 2006. That same year, PBS launched an animated series using the same name, which proved popular with young viewers.

Robert E. Schnakenberg

For More Information

Berg, Julia. *H. A. Rey: Young at Heart.* Minneapolis: Abdo & Daughters, 1994.

Curious George. http://www.curiousgeorge.com/#/home (accessed July 22, 2011).

Curious George. http://pbskids.org/curiousgeorge/ (accessed July 22, 2011).

Houghton Mifflin Company. *Happy 60th Birthday, Curious George.* http://www.houghtonmifflinbooks.com/features/cgsite/ (accessed July 22, 2011).

Rey, Margret, and H. A. Rey. *The Complete Adventures of Curious George.* Anniversary ed. Boston: Houghton Mifflin, 2010.

Ebony

Published continuously since 1945, *Ebony* is the largest U.S. mass-circulation magazine written by and for African Americans. With a circulation of more than two million, the full-color monthly, as well as the digest-size *Jet* magazine, is published by the privately held Johnson Publishing Company, one of the nation's largest black-owned businesses.

Ebony's first issue appeared on November 1, 1945, the brainchild of John Harold Johnson (1918–2005), who had been born into poverty in Arkansas. Johnson had acquired his publishing skills as the editor of a weekly news digest for the Supreme Liberty Life Insurance Company, owned by Harry H. Pace (1884–1943). With a $500 loan using his mother's furniture as collateral (that is, pledging that the lender could have the furniture if he could not repay the loan), Johnson founded the *Negro Digest* in 1942. By the end of World War II (1939–45), he was envisioning a magazine that would present positive images to the African-American community, believing that "you have to change images before you can change acts and institutions," as he wrote in *Succeeding Against the Odds.* Inspired by the success of mass-circulation periodicals like **Life** (see entry under 1930s—Print Culture in volume 2) and *Look,* each of whose formula was based on photographic images, Johnson wanted to create a magazine that glorified the accomplishments of Negroes (the term then commonly used to describe African Americans) in the United States and abroad.

Unlike other Afrocentric periodicals that concentrated on social problems, *Ebony* focused on the community's success stories in the business and entertainment worlds. This approach was criticized by some as being elitist, but the magazine was warmly received by its readership. The first issue sold fifty thousand copies, and circulation doubled within the first year. Thanks to advertising support by white-owned companies, led by the Zenith Corporation, *Ebony* was soon able to attract the revenues it needed to become profitable.

Ebony strongly endorsed the **civil rights movement** (see entry under 1960s—The Way We Lived in volume 4) of the 1950s and 1960s. The magazine published newsworthy articles about the struggle for black empowerment in the United States and around the world. Dr. Martin Luther King Jr. (1929–1968) contributed articles as well as a regular column for the magazine. In 1969, one of *Ebony*'s photographers, Moneta Sleet Jr. (1926–1996), became the first black male to be awarded a Pulitzer Prize.

In 2008, Johnson's daughter, Linda Johnson Rice (1958–), succeeded her father as president and chief operating officer of the Johnson Publishing Company. She was not afraid to make necessary changes, revamping the magazine with a glossier look, more fashion spreads, and an emphasis on lifestyle stories in 2003. Such moves did not change decreasing circulation. The global economic downturn that began in 2008 brought declines in advertising and a steep drop in circulation. In addition to increasing *Ebony*'s online presence, Rice reorganized Johnson Publishing Company to keep *Ebony* and *Jet* in print and a leading force in the African American community. She stepped down as CEO in 2010 but remained as the company's chair.

Edward Moran

For More Information

Baeb, Eddie, and Ann Saphir. "Legacy on the Line." *Crain's Chicago Business* (June 22, 2009): 1.

EbonyJet Online. http://www.ebonyjet.com/ (accessed July 23, 2011).

"The *Ebony* Story." *Ebony* (November 1995): 80–87.

Johnson, John H., and Lerone Bennett Jr. *Succeeding Against the Odds.* New York: Warner Books, 1989.

Mullman, Jeremy. "Redo's the Easy Part for *Ebony*: Glossier Look Hasn't Translated into Big Circulation Gains." *Crain's Chicago Business* (June 7, 2004): 4.

Pride, Armistead S., and Clint C. Wilson II. *A History of the Black Press.* Washington, DC: Howard University Press, 1997.

Golden Books

Golden Books are some of the most popular children's books. Originally produced by the Western Publishing Company, which began publishing them in 1942, the Golden Books line of illustrated children's story books have durable covers framed by a familiar gold-colored design. The original Golden Books, created with the Artists and Writers Guild, had forty-two pages and sold for twenty-five cents. Some of the most well-known original titles include *Pat the Bunny,* one of the first touch-and-feel books, *Scuffy the Tugboat,* and *The Poky Little Puppy.*

By the 1990s, the Golden Book line of children's books included more than one thousand titles. Along with the original titles, the Golden Book series has also included tales about familiar characters like **Lassie** (see entry under 1940s—Film and Theater in volume 3), the **Lone Ranger** (see entry under 1930s— TV and Radio in volume 2), and **Rudolph the Red-Nosed Reindeer** (see entry under 1940s—Print Culture in volume 3). Golden Books took advantage of the exclusive rights to publish books with **Disney** (see entry under 1920s—Film and Theater in volume 2) characters. Western Publishing had landed the exclusive publishing rights in 1933. Since the 1970s, the **Muppet** (see entry under 1970s—TV and Radio in volume 4) and ***Sesame Street*** (see entry under 1970s—TV and Radio in volume 4) characters of Jim Henson (1936–1990) have been featured. In the 1990s, Golden Books bought rights to Shari Lewis (1933–1998) productions, including videos and **television** (see entry under 1940s—TV and Radio in volume 3) shows featuring the Lamb Chop and Charley Horse puppets.

In 1996, after several changes in ownership, Western Publishing became known as Golden Books Family Entertainment, Inc. Soon afterwards, it began to add to its familiar Golden Book titles. The company published the *Road to Reading* and *Road to Writing* series that encouraged children to proceed at their own pace in learning language arts. After Golden Books Family Entertainment filed for Chapter 11 bankruptcy, Golden Books changed hands again in 2001 when it sold its book assets to Random House and its film and television properties to Classic Media.

In the early twenty-first century, new Golden Books such as *Kiss Kiss* and *Shwatsit!* appeared. The company also updated both the text and art of old Golden Book titles like the *Pantaloon,* which was originally published in 1951, and *Doctor Squash,* which was originally published in 1952; both were re-issued in 2010.

Edward Moran

For More Information

Anderson, Claudia. "Picture Perfect; Why Golden Books Are Golden." *The Weekly Standard* (June 29, 2009).

Golden Books. http://www.randomhouse.com/golden/ (accessed July 23, 2011).

Jones, Dolores Blythe. *Bibliography of the Little Golden Books: Bibliographies and Indexes in American Literature,* No. 7. Westport, CT: Greenwood, 1987.

Marcus, Leonard S. *Golden Legacy: How Golden Books Won Children's Hearts, Changed Publishing Forever, and Became an American Icon Along the Way.* New York: Golden Books, 2007.

Santi, Steve. *Collecting Little Golden Books: A Collector's Identification & Value Guide.* 5th ed. Iola, WI: Krause, 2003.

Green Lantern

"In brightest day, in blackest night, no evil shall escape my sight! Let those who worship evil's might, beware my power." With those words, the Green Lantern, one of the world's oldest and most popular comic book superheroes, has gone forth to police the universe since 1940. There have been many different Green Lanterns over the years, and many changes made to the character, but his essential nature as a champion of good remains constant.

Other enduring elements of *Green Lantern* comic books include his costume, a skintight green jumpsuit with a distinctive symbol on the chest, and his power ring, the source of all his superheroic abilities. Unlike most other comic book heroes, the Green Lantern is not a unique individual but one of many superbeings who make up the "Green Lantern Corps," a unit that patrols the universe, rooting out evil.

Attesting to the comic character's endurance and popularity, the Green Lantern appeared on a U.S. postage stamp in 2006. © STAMP COLLECTION/ ALAMY.

Over the years, many different men have assumed the role of the Green Lantern. Alan Ladd Scott was the first, or "Golden Age," Green Lantern, making his debut in All-American Comics #16 in April 1940. At first, he battled corrupt politicians and greedy businessmen in fictional Gotham City. With America's entry into World War II (1939–45), however, the Green Lantern joined the fight against America's enemies overseas.

The original *Green Lantern* comic book series was canceled in 1949, but the character returned ten years later in a new series. This time around, Hal Jordan assumed the role of the Green Lantern. The Hal Jordan character became the most popular and longest-running Green Lantern by a wide margin. Other Green Lanterns have included Guy Gardner, John Stewart, and Kyle Rayner.

In 1970, a new creative team took over *Green Lantern* and dramatically changed the direction of the series. Artist Neal Adams (1941–) and writer Denny O'Neil (1939–) injected many of the social concerns of the 1970s into the title. *Green Lantern* thus became one of the first comic book series to address topics like drug addiction and poverty. These landmark issues, which teamed Green Lantern Hal Jordan with Oliver Queen, the Green Arrow, are among the most sought-after and highly praised comic books of all time. The *Green Lantern* series continued to be published in the early twenty-first century, taking on challenging topics like hate crimes against a landmark gay character. A Green Lantern feature film of the same name was released in the summer of 2011. Ryan Reynolds (1976–) took the role of Hal Jordan/Green Lantern.

Robert E. Schnakenberg

For More Information

Beatty, Scott, Daniel Wallace, et al. *DC Comics Encyclopedia: The Definitive Guide to the Characters of the DC Universe.* Rev. ed. New York: DK Publishing, 2008.

Daniels, Les. *DC Comics: Sixty Years of the World's Favorite Comic Book Heroes.* Boston: Little, Brown, 1995.

Dargis, Manohla. "Creatures Galactic and Glacial (Er, Happy Father's Day): Not Easy Being … You Know." *New York Times* (August 13, 2002): E1.

Gustines, George Gene. "A Major Character Becomes a Victim of a Hate Crime." *New York Times* (June 17, 2011): C1.

O'Neill, Dennis, Dick Giordano, and Neal Adams. *The Green Lantern-Green Arrow Collection.* New York: DC Comics, 2000.

Wright, Nicky, and Joe Kubert. *The Classic Era of American Comics.* New York: Contemporary Books, 2000.

Highlights

Generations of Americans have shared a common childhood experience: pleasant hours spent reading the children's magazine *Highlights for Children.* Founded in 1946 by a married couple of teachers, *Highlights* is a general interest magazine for children aged three to thirteen years. Each issue is filled with science facts, jokes, art, and poetry from children around the country. Each issue also contains old favorites like the Hidden Pictures puzzle and cartoons like the silly "Timbertoes" and the ethically oriented "Goofus and Gallant." The magazine's consistently high quality, familiar features, and respectful tone have made it a favorite of both children and parents for more than fifty years.

The founders of *Highlights* were Garry Cleveland Myers (1884–1971) and Carolyn Clark Myers (1887–1980), two Pennsylvania teachers. The Myerses had spent many years developing methods of teaching children and adults to read and write before traveling around the country teaching classes on parenting skills. In the 1930s, Garry began to write an advice column called "Parenting Problems." His advice column appeared in newspapers around the country. The Myerses worked with various publications for children. They became frustrated, however, when business concerns were placed before the welfare of the children who read the publications.

These frustrations led them to decide to start their own magazine. In 1946, *Highlights for Children* was born. Garry Myers was sixty-one years old and his wife Caroline was fifty-nine when they began work on their famous magazine. When they retired, their daughter Betty and her husband Kent Brown took over editing *Highlights.* A clever salesperson, Betty got the idea of placing the magazine in doctors' and dentists' offices, where reading the copies could calm nervous children waiting for their appointments. She also started the practice of selling subscriptions door to door, which continued until 1991. During the 1950s and 1960s, *Highlights* employed four hundred door-to-door salespeople. In comparison, only twenty people actually worked in the office creating the magazine.

In the 1970s, the next generation took over, as Garry and Caroline Myers' grandchildren began to produce *Highlights* and to sell children subscriptions through their schools. The fourth generation of the Myers/Brown family has also begun to work in the family business, and *Highlights* has developed an extensive online presence in the early twenty-first century as another generation of children discovers the publication's charms.

Tina Gianoulis

For More Information

Highlights for Children. http://www.highlights.com/ (accessed July 23, 2011).

Kantrowitz, Barbara. "He-Man Meets Ranger Rick." *Newsweek* (June 30, 1986): pp. 54–56.

Walters, Laurel Shaper. "A 500th Issue for *Highlights.*" *Christian Science Monitor* (July 16, 1993): pp. 13–15.

Rudolph the Red-Nosed Reindeer

The legend of Rudolph the Red-Nosed Reindeer is one of the most recognizable additions to Christmas folklore to have arisen during the twentieth century. As the story goes, Rudolph is initially scorned for his glowing nose and treated as an outcast by his fellow reindeer until he comes to the aid of Santa Claus one foggy Christmas Eve. The red-nosed reindeer has become an annual symbol of the holiday season. The character of Rudolph, which first appeared in 1939, has been immortalized in song, books, toys, holiday decorations, and several **television** (see entry under 1940s—TV and Radio in volume 3) specials.

Rudolph was created in 1939 by Robert May (1905–1976), an advertising copywriter for the Montgomery Ward department-store chain. The store assigned him to compose an original Christmas tale that was to be distributed to shoppers. May based the Rudolph story on his own childhood experience of being taunted by his schoolmates for his slight frame. Montgomery Ward distributed more than two million copies of the tale during the 1939 Christmas season.

The story of Rudolph the Red-Nosed Reindeer has been significantly altered over the years. In May's original version, Rudolph is not a member of Santa's stable. He is teased by his companions but lovingly supported by his parents. One Christmas Eve, Santa arrives and notices that Rudolph's nose could assist his travel through the fog. Santa rewards Rudolph's bravery and the young reindeer is honored by his community. In 1947, May acquired full legal rights to his creation and the Rudolph story became more widely publicized. May commissioned Johnny Marks (1909–1985) to write a song about the reindeer in 1949. The song became an enormous hit for singer Gene Autry (1907–1998) and sold more than two million copies in its first year. It remains a Christmas classic.

In 1964, the *Rudolph the Red-Nosed Reindeer* television special, which was narrated by Burl Ives (1909–1995), further altered the Rudolph legend. In the program, Rudolph begins life in the North Pole and is dismissed by both his reindeer friends and parents. Rudolph runs away and joins a band of "misfit" toys and eventually proves himself to Santa. The TV special is still broadcast each year and has become the version of the Rudolph story most familiar to Americans.

Rudolph's appeal lies in that he is a figure to whom all children can relate. He is an outsider whose special qualities are mocked until he saves the day and wins acceptance. The story of Rudolph the Red-Nosed Reindeer also reveals how closely Christmas and commercialism have become intertwined in the twentieth and early twenty-first century.

Charles Coletta

Santa and Rudolph in a scene from the classic 1964 television special Rudolph the Red-Nosed Reindeer. © PHOTOFEST.

For More Information

Archibald, John. "Rudolph's Tale Left Him Cold." *St. Louis Post-Dispatch* (December 6, 1989): p. 3E.

Frankel, Stanley. "The Story Behind Rudolph the Red-Nosed Reindeer." *Good Housekeeping* (December 1989): p. 126.

Lillard, Margaret. "Rudolph Lit Up Creator's Career." *Los Angeles Times* (December 17, 1989): p. A7.

Murphy, Cullen. "Rudolph Redux." *Atlantic Monthly* (August 1990): p. 18.

"Rudolph the Red-Nosed Reindeer." *CBS.* http://www.cbs.com/specials/rudolph/ (accessed July 23, 2011).

"Rudolph the Red-Nosed Reindeer." *The Enchanted World of Rankin/Bass.* http://www.rankinbass.com/rudolphhome.html (accessed July 23, 2011).

Seventeen

Seventeen is known to U.S. readers as the title of a 1916 novel by Booth Tarkington (1869–1946). It also is the name of a popular monthly magazine for teenage girls that has been continuously published since 1944.

The full title of Tarkington's novel is *Seventeen: A Tale of Youth and the Baxter Family, Especially William.* Once required reading for generations of high school students, the novel is a humorous account of life as seen through the eyes of an adolescent boy growing up in the early part of the twentieth century.

The magazine *Seventeen* helped define the culture of American youth after World War II (1939–45). The magazine was the first publication entirely devoted to the needs and interests of adolescents, more specifically to "young fashions and beauty, movies and music, ideas and people." Founding editor Helen Valentine borrowed its title from Tarkington's novel to appeal to the age group she wanted it to reach. From its start, *Seventeen* was highly successful, with its circulation jumping from one million in 1947 to two and a half million by 1949. By the turn of the twenty-first century, it remains the most widely read magazine amongst teenage girls. In 2010, *Seventeen* sold 2.1 million copies annually.

By urging its advertisers to tailor their promotions specifically to the needs of its adolescent readers, *Seventeen* helped promote the idea that U.S. teenagers represented a distinct market segment. It set high standards for the advertisements it carried. Ads for spike heels and bright nail polish were rejected in favor of products that enhanced the image of the "wholesome" teenaged girl. Editorially, the magazine presented thoughtful articles on education and world affairs, urging its readers to get involved in school and community projects. *Seventeen* also advised its audience on the latest fashion tips, makeup styles, and dating etiquette. Every month, millions of girls turned to its pages to help guide them through the pitfalls of dating and establishing relationships with the opposite sex. With the rise of feminism in the 1960s and 1970s, *Seventeen* published articles encouraging its readers to be more independent and self-reliant. By the 1980s, sexual matters were discussed more openly in its pages, although not with the hipness of rival publications like **Sassy** (see entry under 1980s—Print Culture in volume 5) and *Young Miss.* By the 1990s and early 2000s, *Seventeen* was addressing contemporary issues like **AIDS** (see entry under 1980s—The Way We Lived in volume 5), body issues, technology, and crime, and working to appeal to a more racially and culturally diverse readership.

Edward Moran

For More Information

Massoni, Kelly. *Fashioning Teenagers: A Cultural History of Seventeen Magazine.* Walnut Creek, CA: Left Coast Press, 2010.

McCracken, Ellen. *Decoding Women's Magazines: From Mademoiselle to Ms.* New York: St. Martin's, 1993.

Roberts, Johnnie L., and Aisha Eady. "Ah, to Be Sweet *Seventeen*; The Teen Magazine Stays Loyal to the Good Girls." *Newsweek* (August 20, 2007): 80.

Schrum, Kelly. "'Teens Mean Business': Teenage Girls' Culture and *Seventeen* Magazine, 1944–1950." In *Delinquents and Debutantes: Twentieth-Century American Girls' Cultures.* Edited by Sherrie A. Inness. New York: New York University Press, 1998.

Seventeen. http://www.seventeen.com/ (accessed on July 23, 2011).

Wonder Woman

Wonder Woman, the first and most recognizable female superhero in comic book history, made her debut in *All Star Comics #8* (1941) and has been thrilling generations of readers ever since. William Moulton Marston (1893–1947), a noted psychologist and inventor of the polygraph machine, created the character as an early feminist role model for young girls. He believed male heroes lacked the qualities of maternal love, compassion, and tenderness. Wonder Woman was also designed to appeal to the largely male comic book audience. In *DC Comics: Sixty Years of the World's Favorite Comic Book Heroes,* Les Daniels quotes Marston as saying, "Give them an alluring woman stronger than themselves to submit to and they'll be *proud* to become her willing slaves." Readers were drawn to this attractive heroine who possessed the strength of a powerful man. Soon Wonder Woman was appearing in several popular comic books. Wonder Woman, along with **Superman** (see entry under 1930s—Print Culture in volume 2) and **Batman** (see

Wonder Woman, whether in comic-book form, on TV, or on the big screen, fights crime and injustice. © PHOTOFEST.

entry under 1930s—Print Culture in volume 2), remains among the only comic book characters to be published continuously since the golden age of comics. New Wonder Woman comics and graphic novels are still being published in the early twenty-first century.

Marston and artist Harry Peter (1880–1950) created a unique character whose stories were more modern-day fairy tales than super-heroic adventures. The series was a combination of feminism, psychological theory, Greek and Roman mythology, and American patriotism. According to her 1942 origin story, Wonder Woman began life as Princess Diana of Paradise Island, home to a race of immortal Amazons. Diana was created as a clay statue by the Amazon queen Hippolyta and had been given life and superhuman abilities by the gods of Olympus. When an American pilot named Steve Trevor crashed on the island, Diana nursed him back to health. Hippolyta feared the male's intrusion into her realm and demanded he be returned to America. Upon winning an Olympic contest, Diana was selected to become Paradise Island's emissary to Man's World. In America, she assumed the secret identity of army nurse Diana Prince.

Wonder Woman's mission involved spreading the message of peace, justice, and equality. She faced numerous enemies, including the Cheetah, Giganta, Dr. Psycho, Nazi agent Paula von Gunther, and Ares, the God of War. Wonder Woman did not use excessive force against these villains but instead relied on her intelligence and agility to achieve victory. Her most important weapons against crime and injustice included her invisible robot plane; her magic golden lasso, which compelled those in its snare to tell the truth; and her Amazonian bracelets, which deflected bullets. She would lose her powers if the bracelets were ever chained together. Wonder Woman inspired many young girls to assert themselves, including Gloria Steinem (1934–), who placed the character on the cover of the first issue of **Ms.** (see entry under 1970s—Print Culture in volume 4) magazine in 1972. In 1987, Wonder Woman gained renewed popularity when celebrated comic book artist and writer George Pérez (1954–) took over the feature. In 2007, Gail Simone became the first woman to be an ongoing writer of the Wonder Woman comics.

Wonder Woman has also appeared in comic strips, animated cartoons, and a popular 1970s **television** (see entry under 1940s—TV and Radio in volume 3) program starring Lynda Carter (1951–). The character has further appeared on countless items of merchandise. Wonder Woman has remained a significant American icon because she embodies all the positive qualities of American womanhood: strength, intelligence, beauty, and power. She put forward a feminist message decades before anyone had heard the phrase "girl power."

Charles Coletta

For More Information

Daniels, Les. *DC Comics: Sixty Years of the World's Favorite Comic Book Heroes.* New York: Little, Brown, 1995.

Daniels, Les. *Wonder Woman: The Complete History.* San Francisco: Chronicle Books, 2000.

Dini, Paul, and Alex Ross. *Wonder Woman: Strength of Will.* New York: DC Comics, 2001.

Goulart, Ron. *Ron Goulart's Great History of Comic Books.* Chicago: Contemporary Books, 1986.

Gustines, George Gene. "Wonder Woman Gets a New Voice. And It's Female." *New York Times* (November 27, 2007): E1.

Jimenez, Phil, John Wells, and William Moulton Marston. *The Essential Wonder Woman Encyclopedia.* New York: Ballantine Books, 2010.

Marston, William. *Wonder Woman Archives: Volume 1.* New York: DC Comics, 1998.

"Wonder Woman." *DC Comics.* http://www.dccomics.com/sites/wonderwoman/ (accessed July 23, 2011).

Wonder Woman for DC: An Unofficial Fan Site. http://www.wonderwomanfordc.com/ (accessed July 23, 2011).

1940s

Sports and Games

World War II (1939–45) disrupted professional sports events. After the entrance of American troops into the war in 1941 following the Japanese bombing of Pearl Harbor, many of the nation' finest athletes joined the military. Some teams disbanded when their players went off to war. Most continued with a limited number of players and tight budgets. Even with these wartime cutbacks, sports remained a favorite pastime for Americans. When the war ended, talented players returned, money again poured into sports organizations, and television enlarged the audiences, leading professional sports to once again become a dominant entertainment moneymaker in America.

The war did offer women more opportunities in sports. With so many male athletes fighting for the country, women athletes were encouraged to join the All-American Girls Baseball League, which was popular during the war. Women also attracted attention in golf and tennis.

One of the most important events in sports came in 1947 when Jackie Robinson (1919–1972) signed on to the Brooklyn Dodgers major-league baseball team. Although African Americans had been champions in the boxing arena for some time, Robinson's breaking of the color barrier in baseball was especially important, because baseball was America's favorite sport. By the end of the 1940s, some of the best players in baseball were black. Other sports soon began integration of their own.

In the American household, games were welcome diversions from the war and later remained fun entertainment. The Slinky, a coiled-wire toy that continues to be popular, "walked" down steps to the amusement of kids and adults alike. Scrabble, a word board game, tested the vocabularies and spelling abilities of countless people across the country. Tonka trucks offered children the chance to imagine the life of construction workers with pint-sized dump trucks and tractor toys.

Bowling

Although its origins are in Europe, bowling has long been recognized as the "common man's sport" in the United States. Played in bowling alleys, the game consists of throwing a heavy ball (often weighing ten to sixteen pounds) down a wooden lane in an attempt knock over a set of ten wooden pins set in the form of a triangle. It became especially popular among the American working class because it was an inexpensive sport to play, but it has also attracted people at all levels of income.

Bowling arrived in the United States in the early 1800s, and it developed over the decades into a uniform sport with its own rules, dress, atmosphere, and organization: the American Bowling Congress. By the 1920s, bowling was an established presence in American life, but the heyday of bowling did not occur until the 1940s, 1950s, and 1960s, when the sport became a cultural phenomenon. Part of its success came because working class Americans had more leisure time after World War II (1939–45), and bowling was an inexpensive leisure activity that was fairly easy to learn but challenging enough to keep people working to improve their skill level. It was also promoted on **television** (see entry under 1940s—TV and Radio in volume 3), increasing its visibility. Automated pin setting and ball returns added to the ease of play as well.

More important was bowling's influence on American social life. Bowling was a participatory sport as well as a social one. Although it was competitive, it also fostered team camaraderie because players formed leagues of teams that competed against one another. The pace of the game allowed players to relax between turns, enjoy a beer and some snacks, and talk to their teammates and opponents. Because it was not a contact sport, women were attracted to the game and were welcomed

Bowling, a game that fosters friendships and fun. © RALPH CRANE/GETTY IMAGES.

by men more so than in **baseball** (see entry under 1900s—Sports and Games in volume 1), football, or other rougher sports. Bowling alleys also grew into family entertainment centers with game rooms for children, snack bars, equipment shops, and other amenities. Bowling declined in popularity after 1970 due to competition from other sports and less interest from younger people. Author Robert Putnam, in his book *Bowling Alone,* uses the declining interest in bowling as an indicator of a major shift in American social values away from communal activities to solitary ones, not always with good results. That insight offered further proof of bowling's important place in the history of American leisure and social life. Though bowling alleys can still be found in many communities in the United States in the early twenty-first century, it remains a niche sport that many participants engage in only occasionally. The industry has made efforts to revitalize the sport through the development of family entertainment centers and boutique centers that include not only bowling but other activities and more upscale restaurants and bars.

Timothy Berg

For More Information

Agne-Traub, Charlene E., Joan L. Martin, and Ruth E. Tandy. *Bowling.* 8th ed. Boston: WCB/McGraw-Hill, 1998.

Help with Bowling. http://helpwithbowling.com/history-origins-of-bowling. php (accessed July 24, 2011).

International Bowling Museum and Hall of Fame. http://www.bowlingmuseum. com/Home.aspx (accessed July 24, 2011).

Keirn, Jennifer. "Rolling Along; Centers Emphasizing Entertainment Could Help Spare Industry Once Dominated by Mom-and-Pop Lanes." *Crain's Cleveland Business* (September 24, 2007): 19.

Putnam, Robert. *Bowling Alone: The Collapse and Revival of American Community.* New York: Simon and Schuster, 2000.

Stallings, Howard, and Michael Neese. *The Big Book of Bowling.* Salt Lake City, UT: Gibbs Smith, 1995.

Steele, H. Thomas. *Bowl-O-Rama.* New York: Abbeville Press, 1986.

National Basketball Association

The sport of basketball dates to the late nineteenth century. In 1891, a Young Men's Christian Association (YMCA) Training School instructor named James Naismith (1861–1939) hung a pair of peach baskets on a gymnasium track railing and urged those in attendance to toss balls into the baskets, thus inventing the game. Throughout the early twentieth century, various professional basketball leagues were born, and many quickly failed. Two of the most enterprising were the American Basketball League (ABL), which began in 1925 and folded during the 1930s, and the National Basketball League (NBL), formed in 1937. In 1946 came the formation of the Basketball Association of America (BAA). Three years later, the East Coast–based BAA merged with the Midwest-based NBL. The merger resulted in the formation of the National Basketball Association (NBA), history's most successful and enduring pro basketball league.

At first, the NBA was a hodgepodge of seventeen teams, representing a cross-section of cities from New York and Boston to Syracuse and Sheboygan. Not surprisingly, at the start of the 1950–51 season, seven of the less-competitive teams folded. In its early years, the NBA remained a secondary sports league. Games often were lumbering affairs, dominated by big men such as Minneapolis Laker center George Mikan (1924–) and slowed to a crawl by constant fouling designed to hamper scoring.

To spark interest in the game, the NBA authorized rule changes to speed up play, increase scoring, and encourage athleticism. The Boston Celtics were the immediate beneficiaries. The Celts, coached by the legendary Arnold "Red" Auerbach (1917–2006), featured two players who excelled in the new, fast-break style of play. Bill Russell (1934–), an intimidating center, aggressively blocked shots. Bob Cousy (1928–), a sleek guard, played the new game well. Starting in 1959, the Celtics won eleven NBA titles in thirteen years.

The 1960s and 1970s featured a rivalry between two of the game's most dominant centers: Russell and Wilt Chamberlain (1936–1999). The New York Knicks, NBA champions in 1970 and 1973, were famed for their thoughtful, team-oriented playing style. By now passing, shooting, and nonstop action were synonymous with pro basketball. However, the upstart American Basketball Association (ABA) began signing many top college players, including Rick Barry (1944–) and Julius "Dr. J." Erving (1950–). The NBA-ABA rivalry was extinguished in 1976 when the leagues merged and four ABA teams were allowed to join the NBA.

In the late 1970s and early 1980s, the NBA was losing its hold on the public. There were no compelling rivalries and few charismatic star players. A series of violent off-court incidents and drug abuse among players tarnished the league's reputation. Two multitalented players were single-handedly responsible for the NBA's reemergence: Larry Bird (1956–), of the Boston Celtics, and Earvin "Magic" Johnson (1959–), of the Los Angeles Lakers. These competitors—who met each other in their final collegiate game, the 1979 NCAA championship game between Bird's Indiana State University and Johnson's Michigan State University—maintained a fierce rivalry as professionals. Their teams met in the 1984 championship finals, a thrilling seven-game affair that attracted the largest **television** (see entry under 1940s—TV and Radio in volume 3) audience in NBA history.

In the ensuing years the league expanded, adding teams as far south as Florida and as far north as Canada. The star player of the 1980s and 1990s was **Michael Jordan** (1963–; see entry under 1990s—Sports and Games in volume 5), who joined the Chicago Bulls in 1984. Jordan's graceful leaping ability, congenial personality, and sharp intelligence propelled the Bulls to six NBA championships. Many fans view

Jordan as the NBA's all-time greatest player. He helped to popularize basketball across the globe, transforming the NBA into an international presence.

After Jordan officially retired in 2003, the NBA struggled to find an identity and star that matched his intensity. Players like Kobe Bryant (1978–), who helped the Lakers win five championships between 2000 and 2010, and **LeBron James** (1984–; see entry under 2000s—Sports and Games in volume 6), who played for the Cleveland Cavaliers and Miami Heat, excelled and became the faces of NBA in the 2000s. In the early 2000s, more and more quality players came from outside of North America to play in the NBA, making the league more international. While Yao Ming (1980–) became one of the first prominent Chinese players in the NBA, German native Dirk Nowitzki (1978–) led the Dallas Mavericks to its first NBA championship in 2011, defeating James's Heat. Such players were considered the future of the NBA as the league continued to increase its global outreach.

Rob Edelman

For More Information

Bjarkman, Peter C. *The Encyclopedia of Pro Basketball Team Histories.* New York: Carroll & Graf, 1994.

Decourcy, Mike. *Inside Basketball: From the Playgrounds to the NBA.* New York: Metro Books, 1996.

Deveney, Sean. "Back to the Future: The Kings and Mavericks Are Ahead of Their Time in Acquiring European Talent, Which Enables Teams to Play a Throwback, High-Scoring Style." *Sporting News* (May 13, 2002): 10.

Graf, Christine. "Basketball without Borders: The Globalization of the NBA." *Faces: People, Places and Cultures* (October 2006): 26.

Ham, Eldon L. *The Playmasters: From Sellouts to Lockouts.* Lincolnwood, IL: Contemporary Books, 2000.

Hartman, Christopher. "NBA Draft 2011: Fulfilling the League's Global Outreach with More International Players." *Christian Science Monitor* (June 23, 2011).

Minsky, Alan. *Kings of the Court: Legends of the NBA.* New York: Metro Books, 1995.

"NBA." *ESPN.* http://espn.go.com/nba/ (accessed July 24, 2011).

NBA.com. http://www.nba.com/home/index.html (accessed July 24, 2011).

Rosen, Charles. *The First Tip-Off: The Incredible Story of the Birth of the NBA.* New York: McGraw-Hill, 2008.

Salzberg, Charles. *From Set Shot to Slam Dunk: The Glory Days of Basketball in the Words of Those Who Played It.* New York: Dutton, 1987.

Jackie Robinson (1919–1972)

In 1947, Jackie Robinson broke the "color barrier" in **baseball** (see entry under 1900s—Sports and Games in volume 1), becoming the first African American to play in the major leagues. His aggressive baserunning and timely batting helped lead the Brooklyn Dodgers to a world championship in 1955. He was inducted into the baseball Hall of Fame in 1962.

Before joining the Brooklyn Dodgers, Jackie Robinson, seen here in 1946, played for the Montreal Royals in the minor leagues. © AP IMAGES/JOHN J. LENT.

A native of Cairo, Georgia, Robinson began his baseball career in the **Negro Leagues** (see entry under 1900s—Sports and Games in volume 1). There he drew the attention of Dodgers general manager Branch Rickey (1881–1965), who signed him to a minor league contract in 1945. When Robinson made it to the majors two years later, he faced taunts, discrimination, and even death threats from hostile fans opposed to integration (the bringing together of different races). To his credit, Robinson rose above these threats and became one of the game's leading base stealers and clutch hitters (batters who do well in tense situations). He retired after ten years of playing and continued to speak out about racism in America until his death in 1972. In 1997, baseball decided to honor Robinson by "retiring" his uniform number "42" across the sport (no player could wear that number). In 2007, after declaring that April 15 was Jackie Robinson Day and would be celebrated annually, Major League Baseball (MLB) began allowing players to wear number 42 on that day. More than 200 players wore his number in the first year. By 2011, every MLB player wore Robinson's 42 on April 15 to honor his accomplishments.

Robert E. Schnakenberg

For More Information

Eig, Jonathan. *Opening Day: The Story of Jackie Robinson's First Season.* New York: Simon & Schuster, 2007.

"Jackie Robinson Day: April 15." *MLB.com.* http://mlb.mlb.com/mlb/events/jrd/ (accessed July 24, 2011).

"Major League Baseball Announces Annual Jackie Robinson Day." *Jet* (March 22, 2004): 48.

The Official Site of Jackie Robinson. http://www.jackierobinson.com/ (accessed July 24, 2011).

Rampersand, Arnold. *Jackie Robinson: A Biography.* New York: Knopf, 1997.

"Robinson, Jackie" *National Baseball Hall of Fame.* http://baseballhall.org/hof/robinson-jackie (accessed July 24, 2011).

Tygiel, Jules. *Baseball's Great Experiment: Jackie Robinson and His Legacy.* 25th anniversary ed. New York: Oxford University Press, 2008.

Scrabble

One of the most popular board games in history, Scrabble is a crossword-style game designed for two, three, or four players. Participants make interlocking words by drawing randomly from a stock of one hundred tiles, each bearing a letter of the alphabet. Letters are distributed according to their relative frequency in the language—there are twelve "E's" and nine "A's," for example, but only one "Q" and one "Z." The point value of the letters varies accordingly. By placing the tiles strategically on the game board, players can double or triple the point value of letters and words. Using seven letters in a single play (the number of tiles available for use in a turn) is worth a bonus of fifty points.

Scrabble was invented by Alfred Mosher Butts (1899–1993) during the 1930s, who originally called it Lexiko, then Criss-Cross Words. He developed and manufactured the game himself from his apartment in the New York City borough of Queens, marketing it by word of mouth. In 1947, the rights to the game were acquired by James Brunot (1902–1984), a Connecticut farmer who named it Scrabble. When the game was marketed by New York's Macy's Department Store in 1953, it became an overnight sensation. Sales skyrocketed. Brunot sold the game to the Selchow & Righter Company, which sold 3.8 million sets by the following year. The game was later marketed by Coleco. Scrabble is now sold in the United States by Hasbro. Some two million sets are sold worldwide every year.

A popular board game born of the Great Depression, Scrabble tournaments are held around the world. © SHUTTERSTOCK.COM.

Most players typically use familiar words while playing Scrabble. Competitive players enhance their scores considerably by memorizing lists of little-known words included in "official" Scrabble dictionaries used in tournaments. Official word lists used in the United States and Canada differ from those used elsewhere in the world. The dictionary used in international tournaments contains about forty thousand words that are not considered playable in North America. In recent years, some of the world's Scrabble champions have come from non-English speaking countries like Thailand and Malaysia. Scrabble entered the **Internet** (see entry under 2000s—The Way We Lived in volume 5) age in the early 2000s with an official online version of the game. Scrabble apps were also created for **Facebook** (see entry under

2000s—The Way We Lived in volume 6) and for **smart phones** (see entry under 2000s—The Way We Lived in volume 6) so the game could be played on the go.

Edward Moran

For More Information

Fatsis, Stefan. *Word Freak: Heartbreak, Triumph, Genius, and Obsession in the World of Competitive Scrabble Players.* Boston: Houghton Mifflin, 2001.

Korkki, Phyllis. "Word Games Anytime, No Travel Tiles Required." *New York Times* (February 22, 2011): B3.

Official Scrabble Game from Hasbro. http://www.hasbro.com/scrabble/en_US/ (accessed July 24, 2011).

The Official Worldwide Scrabble Home Page. http://www.scrabble.com (accessed July 24, 2011).

"Scrabble." *Pogo.com.* http://word-games.pogo.com/games/scrabble?guest_country=US (accessed July 24, 2011).

Slinky

The Slinky, a popular springy wire toy, was invented in 1943 by engineer Richard James (1914–1974) while he was working on an antivibration device for ships' instruments. James was fascinated by the way one of the springs he had made "walked" down to the ground when he accidentally knocked it off a shelf. He took it home to show his wife, Betty (1918–2008), and together they promoted it as a toy. The Slinky first went on sale at Gimbel's Department Store in Philadelphia, Pennsylvania, just before Christmas 1945. Much to their surprise, the Jameses sold their entire stock of 400 Slinkys in just 90 minutes. By its fiftieth anniversary, over 250 million Slinkys had been sold. In 2002, it also comes in brightly colored plastic and, if price is no object, fourteen karat gold.

The simplicity of the Slinky, and the strange way it walks down steps and slopes, is what attracts children and adults to the toy. The Slinky is almost unchanged from the design the Jameses first promoted. The metal version has had just one change in over fifty years: The sharp ends of the spring have been blunted for safety reasons. Although it looks simple, the Slinky depends on some serious science. In education, Slinkys are used to explain different kinds of wave forms, as well as forces such as gravity, friction, and inertia. Slinkys also have practical uses. As soldiers

Accidentally invented in 1943, the Slinky became one of the twentieth century's most popular toys. © SHUTTERSTOCK.COM.

in Vietnam discovered, Slinkys make very good radio antennae. A Slinky bent over in the form of an arch makes an excellent letter rack.

The Slinky jingle—"It's Slinky, it's Slinky, for fun it's a wonderful toy …"—is America's longest-running national **television** (see entry under 1940s—TV and Radio in volume 3) commercial campaign, running since 1963. The Slinky has appeared prominently in several movies, including *Hairspray* (1988), *Ace Ventura: When Nature Calls* (1995), and most memorably as Slinky Dog in the ***Toy Story*** (see entry under 1990s—Film and Theater in volume 5) movies. The antivibration device James had been working when he invented the Slinky was a complete flop. However, his accidental creation went on to become one of the best-selling toys in America. With its graceful movements and "slinkety" sound, the Slinky has played a part in the childhood of most Americans born since the end of World War II (1939–45).

Chris Routledge

For More Information

Green, Joey. *The Official Slinky Book: Hundreds of Wild and Wacky Uses for the Greatest Toy on Earth.* New York: Berkley Publishing, 1999.

Harry, Lou. *It's Slinky: The Fun and Wonderful Toy.* Philadelphia: Running Press, 2000.

"The Slinky." *Inventor of the Week.* http://web.mit.edu/Invent/iow/slinky.html (accessed July 24, 2011).

"Slinky Brand." *Poof-Slinky.com.* http://www.poof-slinky.com/ (accessed July 24, 2011).

"Slinky History—Invention of the Slinky." *The Great Idea Finder.* http://www.ideafinder.com/history/inventions/slinky.htm (accessed July 24, 2011).

Wellock, William. "The Sensational Story of the Sleek, Silver Slinky." *The Pennsylvania Center for the Book.* http://www.pabook.libraries.psu.edu/palitmap/Slinky.html (accessed July 24, 2011).

Tonka Trucks

The American enthusiasm for cars and trucks shows itself early in the love of American children for toys modeled after the vehicles. Of these, none is more famous for quality and realism than the Tonka truck. First made by Mound Metalcraft Company of Mound, Minnesota, Tonka is named after that state's Lake Winnetonka. The company manufactured sturdy steel toy trucks with parts that moved and worked but did not break easily. Beginning with the popular steam shovel and the crane in 1947, Mound Metalcraft (under the name Tonka) made many different kinds of trucks replicating both construction and military vehicles. The yellow dump truck, introduced in 1965, has been the most popular Tonka toy ever since.

While children, especially boys, love their Tonka trucks, adults have also begun to collect the miniatures, paying high prices for early models.

The most popular Tonka toy: the yellow dump truck.
© BEATRICE BEAUDRY/ALAMY.

The toys have changed over the years, with a variety of new models offered in plastic as well as metal. In 1996, Tonka was bought by Hasbro Toys, and the company continues to manufacture the toys through the 2000s.

Tina Gianoulis

For More Information

David, Dennis, and Lloyd L. Laumann. *Tonka.* St. Paul, MN: MBI, 2004.

Tonka Home. http://www.hasbro.com/tonka/en_US/ (accessed July 24, 2011).

"Tonka Toy Trucks: They're Not Just for Kids Anymore." *NeatOldToys.com.* http://www.neatoldtoys.com/ (accessed July 24, 2011).

Townsend, Allie. "1950s Tonka Truck." *Time.* http://www.time.com/time/specials/packages/article/0,28804,2049243_2048654_2049126,00.html (accessed July 24, 2011).

1940s

TV and Radio

Radio proved its importance during World War II (1939–45) by providing almost immediate coverage of events. Between 1941 and 1945, Americans tuned in to listen to breaking news from Europe, hearing about major battles and the bombing of Pearl Harbor in Hawaii just moments after the actual events. News reporters such as Edward R. Murrow (1908–1965) and William Shirer (1904–1993) offered insightful commentary and objective, factual news. Their example would influence the news anchors in the new newscast medium—television, commonly called TV—for decades. Radio's golden age ended with the war.

The 1940s were the true beginning of the TV era. Although sets had been available as early as the late 1930s, the widespread distribution and sale of TV sets did not really take off until after the war. Broadcasting companies neglected many of their radio stations and poured money into TV after the war. Soon many radio dramas, variety shows, and comedy programs were available on TV and radio was left with mostly music. For children, new shows like *Kukla, Fran, and Ollie* and *The Howdy Doody Show* offered laughs. One of the most popular early TV programs was a variety show called *Texaco Star Theater,* starring comedian Milton Berle (1908–2002), that started in 1948.

As the decade continued, more and more people bought TV sets. Instead of circling around their radios, people would settle in front of their TVs for news and entertainment. As TV became more popular, the government set up regulations to ensure competition between stations, channels, and programs. The 1950s would see the new medium change dramatically with the introduction of color and other technological advances.

Jack Benny (1894–1974)

Jack Benny was one of the most popular and influential comedians of the twentieth century. He was known for his subtle sense of comic timing, which relied on a long pause and a frozen, pained expression in order to milk laughs. Benny's humor focused on the made-up persona of a wisecracking penny-pincher (one who is very conservative, often cheap, with his or her money). In one of his classic comic sketches, Benny is held up by a burglar who demands, "Your money or your life." After his characteristic lengthy pause, Benny responds, "I'm thinking about it." In another classic bit, when asked his age, Benny always said he was "thirty-nine," a line that grew funnier as the years passed and he was well into old age.

Benny was born Benjamin Kubelsky. Unlike other Jewish entertainers of his time, he did not adopt an ethnic approach to humor. This may be because his roots were in the Midwestern town of Waukegan, Illinois, rather than in the immigrant "melting pot" (racial, social, and cultural mixture) of New York City, where exaggerated Yiddish accents and Semitic jokes were more prevalent. His first appearances were as a teenager, playing the violin in **vaudeville** (see entry under 1900s—Film and Theater in volume 1). When he realized that audiences applauded his stiff demeanor and wrong notes more fervently than his musical ability, Benny became a stage comic and often used his violin-playing as a means of getting laughs. As the century progressed, Benny successfully starred on his own series on the **radio** (see entry under 1920s—TV and Radio in volume 1) and later on **television**

Comedian, violin virtuoso, and radio star Jack Benny.
© JOHN SPRINGER
COLLECTION/CORBIS.

(see entry under 1940s—TV and Radio in volume 3). He also starred in several films.

Audrey Kupferberg

For More Information

Benny, Jack, and Joan Benny. *Sunday Nights at Seven: The Jack Benny Story.* New York: Warner, 1990.

"Jack Benny." *The Museum of Broadcast History.* http://www.museum.tv/rhofsection.php?page=168 (accessed July 23, 2011).

Fein, Irving. *Jack Benny: An Intimate Biography.* New York, Putnam, 1976.

Josefsberg, Milt. *The Jack Benny Show.* New Rochelle, NY: Arlington House, 1977.

Bugs Bunny

Bugs Bunny, the smart-aleck cartoon rabbit, known equally well for his carrots, his quips, and his trademark question—"Eh, what's up, Doc?"—is one of the most popular animated characters ever created.

The rascally rabbit's origins gave no hint of the greatness to come. He first appeared in *Porky's Hare Hunt,* a 1938 Warner Brothers cartoon. He was drawn smaller than he would later become and was also completely white. In his debut, Bugs was given no name; he was simply an unidentified rabbit who turned Porky Pig's hunting expedition into a farce.

The character's appearance and attitude evolved through several more cartoon appearances. Bugs Bunny finally reached the form for which he is best known in 1940's *A Wild Hare.* Directed by Tex Avery (1908–1980), this was the first cartoon to use the line "What's up, Doc?" The tall, gray-and-white rabbit remained unnamed.

That anonymity changed in 1941, when the name "Bugs Bunny" was used for the first time in *Elmer's Pet Rabbit,* directed by Chuck Jones (1912–2002). The name came from Ben "Bugs" Hardaway (1896–1957), an animator at Warner Brothers who had invented the rabbit for *Porky's Hare Hunt.* The cartoonists at Warner had been informally referring to the character as "Bugs' Bunny" for years. The name was now official.

The voice of Bugs Bunny was that of famous voice actor Mel Blanc (1908–1989). Blanc was also responsible for the voices of such characters as Woody Woodpecker, Daffy Duck, Porky Pig, and Barney Rubble.

Bugs Bunny was gaining popularity at about the same time that the United States entered World War II (1939–45), following the Japanese bombing of Pearl Harbor in Hawaii on December 7, 1941. Like many characters at Warner, **Disney** (see entry under 1920s—Film and Theater in volume 2), and the other animation studios, Bugs was used in cartoons that combined entertainment with propaganda. In the two-minute cartoon *Any Bonds Today?* (1942), Bugs is dressed in a Revolutionary War (1775–81) uniform while singing about the benefits of buying war bonds. The year 1944 brought the full-length cartoon *Bugs Bunny Nips the Nips.* As the title suggests, this production was an example of the blatant racism that was widely used to depict the Japanese to American audiences during the war years. ("Nip" was a derogatory term used to refer to the Japanese.) Here, Bugs washes up on a Pacific island that is occupied by Japanese troops who try to capture him. Bugs easily makes fools of them all. In 1945, *Herr Meets Hare* has Bugs popping up in Nazi Germany, where he torments and mocks Nazis Hermann Göring (1893–1946) and Adolf Hitler (1889–1945).

However, Bugs Bunny's greatest contribution to national pride during the war may have been less direct: Bugs always won. Even though he lacked superpowers or big muscles, the rabbit always found a way to prevail over his enemies. Bugs was the cartoon equivalent of a character common in many films produced during the war: a brash young guy, usually working-class and full of "street smarts," who always triumphed in the end. The message embodied in both characters was the same: attitude, quick wits, and "good old American know-how" would always come out on top. This was a comforting message to American audiences, especially when the war was going badly for the United States during 1942 and 1943.

Bugs Bunny's popularity did not decline after the war ended in 1945. He won an Oscar in 1948 for *Knighty-Knight Bugs* (having been nominated twice before). Among theater owners, it was widely believed that a phrase like "2 New Bugs Bunny Cartoons" on a sign was enough to bring in legions of customers, regardless of what the main feature might be.

The carrot that Bugs was often shown munching soon became part of his trademark. The image was so well known that the Utah Celery Company tried to persuade Warner Brothers to substitute Bugs's favorite vegetable with its product. The studio declined politely, just as it did when made a similar offer from the Broccoli Institute of America. Bugs Bunny would keep his carrot.

Television (see entry under 1940s—TV and Radio in volume 3) came into America's homes in the 1950s. Bugs made the transition easily, along with his other Warner Brothers costars like Daffy Duck, Sylvester the Cat, and Elmer Fudd. The cartoons that had been seen only in movie theaters were repackaged and sold to TV stations for broadcast on Saturday mornings (although new Bugs Bunny cartoons continued to appear in theaters until 1964). In addition, *The Bugs Bunny Show* was the first nationally broadcast cartoon program. Shown on Tuesday evenings from 1960 to 1962 (and revived for the 1971–72 season), it combined vintage Warner Brothers cartoons with new animation. Bugs Bunny appeared on television screens again beginning in 2011 as part of Cartoon Network's *The Looney Tunes Show.* The program featured all-new adventures with classic Warner Brothers characters like Daffy Duck; both Bugs Bunny and Daffy Duck were voiced by Jeff Bergman (1960–) in this version.

Bugs Bunny returned to the big screen in 1996 with the feature-length film *Space Jam,* which combined animation with live action. In the film, Bugs and his friends have been kidnapped by aliens. Their captors agree to release them only if Bugs and the other Warner characters can beat the aliens at basketball. Bugs and his team seek help from basketball superstar **Michael Jordan** (1963–; see entry under 1990s—Sports and Games in volume 5) and eventually play their way to freedom. Bugs Bunny and Daffy Duck were also featured in the 2003 film *Looney Tunes: Back in Action,* which also featured a combination of animation and live action.

The spot that Bugs Bunny occupies in American popular culture is so prominent that, in 1998, the U.S. Post Office honored him with his own commemorative stamp.

Justin Gustainis

For More Information

Adamson, Joe. *Bugs Bunny: Fifty Years and Only One Grey Hare.* New York: Henry Holt, 1990.

Evanier, Mark. *Bugs Bunny and Friends: A Comic Celebration.* New York: DC Comics, 1998.

The Looney Tunes Show. http://looneytunes.kidswb.com/ (accessed July 24, 2011).

Lowry, Brian. "The Looney Tunes Show." *Daily Variety* (May 3, 2011): 14.

Preller, James, Leo Benvenuti, and Steve Rudnick. *Bugs Bunny's 'Space Jam' Scrapbook: How I Saved the World.* New York: Scholastic Press, 1996.

Sandler, Kevin S. *Reading the Rabbit: Explorations in Warner Bros. Animation.* New Brunswick, NJ: Rutgers University Press, 1998.

Seiler, Andy. "*Back in Action*? Looney Tunes Never Left." *USA Today* (November 14, 2003): 4E.

The Howdy Doody Show

The Howdy Doody Show (1947–60) is one of the most fondly remembered children's programs from the early years of **television** (see entry under 1940s—TV and Radio in volume 3). To formulate the show, which aired on NBC, singer Robert E. Smith (1917–1998) adopted

Howdy Doody and Buffalo Bob Smith converse with a fair-haired friend during one of their many television broadcasts. © EVERETT COLLECTION.

the basic format of a **radio** (see entry under 1920s—TV and Radio in volume 2) show he had hosted for youngsters. Episodes of the series were initially broadcast weekly in hour-long segments, but the show's popularity with young people led NBC to give it a daily, Monday-through-Friday half-hour slot.

The show's story took place in a made-up circus town called Doodyville. The show featured puppets and fantastic characters who were residents of the imagined village. In Doodyville, Smith became a personable character named Buffalo Bob. The star character was a wooden puppet suspended on strings called Howdy Doody, a charming and cheerful twenty-seven-inch-high freckle-faced marionette with a smiling mouth filled with bright white teeth. Although the show was shown primarily in black-and-white until 1955, Howdy was colorfully attired in blue jeans, a plaid shirt and red bandana, and two-toned cowboy boots. He was joined by other wooden puppets, such as Phineas T. Bluster, the ill-tempered mayor of Doodyville; a simple-minded carpenter named Dilly Dally; and the fanciful creature Flub-a-Dub, who was made up of eight types of animals.

Buffalo Bob's sidekick was a human clown named Clarabell, who never spoke. Clarabell wielded a seltzer bottle that sprayed the bubbly water and honked a horn attached to his belt. He was played for several years by Bob Keeshan (1927–2004), who went on to become the star of another children's television show, *Captain Kangaroo* (see entry under 1950s—TV and Radio in volume 3). Other characters played by humans were Indian Chief Thunderthud, lovely Princess Summerfall Winterspring, Bison Bill, and a wrestler named Ugly Sam. Members of the studio audience—as well as the kids at home—were referred to as the Peanut Gallery. At the beginning of every show, Buffalo Bob would shout out, "Say kids, what time is it?" The Peanut Gallery would answer, "It's Howdy Doody Time!"

An updated version of the show with Buffalo Bob and Howdy Doody was syndicated (sold to many TV markets by a designated distributor) in 1976, but it failed to gain an audience. In 1987, in order to celebrate Howdy Doody's fortieth birthday, a two-hour special was aired, but it, too, failed to capture the excitement of the original shows. Howdy Doody's twin, Double Doody, was donated to the Smithsonian Institution. The original Howdy Doody marionette sold for $23,000 at auction in 1995.

Audrey Kupferberg

For More Information

Davis, Stephen. *Say Kids, What Time Is It?: Notes from the Peanut Gallery.* Boston: Little, Brown, 1987.

"The Howdy Doody Show." *The Museum of Broadcast Communications.* http://www.museum.tv/eotvsection.php?entrycode=howdydoodys (accessed July 23, 2011).

Smith, Buffalo Bob, and Donna McCrohan. *Howdy and Me: Buffalo Bob's Own Story.* New York: Plume, 1990.

Kukla, Fran, and Ollie

Kukla, Fran, and Ollie was a televised puppet show that ran from 1947 through 1957. The puppet show was first shown on the NBC **television** (see entry under 1940s—TV and Radio in volume 3) network. For its final three years, the show appeared on ABC-TV. Kukla and Ollie were the names of two puppets created by Burr Tillstrom (1917–1985). Fran Allison (1907–1989) was the human who chatted with them as they performed on a tiny stage. Kukla (his name is the Russian word for "doll") was an excitable fellow with a huge round nose and receding hairline. Ollie (Oliver J. Dragon) was a self-centered but good-natured dragon. In the

The stars and creator of the Kukla, Fran and Ollie *television show: Kukla, Burr Tillstrom, Fran Allison, and Ollie.* © EVERETT COLLECTION.

show, Kukla never talked, making himself understood by rapid body move-ments, but Ollie had a falsetto voice. These two puppets were the most prominent of the Kuklapolitans, a group of Tillstrom's puppets that in-cluded Madame Ooglepuss, Fletcher Rabbit, Cecil Bill, and Beulah Witch. Tillstrom provided all the voices and manipulated the puppets from behind a small stage as Allison chatted with them while standing at eye level. Musi-cal accompaniment was provided by pianist Jack Fascanato (1915–1994).

Tillstrom became interested in puppetry while a teenager. He per-formed with his puppets in nightclubs, and department stores, and at the 1939–40 **World's Fair** (see entry under 1900s—The Way We Lived in volume 1) in New York. The Kuklapolitans appeared on TV for the first time on October 13, 1947, Tillstrom's thirtieth birthday. On this date, they were joined by Allison, a singer and comedian, on a local Chicago show called *Junior Jamboree*. The title of the program was sub-sequently changed to *Kukla, Fran, and Ollie*. On January 12, 1949, it became the first show broadcast over the national NBC network. It was seen five nights a week at 6:00 PM Central Time. After *Kukla, Fran, and Ollie* ended its run on national TV in 1957, the Kuklapolitans appeared on many TV specials, in syndication, and in live performance.

Edward Moran

For More Information

Brooks, Tim, and Earle Marsh. *The Complete Directory to Prime Time Network and Cable TV Shows, 1946–present.* 9th ed. New York: Ballantine Books, 2007.
"Kukla, Fran & Ollie." *The Museum of Broadcast Communications.* http://www.museum.tv/eotvsection.php?entrycode=kuklafrana (accessed July 23, 2011).
The Kuklapolitan Website. http://kukla.tv/ (accessed July 23, 2011).

News Anchors

When **television** (see entry under 1940s—TV and Radio in volume 2) was in its infancy during the late 1940s and early 1950s, news reports became an important part of daily programming. The major networks set aside a time period each evening to broadcast national and international news. Local stations did the same for local events. As such programs evolved, they consisted of field reporters passing along information on specific events, along with accompanying visual images on 16-millimeter (16-mm) film. Holding each program together was the news anchor, a

constant presence throughout the broadcast. The anchor described news events and introduced field journalists and news clips. The most successful anchors are recognized for their calming, steadying presence, particularly in times of crisis.

The best news anchors have strong journalism backgrounds. For nineteen years beginning in 1962, Walter Cronkite (1916–2009) anchored the evening news on CBS. Cronkite brought to the job flawless journalistic credentials; he had started out as a wire-service correspondent during World War II (1939–45). Fabled for his reassuring demeanor, Cronkite came to be known as "Uncle Walter" and "The Most Trusted Man in

America." He signed off each broadcast by stating, "And that's the way it is." Few questioned the truthfulness of this declaration. When appropriate, Cronkite injected emotion into his broadcast. He did so in times of tragedy and triumph, whether tearfully announcing the death by assassination of President John F. Kennedy (1917–1963) or adding cheerleader-style comments while anchoring coverage of America's space program. On occasion, an anchor of Cronkite's stature may become a news-maker. A trip to Vietnam during the 1968 Tet offensive (a massive surprise attack on South Vietnam by North Vietnamese fighters) helped turn Cronkite against the Vietnam War (1954–1975). During the final moments of a CBS documentary, he called for an end to the fighting, an action that helped turn millions of mainstream Americans against the war.

Cronkite's most direct competition came from NBC, which between 1956 and 1970 featured a pair of popular anchors. Chet Huntley (1911–1974) broadcast from New York, while David Brinkley (1920–2003) was situated in Washington, D.C. Both were veteran journalists. Huntley's sober, deliberate style played off of Brinkley's low-key wit to make their show a consistent ratings winner—usually besting Cronkite's broadcasts during the 1960s. They, too, had their own special way of ending each broadcast, with each declaring, in turn, "Good night, Chet … Good night, David … and good night for NBC News."

Cronkite, Huntley, and Brinkley were not the lone pioneer anchors. John Cameron Swayze (1906–1995), who began on NBC-TV in 1948, was the medium's first superstar anchor. However, Swayze, who opened his broadcasts with a cheerful "And a good evening to you" and closed them with "Glad we could be together," was more a news reader than a journalist. In 1976, Barbara Walters (1931–) became the first woman network news anchor, working beside Harry Reasoner (1923–1991) on ABC. Two years later, ABC's Max Robinson (1939–1988) became the first African American network news anchor. In 2006, Katie Couric (1957–) became the first woman to serve as the sole host of a network weekday evening news show. Other high-profile anchors in the late twentieth and early twenty-first century include: CNN's Bernard Shaw (1940–) and Anderson Cooper (1967–); ABC's Peter Jennings (1938–2005) and Diane Sawyer (1945–); CBS's Dan Rather (1931–), and Scott Pelley (1957–); and NBC's Tom Brokaw (1940–) and Brian Williams (1959–).

Rob Edelman

For More Information

Bliss, Edward, Jr. *Now the News: The Story of Broadcast Journalism.* New York: Columbia University Press, 1991.

Brinkley, David. *David Brinkley: A Memoir.* New York: Alfred A. Knopf, 1995.

Brinkley, David. *Everyone Is Entitled to My Opinion.* New York: Ballantine Books, 1996.

Cronkite, Walter. *A Reporter's Life.* New York: Alfred A. Knopf, 1996.

"Dan Rather: A Storied Life: After 24 Years as Anchor, He Reflects on His Critics, His Career and the Future." *Broadcasting & Cable* (November 29, 2004): 18.

Frank, Reuven. *Out of Thin Air: The Brief Wonderful Life of Network News.* New York: Simon & Schuster, 1991.

Gay, Verne. "CBS Counts on Couric: The First of the Big Three Networks with a Solo Female News Anchor, CBS Is Betting on Katie Couric to Reverse Two Decades of Audience Decline." *Newsday* (September 3, 2006).

Goldberg, Robert, and Gerald Jay Goldberg. *Anchors: Brokaw, Jennings, Rather and the Evening News.* Secaucus, NJ: Carol Publishing Group, 1990.

Matusow, Barbara. *The Evening Stars: The Making of the Network News Anchor.* Boston: Houghton Mifflin, 1983.

Swansburg, John. "The Comic Stylings of Brian Williams: How's an Anchor to Cope When Network Newscasts Keep Losing Ground? Having a Second Career Helps." *New York* (May 2, 2011).

Zimmer, Brian. "Was Cronkite Really the First 'Anchorman'?" *Slate.* (July 18, 2009). Available at http://www.slate.com/id/2223188/ (accessed July 24, 2011).

Road Runner and Wile E. Coyote

Constantly at odds with each other in a series of thirty-five animated cartoons produced by Warner Brothers from 1949 through 1966, Road Runner and Wile E. Coyote still entertain audiences with their familiar escapades in the southwestern desert. The premise of all the cartoons is the same: Wile E. Coyote tries without success to capture the Road Runner. The Road Runner proves more clever than the crafty but bumbling coyote, whose traps inevitably backfire as the bird escapes with his signature "beep-beep" farewell.

The two characters first appeared in the 1949 cartoon short *Fast and Furry-Ous,* created by director Chuck Jones (1912–2002) and story-man Michael Maltese (1908–1981). Their second cartoon, *Beep, Beep,* appeared in 1952. The cartoon "Beep Prepared" was nominated for an Academy Award in 1961. The *Road Runner* cartoons are reminiscent of other Warner Brothers animated shorts that feature combative

In a scene from The Road Runner Show, *Wile E. Coyote closes in on his ever-elusive prey.* © EVERETT COLLECTION.

characters, like **Bugs Bunny** (see entry under 1940s—TV and Radio in volume 3) and Elmer Fudd, or Sylvester the Cat and Tweety Bird. The difference is that Wile E. Coyote is shown using increasingly sophisticated and complex devices in his hopeless attempts at capturing his prey, many of them ordered from the fictional Acme Company. Time and time again, Road Runner eludes the traps. It is Wile E. Coyote who falls over the cliff, is flattened by a locomotive, or has an explosive charge blow up in his face.

The *Road Runner* cartoons were first shown in theaters and on network **television** (see entry under 1940s—TV and Radio in volume 3). In September 1966, *The Road Runner Show* premiered in the CBS Saturday morning lineup of children's shows. The shorts later appeared on cable stations such as TNT and the Cartoon Network, and are also available for viewing online on websites like **YouTube** (see entry under 2000s—The Way We Lived in volume 6).

Edward Moran

For More Information

Friedwald, Will, and Jerry Beck. *The Warner Brothers Cartoons.* Metuchen, NJ: Scarecrow Press, 1981.

Lenburg, Jeff. *The Encyclopedia of Animated Cartoons.* 3rd ed. New York: Facts on File, 2009.

McCorry, Kevin. *The Road Runner Show Page.* http://looney.goldenagecartoons. com/tv/rrshow/ (accessed July 24, 2011).

"Road Runner and Wile E. Coyote." *Looney Tunes—Stars of the Show.* http:// looneytunes.warnerbros.co.uk/stars_of_the_show/wile_roadrunner/wile_ story.html (accessed July 24, 2011).

Studio One

From the late 1940s through the early 1960s, live dramatic presentations were a staple of commercial **television** (see entry under 1940s—TV and Radio in volume 3), helping earn this era the reputation as TV's "golden age." Each week, various anthology series presented classic and original dramas starring familiar older **Hollywood** (see entry under 1930s—Film and Theater in volume 2) stars and hot new up-and-comers. One of the oldest and most distinguished and innovative shows was *Studio One,* which aired on CBS from November 1948 through September 1958.

The hour-long show offered a vast and impressive array of programming. Across the decade, almost five hundred plays were broadcast. Among the most notable early *Studio One* productions: **"Mary Poppins"** (see entry under 1960s—Film and Theater in volume 4) and Somerset Maugham's (1874–1965) "Of Human Bondage" (both of which aired in 1949), and William Shakespeare's (1564–1616) "Julius Caesar" (staged twice in 1949), "Macbeth" (1950), and "The Taming of the Shrew" (1951). Jackie Gleason (1916–1987) and Art Carney (1918–2003), beloved stars of the classic TV sitcom *The Honeymooners* (1955–1956, 1971; see entry under 1950s—TV and Radio in volume 3), played dramatic roles in *Studio One*'s "The Laugh Maker" (1953). **James Dean** (1931–1955; see entry under 1950s—Film and Theater in volume 3), who soon would personify adolescent anxieties on the big screen in *East* *of Eden* (1955) and *Rebel Without a Cause* (1955), had one of his initial important roles in "Sentence of Death" (1953). Fabled stage-and-screen actor Jason Robards Jr. (1922–2000), had his first significant TV part in "A Picture in the Paper" (1955). Even Mike Wallace (1918–), best known as a host of **60 Minutes** (see entry under 1960s—TV and Radio in volume 4), the long-running CBS newsmagazine, acted on *Studio One,* in "For the Defense" (1955). Among the then-emerging actors to appear on the series were Grace Kelly (1928–1982), Charlton Heston (1923–2008), Peter Falk (1927–2011), William Shatner (1931–), Leslie Nielsen (1922–2010), Steve McQueen (1930–1980), and Warren Beatty (1937–).

A generation of directors and writers got their professional starts on *Studio One.* Franklin J. Schaffner (1920–1989), who would win an Academy Award for directing *Patton* (1970), regularly worked on the series. Others who went on to feature film-making careers included Sidney Lumet (1924–2011), George Roy Hill (1922–2002), and Robert Mulligan (1925–2008). Among the writers who penned original teleplays for *Studio One* were Rod Serling (1924–1975), Gore Vidal (1925–), and Reginald Rose (1921–2002). Rose's Emmy Award–winning *12 Angry Men,* one of the higher-profile *Studio One* productions, aired in 1954 and was transferred to the screen by Lumet three years later.

Most significant of all, however, were the contributions of Worthington Miner (1900–1982), the show's first producer. Miner was an innovative force in early TV. He was concerned as much with visual storytelling as with dialogue. To Miner, *Studio One* was a "live performance staged for multiple cameras," rather than for a theater audience. In this regard, he viewed the medium of TV as halfway between live drama and cinema. Miner experimented with camera placement and movement, movable sets, editing, lighting techniques, and actors performing in relation to the camera. All these techniques added immeasurably to the development of TV as a visual medium.

Rob Edelman

For More Information

Barnouw, Erik. *Tube of Plenty: The Evolution of American Television.* 2nd ed. New York: Oxford University Press, 1990.

Raw, Lawrence. "Form and Function in the 1950s Anthology Series: Studio One." *Journal of Popular Film and Television.* (Summer 2009): 90.

"Studio One." *The Museum of Broadcast Communications.* http://www.museum.tv/eotvsection.php?entrycode=studioone (accessed July 23, 2011).

Television

Since World War II (1939–45), television, commonly known as TV, has dominated American popular culture. From the moment of its arrival, TV redefined the way Americans spent their leisure time. In the twenty-first century, TV is the main media outlet for news, sports, entertainment, and politics. The industry is run by multi-billion-dollar corporations. Politicians, celebrities, sports promoters, and the film and music industries compete for the best TV coverage. Advertisers pay millions of dollars each year to promote their products during the most popular shows. From sports to news, from **game shows** (see entry under 1950s—TV and Radio in volume 3) to comedy, drama, and documentaries, TV offers something for almost everyone.

Although the technological principles of TV were established in the 1880s, it was not until 1924 that British inventor John Logie Baird (1888–1946) transmitted images of crude shapes. He did the same trick with moving images in 1926. An American, Ernst F. W. Alexanderson (1878–1975), demonstrated the first home TV set in January 1928. Station WGY began broadcasting to the area around Schenectady, New York, on May 10, 1928. It is doubtful that many people were watching, because few Americans could afford TVs during the **Great Depression** (1929–41; see entry under 1930s—The Way We Lived in volume 2) or World War II. After the war, the effect of TV on American life was dramatic. Americans bought just seven thousand sets in 1946. In 1953, color TV appeared. By 1960, 90 percent of American homes had a TV. Television's influence soon damaged the sales of newspapers, magazines, and books. Many popular titles, such as *Colliers* and the ***Saturday Evening Post*** (see entry under 1900s—Print Culture in volume 1), went out of business in the 1950s. Television helped bring **Hollywood** (see entry under 1930s—Film and Theater in volume 2) to a crisis point in the 1960s, and it took away the audience for the **radio** (see entry under 1920s—TV and Radio in volume 2) drama.

During the late 1940s, over one hundred TV stations were using just twelve VHF (Very High Frequency) TV channels. The introduction of UHF (Ultra High Frequency) pushed public access and community broadcasters away from the high-quality VHF waveband, leaving the "big three" networks—ABC, CBS, and NBC—to take control. The **Public Broadcasting System (PBS)** (see entry under 1960s—TV and

Radio in volume 4) aimed to make TV morally and culturally uplifting, but most Americans preferred the commercial channels. Many watched TV for several hours every day. In the 1970s, **cable TV** (see entry under 1970s—TV and Radio in volume 4) became popular. Cable TV made a much larger number of channels—exclusively covering such topics as music, gardening, history, and sports— available to viewers.

Probably the strongest single influence on American TV is **advertising** (see entry under 1920s—Commerce in volume 2). Advertisers realized that many viewers would watch the "least objectionable" show on air at any given time, regardless of what it was. They used their power over the TV companies to influence the schedules. In the 1950s, inoffensive, simple "situation comedies," or **sitcoms** (see entry under 1950s—TV and Radio in volume 3), dominated American TV. In the 1990s, lightweight news "magazine" shows such as *48 Hours* had taken their place.

At the beginning of the twenty-first century, TV audiences around the world were enthralled by *Survivor* and other "**reality TV**" (see entry under 1990s—TV and Radio in volume 5) shows. Reality competitions also experienced a resurgence in popularity during the early 2010s, with shows like ***American Idol*** (see entry under 2000s—TV and Radio in volume 6) and ***Dancing with the Stars*** (see entry under 2000s—TV and Radio in volume 6) garnering impressive ratings. What all these shows have in common is that they are cheap, easy to produce, and command a huge, uncritical audience. Viewers began wanting more substance as well, with dramas like the award-winning ***Mad Men*** (see entry under 2000s—TV and Radio in volume 6) greatly influencing fashion and culture.

It is impossible to overestimate the effect of TV on American cultural life. Televised coverage of civil rights marches, the first moon walk, and the assassinations of President John F. Kennedy (1917–1963), Martin Luther King Jr. (1929–1968), and Robert Kennedy (1925–1968) all helped define the era of the 1960s. Pictures of the *Challenger* space shuttle disaster in 1986; the Oklahoma City, Oklahoma, bombing in 1995; the **September 11, 2001, terrorist attacks** (see entry under 2000s—The Way We Lived in volume 6) ; and **Hurricane Katrina** (see entry under 2000s—The Way We Lived in volume 6) brought the American public together in tragedy. Major sporting events provide happier experiences. The **Super Bowl** (see entry under 1960s—Sports and Games in volume 4) is by far the most watched TV broadcast. Individual sporting moments such as the record-breaking sixty-second home run hit by Mark McGwire in 1998 have passed into national memory because of TV.

In the 1950s, politicians gradually realized that TV had become an essential tool for attracting voters. For example, Richard Nixon (1913–1994) embraced the medium after losing the 1960 presidential election, using televised debates and appearances to project a well-dressed, polished demeanor that helped him win the 1968 presidential election. His later fall from grace was also shown on TV.

Television's effect on sports has been no less dramatic. Television companies and advertisers hold major stakes in sports from basketball and football to motor racing and golf. Sports teams depend on TV advertising deals for much of their funding. Celebrity athletes earn fantastic salaries in return for becoming walking billboards. Since the 1990s, so-called pay-per-view and interactive digital services have been responsible for a leap in the incomes of athletes, celebrities, and their promoters.

By the 1990s, most people learned about major events from TV. The dangers of this situation are clear. Controlled by advertisers and censored by government, TV does not always provide complete or accurate coverage of important moments in history. Of course, TV has always led a double life. On the one hand, people depend on it for information and entertainment. On the other hand, they complain about violence, sexual content, poor news coverage, and oversimplification of events. Like it or loathe it, television has provided many of the most dramatic visual and cultural memories of the late twentieth and early twenty-first centuries. While its domination of the American cultural landscape began to diminish in the twenty-first century as a result of social media like **Facebook** (see entry under 2000s—The Way We Lived in volume 6) and **Twitter** (see entry under 2000s—The Way We Lived in volume 6), as well as other online viewing resources like **YouTube** (see entry under 2000s—The Way We Lived in volume 6) and news websites, many viewers still regarded television as a primary source of news and entertainment.

Chris Routledge

For More Information

Barnouw, Erik. *Tube of Plenty: The Evolution of American Television.* 2nd ed. New York: Oxford University Press, 1990.

Calabro, Marian. *Zap!: A Brief History of Television.* New York: Four Winds Press, 1992.

Castleman, Harry, and Walter J. Podrazik. *Watching TV: Six Decades of American Television.* 2nd ed. Syracus, NY: Syracuse University Press, 2003.

DeVolld, Troy. *Reality TV: An Insider's Guide to TV's Hottest Market.* Studio City, CA: Michael Wiese Productions, 2011.

Edgerton, Gary R. *The Columbia History of American Television.* New York: Columbia University Press, 2007.

Himmelstein, Hal. *Television Myth and the American Mind.* 2nd ed. Westport, CT: Praeger, 1994.

Hulu. http://www.hulu.com/ (accessed July 24, 2011).

"More Consumers Are Watching TV Broadcasts Online." *US Newswire* (October 15, 2007).

Perenson, Melissa J. "The Best of TV on the Web: How Do You Find Stuff That's Worth Watching?" *PC World* (September 2008): 105.

Poniewozik, James. "Reality TV at 10: How It's Changed Television—and Us" *Time* (February 22, 2010): 92.

Stark, Steven D. *Glued to the Set: The 60 Television Shows and Events that Made Us Who We Are Today.* New York: Free Press, 1997.

Weprin, Alex. "Hoping to Reverse the Online Video (Cash) Flow." *Broadcasting & Cable* (September 14, 2009): 13.

1940s

The Way We Lived

The Great Depression (1929–41) had plunged millions of Americans into poverty. Although New Deal programs had helped many, at the beginning of World War II (1939–45) 40 percent of all American families were living in poverty. The desperate conditions of the Depression left a deep impression on the people living through it. Their personal suffering during the Depression prepared them to endure the mandatory restrictions on food, clothing, and other items that were needed to supply the war effort of the 1940s. Americans rallied behind their soldiers and grew their own vegetables in "victory gardens." They lived frugally even though they could now find jobs and had extra money to spend.

The deprivation caused by the Depression had caused many people to delay marriage. By the 1940s, young lovers rushed to marry before soldiers left for the war. When the soldiers returned after the war, many couples moved into ranch houses in the suburbs and began having children—lots of children. The baby boom had started. By the mid-1940s, the country's economy was prospering; people could find jobs that paid well; families were growing; and people began buying things. Homes, cars (not just family sedans, but hot rods), electric appliances, and other once-luxuries were purchased or financed. People began vacationing more often, going to Las Vegas, Nevada, the gambling capital of the country, or spending spring breaks in sunny locations.

The postwar period did have a downside, however. The end of World War II had divided the world into two major parts: democratic and communist. Countries with opposing types of governance distrusted one another and encouraged their citizens to be wary of others as well. Fear was a common feeling during what came to be called the "Cold War" (1945–91). No bloody battles were fought between such countries, but each prepared for the worst. People built cement bomb shelters dug into their backyards. In the United States, Federal Bureau of Investigation (FBI) agents became revered as super-sleuths tasked with keeping America safe from communists. The fear and distrust generated by the Cold War would not end until the Soviet Union government dissolved in 1991.

Baby Boom

When World War II (1939–45) ended, Americans had endured fifteen years of economic depression and war. Lacking money during the **Great Depression** (1929–41; see entry under 1930s—The Way We Lived in volume 2) and unsure of the future during the war, many young couples put off starting families during these years. With the war over and economic prosperity restored, they no longer had to wait. By 1946, the "baby boom" was on, with more babies being born than ever before. Because of their numbers, baby boomers, those people born between 1946 and 1964 (when the birth rate leveled off), are a generation that has had a great impact on American life and culture.

Between 1946 and 1964, seventy-eight million babies were born in the United States. As these children grew up, their numbers created unique problems. In the late 1940s and early 1950s, nurses, doctors, and hospitals struggled to deal with overcrowding as so many women gave birth. In the 1950s, as these kids reached school age, there were not enough school classrooms and teachers to meet the demand. In the 1960s and early 1970s, these children created the same problems for college and universities. After college, all these students wanted jobs, putting pressure on the job market. As baby boomers began to retire around 2010, many worried that services for the elderly—namely health care and Social Security—would not be able to meet the demand. At every stage of their lives, the baby-boom generation has created unfamiliar complications because of its size.

When the baby boomers were young, their numbers could also create opportunities. All these new kids needed things—diapers and toys at first, school buildings and clothes, records and cars later, and all kinds of products that created a booming economy. For twenty-five years after World War II, the United States enjoyed great economic prosperity. Many baby boomers grew up in material comfort, much more so than their parents, who had suffered through the Depression and World War II.

The baby boom created great demand for housing, which helped create the many new suburban communities that sprung up after 1945. The baby boomers spurred the growth of social and cultural phenomena known as "consumer culture" and "youth culture." Because many baby boomers were economically comfortable as they grew up, they had money to spend on luxuries. They bought lots of records and so helped make **rock and roll** (see entry under 1950s—Music in volume 3) music popular in the mid-1950s and after. They went to the movies, so movies were made about them, most famously *Rebel Without a Cause* (1955), starring **James Dean** (see entry under 1950s—Film and Theater in volume 3), about a troubled teenager bored with life. Books such as ***The Catcher in the Rye*** (1951; see entry under 1950s— Print Culture in volume 3), by J. D. Salinger (1919–2010), captured this teenage anxiety as well. They were also the first generation to grow up with **television** (see entry under 1940s—TV and Radio in volume 3), and TV catered to their needs and experiences. Later, many baby boomers grew bored with the comfortable middle-class lives many of them led. In the 1960s, they experimented with drugs, Eastern religions, and alternative lifestyles. The **hippie** (see entry under 1960s—The Way We Lived in volume 4) counterculture was most famously displayed at the **Woodstock** (see entry under 1960s—Music in volume 4) Music Festival in 1969.

The boredom many baby boomers felt with their comfortable lives also led them to examine and question some of the big problems in American life. That discontent was partly responsible for creating some of the most sweeping social changes in American life. Although their own lives were comfortable, they began to notice that others, even of their own generation, were not as fortunate. The term "baby boomer" is in many ways a stereotype, one that describes white, middle-class, suburban kids but leaves out poor and minority communities. In the early 1960s, as the first boomers went off to college, they were troubled by racial segregation and discrimination, issues that were brought to light by the African American **civil rights movement** (see entry under 1960s—The Way We Lived in volume 4) of the time. Some baby boomers joined with African Americans in this struggle.

Politically, baby boomers were troubled by the **Cold War** (the political and military standoff between the United States and the Soviet Union that began in 1946 and ended in 1991; see entry under 1940s—The Way We Lived in volume 3) and the threat nuclear weapons presented to everyone's lives. They also began to protest American involvement in the Vietnam War (1954–75), an outgrowth of the Cold War. Many of the baby boomers could avoid the war at first by attending college. Many of the poorer baby boomers who could not go to college fought in Vietnam. Fifty-eight thousand died in that military engagement. Baby boomers protested the war in greater numbers during the 1960s, helping to finally end it. The social protest of the 1960s, with its distrust of authority and dissatisfaction with social injustice, was due in large part to the baby-boom generation.

As the baby-boom generation matured in the 1970s and 1980s, many left behind their youthful rebellion and became what were called **"yuppies"** (see entry under 1980s—The Way We Lived in volume 5), slang for young urban professionals. Although many baby boomers had once criticized the boredom of affluence, as they began their own families, the boomers sought secure and high-paying jobs that would provide them with their own affluent lifestyles, although the economic crisis of the late 2000s affected them significantly. At every stage of their lives, members of the baby-boom generation have proved to be a powerful force in American political, social, and cultural life.

Timothy Berg

For More Information

Gitlin, Martin. *The Baby Boomer Encyclopedia.* Santa Barbara, CA: Greenwood Press, 2011.

Gitlin, Todd. *The Sixties: Years of Hope, Days of Rage.* Rev. ed. New York: Bantam Books, 1993.

Hamilton, Neil A., et al., eds. *Atlas of the Baby Boom Generation.* Detroit: Macmillan Reference USA, 2000.

Jones, Landon Y. *Great Expectations: America and the Baby Boom Generation.* New York: Coward, McCann & Geoghegan, 1980.

Light, Paul Charles. *Baby Boomers.* New York: Norton, 1988.

Lynch, Frederick R. *One Nation under AARP: The Fight Over Medicare, Social Security, and America's Future.* Berkeley: University of California Press, 2011.

Makower, Joel. *Boom!: Talkin' About Our Generation.* Chicago: Contemporary Books, 1985.

Owram, Doug. *Born at the Right Time: A History of the Baby Boom Generation.* Toronto: University of Toronto Press, 1996.

Zeitz, Joshua. "Boomer Century: What's Going to Happen When the Most Prosperous, Best-Educated Generation in History Finally Grows Up?" *American Heritage* (October 2005): 32.

The Bomb

Since the first atomic bomb was detonated in a test in the desert of New Mexico in early 1945, the United States, and the world, has had to live with the constant threat of thermonuclear destruction. More than just a

The atomic bomb, nicknamed "Fat Man," detonates over Nagasaki, Japan, on August 9, 1945, helping to bring an end to World War II. © BETTMANN/ CORBIS.

military weapon, atomic weapons, or simply, "the bomb," have had an extensive influence on American culture after 1945.

As World War II (1939–1945) began in Europe, prominent scientists, including Albert Einstein (1879–1955), urged U.S. president Franklin D. Roosevelt (1882–1945) to begin a program to build an atomic bomb. The scientific theories necessary to create an atomic bomb had been around since 1905, but the news that Germany, the clear aggressor in the war, was moving to build an atomic bomb created a special urgency. President Roosevelt authorized the program, known as the Manhattan Project, in December 1941, just before the United States entered the war. Working in extreme secrecy, scientists developed the bomb and first tested it at Alamogordo, New Mexico, on July 16, 1945. The bomb was used against humans only twice: at Hiroshima, Japan, on August 6, 1945, and at Nagasaki, Japan, on August 9, 1945.

After the war, atomic weapon technology was developed further. A newer, more powerful version, the hydrogen bomb, was first tested in 1949. By this time, a **Cold War** (1945–91; see entry under 1940s—The Way We Lived in volume 3) had developed between the United States and the Soviet Union. When the Soviet Union detonated its first atomic bomb in 1949, an arms race (a prolonged effort to invent more advanced military technology than an opposing force) developed that would have an inescapable impact on American culture. With the development of intercontinental ballistic missiles (ICBMs), nuclear bombs could be carried to far-off places by unmanned rockets. With these missiles and bombs aimed at each other, a standoff began between the United States and the Soviet Union. The moment of greatest tension during this standoff occurred in October 1962, during the Cuban Missile Crisis. The Soviet Union attempted to put ICBMs in Cuba, just ninety miles off the coast of Florida. During this crisis, the world came as close as it has ever come to initiating a full-scale nuclear war.

Living with the fear of the bomb was not a burden reserved solely by American political leaders. Uncertainty about potential use of the bomb affected almost everyone in the United States. With Cold War tensions high in the 1950s and early 1960s, concern over the bomb reached, quite literally, into everyone's backyard. Many Americans built underground bomb shelters in their yards as safe havens from a nuclear attack. These metal or concrete containers contained canned food and water and simple bunks. The idea was that, upon the event of a nuclear-attack alert, a family could descend into their shelter and wait out the attack for several weeks until it was safe to emerge again. Whether or not they would really provide protection mattered less than the feeling of safety the shelters supplied. In schools during the 1950s and beyond, children were instructed on how to prepare for a nuclear attack. "Duck and cover" drills were routinely conducted. During the drills, the children would get under their desks, cover their heads, and curl up into a ball. Public-safety films instructed adults on how to protect themselves from nuclear attack.

Those fears also found their way into popular culture. Novels such as *On the Beach* (also a popular film) by Nevil Shute (1899–1960) and *Alas, Babylon* by Pat Frank (1907–1964) dramatized the aftermath of a nuclear war on ordinary people. The 1963 film **Dr. Strangelove** (see entry under 1960s—Film and Theater in volume 4), directed by Stanley Kubrick (1928–1999), was a darkly humorous parody of the entire military, government, and nuclear-science establishment. In his portrayals of idiotic military and political leaders, Kubrick pointed out the absurdity of atomic weapons. The film *Fail-Safe,* from 1964, was a more serious take on the same subject. It told the story of American bombers mistakenly sent to bomb the Soviet Union with no way to recall them. In 1983, the made-for-television film *The Day After* created quite a controversy in its depiction of the nuclear bombing of a Midwestern city and the efforts of the survivors to struggle through the aftermath. Coming during a time of increased activism against nuclear weapons in the early 1980s, *The Day After* reminded people that nuclear war was still a very real threat.

Although the Cold War ended with the collapse of the Soviet Union in 1991, the threat of the bomb has not gone away. As of the early twenty-first century, eight nations were in verified possession of nuclear weapons, while others, such as Israel and Iran, were widely suspected of maintaining atomic armament programs. By the turn of the twenty-first century—especially in the aftermath of the **September 11, 2001, terrorist attacks** (see entry under 2000s—The Way We Lived in volume 6) on the World Trade Center in New York City and the Pentagon in Washington, D.C.—the nuclear threat now seems to lie less with full-scale nuclear attack than with a single bomb unleashed by a terrorist group or an unstable nation. Until humanity achieves the complete dismantling of all nuclear weapons, living with the bomb will continue to be a part of everyday life.

Timothy Berg

For More Information

Boyer, Paul. *By the Bomb's Early Light: American Thought and Culture at the Dawn of the Atomic Age.* New York: Pantheon, 1985.

Crowley, Michael, and Eric Adams. "Can Terrorists Build the Bomb? It's the Ultimate Nightmare: A Nuclear Attack in the U.S. Masterminded by Terrorists. Here's How That Could Happen—And How We Can Prevent It." *Popular Science* (February 1, 2005): 58.

Frank, Pat. *Alas, Babylon.* New York: Bantam, 1959.

Harris, William, Craig Freudenrich, and John Fuller. "How Nuclear Bombs Work." *How Stuff Works.* http://www.howstuffworks.com/nuclear-bomb.htm (accessed July 24, 2011).

Karpin, Michael. *The Bomb in the Basement: How Israel Went Nuclear and What That Means for the World.* New York: Simon & Schuster, 2006.

Powaski, Ronald E. *March to Armageddon: The United States and the Nuclear Arms Race, 1939 to the Present.* New York: Oxford University Press, 1987.

Reed, Thomas C., and Danny B. Stillman. *The Nuclear Express: A Political History of the Bomb and Its Proliferation.* Minneapolis: Zenith, 2009.

Seddon, Tom. *Atom Bomb.* New York: Scientific American Books for Young Readers, 1995.

Shute, Nevil. *On the Beach.* New York: William Morrow, 1957.

Whitfield, Stephen J. *The Culture of the Cold War.* 2nd ed. Baltimore: Johns Hopkins University Press, 1996.

Younger, Stephen M. *The Bomb: A New History.* New York: Ecco Press, 2009.

Cold War

The tension between the democratic and the communist countries, called the Cold War, dominated American political and cultural life between 1945 and 1991. World War II (1939–45) left only two major superpowers standing: the United States and the Soviet Union. Although they had been allies in World War II, the countries had very different political systems. Each sought to dominate the postwar world. This struggle divided the world into two major groups: democratic nations led by the United States and communist nations led by the Soviet Union. Rather than existing peacefully, with each side content to operate under its own system of government, both the United States and the Soviet Union felt threatened by one another. The United States desired as many free trading partners as possible to keep the U.S. capitalist system expanding. The Soviet Union believed in the communist system, under which the state controls the economy and production methods and owns all property. Furthermore, the Soviet Union believed that capitalism, an evil system from its perspective, was doomed to fail. The Soviet Union sought to speed up that process by encouraging more nations to become communist.

Because both the Americans and the Soviets had the atomic **bomb** (see entry under 1940s—The Way We Lived in volume 3) after 1949, they did not want to fight a "hot" war against each other for fear of destroying the world. Not wanting to destroy humanity, they engaged in a "cold" war. Rather than fighting each other directly, they fought through other, smaller nations, as they did in the Korean War (1950–53) and Vietnam War (1954–75). They also threatened each other in a high-stakes game of bluffing (as in the Berlin Airlift of 1948, the Cuban Missile Crisis of 1962, and other smaller standoffs). Both sides made sure the other feared utter destruction if direct military conflict broke out. This process continued until the collapse of the Soviet Union in 1991.

The Cold War had a profound influence on American culture. Its influence colored many novels, films, **television** (see entry under 1940s—TV and Radio in volume 3) programs. Readers learned of the horrors of nuclear war in *Alas Babylon* (1959) by Pat Frank (1907–1964); of communist brainwashing in *The Manchurian Candidate* by Richard Condon (1915–1996); and of political intrigue in *Advice and Consent* by Allen Drury (1918–1998). In the 1940s, **Hollywood** (see entry under 1930s—Film and Theater in volume 2) had produced a few films that celebrated the wartime alliance between the United States and the Soviet Union. As animosity between the countries grew during the Cold War, new films highlighting the Soviets as a "Red Menace" were released ("Red" is a nickname for communist). These films include *I Married a Communist* (1950) and *Invasion U.S.A.* (1952).

In the 1960s, the film *Fail-Safe* (1964) imagined a computer glitch sending American planes to bomb Moscow, the Soviet capital. That same year, ***Dr. Strangelove*** (see entry under 1960s—Film and Theater in volume 4), directed by Stanley Kubrick (1928–1999), used a plot similar to *Fail-Safe* to satirize American obsession with the Cold War. The film's final image shows actor Slim Pickens (1919–1983) riding a falling atomic bomb as if it was a bucking bronco, hooting, hollering, and waving his hat as he fell to earth. The communist threat proved a popular topic well into the 1980s. *Rambo: First Blood Part II* (1985) tells the story of a man who goes back to Vietnam to rescue American prisoners of war held by the communist North Vietnamese. *Red Dawn,* a 1984 film about a Soviet invasion of the United States, focuses on a group of teenagers who fight against the Soviets. The Cold War also spurred interest in spy novels and films. British spy character James Bond, created by Sir Ian Fleming (1908–1964), proved a big hit at the box office in films such as *From Russia with Love* (1963). Other spy films followed, including *The Ipcress File* (1965) and *The Spy Who Came in from the Cold* (1965). Television also reflected the Cold War in such shows as *I Spy,* costarring **Bill Cosby** (1937–; see entry under 1980s—TV and Radio in volume 5) and Robert Culp (1930–2010). *The Man From U.N.C.L.E,* a spoof of **James Bond films** (see entry under 1960s—Film and Theater in volume 4), enjoyed some popularity in the mid-1960s. *Get Smart* was a humorous take on the Cold War with a bumbling spy played by Don Adams (1926–2005).

The Cold War also invaded family and school life. The threat of nuclear war spurred many people to build bomb shelters in their yards. These concrete shelters, about the size of small school buses, were buried in the yard with only a small air vent and an entry tunnel showing above ground. Inside, they contained sleeping cots, canned food, water, and other emergency supplies. School children were taught how to protect themselves against a nuclear attack. In the film *Duck and Cover,* a cartoon character named Bert the Turtle instructed kids to "duck and cover," much like a turtle does, in the case of a nuclear explosion. Children went through duck-and-cover drills at school. At the sound of a siren, they would have to duck and cover under their desks.

Looking back at this time period, some of the hysteria over the Cold War in popular culture might seem a little crazy, but the fear of communism and nuclear conflict that was at the heart of the Cold War was something that many people took very seriously. The fear that often gripped the nation was at its worst in the late 1940s and 1950s, but it only dissipated completely when the Soviet Union dissolved in 1991.

Timothy Berg

For More Information

Barrass, Gordon S. *The Great Cold War: A Journey Through the Hall of Mirrors.* Stanford, CA: Stanford University Press, 2009.

Barson, Michael. *"Better Dead Than Red": A Nostalgic Look at the Golden ears of Russiaphobia, Red-Baiting, and Other Commie Madness.* New York: Hyperion, 1992.

Brands, H. W. *The Devil We Knew: Americans and the Cold War.* New York: Oxford University Press, 1993.

"The Cold War and Red Scare in Washington State." *Center for the Study of the Pacific Northwest.* http://www.washington.edu/uwired/outreach/cspn/Website/Classroom%20Materials/Curriculum%20Packets/Cold%20War%20&%20Red%20Scare/Cold%20War%20and%20Red%20Scare.html (accessed July 24, 2011).

"Cold War." *BBC History.* http://www.bbc.co.uk/history/worldwars/coldwar/ (accessed July 24, 2011).

Cold War Museum. http://www.coldwar.org/ (accessed July 24, 2011).

Dickstein, Morris. *Gates of Eden: American Culture in the Sixties.* Rev. ed. New York: Penguin Books, 1989.

Henriksen, Margot A. *Dr. Strangelove's America: Society and Culture in the Atomic Age.* Berkeley: University of California Press, 1997.

Mann, James. *The Rebellion of Ronald Reagan: A History of the End of the Cold War.* New York: Viking, 2009.

May, Elaine Tyler. *Homeward Bound: American Families in the Cold War Era.* Rev. ed. New York: Basic Books, 2008.

Whitfield, Stephen J. *The Culture of the Cold War.* Baltimore: Johns Hopkins University Press, 1991.

Federal Bureau of Investigation

J. Edgar Hoover, pictured here in 1948, served as director of the Federal Bureau of Investigation (FBI) from 1924 to 1972. © BETTMANN/CORBIS.

In 1908, Charles Bonaparte (1851–1921), the attorney general for President Theodore Roosevelt (1858–1919), founded the Bureau of Investigation. (It was renamed the United States Bureau of Investigation in 1932 before it wound up as the Federal Bureau of Investigation [FBI] in 1935.) The organization's aim was to investigate federal crimes for the Department of Justice with a small force of federal agents. J. Edgar Hoover (1895–1972), director of the FBI from 1924 until his death in 1972, created the FBI's most enduring image as a bureau of dedicated sleuths.

The FBI enjoyed a series of high-profile successes in its early years, nabbing such famous criminals as "Machine Gun" Kelly (1895–1954) and "Pretty Boy" Floyd (1904–1934) in the early 1930s. In 1934, after a year-long manhunt, the FBI found and killed notorious bank robber John Dillinger (1903–1934). During the late 1930s and 1940s, as World War II (1939–1945) erupted in Europe and spread, the FBI's mission was broadened to include investigations into potential communist or fascist threats within the United States. The FBI successfully uncovered two German spy rings in the United States during this time.

After World War II, the U.S. government's concern about the threat posed by the Soviet Union and communism led to a great expansion of the FBI's investigations. Under Hoover's direction, FBI agents developed extensive, secret files about a wide range of public figures. Some of the information the agents gathered was collected through illegal means; however, because the FBI had so much personal, potentially embarrassing information about so many people, few were willing to challenge Hoover or his methods.

The FBI's crime-fighting prowess inspired fictional characters and adventures in multiple media. The first comic strip about an FBI hero was *Secret Agent X-9* (1934), created by **detective fiction** (see entry under 1930s—Print Culture in volume 2) writer Dashiell Hammett (1894–1961). **Pulp magazines** (see entry under 1930s—Print Culture in volume 2) of the era were soon full of exciting (and often quite unlikely) FBI agent adventure stories.

The bureau's hard-nosed government men (nicknamed G-men) were first featured in film as heroes in *G-Men* (1935), starring **James Cagney** (1899–1986; see entry under 1930s—Film and Theater in volume 3). Other FBI movies soon followed, including *Public Hero Number One* (1935), *Let 'em Have It* (1935), and *Public Enemy's Wife* (1936).

The FBI's counterintelligence role in World War II added to the bureau's popular legend. Films like *Confessions of a Nazi Spy* (1939) and radio shows such as *The FBI in Peace and War* (1944–58) glamorized the hunt for Nazi agents in the United States. The FBI's active contributions to the anticommunist purges of the 1950s were fictionalized in such radio series as *I Was a Communist for the FBI* (1952–53). Hoover's own nonfiction book, *Masters of Deceit* (1958), helped define the FBI in American popular culture at the time. In the book, Hoover deftly creates a picture of the world as a terrifying place (filled with dangerous communists) from which only G-men can protect America.

From the beginning of fictional depictions of G-men in comics, **radio** (see entry under 1920s—TV and Radio in volume 2), **television** (see entry under 1940s—TV and Radio in volume 3), and film, the FBI had a strong hand in shaping the characters and the stories. One of the most popular fictional FBI agents was Chip Hardesty, created for the film *The FBI Story* in 1959. Starring Jimmy Stewart (1908–1997) as Hardesty, the film traces Hardesty's four-decade-long career with the FBI, which involves him in many of the bureau's most famous cases. The bureau had substantial input into the film, and even more in the TV series *The FBI,* which ran from 1965 to 1973. Each script required FBI approval before filming.

The FBI has continued to be featured in print, television, and films into the twenty-first century. The film *Mississippi Burning* (1988) dramatized (inaccurately, some critics claimed) the bureau's hunt for the murderers of three civil rights workers in 1964. *The Silence of the Lambs* (1991) won several Academy Awards for its story of a female FBI agent (Jodie Foster, 1962–) in search of a serial killer and prompted a surge in FBI applications by women. In the 1990s, TV series such as *Twin Peaks* (1990–91) and *The X-Files* (1993–2002) featured FBI agents working to investigate paranormal happenings. TV series in the early 2000s such as *Without a Trace* (2002–09) featured FBI agents working in a missing persons unit, while *Criminal Minds* (2005–) focused on FBI profilers and their cases. In 2011, Hoover was the subject of a controversial biographical film, *J. Edgar,* directed by Clint Eastwood (1930–). The film, starring Leonardo DiCaprio (1974–) in the title role, explores persistent rumors that the former FBI director was homosexual.

Justin Gustainis

For More Information

Charles, Douglas M. *J. Edgar Hoover and the Anti-interventionists: FBI Political Surveillance and the Rise of the Domestic Security State 1939–1945.* Columbus: Ohio State University Press, 2007.

Federal Bureau of Investigation. http://www.FBI.gov (accessed July 24, 2011).

Grabianowski, Frank. "How the FBI Works." *How Stuff Works.* http://people.howstuffworks.com/fbi.htm (accessed July 24, 2011).

Jeffreys-Jones, Rhodri. *The FBI: A History.* New Haven, CT: Yale University Press, 2007.

Kelly, Jack. "'The Most Dangerous Institution': For Nearly a Hundred Years, the FBI Has Been Fighting for America—with Its Discipline and at Odds with Its Shadowy, Extralegal Tactics." *American Heritage* (August-September 2002): 30.

Kessler, Ronald. *The Bureau: The Secret History of the FBI.* New York: St. Martin's Press, 2002.

Powers, Richard Gid. *G-Men: Hoover's FBI in American Popular Culture.* Carbondale: Southern Illinois University Press, 1983.

Theoharis, Athan G., Tony G. Poveda, Susan Rosenfield, and Richard Gid Powers. *The FBI: A Comprehensive Reference Guide.* New York: Oryx Press, 1999.

Hot Rods

A hot rod is a factory-made automobile that has been remodeled to make it faster, flashier, and more interesting. Ever since cars were first mass produced, car owners have altered their cars to put their own personal mark on their vehicle. Even Henry Ford (1863–1947) himself, who produced the first factory-made cars, modified his own **Model T** (see entry under 1900s—Commerce in volume 1), making it lighter and faster for racing.

The term hot rod may have been a shortened version of "hot roadster," as sporty roadsters were among the first cars to be cut down and souped up for racing in the 1930s. Young men of the Depression era (1929–41) could not afford new cars. Those who wanted flashy, fast cars had to make them from the bodies of old cars that could be purchased cheaply. After World War II (1939–45), many young soldiers returned

A fancy paint job adds to the allure of a hot rod. © CAR CULTURE COLLECTION/GETTY IMAGES.

from battle with new mechanical skills and an urge for adventure. Hot rod culture began to take root, especially in southern California, where miles of dry lake beds outside Los Angeles provided room to race the fast cars. Mechanics like Lee Chapel and George Wright opened "speed shops." In these shops, they created their works of art, hot rods that were meant to race not in circles on a track, but in long, straight-lines sprints called "drag races."

Soon, wild young hot rodders did not bother heading for dry lakes but instead gathered to race on the streets of the city, prompting Los Angeles newspapers to start a campaign against the "hot rod menace." The Southern California Timing Association, which had formed in 1938 to help regulate hot rod races, tried to calm the conflict over hot rodding. In 1948, the association held a big hot rod show in Los Angeles to demonstrate that hot rods were not just for hoodlums. That same year *Hot Rod* magazine was published for the first time. Its editor, Wally Parks (1913–2007), started the National Hot Rod Association in 1951. Hot rodding had always been a social activity. Dozens of hot rod clubs, with names like Outriders and Night Flyers, formed around the country.

The 1970s saw a different era in hot rodding as creative mechanics began to create "street rods." Street rods are cars with vintage bodies, but they also contain modern engines and many modern features, such as air conditioning and **compact disc** (see entry under 1980s—Music in volume 5) players. In the late 1990s, the Chrysler Corporation took the phenomenon a step further by marketing a factory-made street rod, the PT Cruiser, a modern car with a sporty but retro design (a retro design is in the style of an earlier time). A convertible version was introduced in 2005, though production of the PT Cruiser ended in 2010 after selling nearly 1.4 million cars. Hot rod shows were revived in the early 2000s, with major events being held in cities like Las Vegas.

Tina Gianoulis

For More Information

"Chrysler Parks Its Retro Cruiser after a Decade." *Automotive News* (July 12, 2010): 26.

Ganahl, Pat. "The Emergence of the Hot Rod." *Hot Rod* (January 1998): 130–36.

Ganahl, Pat. *Hot Rods and Cool Customs.* New York: Abbeville Press, 1995.

Hot Rod (40th anniversary edition; January 1988).

Hot Rods Magazine. http://www.hotrod.com/index.html (accessed July 24, 2011).

Hot Rods Online. http://www.hotrodsonline.com/ (accessed July 24, 2011).

Schuette, Sarah L. *Hot Rods*. Mankata, MN: Capstone Press, 2007.

Yates, Brock. "Hot Rods Redux: Hot Rods as Folk Art." *American Heritage* (July 1999): 68–76.

Las Vegas

Las Vegas, located in southwestern Nevada, is the gambling capital—the place most gamblers dream of visiting—of the United States. Surrounded by a combination of mountains and desert, it is a city of glitz, neon-lit streets, and luxurious casinos that attract visitors to wager their money and, perhaps, if luck shines on them, win huge jackpots.

Las Vegas was established by a land grant in 1835. The area originally was called Nuestra Señora de los Dolores de Las Vegas Grandes (Our Lady of the Sorrows of the Great Meadows). The name was eventually shortened to Las Vegas (The Meadows). The area soon was charted by explorer John C. Frémont (1813–1890). Las Vegas became a trading post along the Santa Fe Trail. The Mormons also colonized it. Just after the turn of the twentieth century, Las Vegas was a small watering hole with several hotels and stores, a saloon, and a few thousand residents.

Most of Las Vegas's development before World War II (1939–45) came about in the early 1930s, in conjunction with construction of the Boulder Dam, located 40 miles away on the Nevada-Arizona border, and the legalization of gambling throughout most of Nevada. However, by 1941, only a handful of casinos and hotels had been constructed in the city. Then, with the opening of two hotels—the El Rancho, a 63-room resort, in 1941, and the Hotel Last Frontier, a 107-room facility, the following year—came the birth of what today is known as the Las Vegas Strip.

New York mobster Benjamin "Bugsy" Siegel (1906–1947) sensed that Las Vegas was an untapped source of riches for organized crime. In 1946, just after the end of the war, he oversaw construction of the Flamingo, an extravagant gambling house-nightspot-hotel that ushered in the city's modern era. Other lavish casinos followed, including the Thunderbird, the Sahara, the Sands, the Dunes, the Desert Inn, and the Riviera. The casinos sported mammoth swimming pools, thousands of rooms, gaudy decor, and nightclubs that spotlighted the era's top entertainers. Mobsters ruled the town through the 1950s, with millions of illegitimately acquired dollars pouring through Las Vegas. The Federal Bureau of Investigation (FBI) (see entry under 1940s—The Way We Lived in volume 3) eventually began cracking down on the gangsters who were most openly operating the casinos.

In 1966 the legendary, eccentric aviation pioneer Howard Hughes (1905–1976) moved into the fifteenth-floor penthouse of the Desert Inn. The following year, he purchased the hotel for $14 million and also bought several other hotels and casinos, the city's airport, and additional prime real estate. A reputable businessman finally controlled much of Las Vegas. Eventually, the city's image became more corporate and more positive. In 1971, Hilton became the first hotel chain to open a branch in Las Vegas. Others followed; the most impressive among them being the massive MGM Grand.

In 2002, Las Vegas contained over thirty-five thousand hotel rooms. Thirty million people visited the city each year. Though the city suffered during the early twenty-first century economic downturn, more than thirty-seven million visitors came to Las Vegas in 2010. The Nevada Gaming Commission and the FBI watch over Las Vegas's gambling operation. According to those agencies, little, if any, mob involvement remains.

Rob Edelman

For More Information

Balboni, Alan Richard. *Beyond the Mafia: Italian Americans and the Development of Las Vegas.* Reno: University of Nevada Press, 1996.

Berman, Susan. *Lady Las Vegas: The Inside Story Behind America's Neon Oasis.* New York: TV Books, 1996.

Gragg, Larry. "Las Vegas: Who Built America's Playground?" *History Today* (February 2007): 51.

Land, Barbara, and Myrick Land. *A Short History of Las Vegas.* 2nd ed. Reno: University of Nevada Press, 2004.

Las Vegas Convention and Visitors Authority. http://www.visitlasvegas.com/ (accessed July 24, 2011).

McCracken, Robert D. *Las Vegas: The Great American Playground.* Reno: University of Nevada Press, 1997.

Official City of Las Vegas Web Site. http://www.lasvegasnevada.gov/ (accessed July 24, 2011).

Official Site for Las Vegas Meetings and Travel Professionals. http://www.lvcva.com/index.jsp (accessed July 24, 2011).

Levittown

Levittown was the first successful large-scale suburban housing development in the United States. **Suburbs** (see entry under 1950s—The Way We Lived in volume 3) existed to some extent in the 1800s, but they were mostly for rich people. When it opened in 1948 on Long Island outside New York City, Levittown brought suburban living to ordinary middle- and working-class Americans.

When World War II (1939–45) ended, the U.S. economy was booming. The **Great Depression** (1929–41; see entry under 1930s—The Way We Lived in volume 2) was over, and people looked forward to plentiful jobs and good times. Millions of people, many just returned from the war, wanted to start a new life. Many were tired of living in cramped city apartments. They wanted fresh air, grass, and safe places for their kids to play. Housing developers William Levitt (1907–1994) and his brother

The Levitt family outside their Levittown home on Long Island, New York, in 1950.
© BERNARD HOFFMAN/TIME LIFE PICTURES/GETTY IMAGES.

Alfred recognized these needs and came up with a new way to meet them. In 1946, they purchased fifteen hundred acres of potato fields in Nassau County, Long Island, and built six thousand small houses there. By 1951, over fifteen thousand houses had been built. The key to their success was in their production methods. They applied the assembly-line process, pioneered by car-maker Henry Ford (1863–1947), to house building. Teams of workers moved from one house site to the next performing the same task over and over. One team prepared the site and laid a concrete foundation. The next team put up prefabricated walls. Another team put in plumbing fixtures, another did the electrical work, and so on, until everything was done and the house was ready. This system was possible because all the Levitt houses were largely the same. At one point, Levitt's teams were starting and finishing 150 houses a day.

This new neighborhood, called Levittown, was immediately successful. The homes were inexpensive, and they quickly filled up with young couples and their children. Although critics complained of the dull sameness of Levittown, people liked having their own homes in a friendly neighborhood. Kids loved that there were always other playmates nearby. Although Levittown was immensely successful, its importance lies in its prominence as a model copied by builders across the United States. The modern suburb, and much of modern America, owes a great deal to the example of Levittown.

Timothy Berg

For More Information

Boulton, Alexander O. "The Buy of the Century." *American Heritage* (July-August 1993): 62.

Gans, Herbert. *The Levittowners: Ways of Life and Politics in a Suburban Community.* New York: Pantheon Books, 1967.

Jackson, Kenneth T. *Crabgrass Frontier: The Suburbanization of the United States.* New York: Oxford University Press, 1985.

Levittown Historical Society. http://www.levittownhistoricalsociety.org/index.html (accessed July 23, 2011).

Wagner, Richard, and Amy Duckett Wagner. *Levittown.* Mount Pleasant, SC: Arcadia, 2010.

Spring Break

The end of the winter has long been an occasion for celebration in many different cultures around the world. Purim, Passover, Mardi Gras, and Easter are all ancient celebrations that replaced even more ancient celebrations of the renewal of life, warmth, and growth that comes with spring. The week-long spring break from school has become a modern tradition, beloved by some, dreaded by others.

Spring vacation gives students a break from the tensions of schoolwork, but the warm weather also seems to bring with it an irresistible urge to party. For college students especially, spring break has become a sort of coming-of-age ritual. At the threshold of adulthood, but not quite there, hundreds of thousands of college students each year head to warm beaches or skiing hot spots for a week of fun—the wilder the better. Drunkenness, casual sex, and vandalism are frequently a part of the spring break "scene" in cities like Panama City, Florida, and Cancún, Mexico.

The tradition of celebrating spring break by heading south for a good time with other vacationing students began in 1936. The swim coach at Colgate University in Hamilton, New York, took the college swim team to train in Fort Lauderdale, Florida. During the following years the students kept coming back, and the tradition spread. By 1953, 15,000 students were filling the hotels and beaches of Fort Lauderdale; by 1985, the number had grown to 350,000. The 1980s were the peak period for wild spring break parties, when resort destinations like Daytona Beach, Florida, and South Padre Island, Texas, were crammed with vacationing students. Since then, many cities have taken measures to reduce and control crowds. Even students themselves have looked for alternatives to the party scene. Many join organized programs to fill their spring break doing charity work.

Novels and films have both documented and advertised the rise of spring break in the 1960s and its peak in the 1980s. The beach party films of the 1960s represent the lighthearted side of the phenomenon, as does the 1983 film *Spring Break*. The classic spring break story is told in *Where the Boys Are* by Glendon Swarthout (1918–1992). The 1958 novel about college students on vacation in Fort Lauderdale was made into a popular film in 1960 and again in 1984. Stories and films about spring break continued to be made into the twenty-first century, like the feature film *From Kelly to Justin* (2003) and the television movie *Spring Break Shark Attack* (2005).

Tina Gianoulis

For More Information

Mangan, Katherine S. "For Spring Break, Thousands of Students Are Volunteering in the Gulf Coast." *Chronicle of Higher Education* (March 17, 2006).

Marsh, Bill. "The Innocent Birth of the Spring Baccanal." *New York Times* (March 19, 2006): WK3.

Sheffield, Skip. "A Spring Break History." *Knight-Ridder/Tribune News Service* (March 24, 1994).

"Spring Break—And Not a Beer Bash in Sight: Student Volunteerism During Spring Break." *Business Week* (April 19, 1999): 4–6.

Waldrop, Judith. "Spring Break." *American Demographics* (March 1993): 52–55.

Williams, Alex. "Before Spring Break, The Anorexic Challenge." *New York Times* (April 2, 2006): ST1.

Teen Idols

Teen idols are an offshoot of mass-marketed twentieth-century popular culture. Most often, teen idols are movie and **television** (see entry under 1940s—TV and Radio in volume 3) actors or pop singers and singing groups. Adolescent heartthrobs may be teens themselves, but rarely are they far beyond their early- to mid-twenties. Some are traditionally handsome, but most are best described as "super-cute." Their fans are preteen and adolescent girls who scream and faint in their presence. For youngsters, the idol is a romanticized love-object. Teen idols are marketed and sold to their target audience, who are ever-eager to purchase their records, buy tickets to their movies and concerts, and own anything with their images plastered on it, from teen-oriented magazines to—late in the century—posters, **T-shirts** (see entry under 1910s—Fashion in volume 1), pins, and lunch boxes.

In the late 1920s, actor-singer Rudy Vallee (1901–1986) induced swoons (fainting and collapsing) among teen girls when he sang through a megaphone. However, the true pioneer among teen icons was **Frank Sinatra** (1915–1998; see entry under 1940s—Music in volume 3). Back in the mid-1940s, he serenaded his teen audiences with dreamy, romantic ballads. These girls were known as **bobbysoxers** (see entry under 1940s—Fashion in volume 3), after the type of

Teen idols Frankie Avalon (left) and Fabian relax beside the pool in between performing and fleeing screaming fans. © CORBIS.

socks that were then in style. They swooned over Sinatra, just as their mothers had over Vallee. The next set of teenagers, still wearing bobby socks, did the same when **Elvis Presley** (1935–1977; see entry under 1950s—Music in volume 3) performed, during the rise in popularity of **rock and roll** (see entry under 1950s—Music in volume 3) and the emergence of American teen culture in the mid-1950s. Presley's appeal was far more sexual than Sinatra's. Girls were attracted to his swiveling hips and curling lip, and his hit songs were as rowdy ("Hound Dog," "Jailhouse Rock") as they were romantic ("Love Me Tender"). Other late 1950s–early 1960s "pretty-boy" rock-and-roll teen idols included Frankie Avalon (1939–), Ricky Nelson (1940–1985), Fabian (1942–), and Bobby Rydell (1942–). Some, like Presley, had staying power. For most, though, the fame was relatively short-lived.

Across the decades, rock groups from New Kids on the Block to *NSYNC to Justin Bieber (1994–) have become teen idols. However, the **Beatles** (see entry under 1960s—Music in volume 4) have had the most enduring fame and cultural impact. Around 1964 and 1965, the burning questions among adolescent girls were which Beatle was the cutest and which was the most lovable. Furthermore, the moptop **hairstyle** (see entry under 1900s—The Way We Lived in volume 1) the band members wore became the driving force behind the mass acceptance of long hair as a male fashion statement. In this regard, the Beatles' influence on pop culture transcended their teen-idol status.

The 1960s and 1970s saw a generation of young TV stars emerge as real teen heartthrobs. Among them were Richard Chamberlain (1935–), who played *Dr. Kildare* (1961–66; see entry under 1960s—TV and Radio in volume 4); David Cassidy (1950–) of *The Partridge Family* (1970–74; see entry under 1970s—TV and Radio in volume 4); and John Travolta (1954–) of *Welcome Back, Kotter* (1975–79). Travolta cemented his teen-idol status when he appeared on screen as disco king Tony Manero in *Saturday Night Fever* (1977; see entry under 1970s— Film and Theater in volume 4). A decade earlier, **James Dean** (1931–1955; see entry under 1950s—Film and Theater in volume 3) became a teen icon while playing anxiety-ridden adolescents in *East of Eden* (1955) and *Rebel Without a Cause* (1955). In the 1990s, Leonardo DiCaprio (1974–), a young film actor and Academy Award nominee (for *What's Eating Gilbert Grape,* 1993), won teen heartthrob status in the wake of a single screen role: He played an heroic but ill-fated passenger aboard the ***Titanic*** (1997; see entry under 1910s—The Way We Lived in volume 1). With his starring role as Edward Cullen in the film adaptation of the popular ***Twilight*** (see entry under 2000s—Print Culture in volume 6) series of novels by Stephenie Meyer (1973–), Robert Pattinson (1986–) became a teen idol in the early 2000s, as did Daniel Radcliffe (1989–), who took on the titular role in the films based on the ***Harry Potter*** series (see entry under 2000s—Print Culture in volume 5) of books by J.K. Rowling (1965–). Additionally, teen idols may enter areas of show business other than the one that initiated their popularity. Handsome movie actor Tab Hunter (1931–), a 1950s teen icon, cut records, as did Chamberlain and Travolta, while musical performers from Sinatra and Presley onward starred on screen.

Rob Edelman

For More Information

Brown, Peter Harry, and Pat H. Broeske. *Down at the End of Lonely Street: The Life and Death of Elvis Presley.* New York: Dutton, 1997.

Caramanica, Jon. "Twilight of the Teen Idol." *New York Times* (February 20, 2011): 3.

Gilmore, John. *Live Fast—Die Young: Remembering the Short Life of James Dean.* New York: Thunder's Mouth Press, 1997.

Kelly, Sarah. *Teen Idols.* New York: Pocket Books, 2002.

MacDonald, Ian. *Revolution in the Head: The Beatles' Records and the Sixties.* 3rd ed. Chicago: Chicago Review Press, 2007.

Norman, Philip. *Shout! The Beatles in Their Generation.* Rev. ed. New York: Fireside/Simon & Schuster, 2006.

Teen Idols. http://teenidols.student.com/ (accessed July 24, 2011).

Teen Idols 4 You. http://www.teenidols4you.com/ (accessed July 24, 2011).

Zielbauer, Paul. "In Connecticut, Chasing Pop Stardom with Voice Lessons and Arm Curls." *New York Times* (February 14, 2002): B1.

UFOs

Unidentified flying objects (UFOs) have been noted by observers of the night sky since people first raised their eyes to gaze at the stars. However, the idea that these unidentified objects might be visitors from other planets originated with the age of science and technology that followed World War II (1939–45). The excitement and fear caused by this new technological age led to an exciting and frightening new belief: that there are intelligent beings on other planets who wish to communicate with us. Some view this idea as simple common sense, reasoning that in all the vastness of the universe, there must be other planets with beings similar to humankind. Others see the belief in life on other planets as superstitious nonsense with no scientific proof to back it up. These skeptics insist that UFOs can always be identified as military aircraft, research balloons, unusual weather phenomena, or simply as hoaxes, fabricated by their so-called observers.

One common response of those who believe in visitors from outer space has been fear of attack. In 1898, H. G. Wells (1866–1946) published his science-fiction work *The War of the Worlds* (see entry under 1930s—TV and Radio in volume 2), which was about an attack on Earth by aliens from Mars. When his work was broadcast as a radio play in 1938, it caused panic among many who heard it. Radio listeners believed it was a newscast about a real assault. Fears were heightened during the wartime 1940s, when UFO sightings began in earnest, as U.S. citizens were encouraged to scan the skies for enemy aircraft. Along with the usual airplanes and weather balloons, watchers began to report sightings of objects they could not identify or explain. New rocket technology developed during the war seemed to increase the possibility of space travel. The 1947 sightings of "flying saucers" over Mt. Rainier in the state of Washington and rumors of alien bodies recovered from a spaceship crash in Roswell, New Mexico, gave further support to the idea that human beings were not alone in the universe.

The **Cold War** (1945–91; see entry under 1940s—The Way We Lived in volume 3) years fostered the idea of hidden enemies. The number of UFO sightings reported continued to rise throughout the 1950s and 1960s. These sightings led to the creation of organizations for believers like the Unaris Educational Foundation and the Mutual UFO Network. The Mutual UFO Network still publishes a monthly journal and seeks volunteer UFO investigators.

Another element of the UFO phenomenon is the idea of alien abduction. There have been many books on the subject, notably *The Interrupted Journey* (1966) by John G. Fuller (1913–1990) and *Communion* (1987) by Whitley Strieber (1945–). These books tell the stories of those who say they have been kidnapped and experimented on by aliens. The mystery of UFOs continues to intrigue people worldwide.

Tina Gianoulis

For More Information

Evans, Hilary. *Coming from the Skies: Our Neighbors from Above.* Philadelphia: Chelsea House, 2001.

Extraterrestrial Contact—Scientific Study of the UFO Phenomenon. http://www.ufoevidence.org/ (accessed July 26, 2011).

Jastrow, Robert. "The Case for UFOs." *Science Digest* (November-December 1980): pp. 82–86.

Keen, Judy. "Probing Odds of Alien Visitors." *USA Today* (November 24, 2010): 3A.

Mansueto, Anthony. "Visions of Cosmopolis: Belief in UFOs." *Omni* (October 1994): pp. 64–71.

Mutual UFO Network. http://www.mufon.com (accessed July 26, 2011).

Netzley, Patricia D. *UFOs.* San Diego: Lucent Books, 2000.

Patton, Phil. "Something in the Sky." *Popular Mechanics* (March 2009): 54.

Randle, Kevin D. *Crash: When UFOs Fall from the Sky.* Franklin Lakes, NJ: New Page Books, 2010.

Reece, Gregory L. *UFO Religion: Inside Flying Saucer Cults and Culture.* London: I. B. Tauris, 2007.

1950s

Pop Culture in a Decade of Conformity

The 1950s are most often remembered as a quiet decade characterized by conformity, stability, and normalcy. After the tumult of the 1930s and 1940s, with their sustained economic depression (1929–41) and global conflict (1939–45), the 1950s did seem quiet. America was at peace once the conflict in Korea (1950–53) ended. The economy was booming, bringing millions of Americans into the middle class; politics were stable and the president, World War II hero Dwight D. Eisenhower (1890–1969), was beloved by many. For most Americans, the 1950s marked a return to normalcy after the crazy war years. Americans had children in record numbers, continuing a "baby boom" that had begun in the 1940s. They also moved to suburbs in record numbers, and the home construction industry boomed to meet their demand. Popular TV shows of the period like *Leave It to Beaver* (1957–63), *Father Knows Best* (1954–63), and *The Adventures of Ozzie and Harriet* (1952–56) all reflected back to America this calming sense of happy normalcy.

These signs of normalcy and quiet prosperity do not obscure the fact that the 1950s saw real social change and awakening—and a remarkable explosion of pop culture. America's population soared during

1950s At a Glance

WHAT WE SAID:

Beatnik: A person who was very cool, especially one who rejected mainstream values and lived a spontaneous, free-wheeling life. Also called beat.

Cat: A cool guy, used for years among jazz musicians.

Cherry: Used by hot rodders to express approval for a beautifully restored car. Looking at a souped-up Model A Ford, one might say "That A-bomb is cherry!"

Chick: A cool girl, used for years among jazz musicians.

Cool: A multipurpose word used to express approval of someone or something, cool has been used throughout American history but gained wide usage in the 1950s.

Cooties: An invisible curse carried by social outcasts. Preteen boys often worried that girls had cooties.

First base: Among teenagers, getting to first base meant kissing, with the terms "second base," "third base," and "going all the way" meaning ever greater sexual progress.

The fuzz: The police.

"Just the facts, ma'am": This expression became popular thanks to its usage by Sgt. Joe Friday on the popular TV show *Dragnet.*

Knuckle sandwich: A fist delivered to the mouth of an opponent in a fight: "How would you like a knuckle sandwich?"

Passion pit: A drive-in movie where teenagers would go to neck (make out) with their dates.

Square: Someone who was uncool.

Squaresville: One of several slang terms ending in "-ville," this one meant the place where uncool people— squares—came from.

Turf: The territory controlled by a youth gang.

WHAT WE READ:

Mickey Spillane adventure novels: Spillane's books featured the fast gun and romantic exploits of detective Mike Hammer. By mid-decade, seven of the ten best-selling novels in American history were written by Spillane.

The Betty Crocker Picture Cookbook **(1950):** Though it never reached #1 on the *New York Times* best-seller list, this popular cookbook was the single best-selling book of the decade.

From Here to Eternity **(1951):** James Jones's World War II book about life on an army base in Hawaii was filmed in 1953 as a popular movie starring Burt Lancaster, Montgomery Clift, Deborah Kerr, Donna Reed, and Frank Sinatra. The

the decade, from 150 million Americans in 1950 to over 178 million in 1960. School districts raced to build schools for the baby-boom students who were heading their way.

A compelling social and cultural force during the decade was the Cold War (1945–91), the name given to the long battle for supremacy between the United States and the Soviet Union. The Cold War book stayed on the *New York Times* best-seller list for twenty weeks and the movie won several Academy Awards, including Best Picture.

***The Caine Mutiny* (1951):** One of the longest-lasting best-sellers of all time, this war novel by Herman Wouk held its place on the *New York Times* list for 48 weeks. The book also won the Pulitzer Prize.

***The Power of Positive Thinking* (1952):** This inspirational self-help book by author Norman Vincent Peale holds the record for the longest reign as the #1 best-seller in America: it spent 98 weeks atop the *New York Times* list.

***Sexual Behavior in the Human Female* (1953):** Although the book was denounced as a threat to American morals, the follow-up to Alfred Kinsey's report on the sexual behavior of males became a best-seller.

***Playboy* (1953–):** The first mass-market men's magazine, founded in Chicago, Illinois, by Hugh Hefner, rocketed to popularity when it published nude pictures of rising movie star Marilyn Monroe. The magazine promoted the *Playboy* lifestyle of free sexuality and conspicuous consumption, and its nude Playmates became symbols of the sexy girl-next-door.

***Sports Illustrated* (1954–):** The first glossy weekly magazine about sports, this production of the Time-Life company soon became the most popular sports magazine of the century.

The magazine introduced the first swimsuit issue in 1964.

***Lolita* (1955):** This novel by Russian-born author Vladimir Nabokov remains one of the most notorious novels of the century. It tells the story of an aging man's love affair with a twelve-year-old girl in terms that were deemed obscene by four American publishers. The book was turned into a movie in 1962 and again in 1997.

***Peyton Place* (1956):** This sensational novel by Grace Metalious revealed the adultery, incest, murder, and petty infighting taking place in a small town in New England. The book was later made into a movie and a TV series, as well as sequels in print and on film.

***The Hidden Persuaders* (1957):** This book by journalist and social critic Vance Packard revealed the ways that the advertising and public relations industries manipulate people's opinions. It is credited with raising people's skepticism about the advertising images with which they were increasingly bombarded.

WHAT WE WATCHED:

***Texaco Star Theater* (1948–53):** This variety show became the most popular program on TV in the early 1950s thanks to the antics of Milton Berle, a comedian who often dressed up as a woman and became known as "Mr. Television" and "Uncle Miltie."

influenced all areas of American life. It encouraged Americans to improve the quality of public education, because they believed that their children needed to be better informed and more skilled to compete against the Soviet menace. American government and industry invested heavily in science and technology, in part because Americans believed that one way to win the Cold War was to develop more powerful bombs

1950s At a Glance (continued)

***The Ed Sullivan Show* (1948–71):** The most popular variety show of the 1950s and 1960s was hosted by the awkward Ed Sullivan, who acted as the perfect foil to guests that included the top celebrities of the day.

***I Love Lucy* (1951–57):** The first of several shows starring comedienne Lucille Ball, this sitcom depicted the zany antics of housewife Lucy Ricardo, her showman husband Ricky (Desi Arnaz), and their next-door neighbors Fred and Ethel Mertz (played by William Frawley and Vivian Vance).

***Bwana Devil* (1952):** Audiences wore colored glasses to see the startling effects of the first 3-D movie.

***Dragnet* (1952–59):** "Just the facts, ma'am," was all Los Angeles Police Department sergeant Joe Friday wanted in this classic and popular cop show starring Jack Webb.

***The $64,000 Question* (1955–58):** The most popular of the mid–1950s game shows had a featured contestant answer a series of questions leading up to the final, $64,000 question. This was one of several quiz shows that came under question by federal investigators who discovered that some of the programs were rigged.

***Gunsmoke* (1955–75):** The longest running Western drama on TV and the longest running prime-time TV show with continuing characters, *Gunsmoke* began as a radio drama in 1952 and was one of the nation's most beloved programs. The show, which starred James Arness as Marshal Matt Dillon, spawned several movies and a range of merchandise and toys.

***My Fair Lady* (1956):** The decade's most successful musical, in a decade when musicals packed theaters; it broke attendance records in New York City.

***The Ten Commandments* (1956):** The movie studios reacted to the popularity of television by producing spectacular epics such as this monumental Biblical story of the life of Moses. The sixth highest grossing film of all time (adjusted for inflation), *The Ten Commandments* has been shown annually on television for decades.

***Ben-Hur* (1959):** The most spectacular of all the religious epics, this film version of *Ben-Hur* starred Charlton Heston as the avenging Roman slave and featured a chariot race that took four months to rehearse and three months to produce.

***North by Northwest* (1959):** This Alfred Hitchcock-directed tale of suspense and mistaken identity starred Cary Grant and contained some of the most exciting scenes ever seen on screen.

***Some Like It Hot* (1959):** This comedy proved to the world that Marilyn Monroe was more than

and more sophisticated technology. Even the massive investments in the national highway system were justified for the speed with which they would allow military goods to flow in the case of nuclear attack.

The Cold War had its dark side as well. Simply put, people were paranoid. They feared that wild-eyed, godless communists (those who adhere to a system of government in which the state controls the economy just a sex symbol. Monroe teamed with co-stars Tony Curtis and Jack Lemmon in one of the most acclaimed film comedies of the century.

WHAT WE LISTENED TO:
"Goodnight Irene" (1950): One of the many hits by The Weavers, a folk-pop group that paved the way for the folk revival of the 1960s.

"How Much Is That Doggie in the Window?" (1953): Every decade has its novelty song, and for the 1950s it was this goofy hit by Patti Page, the best-selling female singer of the decade.

"Rock Around the Clock" (1955): Performed by Bill Haley and the Comets, this song became the first rock 'n' roll hit when it became the country's #1 single on July 9, 1955.

"Heartbreak Hotel" (1956): Elvis Presley had his first major hit with this song, and he topped the charts for two solid years with such songs as "Don't Be Cruel," "Jailhouse Rock," "Hound Dog," and "All Shook Up."

"My Prayer" (1956): The Platters became the first African American group to have a #1 hit with this 1956 song.

"Wake Up Little Suzie" (1957): This popular song by the Everly Brothers was banned in Boston, Massachusetts, because it contained lyrics then considered provocative.

"Venus" (1959): This corny love song by teen idol Frankie Avalon was typical of the softer, romantic pop songs of the late 1950s.

WHO WE KNEW:
Lucille Ball (1911–1989): This popular star of *I Love Lucy*—the leading sitcom of the 1950s—and several other situation comedies was the most ad-mired and beloved comedienne of the 1950s, and perhaps of the entire twentieth century.

Milton Berle (1908–2002): The man known as "Uncle Miltie" and "Mr. Television" be-came America's first television star thanks to his position as host of the popular variety show *The Texaco Star Theater*. Berle had a long career that included early work on the vaudeville stage, roles in movies, and a long career on television.

Dwight D. Eisenhower (1890–1969): This popular World War II hero became president in 1953, providing an air of comfortable stability that seemed well-suited to the decade. In politi-cal campaigns, Americans rallied around their favorite son with the slogan "We Like Ike."

Alan "Moondog" Freed (1921–1965): This pioneer of radio disc jockeying coined the phrase "rock 'n' roll" for the new kind of music he was playing on the Cleveland, Ohio, radio station WJW. Freed soon spun rock 'n' roll records at WINS in New York and became a national celebrity.

and production methods and owns all property) would invade their schools, marry their daughters, or—in their darkest nightmares—drop atomic bombs and turn the country into a nuclear wasteland. Bomb shelters were built in huge numbers. U.S. senator Joseph McCarthy (1909–1957) of Wisconsin led an anticommunist "witch hunt" that eventually led to blacklists in the movie industry.

1950s At a Glance (continued)

Jack Kerouac (1922–1969): A leading figure in the Beat movement (a literary movement that valued spontaneous expressions of feeling over order and form), Kerouac's novel *On the Road* (1957) captured the spirit of youths who longed to escape the conventional lives of their parents.

Joseph McCarthy (1909–1957): The most famous communist hunter of the 1950s, this U.S. senator from Wisconsin led the charge to search out communist influences in the American government and became a symbol of American extremism. His witch-hunting tactics and careless ruining of reputations resulted in the term "McCarthyism."

Edward R. Murrow (1908–1965): Credited with virtually inventing modern radio and television news, Murrow began his career with radio reports of the coming of World War II in Europe. He went on to set the standard for television news coverage with his programs *See It Now* (1951–58) and his news coverage for CBS. Murrow won the respect of the world when he publicly challenged the fervent communist-hunting tactics of U.S. senator Joseph McCarthy.

Ethel and Julius Rosenberg (1915–1953; 1918–1953): This quiet couple became a Cold War symbol when they were convicted and executed for conspiracy to commit treason after they passed secret documents concerning the American atomic bomb tests to contacts in the Soviet Union. Their execution sparked protests around the world.

Jonas Salk (1914–1995): This research scientist gained international acclaim as a medical hero following his development of a vaccine against the crippling disease polio in 1955.

Against this conflicting backdrop of contented normalcy and debilitating fears, new forms of popular culture flowered. Topping the list was the birth of rock and roll, a new form of music that combined black and white musical forms into a powerful new kind of music that thrilled American youth. Elvis Presley (1935–1977) was the king of rock 'n' roll, but there were also a dozen princes—including Chuck Berry (1926–), Little Richard (1932–), Jerry Lee Lewis (1935–), and many others. Their music blared from the radios of hot rod cars parked at drive-in diners throughout America.

Television came into its own in the 1950s. Millions of Americans purchased TV sets and the big three networks—ABC, CBS, and NBC—produced a wealth of new programming, including situation comedies, westerns, variety shows, and dramas. Among the most popular shows were *Gunsmoke* (1955–75), *Wagon Train* (1957–65), *Have Gun Will Travel* (1957–63), *Make Room for Daddy* (retitled *The Danny Thomas Show* in 1957; ran 1953–65), *Father Knows Best* (1954–63), and

77 Sunset Strip (1958–64). The movie industry had to adjust to the fact that many Americans now sought their entertainment at home, so they produced bigger, more spectacular, and more exciting films than before. With TV producing wholesome family entertainment, the film industry could devote some of its energies to producing racier fare for adults.

The popularity of sports also boomed in the 1950s, helped along by the widespread broadcast of sports on TV. The New York Yankees' decade-long dominance of professional baseball was the big story, followed closely by the increasing integration (blacks were no longer banned) in baseball and other sports. Professional football finally outstripped college football in popularity. Professional basketball experienced growing audiences. America's sports craziness was further encouraged by the country's first sports weekly, *Sports Illustrated*. No quick survey can do justice to the variety and energy of 1950s popular culture.

1950s

Commerce

The American economy, having fully recovered from World War II (1939–45), experienced booming business in the 1950s. With a gross national product (also called the GNP; the sum of the value of goods and services produced in the country) of $284.6 billion, the United States was by far the largest economy in the world. By the end of the decade, the GNP stood at $482.7 billion. Government, businesses, and unions worked together to keep the economy humming, but perhaps the biggest force in the economy during the decade was the consumer.

With more disposable income than ever before, American consumers bought a widening array of goods that gave them the highest standard of living in the world. The ability of American companies to produce a dizzying variety of goods, coupled with the availability of disposable income, created what is called a "consumer society" or "consumer culture." This is a culture where consuming and acquiring goods becomes a marker of social status and a way of creating meaning in people's lives. Though the roots of American consumerismlie earlier in the century, the 1950s was the decade when America truly became a consumptive culture.

There were a number of exciting new products to buy in the 1950s. American automakers produced new, flashy models of cars; among the most popular were the Chevrolet Corvette and the Ford Thunderbird.

A German automaker, Volkswagen, began to market a strange new vehicle called the Beetle, a fuel-efficient car that became very popular in the 1960s. Timex introduced a wristwatch that could "take a licking and keep on ticking." Saran Wrap preserved food in refrigerators across the country. One of the most famous products of the decade was the Barbie doll, introduced in 1959. Each of these products and many more were backed by advertising campaigns that saturated magazines, radio, and television. Advertising grew increasingly important as a way to guide consumption in America.

The 1950s also saw changes in the way Americans purchased goods. One of the most striking innovations in retail shopping was the emergence of the mall. By collecting a variety of specialty shops in one concentrated shopping area, malls changed the landscapes of American cities and the shopping habits of American consumers. Another important factor was the credit card, which was invented in 1950. The ease with which consumers could purchase goods at nearly any store fueled the economy of the United States from that moment on, and was a fundamental part of the growth of the American consumer culture.

Barbie

The Barbie doll is the best selling fashion doll of all time. By 1998, Mattel Inc., the producer of the doll, estimated that the average American girl between the ages of three and eleven owned ten Barbie dolls. More than just a toy, the Barbie doll has become an American cultural icon (a symbol of American culture).

The Barbie doll's status as an icon stems from its use as a model for young girls' real-life hopes and dreams for their own adult lives. Debates rage over whether or not the doll is an appropriate role model for girls in discussions about women's relationship to fashion, their independence in the workplace, their interactions with men, and their body image. The doll has been made fun of by musicians and comedians and criticized by feminist scholars. Despite such controversy, children throughout America and the world have embraced the doll enthusiastically.

The Barbie doll's creator, Ruth Handler (1916–2002), developed the doll after noticing her daughter, Barbara, creating imaginative teenage and adult lives for her paper dolls. Backed by Mattel, the successful toy company Ruth ran with her husband Elliot, Ruth introduced the first Barbie doll at the 1959 New York Toy Fair. It was the first American doll sold as a "teenage fashion model."

The emphasis on fashion and the "age" of the doll were unique to the toy world at the time. The Barbie doll celebrated high fashion and offered young girls an opportunity to participate in the emerging world of design that was being covered by women's magazines. Mattel offered finely sewn outfits that copied the most desirable fashions of the time. Unlike baby dolls, the 11½-inch Barbie doll had full breasts, a tiny waist, and curvy hips. The fashionable outfits draped beautifully over the doll's curves, but some critics worried that young girls who played with the doll would develop unrealistic ideas about how their own bodies should look. The controversy over this issue has not faded over the more than fifty years of the doll's history.

While the teenage fashion model identity of the Barbie doll remains, the doll has also been marketed as an adult capable of pursuing a career. Introduced during a period when most women stayed home to raise families, Mattel offered glamorous wedding dresses for the Barbie doll, but it also created dolls and accessories that allowed young girls to imagine an adult life separate from raising a family. In the 1960s, children could dress Barbie as a doctor, a nurse, and an airline flight attendant. Within a decade of the doll's introduction, the career costumes available for it multiplied rapidly, faster at first than actual opportunities for women did. When the first men walked in space in 1965, Mattel introduced Barbie Astronaut, long before women were able to join the U.S. space program. The Barbie doll could also be a surgeon (1973); an Olympic athlete (1975); a United Nations International Children's Emergency Fund (UNICEF) ambassador (1989); an army, air force, navy, or marine corps recruit (1989, 1990, 1991, 1992); a police officer (1993); a paleontologist (1997); a presidential candidate (2000); and a veterinarian (2005), to name a few.

Barbie, as she looked in 1959 and on her 50th birthday.
© MAURICIO GAMBARINI/EPA/ CORBIS.

The pink aisle in most toy stores provides an immediate example of the choices a Barbie doll offers children to play out their individual fantasies. Although sometimes criticized for promoting excessive purchasing, the Barbie doll and its many accessories offer more choices for children than does any other toy on the market.

Though the first Barbie dolls were all Caucasian, by the early 1980s, the Barbie doll was also offered in a growing variety of ethnicities, beginning with black and Hispanic Barbie dolls. The Dolls of the World Collection included dolls from over fifty countries by 2001 and 140 different Barbies by 2011.

While some critics wish to blame the Barbie doll for encouraging young girls to dislike their own physical attributes, to obsess about making themselves appealing to men, or to shop excessively, others see the doll as a blank slate on which children can create their own realities. For many, the Barbie doll dramatizes the conflicting but abundant possibilities for women. Perhaps because there are so many opportunities for American women at the end of the twentieth century, the Barbie doll—fueled by Mattel's "Be Anything" campaign—continues to be popular. Mattel sold the doll in more than 150 countries by the end of the twentieth century. According to Mattel, two Barbie dolls are sold worldwide every second.

Sara Pendergast

For More Information

Barbie Collector. http://www.barbiecollector.com/ (accessed July 24, 2011).

Barbie.com. http://www.barbie.com (accessed July 24, 2011).

Billy Boy. *Barbie!: Her Life & Times, and the New Theater of Fashion.* New York: Crown, 1987.

Gerber, Robin. *Barbie and Ruth: The Story of the World's Most Famous Doll and the Woman Who Created Her.* New York: Collins Business, 2009.

Handler, Ruth, with Jacqueline Shannon. *Dream Doll: The Ruth Handler Story.* Stamford, CT: Longmeadow, 1994.

Lord, M. G. *Forever Barbie: The Unauthorized Biography of a Real Doll.* New York: William Morrow, 1994.

Stone, Tanya Lee. *The Good, the Bad, and the Barbie: A Doll's History and Her Impact on Us.* New York: Viking, 2010.

Tosa, Marco. *Barbie: Four Decades of Fashion, Fantasy, and Fun.* New York: Abrams, 1998.

Verbeten, Sharon Korbeck. "Barbie's Legendary Aura: Taking a Brand to Heart." *Antique Trader Weekly* (October 20, 2010): 22.

Westernhouser, Kitturah B. *The Story of Barbie Doll.* 2nd ed. Paducah, KY: Collector Books, 1999.

Credit Cards

At the beginning of 2000, *Kiplinger's Personal Finance Magazine* asked its readers to name which modern financial change had the most effect on them personally. The vast majority named the invention of credit cards. These small plastic rectangles, which most businesses now accept as an alternative to cash, have become an everyday feature of modern life. The cards allow shoppers to take a purchase home one day and pay for it later. Credit cards have brought convenience to those who use them. They have also changed the way people both spend and save money and have therefore brought enormous changes to the global economy.

Department stores first introduced the charge card in the 1920s, usually in the form of a small metal plate imprinted with the customer's name. These "charge plates" inspired loyalty to the store that issued them because they could only be used at that store. In 1950, a New York man named Frank McNamara (1917–1957) had the idea of starting a credit company that would allow its customers to charge at many different places. His company, the Diners Club, collected a fee from participating restaurants and issued a card that allowed members to charge meals at all those restaurants.

The next step came in 1958, with the Bank Americard (now called Visa), issued by Bank of America. This card was accepted by many stores and businesses, and it added an exciting new feature. Instead of paying the total bill at the end of each month, as had been the usual policy with credit, customers could pay only a portion of their bill, rolling the remaining amount over to future months. For this privilege, however, users paid high interest rates (fees charged for borrowing the company's money). Other cards continued this profitable policy, notably the Master Charge (later renamed MasterCard), which was introduced in 1966.

Not everyone greeted the arrival of credit cards with enthusiasm. Many, including U.S. congressman Wright Patman (1893–1976) of Texas, called in the 1960s for an end to the practice of extending such easy credit. Patman argued that people would spend more money than they had and never learn to save or manage their finances. Credit cards have since become increasingly easier to get and use. There are still many who fear that they allow working people to become trapped by their debts. Others worry that credit cards encourage a society that values easy spending and consuming more than it values hard work and saving.

However, the use of credit cards continues to grow. In 1965, as the industry was getting its start, 5 million Americans had credit cards. By 1996, more than 1.4 billion cards were in circulation, charging $991 billion worth of purchases each year. Some kinds of shopping, such as automobile rentals and online purchases, are almost impossible without a credit card. The widespread use of credit has given birth to its own brand of crime. Credit card theft and credit card fraud (using trickery and cheating) have become major problems.

By 2005, some countries, such as Japan, saw physical credit cards replaced by **cellular phones** (see entry under 1990s—The Way We Lived in volume 5). Users' credit card information is stored in the phone, which is swiped over a special reader to complete the transaction. The technology was used in the United States on a trial basis by 2009, and was expected to become more widespread soon afterward.

Tina Gianoulis

For More Information

Berlin, Leslie. "Phones as Credit Cards? Americans Must Wait." *New York Times* (January 25, 2009): pp. 4.

Ecenbarger, William. "Plastic Is as Good as Gold." *Reader's Digest* (May 1989): pp. 37–43.

Green, Meg. *Everything You Need to Know about Credit Cards and Fiscal Responsibility.* New York: Rosen, 2001.

Mandell, Lewis. *The Credit Card Industry: A History.* Boston: Twayne, 1990.

Miller, Ted, and Courtney McGrath. "Power to the People." *Kiplinger's Personal Finance Magazine* (January 2000): pp. 82–85.

Nocera, Joseph. *A Piece of the Action: How the Middle Class Joined the Money Class.* New York: Simon & Schuster, 1994.

Ritzer, George. *Expressing America.* Thousand Oaks, CA: Pine Forge Press, 1995.

Shepherdson, Nancy. "Credit Card America: How We Became a Nation of Instant, Constant Borrowers." *American Heritage* (Vol. 42, no. 7, November 1991): pp. 125–33.

Malls

● ●

Americans love to shop. The United States has for many decades been a consumer culture, one dedicated to acquiring things and enjoying material abundance. Over time, however, the ways and places Americans

A New Jersey mall: comfort and convenience under one roof. © EMILE WAMSTEKER/BLOOMBERG/GETTY IMAGES.

have shopped have changed, altering the American landscape and how Americans spend their time. One of the most important changes was the development of the shopping mall.

Prior to the development of shopping malls, Americans shopped in individual stores in the centers of towns and cities. Major cities were known as the homes of large department stores such as Macy's in New York City and Hudson's in Detroit, Michigan. These large department stores were in some ways the forerunners of shopping malls because they carried everything under one roof. Once inside, people could shop in comfort, away from the heat and rain of summer or the cold and snow of winter. More Americans moved away from central cities to the **suburbs** (see entry under 1950s—The Way We Lived in volume 3), however. Stores followed them, eventually forming malls to replicate the urban shopping experience, but in a cleaner, more convenient, and comfortable way. The first modern shopping center was Country Club Plaza, developed by J. C. Nichols (1880–1950) in Kansas City, Missouri, in 1924. This was basically a strip of shops serving Nichols' suburban housing development nearby. In 1956, the Southdale Shopping Center opened in Minneapolis, Minnesota. Southdale was the first completely enclosed, climate-controlled mall. It prompted a host of imitators nationwide. In 1945, there were only eight malls nationwide; by the 1970s, there were more than three thousand.

Over time, malls became much more than places to shop. More and more they came to replace the dense urban shopping districts. Along with shops, malls contained restaurants, including "food courts" with a range of **fast food** (see entry under 1920s—Food and Drink in volume 2) restaurants, video arcades, comfortable seating, and plants and fountains. Special events were designed to draw in customers and keep them there so they would spend more money. The **Mall of America** (see entry under 1990s—Commerce in volume 5), near Minneapolis, took all of this a step further by enclosing an amusement park within its enormous space. Malls also became a focal point for teen culture, with teenagers going to the mall for hours at a time, shopping for a while, but also seeing friends and hanging out. By the 1980s, malls were being criticized. They were viewed as helping to destroy the vitality of older urban shopping districts and contributing to suburban sprawl, destroying farmland and natural areas. By the 1980s, however, malls had become an inescapable part of the American landscape and culture. As brick-and-mortar stores such as those found in malls lost more and more business to online shopping websites like **Amazon.com** (see entry under 2000s—Commerce in volume 6) in the early 2000s, some malls struggled and even closed, but the mall shopping experience remained widely available and common in the United States.

Timothy Berg

For More Information

Jacobs, Jerry. *The Mall: An Attempted Escape from Everyday Life*. Prospect Heights, IL: Waveland Press, 1984.

Kowinski, William. *The Malling of America: An Inside Look at the Great Consumer Paradise*. New York: Morrow, 1985.

Mall of America. http://www.mallofamerica.com/home/ (accessed July 27, 2011).

Saran Wrap

Saran Wrap is a clear, flexible plastic wrap used primarily by consumers to preserve the freshness of food items. It is a trademark of the Dow Chemical Company, which has marketed the product since 1953. Introduced to the public in 1953 as Dow's first consumer product, Saran Wrap was the outgrowth of research and development that had produced many plastics created during World War II (1939–45). Since then, Saran Wrap and similar brands have largely replaced waxed paper as the preferred wrapping for lunchbox sandwiches, leftovers, or refrigerated meats, fruits, and vegetables.

Due to its chemical makeup, Saran Wrap can stand up to extreme temperatures. It can be used in the freezer as well as in a microwave oven (although it is not recommended while microwaving foods with high sugar content). This toughness is a major reason for its usefulness and popularity. Dow further points out that "in developing countries where refrigeration is scarce, meat products are extruded into a sausage covered with Saran film that can be shipped and stored without refrigeration for up to six months."

In a memorable comic bit entitled "The 2,000-Year-Old Man," comedian Mel Brooks (1926–) was asked to name the world's greatest invention. He answered, "In 2,000 years? Saran Wrap," echoing a sentiment of adoration for the product shared by many Americans.

Edward Moran

For More Information
Dow Chemical Corporate Website. http://www.dow.com/ (accessed July 27, 2011).

Green, Joey. "Saran Wrap." *Joey Green's Wackyuses.com.* http://www.wackyuses. com/wf_saran.html (accessed February 26, 2002).

Plastic Wrap by Saran. http://www.saranbrands.com/ (accessed July 27, 2011).

Timex Watches

One of the most famous wristwatch brands is Timex, the brand that "takes a licking and keeps on ticking," according to a memorable ad. When the U.S. Time Company, whose roots date to the 1850s, introduced the Timex in 1950, it revolutionized the time-keeping industry. The wristwatches allowed people to easily tell the time. They were also simply designed, inexpensive, and durable. These improvements played into what was to become one of the most celebrated TV advertising campaigns of all time.

Timex wristwatches were initially promoted exclusively in print. Such ads depicted the timepieces attached to the bat of **baseball** (see entry under 1900s—Sports and Games in volume 1) legend Mickey Mantle (1931–1995), affixed to a turtle and to a lobster's claw, frozen in an ice cube, and twirling inside a vacuum cleaner. In the mid-1950s, John Cameron Swayze (1906–1995), a veteran newscaster, began presiding over a series of **television** (see entry under 1940s—TV and Radio in volume 3) commercials in which the wristwatch was subjected to intricate "torture tests." A Timex might be crushed by a jack-hammer, tossed about in a dishwasher, or strapped to a diver who plunges off a cliff. After this mistreatment, Swayze held the still-operating wristwatch up to the camera. He then declared that it "takes a licking and keeps on ticking," a catch-phrase that quickly entered the pop-culture vocabulary. The success of the ads resulted in Timex wristwatch sales surpassing the five million mark by 1958. By the end of the decade, one in every three wristwatches sold in the United States was a Timex.

Across the decades, thousands of viewers wrote the company, proposing scenarios for future torture tests. The ad campaign ended in 1977, with a "failure" that had been planned in advance. In the commercial, an elephant stomped on—and completely crushed—a Timex, at which point Swayze informed the television audience, "It worked in rehearsal."

Rob Edelman

For More Information

Glasmeier, Amy. *Manufacturing Time: Global Competition in the Watch Industry, 1795–2000.* New York: Guildford Press, 2000.

McDermott, Kathleen. *Timex: A Company and Its Community, 1854–1998.* Middlebury, CT: Timex, 1998.

Timex Corp. "Company Timeline." *Timex.* http://www.timex.com/info/CompanyTimeline (accessed July 27, 2011).

Trading Stamps

Similar in appearance to postage stamps, trading stamps are small, adhesive-backed coupons. These stamps were once frequently given to consumers when they purchased merchandise from certain retailers.

The trading stamps were pasted in small books that could later be redeemed for other merchandise. Retailers commonly gave out one stamp for each purchase of ten cents. The first stamps were issued in 1890 by Schuster's Department Store in Milwaukee, Wisconsin. Schuster's gave the stamps to cash-paying customers to encourage them to forgo charging their purchases. The most prominent trading stamps were S&H Green Stamps, first issued by the Sperry & Hutchinson (S&H) Company in 1896. Other major trading-stamp brands included Top Value, King Korn, Triple S, Gold Bell, and Plaid.

S&H calls trading stamps "America's first frequent shopper program and grandfather of marketing programs such as frequent-flyer miles." During the prime years of trading stamps in the 1950s and 1960s, when they were offered by most large grocery chains and gasoline stations, S&H printed three times as many stamps as the U.S. Post Office. S&H claims that its 1964 catalog was the largest single publication in the United States. As he did with the **Campbell's Soup** (see entry under 1910s—Food and Drink in volume 1) can, pop-artist Andy Warhol (1928–1987) created a series of S&H Green Stamp paintings that confirmed their role as icons (symbols) of popular culture.

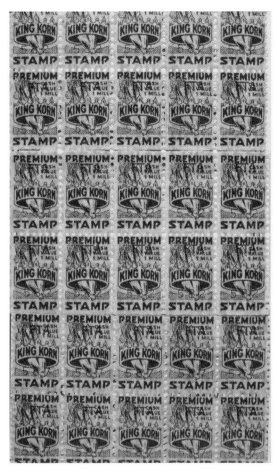

A sheet of King Corn trading stamps. © BLANK ARCHIVES/ GETTY IMAGES.

Trading stamps fell out of favor after the 1970s with the rise of cents-off coupons and other promotions. In 1999, S&H reinvented the trading-stamp concept in digital form, called S&H Greenpoints, describing them as "the new incentive and rewards currency for the next generation of loyalty marketing." Like trading stamps, Greenpoints were issued by participating merchants to consumers who could redeem them through a catalog or via the S&H Web site. Consumers could choose merchandise, discounts, frequent flyer miles, or contributions to a charity. The S&H Greenpoints program continues to be active in the early twenty-first century.

Edward Moran

For More Information

Fox, Harold W. *The Economics of Trading Stamps.* Washington, DC: Public Affairs Press, 1968.

Sperry and Hutchinson Company. *Answers to Some Frequently Asked Questions about the Sperry and Hutchinson Company and S & H Green Stamps.* New York: Sperry and Hutchinson, 1970.

S&H Greenpoints. http://www.greenpoints.com/account/act_default.asp (accessed July 23, 2011).

Volkswagen Beetle

The Volkswagen (VW) Beetle, a small car with an odd, rounded shape that resembled an insect, is one of the more unusual success stories in the history of the automobile. It first arrived in the United States from Germany in the early 1950s. The little rounded car was very out of place amid all the giant cars the American automotive industry was producing

A 1954 model Volkswagen Beetle drives by a gas station. © CHARLES FENNO JACOBS/TIME LIFE PICTURES/GETTY IMAGES.

in Detroit, Michigan. Over time its popularity grew, earning many fans and making an everlasting mark on America's roads.

The Beetle was first developed in Germany by Ferdinand Porsche (1909–1998) in the 1930s during the Nazi era as an inexpensive car for ordinary people to own (*Volkswagen* means "people's car" in German). After World War II (1939–45), Volkswagen began shipping cars to the United States. When they arrived there, they were certainly an oddity. At a time when American cars were big and boxy, were often outfitted with huge fins, and got terrible gas mileage, the VW Beetle turned all those standards upside down. The Beetle was small and rounded, with an easy-to-repair, air-cooled engine in the back of the car (rather than the front, as with other cars) and a price that was far below that of most American cars ($1,545 in 1959). The VW Beetle also got great gas mileage—more than thirty miles per gallon—at a time when American cars rarely got more than ten miles per gallon. At first, the Beetle appealed to only a small portion of the car-buying public. Over time, however, the car caught on.

The Beetle's popularity was boosted by a brilliant advertising campaign. Volkswagen hired the American advertising firm Doyle Dane Bernbach (DDB) in 1959 to do its advertising. Knowing full well that they could never convince the American public the Beetle was more beautiful or more powerful than American cars, they played up the Beetle's quirky features. They used such slogans as "Ugly is only skin deep" and "A face only a mother could love" to describe the Beetle. Because the Beetle cars did not change much from year to year, unlike American cars, one ad simply offered a blank space with the words, "We don't have anything to show you in our new models." The ads helped create an almost cult-like following for the Beetles. Over the years, the number of Beetle lovers increased. Stories spread about Beetles that got fifty miles per gallon or survived floods and disasters that would have disabled other cars.

The real impact of the VW Beetle on American culture came in the ways it was used and in the intense devotion its owners showed to the car. One owner said that "owning a VW is like being in love. It's a member of the family." Amid highways covered in the large cars of Detroit in the 1950s and 1960s, it took some courage to buy an odd-looking German car. In the early years, Beetles were rare and spotting another one on the road often resulted in a honk of the horn or a wave in fellowship. By the 1960s, when Beetles were more common, they became associated with young people and youth culture. The VW Microbus, cousin to the Beetle, was a particular favorite. **Rock and roll** (see entry under 1950s—Music in volume 3) bands could haul all their members and instruments to concerts in them. Surfers could sleep in their vans along with their surfboards. **Hippies** (see entry under 1960s—The Way We Lived in volume 4) would travel around the country in them. Frequently, they hand-painted their VWs in multiple colors and adorned the back of the cars with stickers for bands such as the **Grateful Dead** (see entry under 1960s—Music in volume 4). The Beetle also became the source of college games, including the "Volkstote," where students raced to carry the car by hand for one hundred feet. People have also put the cars to unusual uses, driving them across water for forty minutes or more (because they float very well) and using the engines in home-built airplanes. Such feats only added to the mystique of the vehicle.

Over the years, the VW Beetle remained largely the same, although variations on the basic Volkswagen theme were introduced: the microbus, the station wagon, the Karmann Ghia convertible, and other models. After 1973, when American cars got smaller in response to the oil crisis, the popularity of the Beetle began to decline. The company ceased production for the U.S. market in 1978, although they were still produced and sold in Mexico afterward. The Beetle was revived, however, in 1998, and remained popular in the early 2000s. The updated version maintained the rounded body of the original Beetle, but featured a stronger engine and more luxurious features. It even came with a small flower vase near the steering wheel, just to let everyone know it still had a sense of humor. Its success proved that the American public had not lost its love for that odd German car with the funny shape and that the VW Beetle would still hold a beloved place in American culture for years to come.

Timothy Berg

For More Information

Copping, Richard. *Volkswagen Beetle: A Celebration of the World's Most Popular Car.* Sparkford, U.K.: Haynes, 2010.

Hiott, Andrea. *Thinking Small: The Long, Strange Trip of the Volkswagen Beetle.* New York: Ballantine Books, 2012.

McLeod, Kate. *Beetlemania: The Story of the Car That Captured the Hearts of Millions.* New York: Smithmark, 1999.

Seume, Keith. *VW Beetle: A Comprehensive Illustrated History of the World's Most Popular Car.* Osceola, WI: Motorbooks International, 1997.

Steinwedel, Louis William. *The Beetle Book: America's 30-Year Love Affair with the "Bug."* Englewood Cliffs, NJ: Prentice-Hall, 1981.

1950s

Fashion

Newly confident in themselves after winning World War II (1939–45) and establishing an economy that was the envy of the world, Americans in the 1950s began to develop a fashion sense that was independent from that of the rest of the globe and focused on youth. The most notable youth fashions were quite simple. For boys, an outfit consisting of a pair of blue jeans and a white T-shirt symbolized the spirit of rock and roll and was worn by movie idols James Dean (1931–1955) and Marlon Brando (1924–2004). For girls, a tight sweater, a poodle skirt (a long, full skirt with the image of a poodle on it), bobby socks (ankle-high socks), and saddle shoes (sturdy shoes with a contrasting band of color) were all the rage. These looks were closely associated with the 1950s; they were featured in the wave of nostalgia in the 1970s in such movies as *American Graffiti* (1973) and *Grease* (1978), and in TV shows like *Happy Days* (1974–84).

Women's fashions began to grow independent from the influence of Paris and London in the decade. The "New Look," which is most associated with women's high fashion, began with French designer Christian Dior (1905–1957) in the late 1940s but was modified to suit American tastes. Women were fond of clothes that emphasized the female figure, with closely tailored bustlines, slender waists, and padded hips. Women also wore plenty of makeup.

Men, on the other hand, were not very concerned with fashion. At work, they wore what amounted to a uniform: a gray flannel suit. Conservatively tailored and worn with a white shirt and tie, this standard suit style was so popular that it became a symbol for the businessman's conformity (acting in agreement with established social views), as criticized in the famous book *The Man in the Gray Flannel Suit* (1955) by Sloan Wilson (1920–2003). Younger, less formal men made the loafer, a slip-on leather shoe, the most popular style of footwear in the United States.

Jeans

Blue jeans have been a part of American culture for over 125 years. They have become not only an expression of American fashion but also an element of American identity recognized around the world. Jeans were first worn in the nineteenth century as work clothes, customized to address the needs of gold rush miners in California. They have evolved through the decades to represent the rugged individualism of the American West, the nonconformity of the rebel, and the height of designer fashion.

The first jeans were made by a joint venture involving a Bavarian immigrant shop owner named Levi Strauss (c. 1829–1902) and a San Francisco tailor named Jacob Davis. Davis had designed a pair of work pants with metal rivets on the pockets and seams to help them hold up under the rough use of the California miners, who filled their pockets with heavy ore samples. Strauss supplied the money to buy a patent for the new work pants, which they called "waist overalls." They made their pants out of a sturdy new fabric from France, called *serge de Nimes* (pronounced sairzh duh NEEM). The French term was soon shortened in America to "denim."

Strauss' denim work overalls were worn by miners and cowboys all across the west. In the late 1920s and early 1930s, they gained a different kind of popularity when moviegoers saw them on the stars of **Western** (see entry under 1930s—Film and Theater in volume 2) films, like **John Wayne** (1907–1979; see entry under 1930s—Film and Theater in volume 2) and **Gary Cooper** (1901–1961; see entry under 1930s—Film and Theater in volume 2). During World War II (1939–45), the Navy and the Coast Guard used them as part of their official uniform. After the war, they became available for the first time east of the Mississippi. In the 1950s and 1960s, jeans became the official uniform of rebellion, as stars like Marlon Brando (1924–2004) and **James Dean** (1931–1954; see entry under 1950s—Film and Theater in volume 3) wore them with **T-shirts** (see entry under 1910s—Fashion in volume 1) and leather jackets. Teenagers of the era rushed to buy the newly hip pants. Parents and teachers were just as determined to forbid them in schools and other respectable places. In the 1950s, the waist overalls began to be called jeans, a more relaxed name for pants that were no longer simply work clothes.

Perhaps because of their comfort, which only increases with age, or maybe due to their adaptability, jeans have remained a staple of the American casual wardrobe, especially for young people. In the politically radical late 1960s and early 1970s, the look became patched and faded. In the 1980s, punks wore torn jeans, sometimes only held together by threads, while the wealthy paid hundreds of dollars for jeans from famous fashion designers. Although basic blue jeans are still a standard garment in the twenty-first century, collectors pay high prices to own a pair of Strauss and Davis' original waist overalls.

Tina Gianoulis

For More Information

Adkins, Jan. "The Evolution of Jeans: American History 501." *Mother Earth News* (No. 124, July-August 1990): pp. 60–65.

Caro, Joseph J. "Levi's: Pants That Won the West." *Antiques and Collecting Magazine* (Vol. 98, no. 11): pp. 38–43.

Gromer, Cliff. "Outdoors Levi's Jeans." *Popular Mechanics* (Vol. 176, iss. 5, May 1999): pp. 94–98.

Harris, Alice. *The Blue Jeans.* New York: PowerHouse Books, 2002.

Harris, Michael Allen. *Jeans of the Old West: A History.* Atglen, PA: Schiffer, 2010.

Sullivan, James. *Jeans: A Cultural History of an American Icon.* New York: Gotham Books, 2006.

"True Blue." *Esquire* (Vol. 122, no. 1, July 1994): pp. 102–7.

Weidt, Maryann N. *Mr. Blue Jeans: A Story About Levi Strauss.* Minneapolis: Carolrhoda Books, 1990.

Levi's

Levi's denim blue **jeans** (see entry under 1950s—Fashion in volume 3) are made by Levi Strauss & Company of San Francisco, California. They were originally produced as tough trousers made from tent canvas. The rugged pants were intended for miners in the California gold rush, cowboys, and farm workers. Levi Strauss (c. 1829–1902) himself emigrated to California from Germany in 1850. In 1853, his company began making the denim jeans that became the famous shrink-to-fit "501" style of jeans.

Although the company made other garments, by the 1950s it was the "501" jeans that people meant when they used the term "Levi's." With their button fly, real copper rivets and the red "Levi's" tag sewn into the right back pocket, Levi's became the must-have brand of denim jeans. Their link to rougher, more "authentic" times only made them more desirable. In the 1980s, clever 1950s-style **television** (see entry under 1940s—TV and Radio in volume 3) **advertising** (see entry under 1920s—Commerce in volume 2) once more connected Levi's with a simpler past. It also helped turn the company into the biggest pants manufacturer in the world.

Chris Routledge

For More Information

Downey, Lynn. *501: This Is a Pair of Levi's Jeans—The Official History of the Levi's Brand.* San Francisco: Levi Strauss and Co., 1995.

Downey, Lynn. *Levi Strauss & Co.* Charleston, SC: Arcadia, 2007.

Levi Strauss and Co. http://levistrauss.com/ (accessed July 27, 2011).

Weidt, Maryann N. *Mr. Blue Jeans: A Story About Levi Strauss.* Minneapolis: Carolrhoda Books, 1990.

1950s

Film and Theater

The biggest problem facing the movie industry in the 1950s was the TV. As sales of television sets increased, more and more Americans stayed at home, and thus away from cinemas. This was not the movie studios' only problem, however. A 1948 Supreme Court ruling had led to the major studios selling off all their theater holdings in 1951. No longer could movie studios afford to exert complete control over which movies were shown in which theaters. With TV and the breakup of what was known as the "studio system," moviemakers faced real competition.

Movie studios responded to this new era in a variety of ways. They made fewer movies. In 1954, the seven major studios released fewer than 100 movies, down from over 320 movies per year in the late 1940s. The movies they made, however, were bigger and more dramatic, providing the kinds of entertainment that TV could not. Films like *The Robe* (1953), *The Ten Commandments* (1956), and *Ben-Hur* (1959) featured magnificent sets, huge casts, and epic story lines.

Freed from the production codes that dictated the "moral content" of films, moviemakers also began to explore more daring topics. *North by Northwest* (1959), directed by Alfred Hitchcock (1899–1980), offered suspense. *Some Like It Hot* (1959) offered bawdy humor—and plenty of views of a scantily clad Marilyn Monroe (1926–1962). Science-fiction films like *The Day the Earth Stood Still* (1951) and *Invasion of the Body Snatchers* (1956) offered thrills and chills. One of the decade's biggest surprises was a monster movie from Japan titled *Gojira* (1954)—better known in the United States as *Godzilla*. Godzilla was big, but several real-life stars got more attention, including Monroe, Cary Grant (1904–1986), Grace Kelly (1929–1982), James Dean (1931–1955), and Elizabeth Taylor (1932–2011).

The Day the Earth Stood Still

Featuring a memorable line still popular among film enthusiasts, the 1951 film *The Day the Earth Stood Still* helped usher in a new era in science fiction. A "flying saucer" movie with a message, it was widely imitated, but never duplicated, throughout the decade.

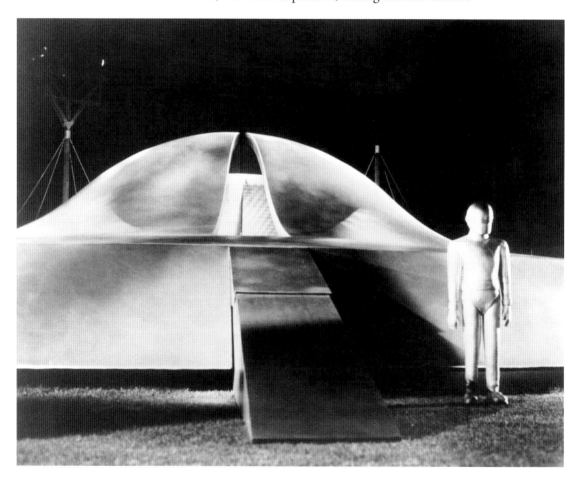

Gort awaits in the ground-breaking 1951 science fiction film The Day the Earth Stood Still. © 20TH CENTURY FOX FILM CORP./ EVERETT COLLECTION.

When *The Day the Earth Stood Still* opened in theaters in September 1951, the United States and the Soviet Union were locked in a nuclear arms race. Each side distrusted the other. Both were in the process of developing enough atomic firepower to destroy the entire planet. The film, like many great science-fiction stories, addressed these important issues in fantasy form. The plot concerns a flying saucer that lands in Washington, D.C., containing the alien Klaatu and his robot companion Gort. Klaatu has come to Earth with a peaceful message about the danger of using nuclear weapons, but the prejudices of Earth people soon get the better of them. Suspicious of his motives, they kill Klaatu. The alien is brought back to life by robot Gort, who in turn threatens to go on a destructive rampage. Klaatu restrains him, using the movie's famous phrase: "Klaatu barada nikto," meaning: "Don't kill." At the end of the film, Klaatu addresses a world audience, warning that unless the people of Earth stop building nuclear bombs, Gort and the rest of the robots from Klaatu's world will destroy the planet. "The choice," declares Klaatu, "is yours."

The Day the Earth Stood Still became an instant classic. It boasted an exciting story, good performances, and superb special effects. Many of the sci-fi movies of the 1950s copied elements, such as alien visitation and the use of robots, directly from the film. The message of *The Day the Earth Stood Still* made it stand out from other sci-fi pictures of the period. It questioned the nuclear-arms race while also condemning mankind's fear of strangers and the unknown. Thanks to its message of hope and tolerance, the film won the Golden Globe award for "Best Film Promoting International Understanding." The film's director, Robert Wise (1914–2005), went on to direct such science-fiction classics as *The Andromeda Strain* (1971) and **Star Trek** (1979; see entry under 1960s—TV and Radio in volume 4).

Robert E. Schnakenberg

For More Information

Meehan, Paul. *Saucer Movies: A UFOlogical History of the Cinema.* New York: Scarecrow Press, 1998.

Pringle, David, ed. *The Ultimate Encyclopedia of Science Fiction.* London: Carlton, 1996.

Staskowski, Andréa. *Science Fiction Movies.* Minneapolis: Lerner, 1992.

Warren, Bill. *Keep Watching the Skies!: American Science Fiction Movies of the Fifties.* Jefferson, NC: McFarland, 1982.

James Dean (1931–1955)

Actor James Dean in a still from the 1955 film East of Eden. © EVERETT COLLECTION.

In his all-too-brief life—he was just twenty-four when he died in a crash of his stylish Porsche automobile—actor James Dean came to symbolize middle-class adolescent alienation, 1950s-style. After appearing briefly on **Broadway** (see entry under 1900s—Film and Theater in volume 1) and **television** (see entry under 1940s—TV and Radio in volume 3) and playing bit parts in several films, Dean starred in three motion pictures: *East of Eden* (1955), *Rebel Without a Cause* (1955), and *Giant* (1956), earning Best Actor Academy Award nominations for the first and last. In each, he was the personification (human representation) of the anxious American youth of the mid-1950s. He was cast as a brooding, vulnerable adolescent whose presence was unsettling during what otherwise was an era of prosperity and conformity (acting in agreement with established social views) after World War II (1939–45).

Dean's stardom lasted a little over a year. His time in the limelight was as strikingly brief as any major star in motion-picture history. His early death, coupled with his unfulfilled potential, immediately transformed him into an American cultural icon, a symbol of American culture—a status that continues into the twenty-first century.

Rob Edelman

For More Information

Gilmore, John. *Live Fast—Die Young: Remembering the Short Life of James Dean.* New York: Thunder's Mouth Press, 1997.

The Official Website of James Dean. http://www.jamesdean.com/ (accessed July 27, 2011).

Perry, George. *James Dean.* Bath, England: Palazzo Editions, 2012.

Riese, Randall. *The Unabridged James Dean: His Life and Legacy from A to Z.* Chicago: Contemporary, 1991.

Schroeder, Alan. *James Dean.* New York: Chelsea House, 1994.

Francis the Talking Mule

Long before **Mister Ed** (see entry under 1960s—TV and Radio in volume 4), the talking horse who ruled America's TV screens, another talking animal won over audiences with his sassy comebacks and helpful demeanor. Francis the Talking Mule, usually voiced by actor Chill Wills (1902–1978), helped his bumbling sidekick Donald O'Connor (1925–2003) out of humorous situations in a popular series of movie comedies in the 1940s and 1950s.

The last forty years of the twentieth century saw an increase in the number of "talking animal" movies and **television** (see entry under 1940s—TV and Radio in volume 3) shows, from the talkative horse Mr. Ed, who ruled the stable on CBS in the 1960s, to Babe, the chatty pig who starred in his own Oscar-nominated film in 1995. Comedian Eddie Murphy (1961–) dealt with a whole host of talking animals in his *Dr. Dolittle* movies beginning in 1998. However, none of this form of entertainment would have been possible without the trail blazed by Francis, the first live-action talking animal in **Hollywood** (see entry under 1930s—Film and Theater in volume 2). Critics dismissed the comedies as silly, but audiences responded well, and a new comedy genre was born.

All told, Francis made seven features for Universal Studios between 1949 and 1956. In *Francis* (1949), his screen debut, the chattering mule rescued a soldier (O'Connor) on a secret mission in Burma (the country now known as Myanmar) during World War II (1939–45). The second feature, *Francis Goes to the Races* (1951), involved him in shenanigans at a horse track. *Francis Goes to West Point* (1952) was a collegiate comedy with an exciting climax set at the annual Army-Navy football game. *Francis Covers the Big Town* (1953) depicted O'Connor as a newspaperman saved from a murder charge by a heroic Francis. *Francis Joins the WACs* (1954) had O'Connor rejoin the military, with the babbling burro in tow. The next year's *Francis in the Navy* was O'Connor's last film in the series, a seafaring romp that also featured a young Clint Eastwood (1930–). The final film in the Francis series was 1956's *Francis in the Haunted House*. Mickey Rooney (1920–) took over for O'Connor in the sidekick role, while Paul Frees (1920–1986) assumed the voice of Francis. The horror comedy had Francis frustrating some art forgers.

So how did Francis "talk"? Years later, it was revealed that technicians actually pulled threads attached to the animal's mouth to make his lips move. The voice-over was later synchronized (perfectly timed) to Francis's lip movements. It was a simple trick, but the illusion it created kept audiences roaring with laughter for the better part of a decade.

Robert E. Schnakenberg

For More Information

Brode, Douglas. *Films of the Fifties.* Secaucus, NJ: Citadel Press, 1976.
Edelson, Edward. *Great Animals of the Movies.* Garden City, NY: Doubleday, 1980.
Rothel, David. *Great Show Business Animals.* San Diego: A. S. Barnes, 1980.

Godzilla

Brought to life by atomic radiation, the giant fire-breathing lizard known as Godzilla has been terrifying movie audiences since the 1950s. The Japanese character's fame spread around the world as Godzilla films were dubbed into many languages. Perhaps only **King Kong** (see entry under 1930s—Film and Theater in volume 2) exceeds Godzilla in popularity among gigantic movie monsters.

Godzilla is called *Gojira* in his native Japan, where he first appeared in a 1954 feature. Created by filmmakers at Toho Studios, including director Ishiro Honda (1911–1993), Godzilla was meant to symbolize Japanese fears of nuclear devastation following their experience in World War II (1939–45). The original film, in which the crazed atomic lizard demolishes the city of Tokyo, struck a chord with Japanese audiences and earned more than $7 million at the box office. In 1956, the film was released in the United States in a dubbed version (that is, a version with a different sound track, usually in a different language) entitled *Godzilla, King of the Monsters.* American actor Raymond Burr (1917–1993) from TV's **Perry Mason** (1957–66; see entry under 1930s—Print Culture in volume 2) and *Ironside* (1967–75) appeared in new footage explaining Godzilla's rampage to English-speaking audiences.

Godzilla proved such a hit worldwide that many sequels were made. In them, Godzilla invariably fights other monsters, including Rodan, a flying lizard, and his own robot double Mechagodzilla. Over time, Godzilla lost his appetite for destruction and became a "good guy," saving Japan from attack by other creatures. Twice, **Hollywood** (see entry under 1930s—Film and Theater in volume 2) has tried to adapt

The monster Godzilla on yet another rampage. © THE KOBAL COLLECTION/ART RESOURCE, NY.

Godzilla to suit American tastes, with *Godzilla 1985* and again in 1998 with a big-budget *Godzilla* starring Matthew Broderick (1962–). Both films proved critical and commercial disappointments.

Away from the movie screen, Godzilla has become a beloved part of popular culture. In 1978, he served as the host of his own animated series *Super Power Hour* on Saturday morning **television** (see entry under 1940s—TV and Radio in volume 3). Godzilla toys, games, and models have been big sellers for more than thirty years. Godzilla has even been the subject of popular songs. The 1977 Blue Oyster Cult hit "Godzilla" sang the praises of the cinematic lizard. In 1998, Puff Daddy and Jimmy Page recorded "Come with Me," a Godzilla-themed rewrite of the **Led Zeppelin** (see entry under 1970s—Music in volume 4) song "Kashmir" for the *Godzilla* film soundtrack. In 2004, Godzilla was honored with his own star on the Hollywood Walk of Fame. The most recent big-screen feature of the "king of the monsters" may have proved a dud, but few doubt he will one day reclaim his throne. Audiences, it seems, have a simple message when it comes to Godzilla: long live the king.

Robert E. Schnakenberg

For More Information

Harmon, Jim. *The Godzilla Book.* San Bernardino, CA: Borgo Press, 1986.

Lees, J. D., et al. *The Official Godzilla Compendium.* New York: Random House, 1998.

Lovece, Frank. *Godzilla!: The Complete Guide to Moviedom's Mightiest Monster.* New York: Morrow, 1998.

Ryfle, Steve. *Japan's Favorite Mon-Star.* Toronto: ECW Press, 1999.

Tsutsui, William M. *Godzilla on My Mind: Fifty Years of the King of Monsters.* New York: Palgrave Macmillan, 2004.

Marilyn Monroe (1926–1962)

Born Norma Jeane Mortenson in Los Angeles, California, Marilyn Monroe's rise to fame is a classic rags-to-riches story. Abused and neglected as a child, she grew up in foster homes. After signing a contract with 20th Century-Fox in 1946, she quickly became a top celebrity. **Hollywood** (see entry under 1930s—Film and Theater in volume 2) was quick to capitalize on Monroe's blend of dangerous sexuality and girl-next-door innocence. However, films like *Gentlemen Prefer Blondes* (1953), *The Seven Year Itch* (1955), and *Some Like It Hot* (1959) also reveal a fine actress with expert comic timing.

Always drawn to powerful men, Monroe's husbands included baseball star Joe DiMaggio (1914–1999) and playwright Arthur Miller (1915–2005). In her last years, gossip linked her with President John F. Kennedy (1917–1963) and his brother, politician Robert Kennedy (1925–1968). Monroe's death by a self-administered drug overdose followed several years of mental collapse, alcoholism, and drug abuse. Decades later, her image is everywhere, adorning objects from **T-shirts** (see entry under 1910s—Fashion in volume 1) to posters to ashtrays to ladies' underwear and nightgowns. Marilyn Monroe lives on as one of the twentieth century's most notable sex symbols.

Chris Routledge

For More Information

Forever-Marilyn.com. http://forever-marilyn.com/ (accessed July 27, 2011).

Krohn, Katherine E. *Marilyn Monroe: Norma Jeane's Dream.* Minneapolis: Lerner, 1997.

Lefkowitz, Frances. *Marilyn Monroe.* New York: Chelsea House, 1995.

Monroe, Marilyn, with Ben Hecht. *My Story.* New York: Stein and Day, 1976.

Spoto, Donald. *Marilyn Monroe: The Biography*. New York: HarperCollins, 1993.

Taraborrelli, J. Randy. *The Secret Life of Marilyn Monroe*. New York: Grand Central Pub., 2009.

Victor, Adam. *The Marilyn Encyclopedia*. New York: Overlook Press, 1999.

North by Northwest

North by Northwest, a fast-moving 1959 thriller, is widely regarded as one of the best films made by legendary director Alfred Hitchcock (1899–1980). It contains several of the usual Hitchcock film-making touches, but "the Master" never did them better than in this movie. *North by Northwest* contains an innocent man accused and on the run, a cool and obscure blonde, and a mysterious object (called by Hitchcock in interviews "the MacGuffin") that all the major characters strive to acquire. It also features one of Hitchcock's best casts: **Cary Grant** (1904–1986; see entry under 1930s—Film and Theater in volume 2), Eva Marie Saint (1924–), James Mason (1909–1984), and Martin Landau (1931–), among others.

In *North by Northwest,* advertising executive Roger Thornhill (played by Grant) is mistaken by thugs for an American intelligence agent named George Kaplan and abducted. He is taken to the home of Philip Vandamm (Mason), master spy in the service of a foreign power. Vandamm ignores Thornhill's protests of mistaken identity and threatens to interrogate his unwilling guest—through torture, if necessary. Thornhill escapes, but the spies are close behind. They include Eve Kendall (Saint), who is Vandamm's fiancée. Her loyalties, however, seem inconsistent, and Thornhill is unsure through most of the film whose side she is really on. The climax is played out atop Mount Rushmore, which explains the film's working title: *The Man in Lincoln's Nose.*

The film contains one of Hitchcock's most famous scenes. Following directions to a meeting, Thornhill finds himself alone in the middle of flat farm country. Nothing is moving for miles around, except for a distant biplane dusting crops. Suddenly the plane heads for Thornhill, drops down to 20 feet or so, and attacks. Thornhill runs, trying to dodge both the plane and the bullets being fired at him from its cockpit.

The sophisticated hero, the series of chases and narrow escapes, the beautiful woman who cannot be trusted—these aspects of *North by Northwest* influenced filmmaking for decades to come, from **James Bond films** (see entry under 1960s—Film and Theater in volume 4) to *Indiana Jones* movies (see entry under 1980s—Film and Theater in volume 5) and beyond.

North by Northwest was nominated for several major Academy Awards, but 1959 was also the year that *Ben-Hur* was released. In the awards, Grant and his bi-plane proved no match for Charlton Heston (1924–2008) and his Roman chariot.

Justin Gustainis

For More Information

Auiler, Dan, and Stephen Rebello. *North by Northwest: The Making of Hitchcock's Classic Thriller.* London: Titan, 2000.

Lehman, Ernest. *North by Northwest* (Faber Classic Screenplay Series). New York: Faber and Faber, 2000.

On the Waterfront

On the Waterfront (1954), the Academy Award–winning drama directed by Elia Kazan (1909–2003) and starring Marlon Brando (1924–2004), is a classic American film. It is also noted for being a thinly veiled allegory (a story that disguises yet another story): *On the Waterfront* symbolically describes the **blacklisting** (see entry under 1950s—The Way We Lived in volume 3) activities in **Hollywood** (see entry under 1930s—Film and Theater in volume 2) at the time and mirrors the era in which it was produced.

On the Waterfront is the story of Terry Malloy (Brando), a young ex-boxer and dockworker. Malloy's older brother Charley (Rod Steiger, 1925–2002) is the lawyer and mouthpiece for the corrupt labor union that rules the waterfront. The union is headed by racketeer (person involved in an organized illegal enterprise) Johnny Friendly (Lee J. Cobb, 1911–1976). At the outset, Terry is inadvertently involved in luring to his death Joey Doyle, a dockworker who has threatened to expose the union to a government committee investigating water-front crime. Then Terry is served with a subpoena (a legal document that orders a person to appear before investigators). As the story progresses, Terry must decide if he will testify and help bring down Friendly and his underlings or refuse and maintain the underworld's power. He heroically decides to testify, which leads to Friendly's downfall.

Actor Marlon Brando in a still from the Elia Kazan–directed 1954 film On the Waterfront. © THE KOBAL COLLECTION/ART RESOURCE, NY.

On the Waterfront is a prime example of how a film may be used as a political and personal tool. The film's plot and the dilemma of Terry Malloy directly relate to the Hollywood blacklist. After World War II (1939–45), the House Un-American Activities Committee (HUAC) was investigating alleged communist influence in the motion picture industry. Those who were called before HUAC were routinely asked, "Are you now or have you ever been a member of the Communist Party?" They were expected to answer "yes" and plead for forgiveness. They were also expected to "name names," that is, to identify others they knew to be Communist Party members. If they refused to fully cooperate, they were blacklisted (kept from being hired) from motion pictures, **television** (see entry under 1940s—TV and Radio in volume 3), and **radio** (see entry under 1920s—TV and Radio in volume 2).

Kazan and Budd Schulberg (1914–2009), author of the *On the Waterfront* screenplay, were both called before HUAC. Both chose to name names. In his 1988 autobiography, Kazan acknowledged the allegorical nature of *On the Waterfront* when he wrote, "When Brando, at the end, yells at Lee Cobb, the mob boss, 'I'm glad what I done—you hear me?—glad what I done!' that was me saying, with identical heat, that I was glad I'd testified as I had. . . . So when critics say that I put my story and my feelings on the screen, to justify my informing, they are right."

However, it may be argued that, in *On the Waterfront,* Terry Malloy is testifying against racketeers who are clearly defined villains. The investigators all are depicted in a positive light, as hard-working crimefighters. Yet in real life, Kazan and Schulberg testified against Americans who were not lawbreakers, who were being hounded by the politically conservative members of HUAC because of their liberalism and leftist political beliefs.

Kazan alleged that he named names because communism was a threat to America and needed to be exposed and destroyed. His critics, meanwhile, claimed—and still claim—that he did so solely to save his career.

Rob Edelman

For More Information

Braudy, Leo. *On the Waterfront.* London: British Film Institute, 2005.

Kazan, Elia. *A Life.* New York: Knopf, 1988.

Navasky, Victor S. *Naming Names.* New York: Viking Press, 1980.

On the Waterfront (film). Columbia Pictures, 1954.

Schulberg, Budd. *On the Waterfront: The Final Shooting Script.* Carbondale: Southern Illinois University Press, 1980.

Peyton Place

Little did Grace Metalious (1924–1964) realize that, when she authored *Peyton Place* (1956), a novel set in the fictional New England title town, she would be creating a financial gold mine. Metalious was a thirty-two-year-old Gilmanton, New Hampshire, housewife with three children, a high school education, and no previous experience as a writer. The story she told involved scandal and sin in the small town. Peyton Place became one of the most famous fictional places in America. It eventually became the setting of a second novel, two hit movies, one ground-breaking prime-time **television** (see entry under 1940s—TV and Radio in volume 3) series, one daytime **soap opera** (see entry under 1930s—TV and Radio in volume 2), and two made-for-TV movies.

In *Peyton Place,* Metalious tells the story of Allison MacKenzie, an adolescent whose mother, Constance, operates a dress shop. Constance claims that she is a widow, but it eventually is revealed that she never wed Allison's father. Constance and Allison are surrounded by a full cast of characters. Among them are Betty Anderson, Allison's flirtatious schoolmate; Rodney Harrington, a spoiled rich boy; Selena Cross, Allison's best pal, who comes from a poor family; and Michael Rossi, the new high school principal. The novel spotlights these and other characters in various plots and subplots, revealing their less-than-stellar pasts and dirty little secrets.

Upon its publication, *Peyton Place* earned generally unfavorable reviews from critics. Readers, however, were captivated by it, and it became a **best-seller** (see entry under 1940s—Commerce in volume 3). In fact, the book was the third top-selling novel of 1956 and the second top-seller of 1957. By 1965, it had become the highest-selling novel in U.S. history, a mark since surpassed. Metalious also authored a sequel, *Return to Peyton Place* (1959).

The movie *Peyton Place* (1957) came a year after the book's release. The six-figure sum Metalious earned for the screen rights was the largest paid at that time for a first novel. The film was as successful as the book and was the top box office hit of its year. Although it is not considered a cinema classic, at the time the film did receive nine Academy Award nominations, including Best Picture and Best Actress (Lana Turner [1921–1995], cast as Constance MacKenzie).

The first film was followed by the screen version of *Return to Peyton Place* (1961). The property resurfaced with *Peyton Place,* the television series (1964–69), which was broadcast on ABC. The series is noteworthy as prime-time television's first official soap opera. Until the premier of TV's *Peyton Place,* programs featuring melodramatic stories whose plot lines continued from show to show and week to week only were aired during the daytime. Additionally, *Peyton Place* was the first prime-time series to be broadcast twice a week, and then three times a week between 1965 and 1967. Two young actors emerged as stars: Mia Farrow (1945–), cast as Allison MacKenzie, and Ryan O'Neal (1941–), playing Rodney Harrington. Next came a daytime soap opera, *Return to Peyton Place* (1972–74), airing on NBC. Two television movies, *Murder in*

Peyton Place (1977) and, inevitably, *Peyton Place: The Next Generation* (1985), followed.

Audrey Kupferberg

For More Information

Metalious, George, and June O'Hara. *The Girl from "Peyton Place": A Biography of Grace Metalious.* New York: Dell, 1965.

Metalious, Grace. *Peyton Place.* New York: Messner, 1956.

Peyton Place (film). Twentieth Century-Fox, 1957.

Return to Peyton Place (film). Twentieth Century-Fox, 1961.

Rosin, James. *Peyton Place: The Television Series.* Philadelphia: Autumn Road, 2010.

Toth, Emily. *Inside Peyton Place: The Life of Grace Metalious.* Garden City, NY: Doubleday, 1981.

Shane

In 1953, George Stevens (1904–1975) directed the classic **Western** (see entry under 1930s—Film and Theater in volume 2) *Shane*. The movie was a critical and popular success in its own time, but over the years its place in popular culture has grown even stronger. The film has an enduring ability to tap into Americans' nostalgia for a simpler, less complicated time, in which good and evil were well-defined and easily distinguishable and regular folks could win out over the big guys.

The film's title character, played by Alan Ladd (1913–1964), is among the most iconic of Western heroes. He is individualistic and self-sufficient, arriving alone and ultimately leaving alone. He is a friendly and well-mannered buckskinned gunslinger. He does not quite fit into society but is still able to walk the border between the wild and civilization. Although not a lawman, over the course of the film Shane becomes a force for moral justice who acts because the law cannot.

Shane was among the first of a new kind of Western that emerged in the 1950s, the "adult" or "psychological" Western. Simply put, these films concentrate on the psychological and moral conflicts of the hero and his relationship to society. *Shane* presents a gritty and unrelenting portrait of the harshness faced by settlers in the American West. This view is perhaps best highlighted by a scene in which the evil Wilson shoots down the inexperienced Torrey. Moviegoers heard Wilson's laughter and saw the overmatched Torrey falling dead face first in the mud.

They could not help but think that this was a much more likely scenario for a gunfight than the cleaned-up versions of shootouts presented in earlier Westerns.

Shane wins out in the end, protecting the values of civilization against brutality, but he gets shot. As he rides off into the distance, viewers do not know whether he'll live or die. The young boy Joey Starrett cries out after him, "Shane, come back!" It is a mythic ending, but it is also tinged with tragedy. The self-sufficient and nonconformist Shane simply does not fit in the society he has helped to protect. Shane's departure signals the death of a part of America's collective past; like Joey, audiences are left hollow, lamenting his passing and longing for his return.

Robert C. Sickels

For More Information

Countryman, Edward, and Evonne von Heussen-Countryman. *BFI Film Classics: Shane.* London: BFI Publishing, 1999.

Hine, Robert V. *The American West: An Interpretive History.* 2nd ed. Boston: Little Brown, 1984.

McGee, Patrick. *From Shane to Kill Bill: Rethinking the Western.* Malden, MA: Blackwell, 2007.

Stevens, George, director. *Shane* (video). Hollywood: Paramount Home Video, 1979.

3-D Movies

For an all-too-brief period in the early 1950s, three-dimensional (3-D) movies enjoyed huge popularity among American moviegoers. Motion picture images are by their nature flat and two-dimensional. In a 3-D film, an illusion of depth and perspective is created with the help of special glasses. Use of these special glasses results in an image's foreground appearing to stand apart from its background. In a 3-D film, an animal could be made to appear to leap off the screen and into the audience. A knife-tossing villain or spear-throwing warrior could appear to be actually hurling the weapon at the viewer.

In the early 1950s, movie ticket sales were falling fast as Americans in great numbers were moving from the cities to the **suburbs** (see entry under 1950s—The Way We Lived in volume 3), where there were fewer movie houses. **Television** (see entry under 1940s—TV and Radio in volume 3) sales were skyrocketing. Potential audiences saw little reason to

Moviegoers enjoying the 3-D experience. © RANDY FARIS/CORBIS.

spend money on a babysitter, a restaurant meal, and movie tickets when free entertainment at home, in the form of one's TV set, could be had. In order to lure patrons back to movie houses, the motion picture industry employed gimmicks to bring viewers sights and sounds they neither could see nor hear at home. One such tool was 3-D, which resulted in more realistic—and potentially more entertaining—movie images.

Three-dimensional movies evolved from **stereoscopy** (see entry on stereoscopes under 1900s—Commerce in volume 1), a technique developed in the nineteenth century for the viewing of still images. In stereoscopy, a three-dimensional illusion is produced via the use of a stereoscope, an optical device that offers up slightly different images to both eyes, resulting in what appears to be a 3-D picture. Over the years, the stereoscopy technique evolved. During the first decades of the twentieth century, scores of stereoscopic moving image systems had been developed, but none were commercially marketable. In the 1950s, the technique was adapted to feature-length Hollywood productions. The first 3-D feature of the period was *Bwana Devil* (1952), an action tale set in Africa and spotlighting murderous, man-eating lions. The most popular 3-D film was *House of Wax* (1953), a horror film starring Vincent Price (1911–1993) as a sculptor who commits murders and transforms his victims into wax museum figures.

Not all 3-D films were horror chillers or adventure yarns. *Kiss Me Kate* (1953), a hit **Broadway** (see entry under 1900s—Film and Theater in volume 1) musical composed by Cole Porter (1893–1964) and based on *The Taming of the Shrew* by William Shakespeare (1564–1616), was shot in 3-D. Even Alfred Hitchcock (1899–1980), the medium's celebrated master of suspense, directed a 3-D film: *Dial M For Murder* (1954), the tale of a man who plots his wife's killing. In order to view a 3-D movie, filmgoers had to wear throwaway glasses outfitted with one red and one blue lens, which allowed each eye to distinguish only specific parts of the on-screen image.

Originally, 3-D was just a fad. The initial thrill of watching three-dimensional images soon waned. The technique's costs and limitations, coupled with the discomfort of wearing the glasses, resulted in the industry abandoning 3-D film production. The technique was reintroduced for a short time in 1980s horror films and employed again a decade later in limited-release IMAX 3-D movies.

In the early 2000s, 3-D became more common again, not only in movie theaters but also on televisions and **cellular telephones** (see entry under 1990s—The Way We Lived in volume 5). Because of improvements to technology, 3-D could be added in the post-production period of films, leading to the release of many films in both regular and 3-D formats. 3-D cameras also advanced, leading to extraordinary films shot in real 3-D, such as the award-winning *Avatar* (2009; see entry under 2000s—Film and Theatre in volume 6). Between 2007 and 2009, twenty-five 3-D films were released, and more than double that number between 2010 and 2011. 3-D televisions also became available, with networks like **ESPN** (see entry under 1970s—TV and Radio in volume 4) airing some of their coverage in 3-D. More than one million 3-D televisions were sold in the United States in 2010. In 2011, the cellular telephone hardware producer LG introduced the first 3-D cell phone, the Optimus, which, like some of the 3-D televisions, did not require special glasses to enjoy 3-D images. Once thought to be essentially a gimmick technology, 3-D seemed to be here to stay in the early twenty-first century.

Rob Edelman

For More Information

Darrah, William C. *The World of Stereographs.* Gettysburg, PA: Darrah, 1977.

DiOrio, Carl. "At Confab, Glasses Are Half Full: 'Consumer Demand Is Clear' as Optimism Reigns at First 3D Experience." *Hollywood Reporter* (September 27, 2010): pp. 7.

Earle, Edward W., ed. *Points of View, the Stereograph in America: A Cultural History.* Rochester, NY: Visual Studies Workshop, 1979.

Gikas, Mike. "LG Optimus, the World's First 3D Smart Phone." *ConsumerReports.org.* (February 14, 2011; accessed on July 27, 2011).

Graser, Marc, and David S. Cohen. "A Wary Eye: Auds Slow to Buy 3D." *Variety* (January 11, 2011): pp. 1.

Hayes, R. M. *3-D Movies: A History of Wonders of Stereograph Cinema.* Jefferson, NC: McFarland, 1998.

Jones, John. *Wonders of the Stereograph.* New York: Knopf, 1976.

Lord, Peter, and Brian Sibley. *Creating 3-D Animation: The Aardman Book of Filmmaking.* Rev. ed. New York: Harry N. Abrams, 2004.

Waldsmith, John. *Stereo Views: An Illustrated History & Price Guide.* 2nd ed. Iola, WI: Krause, 2002.

Wing, Paul. *Stereoscopes: The First One Hundred Years.* Nashua, NH: Transition, 1996.

1950s

Food and Drink

Although most Americans continued to eat as they always had—at home, with freshly prepared foods—several important trends in American culinary habits began to emerge in the 1950s: standardization and franchising. The symbol of both these trends was the most noted restaurant chain of the century: McDonald's. Founded in 1948, McDonald's expanded across America in the 1950s through a system known as franchising. Franchising offered individual owners the opportunity to own a profitable restaurant if they would follow the McDonald's business formula.

The McDonald's formula was simple: Offer hamburgers, French fries, and milkshakes at a reasonable price, and make sure that the customer receives the same product every time at every restaurant. It helped the restaurant chain sell "billions and billions" of burgers—according to one of it's slogans—and it spawned a number of imitators across the country, most notably Burger King.

Food was becoming standardized in other ways as well, particularly with the rise of frozen, pre-prepared meals, often known as TV dinners. These complete meals could be pulled from the freezer, heated in the oven, and enjoyed in front of the TV in less than an hour and with very little effort. In 1954, just the second year of their existence, Swanson sold ten million TV dinners.

The eating habits of the 1950s have since been depicted in a number of movies and TV shows. The center of both the nostalgic film *American Graffiti* (1973) and the long-running TV series *Happy Days* (1974–84) was the local diner where teenagers gathered to eat hamburgers and fries. These and countless other pop culture references indicate that hamburgers and fries were the food of the decade.

Burger King

Burger King, along with **McDonald's** (see entry under 1940s—Food and Drink in volume 3), has created the image of the American "hamburger chain." It mostly serves up **hamburgers** (see entry under 1950s—Food and Drink in volume 3), **French fries** (see entry under 1950s—Food and Drink in volume 3), and shakes. The chain lures customers with clever marketing campaigns and, starting in the 1970s, with what became perhaps the company's most famous jingle: "Have it your way at Burger King."

The first Burger King was opened by James McLamore (1926–1996) and David Edgerton (1928–) in Miami, Florida, in 1954—a year before McDonald's was franchised—selling hamburgers for eighteen cents. Three years later, Burger King introduced what would become its most famous burger, the Whopper, at a price of thirty-seven cents. The chain was eventually nicknamed the "Home of the Whopper."

As of 2011, there were 12,300 Burger Kings in the United States and 76 countries around the world. In the twenty-first century, at least 1.6 billion Whoppers are sold each year. Still, the company ranks a distant second to McDonald's in sales worldwide.

Rob Edelman

For More Information

Burger King. *Company Info.* http://www.bk.com/en/us/company-info/index.html (accessed July 27, 2011).

Burger King. *Investor Relations.* http://investor.bk.com/phoenix.zhtml?c=87140&p=irol-IRHome (accessed July 27, 2011).

McLamore, James W. *The Burger King: Jim McLamore and the Building of an Empire.* New York: McGraw-Hill, 1998.

French Fries

French fries are thin strips of deep-fried potato topped with a choice of condiments. Perfect as a snack or a side dish, French fries have long been a staple of **fast-food** (see entry under 1920s—Food and Drink in volume 2) restaurants like **McDonald's** (see entry under 1940s—Food and Drink in volume 3).

Most experts trace the origin of the French fry to eighteenth-century Belgium, not France. Wherever they were first made, however, fries quickly became a taste sensation all over Europe. At first, they were served only in restaurants, but street vendors in cities like Paris and Brussels soon began selling them as well. In modern times, French fries are still a popular street snack in Europe. They are known as "patat" in Holland, "chips" in England, and "pommes frites" in France. Throughout the world, such condiments as ketchup, vinegar, and mayonnaise are used to enhance the taste of French fries.

The French-fry craze slowly spread across the Atlantic Ocean to America. After developing a love of *pommes frites* while serving as the U.S. minister to France, Thomas Jefferson (1743–1826) served them to guests at his home in Virginia upon his return to America in 1789. However, the French fry did not really catch on with the public until the twentieth century, when soldiers returning from World War I (1914–18) brought back a hunger for the deep-fried potato treat. In the 1950s, American fast-food chains like McDonald's developed systems for deep-frying large quantities of French fries each day. This mass production allowed French fries to grow in popularity as the perfect accompaniment to **hamburgers** (see entry under 1950s—Food and Drink in volume 3) and other fast food. Doctors and other health professionals condemned the fatty snack as unhealthy, but Americans began consuming fries in large quantities. They particularly liked the McDonald's variety, which became the standard of quality. The burger chain even developed a potato computer to monitor the temperature of the frying oil and to notify the operator when a batch of fries was perfectly cooked.

By the turn of the twenty-first century, French fries accounted for more than one-fourth of all potatoes sold in the United States. In 1998, McDonald's made more than 6.8 million pounds of French fries each day. French fries had become identified so closely with American hamburger meals in the twenty-first century that in Japan and Southeast Asia they were promoted as "American fries."

Robert E. Schnakenberg

For More Information

Graulich, David. *The French Fry Companion.* New York: Lebhar-Friedman Books, 1999.

Meltzer, Milton *The Amazing Potato: A Story in Which the Incas, Conquistadors, Marie Antoinette, Thomas Jefferson, Wars, Famines, Immigrants, and French Fries All Play a Part.* New York: HarperCollins, 1992.

The Official French Fries Pages. http://www.officialfrenchfries.com/ (accessed July 27, 2011).

Salaman, Redcliffe N. *The History and Social Influence of the Potato.* Cambridge: Cambridge University Press, 1985.

Schlosser, Eric. *Fast Food Nation.* New York: Houghton Mifflin, 2001.

Hamburger

Typically served with **French fries** (see entry under 1950s— Food and Drink in volume 3) and a soft drink, the hamburger ranks with the **hot dog** (see entry under 1900s—Food and Drink in volume 1) and apple pie as one of America's truly national foods.

The ever-popular hamburger. © STUDIO 1231/ SHUTTERSTOCK.

Named for the style of steak found in the German city of Hamburg, the hamburger consists of a ground-beef patty usually served on a soft round bun, often garnished with a pickle. "Billions and billions" have been served by the **McDonald's** (see entry under 1940s—Food and Drink in volume 3) restaurant chain alone, with uncounted others prepared by other restaurants, large and small. The hamburger was the favorite snack of Wimpy, a character in the old ***Popeye*** (see entry under 1920s—Print Culture in volume 2) comic strip, whose favorite expression was "I will gladly pay you Tuesday for a hamburger today." Inventive short-order cooks and backyard barbecuers have developed many variations, such as the cheeseburger.

Edward Moran

For More Information

McDonald, Ronald L. *The Complete Hamburger: The History of America's Favorite Sandwich.* Secaucus, NJ: Carol Publishing, 1997.

Ozersky, Josh. *The Hamburger: A History.* New Haven, CT: Yale University Press, 2008.

Tennyson, Jeffrey. *Hamburger Heaven: The Illustrated History of the Hamburger.* New York: Hyperion, 1993.

TV Dinners

"It's a TV dinner. You are supposed to watch TV while you eat it." This is how a Polish immigrant explains this American phenomenon to his newly arrived cousin in the 1985 film *Stranger Than Paradise.* In fact, TV dinners, invented in 1953, represented much of what was new and technologically exciting in 1950s American culture. A marvel of modern, streamlined efficiency, the TV dinner combined home refrigeration and **television** (see entry under 1940s—TV and Radio in volume 3), two of the decade's most popular new inventions. Besides that, they allowed Mom to take a break from preparing the family meal and to sit down with the family to eat in front of the television. This shift in focus from gathering around the dinner table to gathering around the television would change American family life forever.

TV dinners originated as a creative solution to a business problem. C. A. Swanson and Sons was a poultry supplier that had sold chickens and turkeys nationwide since the 1920s. In the late fall of 1953, the company found itself with 260 tons of turkey that had not sold during the Thanksgiving season. As the turkeys rode back and forth across the country in refrigerated train cars, Swanson executive Gerry Thomas (1922–2005) tried to think of a solution. The lightweight aluminum tray in which his food was served on an airline flight gave him an idea. He quickly designed a molded aluminum tray with four separate compartments. Then he pitched an idea to Clark Swanson, one of the owners of the company. He proposed that the manufacturer put a different food in each compartment and package the whole thing as an individual **frozen dinner** (see entry under 1930s—Food and Drink in volume 2). Tying the meal in with television could give it the appeal of a modern trend.

Thomas's idea was a radical notion at a time when Americans were used to eating only home-cooked meals prepared from fresh ingredients. Few people owned televisions and even fewer had freezing compartments in their **refrigerators** (see entry under 1910s—The Way We Lived in volume 1). Swanson and Thomas had no idea if people would accept the new dinners, but they used up their leftover turkeys making five thousand dinners with cornbread stuffing, buttered peas, and gravy. They packaged them in a box designed to look like a television screen and sold them for ninety-nine cents each.

The TV dinner concept struck a chord with American families. The first five thousand dinners sold quickly. During the next year, Swanson produced and sold ten million dinners. By 2010, Swanson and other manufacturers were selling more than ten million dinners a week, making TV dinners a $4.5-billion-a-year industry.

Tina Gianoulis

For More Information

Gardner, Marilyn. "Dining for 45 Years with an American Icon." *Christian Science Monitor* (April 7, 1999): pp. 15–16.

I'll Buy That! 50 Small Wonders and Big Deals That Revolutionized the Lives of Consumers. Mount Vernon, NY: Consumers Union, 1986.

McLaughlin, Michael, and Katie O'Kennedy. "1950s: Tupperware, TV Dinners and Rock 'n' Roll." *Bon Appetit* (September 1999): pp. 190–99.

Shaffer, Jeffrey. "Swanson's in the Cozy Cathode Glow: Growing Up with Swanson's TV Dinners." *Christian Science Monitor* (April 16, 1999): p. 11.

1950s

Music

Music in the 1950s was dominated by the birth of rock and roll. Rock and roll was a powerful new form of music that combined elements of rhythm and blues (R&B), pop, blues, and hillbilly music to create a sound that truly shook America. Musician Ray Charles (1930–2004) described the music this way: "When they get a couple of guitars together with a backbeat, that's rock and roll." Rock and roll was raw, powerful, and compelling; it drew young people onto dance floors and into record stores in a way that no music had done before.

The undisputed king of rock and roll in the 1950s was Elvis Presley (1935–1977). Presley's hip-shaking stage performances made teenage girls swoon. Other rock stars of the day included Fats Domino (1928–), Chuck Berry (1926–), Little Richard (1932–), Jerry Lee Lewis (1935–), Buddy Holly (1936–1959), and Johnny Ray (1927–1990).

Rock and roll was a social as well as a musical force. In an era when much of American culture was segregated (blacks and whites were distinctly separated), rock and roll was integrated. Blacks and whites played in bands together, recorded each other's songs, and were played on the same radio stations. Rock and roll was made popular by a new kind of radio programmer called a disc jockey. Disc jockeys chose the music that they played and helped introduce new rock bands to thousands of devoted listeners. The most popular of the disc jockeys, like Alan Freed

(1922–1965) and, later, Wolfman Jack (1938–1995), became celebrities themselves.

Jazz was also undergoing a process of transformation. In the 1940s, jazz had been the music of urban hipsters. The jazz of the 1940s was heard in nightclubs, most often in black neighborhoods. In the 1950s, jazz was brought out of the cities and into new respectability in popular jazz festivals. The Newport Jazz Festival (after 1986, called the JVC Jazz Festival), held in Newport, Rhode Island, became the granddaddy of American jazz festivals and attracted twenty-six thousand fans in its second year. Soon, however, the hippest jazz players boycotted the festival. Many of them returned to playing before small audiences who they thought better understood and appreciated their increasingly difficult and intellectual music.

Disc Jockeys

The rise of **radio** (see entry under 1920s—TV and Radio in volume 2) as an entertainment medium in the 1920s and 1930s resulted in the advent of the disc jockey (or DJ) as an influential on-air personality. Not only did disc jockeys play records; they spoke directly to listeners as they introduced the music, read commercials, and made announcements, essentially serving as a relatable link between the audience and the programming.

Initially, disc jockeys were not skilled announcers, but technicians who operated the broadcast equipment and doubled as on-air voices. The most influential of the early professional DJs was Martin Block (c. 1901–1967), a staff announcer at New York's WNEW-AM, who suggested that the station play recorded music. This led to his hosting *The Make-Believe Ballroom,* which became enormously popular during the 1930s and 1940s. Block was its host from 1936 through 1956. On the program, he invited listeners to an imaginary music show and amused them with humor and recorded melodies.

Disc jockeys enjoyed the height of their influence during the 1950s and 1960s. Before that time, the major radio networks—the National Broadcasting Company (NBC), the Columbia Broadcasting System (CBS), and the American Broadcasting Company (ABC)—had control of the airwaves. Before long, however, countless independent radio stations began broadcasting. They lacked the programming resources of the majors and depended upon recorded music to fill their airtime. Thus, the man selecting and playing the records and the relationship he developed with listeners became a key component to the success of a radio station.

Easily the most famous and influential 1950s DJ was Alan Freed (1922–1965). In 1951, while broadcasting in Cleveland, Ohio, Freed began playing **rhythm and blues** (R&B; see entry under 1940s—Music in volume 3) recordings, which he dubbed "rock 'n' roll." Three years later, he moved his "Moondog Rock and Roll Party" to New York. More than anyone else, Freed was single-handedly responsible for making **rock and roll** (see entry under 1950s—Music in volume 3) a dominant force in American youth culture. Just as significantly, he insisted on playing the original recordings of African American performers, rather than the more lukewarm renditions (or "cover" versions) recorded by white singers.

During this period, DJs did more than play records. They managed bands, promoted tours, hosted live rock-and-roll shows, and befriended and advised performers. One New York DJ, Murray Kaufman (known as "Murray the K," 1922–1982), became a key figure in introducing the British rock group the **Beatles** (see entry under 1960s—Music in volume 4) to American audiences in 1964. Indeed, by deciding which music to play or not play, a popular DJ had a great impact on the success or failure of a record.

The power of the disc jockey evaporated somewhat during the "payola" scandal of the late 1950s. A congressional investigation determined that DJs were being bribed by record promoters to play certain songs. This ended the careers of several major DJs, including Freed, who was disliked by many conservatives for introducing what then was known as "race" music to white teenagers.

The growing popularity of FM broadcast bands, beginning in the late 1960s, led to an evolution in the disc jockey persona. Unlike their AM counterparts, the typical FM DJ was quieter, knew more about music, and played songs from albums—33⅓ rpm (revolutions-per-minute) records, or **long-playing records** (see entry under 1940s—Music in volume 3)—in addition to the singles found on 45 rpm records. Additionally, FM stations began hiring women DJs. Eventually, as programmers and market analysts became the ones who selected the music played on radio stations, the power of the DJ eroded.

Rob Edelman

For More Information

Brewster, Bill, and Frank Broughton. *Last Night a DJ Saved My Life: The History of the Disc Jockey.* Rev. ed. London: Headline, 2006.

Chapple, Steve, and Reebee Garofalo. *Rock 'n' Roll Is Here to Pay.* Chicago: Nelson-Hall, 1977.

Gillett, Charlie. *The Sound of the City: The Rise of Rock and Roll.* 3rd ed. London: Souvenir, 2009.

Jackson, John A. *Big Beat Heat: Alan Freed and the Early Years of Rock & Roll.* New York: Schirmer, 1991.

Passman, Arnold. *The Deejays.* New York: Macmillan, 1971.

Williams, Gilbert. *The Legendary Pioneers of Black Radio.* Westport, CT: Praeger, 1998.

Electric Guitar

More than just a technological breakthrough, the electric guitar changed popular music.
© PAULINE ST. DENIS/CORBIS.

No instrument is more associated with American music than the electric guitar. It is the major instrument in **rock and roll** (see entry under 1950s—Music in volume 3), **blues** (see entry under 1920s—Music in volume 2), and **country music** (see entry under 1940s—Music in volume 3). It has been played by some of the great musicians of the **jazz** (see entry under 1900s—Music in volume 1) world as well. Simply stated, the electric guitar is much like an acoustic guitar, except that a magnetic pickup has been added to turn the vibrations of the strings into electrical impulses. When amplified, the electrical impulses produce sound. The electric guitar is more than a piece of technology; it reshaped American popular music in the 1950s and after.

The drive to create an electrified guitar came from the search for a solution to a common problem. Acoustic guitars had a hard time being heard over the noise of a crowded barroom or concert hall. The acoustic version of the instrument could not be heard next to a roaring **big band** (see entry under 1930s—Music in volume 2) full of trumpets and saxophones. By the 1930s, a number of inventors were experimenting with amplified guitars. Companies such as Gibson began marketing them that same decade. Perhaps the most important inventor was Leo Fender (1909–1991), who was the first to mass produce solid-bodied electric guitars. Fender's Stratocaster and Telecaster became very popular models in rock music and in country music. Musician Les Paul (1916–2009) was another great early experimenter with electric guitars, eventually designing his "Les Paul" model of guitar for the Gibson Company. Since the 1950s, the technology for producing electric guitars has changed only slightly. Classic models are still produced, along with hundreds of others.

Few technological inventions have had as much impact on music as the electric guitar has had. Amplification opened up whole new worlds for guitarists. With it, they could be heard as soloists, and amplification allowed many new sounds, using electronic effects, to be produced. The electric guitar's biggest impact was in rock music; in fact, it defined the sound. The hard edge and loud volume was perfect for the rebelliousness of rock and roll. Rock music from the 1950s through the 1990s and beyond featured electric guitars prominently. Chuck Berry (1926–) and Buddy Holly (1936–1959) brought the electric guitar to mass attention in the 1950s. The **Beatles**, the **Rolling Stones** (see these entries under 1960s—Music in volume 4), and the Who were among the many great guitar-based bands to feature electric guitars in the 1960s. Jimi Hendrix (1942–1970) was popular in the late 1960s for the wild sounds he created on his Fender Stratocaster, as was guitar great Eric Clapton (1945–). Electric guitars defined the sound of hard rock, **heavy metal** (see entry under 1980s—Music in volume 5), **punk** (see entry under 1970s—Music in volume 4), and **alternative rock** (see entry under 1990s—Music in volume 5) in the 1970s, 1980s, and 1990s, and continues to be a definitive part of popular music in the twenty-first century. The popularity of the electric guitar has been undiminished since its invention. It continues to be the key instrument in rock and pop music, a tribute to its adaptability and popularity.

Timothy Berg

For More Information

Freeth, Nick, and Charles Alexander. *The Electric Guitar.* Philadelphia: Courage Books, 1999.

Gruhn, George, and Walter Carter. *Electric Guitars and Basses: A Photographic History.* Rev. ed. New York: Backbeat Books, 2010.

Millard, A. J. *The Electric Guitar: A History of an American Icon.* Baltimore, MD: Johns Hopkins University Press, 2004.

Smith, Richard R. *Fender: The Sound Heard 'round the World.* Fullerton, CA: Garfish, 1995.

Wheeler, Tom. *American Guitars: An Illustrated History.* Rev. ed. New York: HarperPerennial, 1992.

B. B. King (1925–)

B. B. King is probably the most popular and successful **blues** (see entry under 1920s—Music in volume 2) singer and guitarist ever to live. His distinctive style, played on his famous guitar named "Lucille," has influenced countless musicians both in blues and **rock and roll** (see entry under 1950s—Music in volume 3) music.

Born Riley B. King in rural Mississippi in 1925, "B. B.," as he was known, heard early blues guitarists and singers and learned to play in their style before developing his own. King began his career in Memphis, Tennessee, playing on street corners and at local clubs. In the mid-1940s, he had his own ten-minute show on WDIA radio in Memphis. King began recording singles in 1949 and scored a hit song with "Three O'Clock Blues" in 1951. King toured constantly, often playing more than 340 nights a year, and developed a loyal fan base. In the 1960s and 1970s, he had hits with "The Thrill Is Gone" and the albums *Live at the Regal* and *Live in Cook County Jail.*

Younger fans discovered King in the late 1980s when he teamed up with Irish rock group U2 on "When Love Comes to Town." In 2000, he recorded the successful *Riding with the King* with rock musician Eric Clapton (1945–), and he won a Grammy award for his 2008 release, *One Kind of Favor.* Also in the early 2000s, King launched his own channel on Sirius Satellite Radio, B. B. King's Bluesville. King continued to regularly play his now-classic sound to blues fans all over the world in the early twenty-first century.

Timothy Berg

For More Information

BBKing.com: The Official Website. http://www.bbking.com/ (accessed July 28, 2011).

Danchin, Sebastian. *Blues Boy: The Life and Music of B. B. King.* Jackson: University of Mississippi Press, 1998.

King, B. B. *Blues All Around Me: The Autobiography of B. B. King.* New York: Avon Books, 1996.

Sawyer, Charles. *The Arrival of B. B. King: The Authorized Biography.* New York: Da Capo Press, 1980.

Elvis Presley (1935–1977)

In the mid-1950s, a new kind of music was taking the youth culture of the United States by storm, winning the hearts and shaking the hips of America's teenagers. That music was **rock and roll** (see entry under 1950s—Music in volume 3). The new style of music was controversial for several reasons. It was loud. It was unruly. Its sounds were rooted in the **rhythm and blues** (R&B; see entry under 1940s—Music in volume 3) of black America. In a reflection of the times, some white middle-class parents viewed rock and roll as nothing less than a communist plot, a scheme to enslave the minds of their naive, easily led children.

Coming to the rescue of rock and roll was Elvis Presley, a good-natured white boy from Memphis, Tennessee (and born in Tupelo, Mississippi). Presley's outward surliness and hip-shaking sex appeal made him an instant twentieth-century cultural phenomenon. Elvis may have been white, but he sure *sounded* black and authentic as he thrilled teens with songs like "Hound Dog," "Jailhouse Rock," "Don't Be Cruel," and other million-selling hits. He immediately transferred his star appeal to the big screen, appearing in a series of wildly popular box-office hits. From his debut in *Love Me Tender* (1956), an otherwise average **Western** (see entry under 1930s—Film and Theater in volume 2) set during the Civil War (1861–65) era, his charismatic screen presence was undeniable.

Though black performers like Chuck Berry (1926–), Little Richard (1935–), and Fats Domino (1928–) may have invented the form, it was Elvis Presley who transformed rock and roll into a style of music for mass audiences. During the late 1950s and early 1960s, Elvis was truly the biggest celebrity in America. Although his career had several downturns, especially when he lost touch with youthful audiences and begin singing easy-listening pop music in the mid-1960s, Elvis remained a star. Throughout the late 1960s and early 1970s, he increasingly performed in Las Vegas, Nevada, and in lavish arena concerts. By the mid-1970s, however, the "King of Rock 'n' Roll" was battling drug abuse and weight problems as his personal life fell apart.

Presley died of a heart attack in 1977 at the age of forty-two, but he has truly lived on in American culture. His Nashville, Tennessee, home "Graceland" is a shrine for his many fans; the U.S. Postal Service issued an Elvis commemorative stamp in 1993; and his albums continue to sell well into the twenty-first century. Amid a small core of Elvis fanatics whose reports of Elvis sightings appear in tabloids, the rumor persists: "Elvis Lives!"

Rob Edelman and Tom Pendergast

For More Information

Daily, Robert. *Elvis Presley: The King of Rock 'n' Roll.* New York: Franklin Watts, 1996.

Gentry, Tony. *Elvis Presley.* New York: Chelsea House, 1994.

Guralnick, Peter. *Careless Love: The Unmaking of Elvis Presley.* Boston: Little, Brown, 1998.

Guralnick, Peter. *Last Train to Memphis: The Rise of Elvis Presley.* Boston: Little, Brown, 1994.

Hampton, Wilborn. *Elvis Presley: A Twentieth-Century Life.* New York: Viking, 2007.

Rubel, David. *Elvis Presley: The Rise of Rock and Roll.* Brookfield, CT: Millbrook Press, 1991.

Woog, Adam. *Elvis Presley.* San Diego: Lucent Books, 1997.

Rock and Roll

One of the most important forces in American culture, rock and roll emerged in the early 1950s as the merger of several styles of black popular music and white popular music, some reaching back into the nineteenth century and before. The two most important of these styles were black **rhythm and blues** (R&B; see entry under 1940s—Music in volume 3) music and white **country music** (see entry under 1940s—Music in volume 3). When they came together in the early 1950s, rock and roll was born. From its beginnings, however, rock and roll was more than just music—it was an attitude of youthful rebellion that expressed itself in music, fashion, art, film, and in many other aspects of American culture. Few forms of popular culture have been as influential.

Although the origins of rock and roll go back into the distant past well before the Civil War (1861–65), the merger of R&B music and country music that began in the late 1940s is the most influential. Prior to the late 1940s, these traditions had existed in largely separate worlds for many generations. By the 1940s, they had begun to cross racial and musical lines and influence each other. After World War II (1939–45) especially, record company executives began to deliberately combine the two kinds of music. For example, Syd Nathan (1904–1968) at King Records in Cincinnati, Ohio, recorded both white country and black R&B musicians. Nathan felt that if a rhythm and blues song proved successful in the black record market, why not have a white singer record it in a country style to sell to whites? The formula proved successful.

Nathan was not alone in doing this kind of switch, and soon artists from both styles were learning from each others' music.

Another factor that helped in the creation of rock and roll was **radio** (see entry under 1920s—TV and Radio in volume 2). Radio waves do not know about racial barriers. They will go into anyone's radio at any time. In the late 1940s and early 1950s, young listeners began to tune in to both white country stations and black R&B stations. It was only a matter of time before someone blended the two formats.

Although he was not the first person to play what would become rock and roll, **Elvis Presley** (1935–1977; see entry under 1950s—Music in volume 3), a young singer from Memphis, Tennessee, was the first person to make the merger of these two styles a huge success. At Sun Records, owner Sam Phillips (1923–2003) was recording both black and white musicians, much like Nathan was doing at King Records. Phillips realized that if he could find a white singer to sing black R&B music, he would have a star on his hands. Elvis was that singer. Elvis brought his love for black R&B and his deep roots in country music together in a winning formula. His early records, including "Mystery Train" and "That's Alright," had both the gutsy flavor of R&B music and the twang of country music. When Elvis moved to RCA Records and released such songs as "Jailhouse Rock," "Heartbreak Hotel," and "Hound Dog," he popularized rock even further. After Elvis, a number of other important artists made rock into a distinct form in the 1950s. The most notable of these artists were Chuck Berry (1926–), Buddy Holly (1936–1959), Bill Haley (1925–1981) and the Comets, Gene Vincent (1935–1971), and Eddie Cochran (1938–1960).

By late 1959, Presley was in the army, Holly had died in a plane accident, and rock had gone into a bit of a decline. Fortunately for American fans, in 1964 rock and roll was revived by the so-called British Invasion, led by the **Beatles** (see entry under 1960s—Music in volume 4). The British rock scene included such important rock groups as the **Rolling Stones** (see entry under 1960s—Music in volume 4), the Who, and the Kinks. The Beatles, who grew up listening to the early rock pioneers such as Presley, Holly, and Berry, reshaped the music. The "Fab Four" wrote their own songs, developed their own look, and created a huge sensation wherever they went. The Beatles were also largely responsible for taking rock and roll beyond the teenage themes of young love. In the mid-1960s, they began writing songs on more mature topics and pushing the sound of rock in radically new directions. Their 1967 album

Sgt. Pepper's Lonely Hearts Club Band redefined what rock music could be by organizing the record around a single concept and music that used many new sounds. The 1960s saw rock move in a number of directions. There was surf music, led by the **Beach Boys** (see entry under 1960s— Music in volume 4), psychedelic rock led by Jimi Hendrix (1942–1970) and the Jefferson Airplane, and visionary rock artists such as **Bob Dylan** (1941–; see entry under 1960s— Music in volume 4).

By the 1970s, rock and roll was established as the major force in American music, eclipsing all other forms in popularity and record sales. The 1970s also saw rock fragment into a number of different directions, from the soft pop-rock of such musicians as the Eagles, James Taylor (1948–), and Joni Mitchell (1943–); to the music of such hard rockers as Alice Cooper (1948–), Aerosmith, and **Led Zeppelin** (see entry under 1970s—Music in volume 4); to the **punk** (see entry under 1970s—Music in volume 4) movement of such bands as the Ramones, the **Sex Pistols** (see entry under 1970s—Music in volume 4), and the Clash; and towards the end of the decade, New Wave as practiced by Talking Heads, Blondie, and another Elvis—Elvis Costello (1955–). These variety of styles proved that rock and roll could be many things to many people.

Rock continued to grow as a commercial presence in the 1980s, 1990s, and early 2000s. Those decades saw a number of innovations. In the 1980s, there were more traditional rock acts like Journey and Foreigner; more eclectic British pop-rock acts such as Culture Club, Duran Duran, and the Eurythmics; and solo superstars such as **Madonna** (1958–; see entry under 1980s—Music in volume 5). In the 1990s, the **alternative rock** (see entry under 1990s—Music in volume 5) movement, led in part by such groups as Pearl Jam and **Nirvana** (see entry under 1990s—Music in volume 5), sprang up to challenge the self-satisfaction of 1980's rock. By the end of the 1990s and into the early 2000s, a number of rock's greatest names from the past, such as Bob Dylan, the Rolling Stones, and former Beatle Paul McCartney (1942–), continued to make viable music right alongside talented newcomers with a rock-influenced sound like **Nickelback** (see entry under 2000s—Music in volume 6), Outkast, Green Day, and even rapper **Eminem** (see entry under 2000s—Music in volume 6). In the early twenty-first century, it seemed that rock and roll, although a simple musical style in many ways, was in reality an endlessly inventive form of music with an enduring cultural impact.

Timothy Berg

For More Information

Altschuler, Glenn C. *All Shook Up: How Rock 'n' Roll Changed America.* New York: Oxford University Press, 2003.

Bashe, Patricia Romanowski, and Holly George-Warren. *The Rolling Stone Encyclopedia of Rock and Roll.* Rev. ed. New York: Fireside, 2005.

DeCurtis, Anthony, and James Henke, eds. *The Rolling Stone Illustrated History of Rock and Roll.* 3rd ed. New York: Random House, 1992.

Gillett, Charlie. *The Sound of the City: The Rise of Rock and Roll.* 3rd ed. London: Souvenir, 2009.

Gilmore, Mikal. *Night Beat: A Shadow History of Rock and Roll.* New York: Doubleday, 1998.

Marcus, Greil. *Mystery Train: Images of Rock 'n' Roll Music.* 5th ed. New York: Plume, 2008.

Palmer, Robert. *Rock and Roll: An Unruly History.* New York: Harmony Books, 1995.

Stuessy, Joe, and Scott Lipscomb. *Rock and Roll: Its History and Stylistic Development.* 6th ed. Upper Saddle River, NJ: Pearson Prentice Hall, 2009.

Top 40

Since 1956, the term "Top 40" has referred to both a ranking of the best selling music singles and to a **radio** (see entry under 1920s—TV and Radio in volume 2) format that features those songs. For a song to be included in the list, it must be among the top 40 records in terms of record sales and radio station airplay nationwide. As they grow or fall in popularity, records can move up or down the list. The length of time a record stays on the Top 40 list indicates its overall "hit" status. For better or worse, Top 40 has proved to be an influential format in the world of radio.

Although some stations had featured lists of songs as far back as the 1930s, the Top 40 as a standard format began in the Midwest during the early 1950s. At that time, before **television** (see entry under 1940s—TV and Radio in volume 4) had become widespread, many people listened to the radio as their primary entertainment. Radio stations competed aggressively for their audiences. Some historians give credit for the birth of Top 40 to Todd Storz (1924–1964) of radio station KOWH in Omaha, Nebraska. After hearing people in a bar play the same songs again and again over a period of a few hours on a jukebox, Storz hit on the idea of doing the same thing on radio. The format proved a success, increasing the ratings at KOWH. Soon, other stations adopted the idea, and Top 40 as a radio format was born. In 1970, disc jockey Casey Kasem (1932–) began hosting a radio program called *American Top 40,* which has been broadcast nationwide for over forty years. Kasem also created several other Top 40 and Top 20 radio shows to showcase music in a variety of genres before he retired in 2009.

The early years of Top 40, the late 1950s, included all kinds of music, from **rock and roll** (see entry under 1950s—Music in volume 3) and **pop music** (see entry under 1940s—Music in volume 3) to **country music** (see entry under 1940s—Music in volume 3) and even some **jazz** (see entry under 1900s—Music in volume 1). In addition to playing the Top 40 hits, **disc jockeys** (see entry under 1950s—Music in volume 3) provided entertainment, held contests and gave out prizes, and turned radio into a broader form of entertainment than just music. In order to keep up the format, disc jockeys had to follow their Top 40 lists carefully to ensure that hit songs were repeated more often the higher they were on the list. That success also became a drawback for Top 40. While playing the hits more often to draw listeners and, thus, to help advertisers increase their profits, the format also kept off the air what many listeners felt were more interesting or different songs. After a while, audiences tired of the format, preferring to listen to one kind of music rather than what was most popular at the moment. Although Top 40 remains an important format, it had lost much of its dominance by the early 2000s. Radio formats fragmented into various styles, including hit country, adult contemporary, classic rock, oldies, alternative, and others.

Timothy Berg

For More Information

DeCurtis, Anthony, and James Henke, eds. *The Rolling Stone Illustrated History of Rock and Roll.* 3rd ed. New York: Random House, 1992.

Fong-Torres, Ben. *The Hits Just Keep On Coming: The History of Top 40 Radio.* San Francisco: Miller Freeman Books, 1998.

Pollock, Bruce. *When Rock Was Young: A Nostalgic Review of the Top 40 Era.* New York: Holt, Rinehart and Winston, 1981.

Whitburn, Joel. *The Billboard Book of Top 40 Hits.* 9th ed. New York: Billboard Books, 2010.

Whitburn, Joel. *Joel Whitburn Presents a Century of Pop Music: Year-by-Year Top 40 Rankings of the Songs & Artists That Shaped a Century.* Menominee Falls, WI: Record Research, 1999.

1950s

Print Culture

The 1950s were a decade of tremendous energy in American writing. American authors gained international prominence thanks to the Nobel Prizes awarded to William Faulkner (1897–1962) in 1950 and Ernest Hemingway (1899–1961) in 1952. Hemingway's *The Old Man and the Sea* even made it onto the bestseller list for a time. Norman Mailer (1923–2007) was one of several young writers who gained attention during the decade, thanks to the success of his war novel *The Naked and the Dead.* Other emerging literary talents included Flannery O'Connor (1925–1964), John Cheever (1912–1982), and J. D. Salinger (1919–2010). Salinger's novel *The Catcher in the Rye* was one of the most influential novels of the decade. A new group of writers known as the Beats, or beatniks, defied cultural norms and produced a variety of works that were sharply critical of mainstream society. *On the Road* by Jack Kerouac (1922–1969) and the poem "Howl" by Allen Ginsberg (1926–1997) are the most famous of the Beat writings. All these writers remain subjects of study in classrooms today.

American magazine publishing was also energized in the 1950s. Older magazines were dying off and new magazines were being born. A number of general-interest magazines ceased publication in the 1950s, including *Collier's* (with a circulation of four million), the *American Magazine, Woman's Home Companion,* and *Liberty.* Loss of advertising was the primary cause of most magazine deaths, as advertisers looked for more specialized publications that would better reach their target audience. A number of these specialized, or "niche market," magazines were started in the 1950s. Specialized magazines included *Sports Illustrated* for the sports fans, *Playboy* for swinging bachelors, *National Enquirer* for gossip hounds, and *MAD Magazine* for fans of twisted humor.

A number of children's favorites were produced in the 1950s as well. Dr. Seuss (Theodor Seuss Geisel, 1904–1991) was in his prime during the decade, publishing *Horton Hears a Who* (1954), *How the Grinch Stole Christmas* (1957), and *The Cat in the Hat* (1957). A popular 1950 song about a dancing snowman named Frosty was soon published as a book and then converted into an animated TV show in 1969. Charles Schulz (1922–2000) began publishing a comic strip called *Peanuts* in 1950 which explored the trials and tribulations of a boy named Charlie Brown and his circle of friends. The gentle strip spoke to Americans young and old and was published for fifty years, with the final strip running in newspapers the day after Schulz died on February 12, 2000.

Beatniks and the Beat Movement

The Beat movement was both a literary and social ideology. In the late 1940s and into the 1950s, a group of writers shared a deep distaste for American culture and society as it existed after World War II (1939–45). These writers included Allen Ginsberg (1926–1997), Jack Kerouac (1922–1969), William F. Burroughs (1914–1997), John Clellon Holmes (1926–1988), and Lawrence Ferlinghetti (1919–). In an era when many Americans were content to pursue consumer culture, the Beats—or Beatniks—sought out experiences that were more intensely "real." Sometimes "real" experiences meant physical pleasures such as sex and drugs or more spiritual pursuits such as Eastern religions, particularly Buddhism.

Of the Beats, the two most important figures were Ginsberg and Kerouac. Ginsberg's poem "Howl" was a biting commentary on the values of postwar America. He described how he "saw the best minds of [his] generation destroyed by madness, starving hysterical naked…." The poem soon became a landmark in the world of postwar poetry and literature. Kerouac's 1957 novel ***On the Road*** (see entry under 1950s—Print Culture in volume 3) chronicled the adventures of Kerouac, his friend Neal Cassady (1926?–1968), Ginsberg, Burroughs, and others. The novel painted a vivid picture of Beat life as the vaguely fictionalized characters sought out "real" experiences as they traveled across America. *On the Road* proved highly influential in its own way, helping to bring Beat values to a broad and mostly young audience. Other important early works from the Beat movement included Holmes' novel *Go* (1952) and Burroughs' *Naked Lunch* (1959).

This small group formed the core of the Beat movement. The terms "Beat" and "Beatnik" soon moved beyond the group and into the mainstream vocabulary, attracting a popular following among disaffected youth. Some of these people followed their own version of the Beat lifestyle, but without producing poetry, novels, and other creative expressions. Once the term became popularized, however, it attracted still more people who knew little of the real Beats, but wanted to look like them. Many adopted a stereotypical version of Beat fashion styles, sporting sandals, black turtlenecks, black berets, and goatee beards. These stereotypes found their way into popular culture, most notably in the **television** (see entry under 1940s—TV and Radio in volume 2) version of the **Dobie Gillis** (see entry under 1950s—TV and Radio in volume 3) stories, *The Many Loves of Dobie Gillis* (1959–63). In it, actor Bob Denver (1935–2005) played beatnik Maynard G. Krebs. As a cultural phenomenon, the Beat movement was short-lived. As a literary movement, it proved highly influential, with Kerouac writing a number of novels and Ginsberg establishing himself as a major American poet in the tradition of Walt Whitman (1819–1892).

Timothy Berg

For More Information

Charters, Ann, ed. *The Portable Beat Reader.* New York: Viking, 1992.

Evans, Mike. *The Beats: From Kerouac to Kesey.* Philadelphia: Running Press, 2007.

Foster, Edward Halsey. *Understanding the Beats.* Columbia: University of South Carolina, 1992.

Ginsberg, Allen. *Howl and Other Poems.* San Francisco: City Lights Books, 1956.

Kerouac, Jack. *On the Road.* New York: Viking, 1957.

Morgan, Bill. *The Typewriter Is Holy: The Complete, Uncensored History of the Beat Generation.* New York: Free Press, 2010.

Watson, Steven. *The Birth of the Beat Generation: Visionaries, Rebels, and Hipsters, 1944–1960.* New York: Pantheon, 1995.

The Catcher in the Rye

Published in 1951, *The Catcher in the Rye* was quickly recognized as one of the most important American novels of the late twentieth century. It has also regularly topped the lists of most banned and censored books. The only novel written by J. D. Salinger (1919–2010), *The Catcher in the Rye* is one of many novels of the time to signal the end of the "American Dream" of success and wealth. Its adolescent hero, Holden Caulfield, battles against what he sees as the "phoniness" of adult American life. *The Catcher in the Rye* enjoys the strange and unusual status of a cult novel that is also required reading on many high school and college reading lists.

Salinger's novel tells the story of how sixteen-year-old Holden Caulfield is expelled from his Pennsylvania boarding school and stays for two days on his own in New York City. Told in his own words, Holden's adventures in the city include being beaten up by a pimp and a homosexual encounter with an old English teacher, Mr. Antolini. Like the Huckleberry Finn character in the novel of the same name by Mark Twain (1835–1910), Holden Caulfield is on a quest. Huck Finn can still find freedom on his raft, but Holden's attempt to avoid becoming "phony" ends in a nervous breakdown. Some readers have taken Holden's views about phoniness to heart. Mark David Chapman (1955–), the killer of singer John Lennon (1940–1980) of the **Beatles** (see entry under 1960s—Music in volume 4), claims to have been inspired by *The Catcher in the Rye* to murder his hero. Chapman has stated that in his view the ex-Beatle had become a hypocrite (a person who seems to support certain beliefs or points of view but does not really) and a "phony."

The Catcher in the Rye has always attracted controversy. It has been attacked for its sexual content, foul language, and even, to some, alleged occultism. Attempts to have the book removed from libraries and classrooms continue into the twenty-first century. For this reason, the novel has long been a favorite of young rebels everywhere. Perhaps because of the controversy that even then surrounded his novel, in the early 1960s Salinger retired from the New York literary scene. Until the end of his life, he rarely gave interviews and lived privately in rural New Hampshire. Meanwhile, his short and often misunderstood novel has gained the status of a modern classic.

Chris Routledge

For More Information

Alexander, Paul. *Salinger: A Biography.* Los Angeles: Renaissance Books, 2000.

Pinsker, Sanford. *The Catcher in the Rye: Innocence Under Pressure.* New York: Twayne, 1993.

Salinger, J. D. *The Catcher in the Rye.* New York: Modern Library, 1951. Multiple reprints.

Salinger.org. http://www.salinger.org (accessed July 27, 2011).

Slawenski, Kenneth. *J. D. Salinger: A Life.* New York: Random House, 2010.

Dr. Seuss

The 2000 movie *Dr. Seuss' How The Grinch Stole Christmas,* starring Jim Carrey (1962–), was a major hit with audiences. The grotesque green-skinned character was actually created more than forty years earlier, however, by the author and illustrator known as Dr. Seuss. His books, with their colorful characters and rhyming language, have entertained children all over the world for decades.

Dr. Seuss was born Theodor Seuss Geisel (1904–1991) in Springfield, Massachusetts. As a child, he made frequent trips to the zoo, where he got the inspiration for many of his animal creations. He had a flair for drawing and later contributed illustrations to his college's humor magazine. In the 1920s and 1930s, Geisel began working as a professional cartoonist and illustrator, mostly for advertising agencies.

Geisel's real ambition was to create his own children's books. In 1936, he published his first, *And to Think That I Saw It on Mulberry Street.* Its colorful drawings and imaginative, rhyming text were to become trademarks of the Dr. Seuss style. He published other books, including the popular *Horton Hatches an Egg* (1940). During World War II (1939–45), Geisel created cartoons in support of the U.S. war effort. He also worked on army training films.

In the 1950s, Geisel enjoyed perhaps his greatest period of success. His books *Horton Hears a Who* (1954), *How the Grinch Stole Christmas* (1957), and *The Cat in the Hat* (1957) were filled with nonsense humor and made-up words and sold millions of copies worldwide. Challenged to write a book using fewer than fifty different words, Geisel created *Green Eggs and Ham* (1960), one of his best-loved classics. Other Geisel books had more serious themes. *The Lorax* (1971) dealt with saving the environment, for example.

Geisel continued writing until his death in 1991. Overall, his books sold more than one hundred million copies and were translated into eighteen languages. Toward the end of his life, Geisel even wrote books for adults, like *Oh, The Places You'll Go!* (1990). Those too became **bestsellers** (see entry under 1940s—Commerce in volume 3). In addition to the aforementioned *Grinch, The Cat in the Hat* (2003) and *Horton Hears a Who!* (2008) were also made into movies.

Robert E. Schnakenberg

For More Information

Morgan, Judith, and Neil Morgan. *Dr. Seuss & Mr. Geisel: A Biography.* New York: Random House, 1995.

Pease, Donald E. *Theodor Seuss Geisel.* New York: Oxford University Press, 2010.

Random House, Inc. *Seussville.* http://www.seussville.com// (accessed July 27, 2011).

Seuss, Dr. *A Hatful of Seuss: Five Favorite Dr. Seuss Stories.* New York: Random House, 1997.

Weidt, Maryann N. *Oh, the Places He Went: A Story About Dr. Seuss.* New York: Carolrhoda Books, 1994.

Frosty the Snowman

During the Christmas season of 1950, a new holiday song was introduced that told the tale of an inanimate snowman that came to life to spread good cheer. Written by Steve Nelson and Jack Rollins, "Frosty the Snowman" became an international hit recording and a permanent part of many people's Christmas celebrations. The lovably jolly snowman, which possessed "a button nose, and two eyes made out of coal," became as recognizable as other nonreligious Christmas symbols like Santa Claus and ***Rudolph the Red-Nosed Reindeer*** (see entry under 1940s—Print Culture in volume 3).

In the Nelson and Rollins song, the snowman comes alive when a magical silk hat is placed upon his head by a group of children. The newly energized snowman and kids proceed to enjoy a winter day devoted to sledding and ice-skating. Their adventure ends as a warm spell forces Frosty to leave for a colder climate, but he promises to return when the weather again becomes cooler. Although Frosty is closely associated with Christmas, the holiday is never mentioned in the song. Still, the song has been included on dozens of Christmas albums by a wide variety of musical artists over the years.

The popularity of the 1950 song led to the publication of a **Golden Book** (see entry under 1940s—Print Culture in volume 3) featuring the character a year later. The children's book, which was written by Annie North Bedford (1915–) and illustrated by Corinne Malvern (1905–1956), was a great success and further increased Frosty's popularity.

In the 1960s, Frosty leapt from the printed page and landed on **television** (see entry under 1940s—TV and Radio in volume 3). The first, and most popular, Frosty-based holiday TV special was simply titled *Frosty the Snowman* (1969). It was narrated by comedian Jimmy Durante (1893–1980). The TV script expanded upon the original song's premise: Frosty is confronted by a washed-up magician who wants the silk top hat that gave Frosty life. The special also teaches children a message about the power of friendship and kindness. Santa appears at the conclusion to take Frosty to his new home at the North Pole. Comedian Jackie Vernon (1925–1987) provided the voice of Frosty on this and other holiday programs.

In 1976, Frosty returned to TV in *Frosty's Winter Wonderland.* In this special, the lonely snowman's friends, who are children, make him a wife named Crystal, whose voice was provided by actress Shelley Winters (1922–2006). **Andy Griffith** (1926–; see entry on *The Andy Griffith Show* under 1960s—TV and Radio in volume 4) served as the narrator of the story. The 1979 holiday season saw the first showing of *Rudolph and Frosty's Christmas in July.* This TV special teamed the snowman with Rudolph the Red-Nosed Reindeer in an adventure in which they confronted the evil wizard Winterbolt. In this *Frosty* episode, it is revealed that Frosty and Crystal now are the parents of a snow-family. Included among the celebrity voices in this program are Red Buttons (1919–2006), Ethel Merman (1908–1984), and Mickey Rooney (1920–). In 1998, Michael Keaton (1951–) starred in *Jack Frost,* a live-action film that was based partly on the *Frosty* tale. The film tells of a neglectful dad who dies and comes back to life as a snowman in his son's front yard.

Charles Coletta

Frosty the Snowman poses in a still from the 1969 television special of the same name.
© GOLDEN BOOKS/PHOTOFEST.

For More Information

Bedford, Annie North, and Corinne Malverne. *Frosty the Snowman.* New York: Simon & Schuster, 1951.

Eckstein, Bob. *The History of the Snowman: From the Ice Age to the Flea Market.* New York: Simon Spotlight Entertainment, 2007.

MAD Magazine

The comic cartoonists at *MAD* magazine have been providing satire and absurd humor to their loyal readers since 1952. What began as a **comic book** (see entry under 1930s—Print Culture in volume 2) evolved over time into a monthly magazine, a series of books, a stage show, and a popular **television** (see entry under 1940s—TV and Radio in volume 3) program. The influence of the *MAD* style of humor can also be seen on the television program ***Saturday Night Live*** (see entry under 1970s— TV and Radio in volume 4), in films such as *The Naked Gun* and *Scary Movie,* and in countless parody ads and TV commercials.

MAD *magazine publisher William Gaines in his office in 1989.* © JACQUES M. CHENET/ CORBIS.

The *MAD* empire was founded by William M. Gaines (1922–1992), a young comic book publisher of the 1940s. Gaines's "Entertaining Comics" (EC) focused mostly on shocking war comics like *Two-Fisted Tales* and gory horror titles like *Tales from the Crypt.* They were very popular, especially with young readers, but government officials began to put pressure on Gaines to cut out the blood and violence. So, in 1952, Gaines enlisted a young cartoonist named Harvey Kurtzman (1924–1993) to create a new kind of comic book, an all-humor title. Kurtzman named the new series *Tales Calculated to Drive You MAD.* It debuted in the fall of 1952.

Over the course of the next three years, the talented Kurtzman put his personal stamp on the new title. He introduced such classic *MAD* features as the movie parody ("Hah!

Noon," a spoof of the Western classic *High Noon* was an early example) and the use of nonsense words like "fershlugginer" in the word balloons. The early *MAD* also spent a lot of time spoofing other comic books, like "Superduperman," its take on **Superman** (see entry under 1930s—Print Culture in volume 2), and the **Batman** (see entry under 1930s—Print Culture in volume 2) parody "Bat Boy." The drawing responsibilities for these illustrated features were divided up among Kurtzman and other soon-to-be legendary artists like Wally Wood (1927–1981), Jack Davis (1926–), and Basil Wolverton (1909–1978). These early issues of *MAD* are considered some of the greatest achievements in comic book history as well as landmarks in American humor. They typically sell for thousands of dollars at collectible shows and auctions.

In 1955, Kurtzman left *MAD* to work for **Playboy** (see entry under 1950s—Print Culture in volume 3) founder Hugh Hefner (1926–). Al Feldstein (1925–) took over as editor, and *MAD* was converted from a comic book to a magazine. The contents changed very little, although the new format attracted contributions from many well-known humorists including Bob and Ray (Bob Elliott, 1923–; and Ray Goulding, 1922–1990), Jean Shepherd (1921–1999), and Ernie Kovacs (1919–1962). In the 1960s, *MAD* began to focus more on parodies of advertising. The magazine itself refused to take ads, allowing it to poke fun at the exaggerated claims of companies selling cigarettes, liquor, or home appliances.

Alfred E. Neuman, the grinning cartoon mascot who appears on every cover of *MAD* magazine, made his first showing in March 1955. He became the cornerstone for *MAD* starting with issue 30 in December 1956. With his big ears, gap-toothed smile, and his trademark expression "What, Me Worry?" he remains the first image that comes to most people's minds when they think of *MAD* magazine. Over the years, Alfred's face has popped up in a number of unlikely places, including a celebrated campaign poster by artist Norman Mingo (1896–1980) promoting "Alfred E. Neuman for President."

Besides Mingo, a number of other artists and writers became regular contributors to *MAD*. Listed on the masthead as "the usual gang of idiots," they supplied some of the magazine's most beloved long-running features. Sergio Aragones (1937–) created the popular "Spy vs. Spy." Al Jaffee (1921–) supplied "Snappy Answers to Stupid Questions" as well as the monthly "fold-in" drawing on the inside back cover. The capable Don Martin (1931–2000) created a variety of bizarre cartoons, often tied together by the premise "One Fine Day…." Many of these recurring features were collected into paperback books and sold by mail order.

Other *MAD* spin-offs, like the feature film *Up the Academy* (1980), the stage revue *The MAD Show,* and the TV series *MADtv* (1995–2009), were met with mixed reception from the magazine's core audience. Nevertheless, *MAD* continued to have an influence beyond its printed pages, as its brand of satirical humor became entrenched in American pop culture. Any TV commercial that spoofs other TV commercials, it could fairly be said, is drawing on the tradition of *MAD* magazine.

MAD remained popular, particularly with teenage readers, even after Gaines's death in 1992. As the century drew to a close, however, sales had dropped dramatically. The number of *MAD* readers fell from 2.3 million in the early 1970s to 500,000 by the 1990s. Some claimed the magazine no longer seemed fresh in a society where the *MAD* style humor is everywhere.

Whatever the reason, *MAD*'s editors in 2001 announced plans to revamp the magazine around the kind of toilet humor popular in such films as *There's Something About Mary* (1998). The publication also began running ads in every issue to increase revenue. In the early 2000s, *MAD* magazine found a home online with a website that included not only information about back and current issues, but also a **blog** (see entry under 2000s—The Way We Lived in volume 6). Another television show, the animated sketch comedy *MAD* (2010–), aired on Cartoon Network. Despite changes over time, *MAD*'s place in the history of American humor is secure.

Robert E. Schnakenberg

For More Information

Beam, Alex. "Declining Sales: What, Mad Worry?" *Boston Globe* (February 20, 2001): p. D1.

Jacobs, Frank. *The MAD World of William M. Gaines.* Secaucus, NJ: Lyle Stuart, 1972.

MAD. http://www.dccomics.com/mad/ (accessed July 27, 2011).

Reidelbach, Maria. *Completely MAD: A History of the Comic Book and Magazine.* Boston: Little, Brown, 1991.

"Usual Gang of Idiots." *MAD for Decades: 50 Years of Forgettable Humor from MAD Magazine.* New York: Barnes & Noble, 2007.

National Enquirer

Best known for its dramatically suggestive headlines, outlandish stories, and aggressive reporters, the *National Enquirer* is eagerly and secretly read in supermarket checkout lines by many more people than the 3.2 million who pay for it each week. Although most readers claim they do not believe most of what the tabloid newspaper prints, they are drawn to its promise of insider knowledge and hot scoops about celebrities, politicians, and aliens from outer space.

The *National Enquirer* got its start as a crime-focused tabloid called the *New York Enquirer* in 1926. (A tabloid is a half-size newspaper that usually contains many photographs and focuses on dramatic and lurid stories.) The *New York Enquirer* was bought in 1952 by Generoso Pope Jr. (1927–1988). Pope recognized that people were drawn to the blood and shock of an accident. Soon he added gory photos and articles to the crime stories in his paper. In the 1970s, he toned down the gore a bit, and included gossipy and sexy stories about celebrities in order to get his paper, now called the *National Enquirer,* placed on newsstands in supermarkets.

The circulation of the *National Enquirer* began to climb, reaching a peak of 5.7 million readers per week in 1977. Competition from other tabloids, like the *Star* and the *Globe,* along with more television coverage of Hollywood gossip, caused sales of the *Enquirer* to decrease during the 1980s. In 1989, Pope's widow sold the paper to American Media (which also owned its rivals the *Star* and the *Globe*) for $412 million. By 1994, circulation had dropped to 3.1 million, and by 2001 it was at 2.1 million. In 2011, it was only just over a million copies.

The *Enquirer* responded to these decreases by changing its focus once again, this time to politics. Originally exposed by a mainstream paper, the Miami *Herald,* it was the *Enquirer* that splashed politician Gary Hart's (1936–) scandalous affair across its pages in the late 1980s to much fanfare. Coverage of political figures increased dramatically in the 1990s. With its aggressive investigative reporters and its policy of sparing no cost to get a story, the *National Enquirer* managed to scoop many more respected newspapers on stories about the affairs of politicians like Bill Clinton (1946–), Jesse Jackson (1941–), and Gary Condit (1948–).

Many celebrities have been angered by the *Enquirer*'s exposés about their lives, and some have taken the tabloid to court. However, the

Enquirer prides itself on its careful research. Although some well-known people, like actress Carol Burnett (1933–), have won settlements against the paper, many others have lost.

Tina Gianoulis

For More Information

Calder, Iain. *The Untold Story: My 20 Years Running the National Enquirer.* New York: Hyperion, 2004.

Cohen, Daniel. *Yellow Journalism: Scandal, Sensationalism, and Gossip in the Media.* Brookfield, CT: Twenty-First Century Books, 2000.

Farhi, Paul. "Three-Headed Baby? Rival Tabloids Joined in Corporate Deal." *Washington Post* (November 3, 1999): p. C1.

Hogshire, Jim. *Grossed-Out Surgeon Vomits Inside Patient! An Insider's Look at Supermarket Tabloids.* Venice, CA: Feral House, 1997.

National Enquirer Online. http://www.nationalenquirer.com/ (accessed July 27, 2011).

"Pass the Pulitzers: The Power of the Tabloid Magazine Press." *Economist* (July 7, 2001): pp. 3–7.

Sloan, Bill. *I Watched a Wild Hog Eat My Baby: A Colorful History of Tabloids and Their Cultural Impact.* Amherst, NY: Prometheus Books, 2001.

Vitek, Jack. *The Godfather of Tabloid: Generoso Pope Jr. and the National Enquirer.* Lexington: University Press of Kentucky, 2008.

Waters, John. "Why I Love the *National Enquirer.*" *Rolling Stone* (October 10, 1985): pp. 43–48.

On the Road

Published in 1957, Jack Kerouac's semiautobiographical novel *On the Road* soon became the bible of the **Beat movement** (see entry on Beatniks and the Beat Movement under 1950s— Print Culture in volume 3) and an inspiration to many young people who felt disconnected from the dominant values of 1950s America. During a time when conformity (acting in agreement with established social views) was the norm, *On the Road* showed another way of living, an on-the-go lifestyle that seemed very exciting to many people. In the decades since its publication, it has continued to do just that.

The novel's main character and narrator was Sal Paradise, based on Kerouac (1922–1969) himself. The other main characters were fictional versions of other important Beat figures, including Allen Ginsberg (1926–1997), William Burroughs (1914–1997), and Neal Cassady

(1926?–1968). Reflecting the Beats' continual search for something new and more significant in American life, the novel relates the experiences of Paradise and his friends during a series of cross-country road trips. Along the way, they meet a host of odd characters, try to meet women, smoke marijuana, stay up all night, and listen to **jazz** (see entry under 1900s—Music in volume 1). Much of the inspiration for the book came from Kerouac's adventures with his close friend Cassady. His friend's erratic, open-to-all-experiences behavior appealed to Kerouac's longing for something more in life.

Because of the strange behavior of the characters and their reckless habits that went against accepted standards for the 1950s, the book created something of a scandal when it came out. Like the **rock and roll** (see entry under 1950s—Music in volume 3) that had emerged two years before, *On the Road* championed odd lifestyles that seemed threatening to many people. Few parents wanted their teenage children to live like Kerouac and his friends. However, for many young people, bored with the self-confining nature of life in suburban 1950s America and dreaming of something more, *On the Road* allowed them to at least glimpse another way of living. The continual search for something better in American culture was something with which many people, then and now, could identify. Kerouac's search made *On the Road* a classic of American literature.

On the Road *author Jack Kerouac in 1962.* © AP IMAGES.

Timothy Berg

For More Information

Charters, Ann. *Kerouac: A Biography.* San Francisco: Straight Arrow Books, 1973.

Charters, Ann, ed. *The Portable Beat Reader.* New York: Penguin, 1992.

Kerouac, Jack. *Lonesome Traveler.* 2nd ed. New York: HarperCollins, 1994.

Kerouac, Jack. *On the Road.* New York: New American Library, 1957. Multiple reprints.

Kerouac, Jack. *On the Road: The Original Scroll.* New York: Penguin, 2007.

The Organization Man

The Organization Man, the 1956 best-selling book from William H. Whyte (1917–1999), described the psychological and social costs of a major trend in American life during the 1950s. The trend was the movement of more people away from blue-collar jobs and toward white-collar office jobs in large corporations. The trend, Whyte argued, came with a price. Succeeding in the corporate world required people to suppress individual thought and initiative and to replace it with an attitude of conformity (acting in agreement with established social views) that sought only to please the boss. To Whyte, this seemed a major shift in the American character. Americans were forsaking the competitive individualism that had propelled the economy and culture of the United States forward, a trend that Whyte argued would not lead to great things.

The Organization Man was a very influential commentary on the problems of conformity that plagued the United States in the 1950s and beyond, one that also found expression in **Hollywood** (see entry under 1930s—Film and Theater in volume 2) films such as *The Man in the Gray Flannel Suit* (1956).

Timothy Berg

For More Information

Glazer, Nathan. "The Man Who Loved Cities." *Wilson Quarterly* (Spring 1999): pp. 27–33.

Whyte, William H. *The Organization Man.* New York: Simon & Schuster, 1956.

Peanuts

An unlucky little boy and his daydreaming beagle form the core of *Peanuts,* the beloved comic strip of Charles Schulz (1922–2000). The comic strip has entertained newspaper readers daily since 1950. Despite creator Schulz's death in 2000, *Peanuts* remains in reruns on many newspapers' comic strip pages and lives on in the form of its timeless humor and instantly recognizable characters.

Originally titled *Li'l Folks, Peanuts* debuted on October 2, 1950. Within a decade, the four-panel strip was appearing in over four hundred newspapers nationwide. Readers quickly took to Schulz's gentle humor

and likable characters. Charlie Brown was the "hero" of the strip, a lovable loser who was repeatedly blocked in his attempts to kick a football by his overbearing neighbor, Lucy Van Pelt. Snoopy, Charlie Brown's pet beagle, became something of a national sensation. The adorable pooch loafed atop his doghouse and imagined himself as a flying ace during World War I (1914–18). Snoopy was joined later by a bird sidekick named Woodstock, who also developed a fan following. Other characters included Linus, a smart but insecure child who carried a "security blanket"; Peppermint Patty, a freckle-faced girl who had a crush on Charlie Brown; and Schroeder, a piano prodigy who idolized German composer Ludwig van Beethoven (1770–1827). Adults were rarely seen.

Comic-strip readers related to the troubles the *Peanuts* gang experienced solving life's problems. The strip's unique blend of animals, children, and homespun philosophy made it unique among comic strips of the 1950s. Popular comic strips of later years, like *Calvin and Hobbes* and *Bloom County,* showed the influence of Schulz's work.

Another way in which *Peanuts* revolutionized the American comic strip was in the area of merchandising. The strip became so popular (in 1984, it was named the world's most widely syndicated comic strip by the *Guinness Book of World Records*) that its characters began appearing on calendars, mugs, **T-shirts** (see entry under 1910s—Fashion in volume 1), and plush toys from coast to coast. Snoopy became the "spokesbeagle" for the Metropolitan Life Insurance Company, as he and the rest of the gang turned up in a popular series of **television** (see entry under 1940s—TV and Radio in volume 3) commercials starting in the 1980s. Spin-offs of the *Peanuts* daily strip also became quite popular. A series of animated TV specials, many centered around major holidays, was launched in the 1960s and is still rerun in the twenty-first century.

Robert E. Schnakenberg

For More Information

Gherman, Beverly. *Sparky: The Life and Art of Charles Schulz.* San Francisco: Chronicle Books, 2010.

Johnson, Rheta Grimsley. *Good Grief: The Story of Charles M. Schulz.* New York: Pharos Books, 1989.

Michaelis, David. *Schulz and Peanuts: A Biography.* New York: Harper, 2007.

Schulz, Charles M. *Celebrating Peanuts: 60 Years.* Kansas City, MO: Andrews McMeel, 2009.

Schulz, Charles M. *Peanuts: A Golden Celebration: The Art and the Story of the World's Best-Loved Comic Strip.* New York: HarperCollins, 1999.

Schulz, Charles M. *Peanuts 2000.* New York: Ballantine, 2000.

Schulz, Charles M., and M. Thomas Inge. *My Life with Charlie Brown.* Jackson: University Press of Mississippi, 2010.

Peanuts: The Official Website. http://www.peanuts.com/ (accessed July 28, 2011).

Playboy

Playboy was the first "skin magazine" to win a degree of acceptance in mainstream America. It did so by providing its male readers with more than just "skin." It also offered an entire lifestyle for the reader to enjoy—at least in his fantasies.

Playboy debuted as a reaction against the repressive standards that ruled popular culture in the 1950s. No nudity, no suggestive language, no sex portrayed outside of marriage, and very little mention of sex even within marriage were allowed in mainstream media.

Hugh Hefner (1926–), who had worked in publishing with little personal success, decided to gamble that the kind of magazine he wanted to read would also appeal to other young men. He borrowed a few thousand dollars and launched *Playboy* in December 1953. The first issue was given a boost by its centerfold: **Marilyn Monroe** (1926–1962; see entry under 1950s—Film and Theater in volume 3), the hottest actress of the decade. She had posed for some nude pictures years earlier while still an unknown, to which Hefner had acquired the rights.

Gradually, the magazine took on its distinctive characteristics: the mini-poster "centerfold" in each issue exhibiting the "Playmate of the Month"; the Playboy Interview, which over the years has included such unlikely subjects as Malcolm X (1925–1965), Yasser Arafat (1929–2004), Fidel Castro (c. 1927–), and then–presidential candidate Jimmy Carter (1924–); and a host of articles. The articles promoted the "good life"—sports cars, elegant clothing, expensive stereo equipment, and fine dining.

In the 1960s, Hefner expanded into other areas, such as the Playboy Clubs (with their "bunnies" as waitresses), casinos, book publishing, and even film production. These did well until the 1980s, when the Playboy empire was hurt by the loss of its gambling license, declining club membership, and competition from imitation magazines such as *Penthouse* and **Hustler** (see entry under 1970s—Print Culture in volume 4).

The empire fell into financial trouble, but it was saved by Christie Hefner (1952–), the founder's daughter, who was made president and chief executive officer (CEO) in 1982. Christie Hefner closed the clubs, dropped the film and book divisions, and began to explore the possibilities of new media, such as videotapes, CD-ROMs, and the Internet. She left the company in 2009. Her father remained involved with the magazine in the early 2000s, when the Playboy empire again faced challenges both financial and from other men's magazines like *Maxim*. In early 2011, the company went private, with Hefner remaining the largest shareholder. He planned to reinvigorate the company while maintaining its long-standing editorial direction. Online and in print, *Playboy* continues to feed the fantasies, sexual and otherwise, of millions of readers around the world.

Justin Gustainis

For More Information

Edgren, Gretchen. *The Playboy Book: Fifty Years.* Los Angeles: Taschen, 2005.

Marek, Lynne. "Battle for the Bunny." *Crain's Chicago Business* (July 19, 2010): pp. 1.

Miller, Russell. *Bunny: The Real Story of Playboy.* New York: Holt, Rinehart and Winston, 1985.

Watts, Steven. *Mr. Playboy: Hugh Hefner and the American Dream.* Hoboken, NJ: Wiley, 2008.

J. R. R. Tolkien (1892–1973)

Born in South Africa, J. R. R. Tolkien lived in Britain from the age of three. He is best known as the author of *The Hobbit* (1937) and the best-selling epic trilogy *The Lord of the Rings* (1954–55). Tolkien's tales of "Middle-earth" draw on ancient Anglo-Saxon legends, culture, and languages. They also address very modern themes of lost tradition, family loyalty, and sense of place. His achievement is to have invented a consistent ancient mythology and to have made it come to life for millions of readers. A big-budget movie treatment of part one of the trilogy—*The Lord of the Rings: The Fellowship of the Ring* was released in 2001; in 2002, it received thirteen Academy Award nominations, winning four of them. The trilogy was completed with *The Lord of the Rings: The Two Towers* (2002) and *The Lord of the Rings: The Return of the King* (2003). Both were popular, critically acclaimed, award-winning films. (See entry on **The Lord of the Rings film trilogy** under 2000s—Film and Theater in volume 6.)

Tolkien's career as an academic lasted thirty-nine years, beginning in 1920. He was the Rawlinson and Bosworth Professor of Anglo-Saxon. Later he became Merton Professor of English at Oxford University. In his waistcoat and tweed jacket, the aging professor made an unlikely cult author during the 1960s. Although his books have many imitators, Tolkien remains in the twenty-first century the most popular of all fantasy writers.

Chris Routledge

For More Information

Bloom, Harold. *J. R. R. Tolkien.* New ed. New York: Bloom's Literary Criticism, 2008.

Carpenter, Humphrey. *Tolkien: A Biography.* Boston: Houghton Mifflin, 1977.

Collins, David R. *J. R. R. Tolkien: Master of Fantasy.* Minneapolis: Lerner, 1992.

Day, David. *Tolkien: The Illustrated Encyclopedia.* New York: Macmillan, 1991.

The Lord of the Rings "Unofficial" Homepage. http://www.thelordoftherings.com/ (accessed July 28, 2011).

Neimark, Anne E. *Myth Maker: J. R. R. Tolkien.* New York: Beech Tree, 1998.

Shippey, Tom. *J. R. R. Tolkien: Author of the Century.* Boston: Houghton Mifflin, 2000.

TV Guide

Back in the 1950s, watching **television** (see entry under 1940s—TV and Radio in volume 3) was replacing listening to the **radio** (see entry under 1920s—TV and Radio in volume 2) and going to the movies as the most popular of all leisure activities. TV stations were sprouting up across the country, and TV programming was expanding. This cultural shift towards TV viewing established a market for a weekly magazine that offered its readers a handy, easy-to-use program schedule guide. That magazine became the aptly titled *TV Guide.*

Prior to going national in 1953, *TV Guide* existed as a regional publication. Today, these editions are called "pre-nationals." After 1953, the regional issues all featured the same covers and articles, but the programming schedules were altered to fit each locality. For example, the New York City and Albany, New York, editions would include the same editorial content, but each city would have different schedules to reflect the changes in local TV station call letters, channel numbers, and programming.

The initial *TV Guide* national edition was dated April 3–9, 1953. The cover featured a photo of Desiderio Alberto Arnaz IV (1953–), the highly anticipated infant son of *I Love Lucy* (see entry under 1950s—TV and Radio in volume 3) stars Lucille Ball (1911–1989) and Desi Arnaz (1917–1986). Above the *TV Guide* logo was the headline "Lucy's $50,000,000 Baby." Across the decades, just about every top television star has on at least one occasion graced the magazine's cover.

Over the years, *TV Guide* featured everything from celebrity interviews to TV series features; crossword puzzles to series reviews; "Insider" and "Grapevine" sections announcing new trends, shows, and stars to a "Cheers & Jeers" page that congratulates or scolds individuals, networks, or stations. The publication's cornerstone, however, was its TV listings. For this reason, *TV Guide* claimed a circulation of as high as 19.7 million in 1975, a number that dropped to 9.9 million by 2001. Across the decades, the magazine's format has been altered, and features and columns have been added or dropped, but its program listing section, which makes up its bulk, has remained a constant.

With the widespread availability of **cable TV** (see entry under 1970s—TV and Radio in volume 4) in the 1990s and the resulting access to hundreds of TV stations within a single market, it became impossible for the print edition of *TV Guide* to list every scheduled television program. As a result, the publication entered the twenty-first century with the TV Guide Channel, a television channel that offered the current and upcoming hour's programs on a continually rolling scroll on the TV screen.

The TV Guide Channel moved away from emphasizing television schedules to original programming, primarily **reality TV** (see entry under 1990s—TV and Radio in volume 5), in 2011, leaving the full television listings grid to its website. Because *TV Guide* continued to lose money and saw its circulation dwindle to two million by 2010, the print edition of *TV Guide* was re-vamped several times in the early 2000s. The result was a less complete schedule and more feature stories, especially related to television and celebrities. The periodical also was re-named *TV Guide Magazine*. In the midst of these changes, *TV Guide* kept its identity as a go-to source of information about television and its programming.

Rob Edelman

For More Information

Harris, Jay S., ed. *TV Guide: The First 25 Years.* New York: Simon & Schuster, 1978.

Hofer, Stephen F. *TV Guide: The Official Collectors Guide.* Braintree, MA: Bangzoom, 2006.

Levine, Stuart. "*TV Guide* Turns to Reality." *Daily Variety* (April 27, 2011): pp. 18.

Moses, Lucia. "Last-ditch Tweaks? *TV Guide* Breaks Up Listings Grid, Adds More Options." *MediaWeek* (April 5, 2010): pp. 45.

Norback, Craig T., and Peter G. Norback. *TV Guide Almanac.* New York: Ballantine Books, 1980.

TV Guide. http://www.tvguide.com/ (accessed July 28, 2011).

Weiner, Ed. *The TV Guide Book.* New York: HarperPerennial, 1992.

1950s

Sports and Games

Public interest in sports intensified during the 1950s. Television brought live sports into the homes of many Americans for the first time. A new magazine, *Sports Illustrated,* was created to provide a weekly source of sports news and photographs. Baseball remained the most popular of American sports, and the New York Yankees continued to dominate the game, winning seven of the nine World Series they played in during the decade. Professional football finally surpassed college football in popularity during the period, thanks in part to the weekly televised broadcasts of games. During the winter, Americans turned to basketball. College basketball remained popular, despite several betting scandals that disgraced the game. The reorganization of the National Basketball Association (NBA) in 1949 gave a boost to professional basketball. Even more important were rule changes in 1954 that made basketball more exciting.

An important trend in sports during the 1950s was integration. Jackie Robinson (1919–1972) had broken the "color line" in professional baseball in 1947. Several black players led their teams in the 1950s, including Roy Campanella (1921–1993), Willie Mays (1931–), Don Newcombe (1926–), Hank Aaron (1934–), and Ernie Banks (1931–). The NBA allowed black players in 1950 and Bill Russell (1934–) of the Boston Celtics became the dominating player of the decade. Black athletes soon participated in professional bowling and in women's tennis. In fact, black player Althea Gibson (1927–2003) won the Wimbledon tennis tournament in 1951. A sure sign that African Americans had been accepted was the disbanding of baseball's Negro American League in 1960.

Organized sports were not the only way that Americans amused themselves. Children were treated to several popular new games during the decade. LEGO building bricks, imported from Denmark, were beloved by American children who could build whatever they imagined with the plastic pieces. The Etch A Sketch provided a blank slate on which kids could create amusing illustrations by turning dials to draw lines. Older kids, especially those living amid the vast paved surfaces of the suburbs, enjoyed skateboards. Teenagers and adults found a new model for physical fitness in the muscled Jack LaLanne (1914–2011), whose feats of strength drew attention to the need for all Americans to keep in good shape. LaLanne's message of physical readiness was well suited to a decade when Americans lived under the cloud of a Cold War (1945–91) with the distant Soviet Union.

Etch A Sketch

The popular toy, Etch A Sketch, was invented in the 1950s by Frenchman Arthur Granjean, who called it "The Magic Screen." In 1959, Granjean took his invention to a toy fair in Germany, where it was purchased by an

Just one of the one hundred million Etch A Sketch toys sold worldwide. © JOHNER IMAGES/ ALAMY.

American firm, the Ohio Art Company. The toy, renamed Etch A Sketch, was first sold in the United States in 1960 and was a huge success.

Etch A Sketch is a plastic rectangle with a translucent screen in the middle and two knobs below the screen. Two knobs—one for horizontal, one for vertical—control the direction of an uninterrupted line that appears on the screen, allowing the user to "draw." Shaking the device renders the screen blank again. Some talented users have used the toy to create complex works of art.

By the twenty-first century, Etch A Sketch was available in traditional, travel-sized, miniature, and glow-in-the-dark versions. New types of Etch A Sketch toys were introduced, such as the Freestyle and the Magic Pad, which allowed users to doodle with different types of controllers. It was also available online. The original Etch A Sketch is the most popular drawing toy ever made, having sold over one hundred million units in seventy countries.

Justin Gustainis

For More Information

Etch A Sketch. http://www.etch-a-sketch.com/ (accessed July 27, 2011).
The Etch A Sketch Book. Palo Alto, CA: Klutz Press, 1996.
Sobey, Ed, and Woody Sobey. *The Way Toys Work: The Science Behind the Magic 8 Ball, Etch A Sketch, Boomerang, and More.* Chicago: Chicago Review Press, 2008.

Jack LaLanne (1914–2011)

Jack LaLanne's image—bouncy, cheerful, and muscular, dressed in a form-fitting jumpsuit—was associated with health and fitness for over sixty years. Although he started his career in the 1930s, at a time when people thought that exercising was odd or even dangerous, LaLanne practically invented the physical-fitness movement in the United States. A hot-tempered high school dropout from Bakersfield, California, mostly known for getting into fights and trouble, LaLanne discovered health food and body building at the age of fourteen and changed the course of his life.

In order to spread the word about how exercise could improve people's lives, LaLanne opened the first fitness club in the United States in 1936. He invented weight machines and exercise programs to help his customers learn to exercise. LaLanne was a pioneer not only in physical fitness but also in the use of showmanship and promotion to spread his ideas.

Comedienne Lucille Ball and some canine friends join fitness expert Jack LaLanne for some exercise. © PHOTOFEST.

He hosted a popular exercise show on **television** (see entry under 1940s—TV and Radio in volume 3) from 1951 to 1985. LaLanne performed dozens of well-publicized physical stunts to draw attention to his cause. For example, on his seventieth birthday he swam a mile and a half in handcuffs, pulling seventy boats behind him. He remained active until the end of his life, dying of respiratory failure in 2011 at the age of 96.

Tina Gianoulis

For More Information

Goldstein, Richard. "Jack LaLanne, 96, Fitness's Father, Dies." *New York Times* (January 24, 2011): pp. A25.
Jack LaLanne. http://www.jacklalanne.com/ (accessed July 27, 2011).

Kita, Joe. "Jack LaLanne Is 85 Years Old, and He Can Still Kick Your Butt." *Men's Health* (June 2000): pp. 98–105.

Lalanne, Jack. *Live Young Forever: 12 Steps to Optimum Health, Fitness, & Longevity.* Mississauga, Ontario: R. Kennedy, 2009.

Ottum, Bob. "Look, Mom, I'm an Institution." *Sports Illustrated* (November 23, 1981): pp. 64–69.

LEGOs

LEGOs are, quite simply, one of the most successful toys of all time. The uncomplicated multicolored plastic blocks interlock and can be rearranged in endless combinations. The durable LEGOs have provided endless hours of creative play for millions of children around the world.

LEGO began in 1932 with carpenter Ole Kirk Christiansen (1891–1958) in Billund, Denmark. Christiansen's business manufactured simple wooden products, including toy blocks he made with leftover wood. In 1934, he adopted the name "LEGO" from the Danish words *Leg Godt,* which mean "play well." The phrase also means "I study" or "I put together" in Latin. This business did well enough for a while, but it really took off in the late 1940s when the company bought a plastic injection-molding machine to make plastic bricks. By 1949, the company was producing two hundred different plastic and wooden toys. In 1955, the business began selling LEGO bricks in organized sets, which they called the "LEGO System of Play." There were twenty-eight sets offered that year.

In 1958, the company introduced the modern version of the LEGO brick that most children are familiar with: raised studs on the tops of the bricks, with depressions underneath to lock onto studs from other bricks. Now there were 102,981,500 different ways of combining six eight-stud bricks of the same color. This allowed for virtually endless variety, and it became very difficult for creative children to exhaust the possibilities. The company offered model sets beginning in 1964. These contained the proper bricks to make complete models of cars, villages, boats, and so on. By 1966, more than 57 sets were offered and more than 706 million blocks were manufactured. In 1967, larger bricks, called DUPLO, were introduced for younger children. The company would later offer more advanced sets, called Technik, for older children, and specialty lines featuring space adventures, pirates, knights and castles, and other themes. In 1968, the company opened its first LEGOLAND theme park

LEGOs can be built into whatever the human mind can conceive. © FUSE/JUPITERIMAGES/GETTY IMAGES.

in Billund, Denmark, showcasing all that could be done with LEGOs. Other parks in England and the United States opened later in the century. The company also held periodic World Cup building championships to see who could build the biggest and best LEGO creations.

LEGO bricks had been an enduring part of the lives of American children for several generations by the end of the twentieth century. Their simplicity offered almost unlimited options for creative play. Unlike other toys that carefully defined what children could do with them, LEGOs encouraged kids to use their imaginations to build ever-more-elaborate and fanciful constructions. Kids could build houses full of many rooms, castles with towers, and entire towns out of the bricks. When LEGO introduced plastic people and wheels to their basic sets, kids could invent entire worlds populated with people driving fancy cars, flying airplanes, and living in gigantic houses. LEGOs were seen as being good for kids because they required thinking. LEGOs encouraged them to use their minds rather than simply sit in front of the **television** (see entry under 1940s—TV and Radio in volume 3) set or play **video games** (see entry under 1970s—Sports and Games in volume 4).

Eventually, LEGO moved beyond the basic building-block sets toward sets that could be built in more limited, specialized ways. With the basic blocks, just about anything could be built. With the more specialized ones, it became harder to break away and build anything other than the models in the set. Eventually, the company introduced computer chips into certain models, such as the LEGO "Mindstorm" sets. Some sets even came with CD-ROMs containing instructions on how to build the models. This was a long way from the basic theme of the early LEGO blocks: simple bricks that required children to be creative in their play. These changes were more than successful, however. By the mid-1990s, LEGO was one of the largest toy manufacturers in the world. By this time, LEGO had become one of the world's most recognized brand names, splashed on building blocks, CD-ROM games, and a magazine. *Fortune* magazine and the British Association of Toy Retailers named LEGO the "toy of the century." With the introduction of buildable action figures known as Bionicles in 2001 and other new products like **video games** (see entry under 1970s—Sports and Games in volume 4) being introduced on a regular basis, LEGO worked to be the toy of the twenty-first century as well.

Timothy Berg

For More Information

Lane, Anthony. "The Joy of Bricks: What Have the Danes Done for Children?" *New Yorker* (Vol. 74, no. 10, April 27/May 4, 1998): pp. 96–103.
LEGO.com. http://www.lego.com/en-us/Default.aspx (accessed July 28, 2011).
Lipkowitz, Daniel. *The LEGO Book.* New York: Dorling Kindersley, 2009.
Wiencek, Henry. *The World of LEGO Toys.* New York: Harry N. Abrams, 1987.

Skateboarding

Since its invention in the late 1950s, skateboarding has had several separate waves of popularity. The style of each wave may have been slightly different, but they all share a youth culture of rebellion and stylish feats of physical skill and daring. Although some parents and coaches tried to make skateboarding a **Little League** (see entry under 1930s—Sports and Games in volume 2) sport in the 1970s, and others have tried to have it

Skateboarding has gone in and out of fashion since the late 1950s but still remains popular among the young. © PT IMAGES/
JUPITERIMAGES/GETTY IMAGES.

outlawed, "boarders" are a highly independent group who have resisted attempts to take their sport from them. Marty McFly, from the 1980s film series *Back to the Future,* and cartoon brat Bart Simpson of ***The Simpsons*** (1989–; see entry under 1980s—TV and Radio in volume 5), are two of the media's best-known flashy skateboarders.

The first skateboards were made in California by surfers who attached roller-skate wheels to short boards and learned to maneuver them. They rode their skateboards the way they rode their surfboards through the waves, shifting their body weight and moving their feet along the board. Soon, boards were being manufactured and sold to children as toys, but the danger involved in rolling at high speeds on concrete sidewalks caused skateboarding to be forbidden in most towns by the end of the 1960s. The 1970s, however, saw an improvement in the design of the original board. Urethane wheels gave boarders more control, and a new generation of young people joined the skateboard craze, performing more acrobatic feats than ever before.

Skateboarding's popularity rose again in the 1980s and in the 1990s, as each new generation of rebel athletes has taken to the boards. Since the 1970s, many communities have tried to improve the safety of skateboarding by building skateboarding parks where boarders can practice their moves away from both traffic and pedestrians. Still, some skateboarders are rebels who often choose to break the rules for late night skates on the concrete ramps of empty parking garages and swimming pools. These boarders are viewed by the police as troublemakers.

Perhaps as a result, skateboarders have created their own subculture, with its own slang, uniform, and magazines. They sometimes wear baggy shorts, **T-shirts** (see entry under 1910s—Fashion in volume 1), and high-top sneakers, and they read *Thrasher, Warp,* and *Skateboarder.*

In the 1990s, skateboarding, as well as other **extreme sports** (see entry under 1990s—Sports and Games in volume 5) such as snowboarding, was given a professional outlet at competitions such as the X-Games, created by **ESPN** (see entry under 1970s—TV and Radio in volume 4), where thrashers compete in downhill racing, slalom racing, and freestyle. Skateboarding continued to be both a vital subculture and a popular competitive sport in the early twenty-first century with well-known stars such as Tony Hawk (1968–) and **Shaun White** (1986–; see entry under 2000s—Sports and Games in volume 6).

Tina Gianoulis

For More Information

Brooke, Michael. *The Concrete Wave: The History of Skateboarding: From the Backyard to the Big Time.* Toronto: Warwick, 1999.

Burke, L. M. *Skateboarding! Surf the Pavement.* New York: Rosen Publishing, 1999.

Cocks, Jay. "The Irresistible Lure of Grabbing Air." *Time* (June 6, 1988): pp. 90–95.

Louison, Cole. *The Impossible: Rodney Mullen, Ryan Sheckler, and the Fantastic History of Skateboarding.* Guilford, CT: Lyons Press, 2011.

Martin, Michael. *History of Skateboarding: From the Backyard to the Big Time.* Mankato, MN: Capstone High-Interest Books, 2002.

Thatcher, Kevin J., and Brian Brannon. *Thrasher: The Radical Skateboard Book.* New York: Random House, 1992.

Sports Illustrated

During the 1950s, a booming economy allowed Americans more leisure time than they had ever known before. Many of these hours were spent following amateur and professional athletics, but fans could only read about these sporting events in their local newspapers. Hoping to cash in on the surge of interest in sports, a new weekly magazine known as *Sports Illustrated (SI)* debuted on August 16, 1954. The magazine single-handedly created the concept of the national sports magazine. It offered in-depth, feature-length sports journalism and dazzling photographic images.

Sports Illustrated was the brainchild of Henry Luce (1898–1967), editor of **Time** (see entry under 1920s—Print Culture in volume 2) and founder of **Life** (see entry under 1930s— Print Culture in volume 2), two other successful weekly magazines. At first, *SI* was more of a generic men's magazine. It focused on sports and such leisure activities as yachting, big-game hunting, and fishing. However, it emerged as a journalistic force in the early 1960s when it narrowed its focus to the four major sports (baseball, football, basketball, and hockey), as well as covering boxing, tennis, and golf. The key to the magazine's success was its incisive, analytical writing. Newspapers reported the mere facts of sporting events. An *SI* article, accompanied by vivid photography, captured the essence of the player, team, or event, with as much of a focus on behind-the-scenes activity as on what occurred on the playing field. *Sports Illustrated* also published issue-oriented articles on topics such as the exploitation of African American athletes, the increasing threat of drug use among athletes, and the right of women to excel on the playing field.

For the more inquisitive and critical sports fan, the magazine became a "must-read." In 1954, its subscriber base was 350,000. Six years later, its circulation was 1 million. It grew to 2 million in the mid-1970s, 3 million in the mid–1980s, and 3.5 million in the late 1980s. Along with sports programming on **television** (see entry under 1940s—TV and Radio in volume 3), the popularity of *SI* helped usher in the era of athletics as big business. Its influence eventually transcended sports, as *SI*'s annual swimsuit issue, first published in 1964 and featuring attractive (and, as the years passed, ever more scantily clad) models, became wildly popular. The swimsuit editions helped cement the celebrity of such models as Cheryl Tiegs (1947–), Christie Brinkley (1954–), Kathy

Ireland (1963–), and Elle Macpherson (1963–). The swimsuit editions were also a contributing factor in the emergence of the **supermodel** (see entry under 1980s—Fashion in volume 5) phenomenon.

With the arrival of all-sports cable networks like **ESPN** (see entry under 1970s—TV and Radio in volume 4), the influence of *SI* lessened. The magazine is still well known in the early twenty-first century for its swimsuit issues, as well as for its writing and photography.

Rob Edelman

For More Information

SI.com. http://sportsillustrated.cnn.com (accessed July 28, 2011).

MacCambridge, Michael. *The Franchise: A History of "Sports Illustrated" Magazine.* New York: Hyperion, 1997.

Michener, James A. *Sports in America.* 12th ed. New York: Random House, 1989.

SI Kids. http://www.sikids.com/ (accessed July 28, 2011).

1950s

TV and Radio

Television was introduced to Americans in 1939 and began to gain a foothold after World War II (1939–45). In the 1950s, the sale of TV sets and the boom in programming made TV America's favorite source of entertainment. Consider the numbers: in 1946, 7,000 TV sets were sold; in 1948, 172,000 sets were sold; and in 1950, 5 million sets were sold. In 1950, just under 20 percent of American homes contained a TV set. Ten years later, nearly 90 percent of homes contained a TV—and some even had color TVs. The number of TV stations, channels, and programs all grew to meet this surge in demand. The 1950s truly were the decade of the television.

Three major networks—the National Broadcasting Company (NBC), the Columbia Broadcasting System (CBS), and the American Broadcasting Company (ABC)—provided the majority of TV program-ming. Early in the decade, the most popular programs were variety shows or serious dramas, such as *Texaco Star Theater, Fireside Theatre, Philco TV Playhouse, Your Show of Shows,* and *The Colgate Comedy Hour.* However, American tastes in TV changed over the decade. By 1959, the top three shows were Westerns—*Gunsmoke, Wagon Train,* and *Have Gun Will Travel*—and other favorites included comedy (*The Red Skelton Show*) and a game show (*The Price Is Right*).

Several important TV standards were set in the 1950s. *I Love Lucy* and *The Honeymooners* set the standard for situation comedies, which would grow to be TV's most dominant form of programming. Game shows like *The Price Is Right* and *The $64,000 Question* were popular and inexpensive to produce. *The Today Show* pioneered the idea of the morning variety show and remains on the air fifty years later. Moreover, TV programmers began to create innovative programs for kids, including *Captain Kangaroo, Leave It to Beaver,* and *The Mickey Mouse Club.* All these shows were loved by advertisers, who profited from their ability to advertise before huge audiences.

Television changed the American entertainment landscape. In towns where TV was introduced, movie attendance and book sales dropped off dramatically. Radio, which had been America's favorite form of at-home amusement, declined in importance in the 1950s. Variety, comedy, and dramatic shows left the airwaves for TV. Radio increasingly focused on news, talk shows, and sports broadcasting. Critics began to worry that TV encouraged passive behavior; that is, it turned people into what later generations would call "couch potatoes." It was a concern that would grow in the coming years.

The Adventures of Ozzie and Harriet

The Adventures of Ozzie and Harriet was the longest-running situation-comedy show in **television** (see entry under 1940s— TV and Radio in volume 3) history. From October 3, 1952, until September 3, 1966, in 435 episodes, the **sitcom** (see entry under 1950s—TV and Radio in volume 3) depicted the family of Ozzie and Harriet Nelson as they dealt with the minor problems of everyday life in a middle-class American **suburb** (see entry under 1950s—The Way We Lived in volume 3).

Usually considered the first TV series about a family, *Ozzie and Harriet* paved the way for similar 1950s series like **Leave It to Beaver** (1957–63; see entry under 1950s—TV and Radio in volume 3) and *Father Knows Best* (1954–62). Like them, *Ozzie and Harriet* focused on family matters, such as whether one of the sons in the family was old enough to have his own key to the house.

The show did not deal with social or political issues, nor did it show its characters being angry or mean. Often the problems in an episode would turn out to be the result of a simple misunderstanding. Overall the show presented a happy, agreeable image of life in America. Indeed, the show came to be seen as a symbol of the harmonious 1950s. The phrase "Ozzie and Harriet" came to be used as shorthand to refer to a time before the upheavals and social conflicts of later decades.

One of the oddities of the show was that its stars all played themselves. The real-life Ozzie and Harriet Nelson played Ozzie and Harriet

Nelson, and their real-life sons played their sons. When the sons grew up and married, their wives got roles on the show, too.

Ozzie, or Oswald George, Nelson (1906–1975) had been a bandleader in the 1930s. He married Harriet Hilliard (1909–1994), the band's singer and a former actress. The two of them began performing skits on the radio show of comedian Red Skelton (1913–1997). Their skits became a radio show called *The Adventures of Ozzie and Harriet* in 1944.

On the radio show, the Nelsons' two sons were at first played by actors, but beginning in 1949 the real Nelson boys, David (1936–2011) and Ricky (1940–1985), played themselves. Ricky, whose actual name was Eric, became a popular singer in his own right and often sang on the show in its later years on TV.

Sheldon Goldfarb

For More Information

"The Adventures of Ozzie and Harriet." *Sitcoms Online.* http://www.sitcomsonline.com/theadventuresofozzieandharriet.html (accessed July 28, 2011).

The Adventures of Ozzie and Harriet. http://timvp.com/ozzie.html (accessed July 28, 2011).

Bashe, Philip. *Teenage Idol, Travelin' Man: The Complete Biography of Rick Nelson.* New York: Hyperion, 1992.

Davidson, Sara. "The Happy, Happy, Happy Nelsons." *Esquire* (June 1971): pp. 97–101, 157–68.

Denis, Christopher Paul, and Michael Denis. "The Adventures of Ozzie and Harriet." In *Favorite Families of TV.* New York: Citadel Press, 1992.

Jones, Peter, writer-director. *Ozzie & Harriet: Adventures of America's Favorite Family* (video). A&E Biography Series, 1998.

Nelson, Ozzie. *Ozzie.* Englewood Cliffs, NJ: Prentice-Hall, 1973.

Alvin and the Chipmunks

In 1958, a singing group known as Alvin and the Chipmunks burst onto the national music scene with two hits, "Witch Doctor" and "The Chipmunk Song (Christmas Don't Be Late)." In the second song, the "chipmunks," with their high, wobbly voices, longed for Christmas to come soon. Their unique singing style was actually created through sped-up recording techniques. The singing captivated the American public and helped the group sell millions of singles. Ever since that first recording, Alvin and the Chipmunks have occupied a rare place in American popular culture as a novelty act that never lost its novelty. The group sold a string of albums and appeared in an animated **television** (see entry under 1940s—TV and Radio in volume 3) series in the 1960s and again in the 1980s.

The Chipmunks were the brainchild of Ross Bagdasarian (1919–1972), a prolific composer, producer, impressionist, and actor who performed under the pseudonym "David Seville." Bagdasarian had already enjoyed some success with several novelty tunes in the late 1950s, but with "Witch Doctor" he stumbled on a gold mine. Bagdasrian used nonsense lyrics (most memorable: "Ooo eee, ooo ah ah, ting tang, walla walla, bing bang") and sped-up vocal tracks to give the singers unique voices—the voices of a trio of chipmunks. The song was an immediate hit. It was followed later in 1958 by "The Chipmunk Song," which sold four million singles in just two months.

The Chipmunks were composed of the mischievous Alvin, brainy Simon, and chubby, silly Theodore. Bagdasarian provided the voices for all the characters as well as the voice of their temperamental manager, Dave Seville. The Chipmunks followed their first hits with a string of albums, beginning with *Let's All Sing with the Chipmunks* (1959) and continuing until the year 2000 with thirty-five albums. After his early success, Bagdasarian decided to bring his characters to television. He formed his own animation company and produced *The Alvin Show* for NBC in 1961. The prime-time series featured the songs and adventures of The Chipmunks. Most of the cartoons focused on Alvin and the trouble he caused for his brothers and manager. The series was canceled due to low ratings after one season, but it appeared for three more seasons as a **Saturday morning cartoon** (see entry under 1960s—TV and Radio in volume 4).

Alvin and the Chipmunks' popularity began to falter in the late 1960s. Albums released in the mid-1960s, like *The Chipmunks Sing The Beatles' Hits* (1964) and *Chipmunks a Go-Go* (1965), on which they performed the songs of the **Beach Boys** (see entry under 1960s—Music in volume 4), Tom Jones (1940–), and Petula Clark (1932–), failed to capture the public's interest. In the early 1980s, Ross Bagdasarian Jr. (1949–) revived his late father's characters and promoted them to **baby boomers,** (see entry under 1940s—The Way We Lived in volume 3) who had grown up with the original recordings. In *Chipmunk Punk* (1980), the gang sang the work of the Cars, Pat Benatar (1953–), and Billy Joel (1949–). Riding a new wave of popularity, Bagdasarian Jr. created a new

TV series titled *Alvin and the Chipmunks*. From 1983 to 1990, *Alvin and the Chipmunks*—a gentler version of the original cartoon— was a mainstay of NBC's Saturday morning cartoon lineup. The latter series also introduced The Chipettes, a group of singing female chipmunks named Jeanette, Brittany, and Eleanor.

While Alvin and the Chipmunks did not appear regularly on television after 1990, they were the stars of both video and film releases in the late 1990s and early 2000s. They starred in two straight-to-video animated releases, *Alvin and the Chipmunks Meet Frankenstein* (1999) and *Alvin and the Chipmunks Meet the Wolfman* (2000). The franchise was revived for the big screen in 2007, with *Alvin and the Chipmunks*. The film was primarily live action, although the three Chipmunks were animated. Actor Jason Lee (1970–) played Dave Seville. *Alvin and the Chipmunks* was a hit and led to two sequels, *Alvin and the Chipmunks: The Squeakquel* (2009) and *Alvin and the Chipmunks: Chip-Wrecked* (2011). Through the years the Chipmunks have stayed in the public consciousness, primarily because their songs—especially "The Chipmunk Song"—remain a mainstay of American musical goofiness.

Charles Coletta

For More Information

Alvin and the Chipmunks! http://www.chipmunks.com/ (accessed July 28, 2011).

"Alvin and the Chipmunks." *Rhapsody.* http://www.rhapsody.com/#/artist/alvin-and-the-chipmunks (accessed July 28, 2011).

The Alvin Show. http://www.toontracker.com/alvin/alvin.htm (accessed July 28, 2011).

Brooks, Tim, and Earle Marsh. *The Complete Directory to Prime Time Network and Cable TV Shows, 1946–present.* 9th ed. New York: Ballantine Books, 2007.

American Bandstand

Originally hosted by Dick Clark (1929–) from a studio in Philadelphia, Pennsylvania, *American Bandstand* was a live, hour-long televised dance show that began national broadcasts on August 5, 1957. It was a highly popular show that exposed a live audience of teenagers **dancing** (see entry under 1900s—The Way We Lived in volume 1) to the

Host Dick Clark and the lucky couples appearing on American Bandstand. © ABC/PHOTOFEST.

latest **rock and roll** (see entry under 1950s—Music in volume 3) records—a formula that helped popularize this musical genre (category) as an emblem of American youth culture. Most of rock and roll's leading artists made guest appearances on *American Bandstand,* including Buddy Holly (1936–1959) and the Crickets, Jerry Lee Lewis (1935–), the Everly Brothers, Johnny Mathis (1935–), Fabian (1943–), Bobby Rydell (1940–), and Frankie Avalon (1940–).

The original version of the show had debuted on WFIL-TV in 1952 as a local program with the name *Bandstand,* hosted by Philadelphia disc jockey Bob Horn (1916–1966). In 1956, Horn was dropped from the show after being arrested for driving while drunk. Horn was replaced by Clark, who had hosted country-and-western music shows on **television** (see entry under 1940s—TV and Radio in volume 3) as well as an easy-listening show for WFIL **radio** (see entry under 1920s—TV and Radio in volume 2). In 1964, when the show moved to Los Angeles, California, *American Bandstand* ceased being a live "after-school" show aired on Monday through Friday afternoons. From that point, it was taped for airing on Saturday afternoon. During the 1980s, competition from **MTV** (see entry under 1980s—Music in volume 5) and music videos made *American Bandstand* seem like a relic from an earlier generation. The durable Clark remained as host until the show finally went off the air for good in October 1987. A syndicated version, *The New American Bandstand,* ran through September 1989.

Even though the show failed to capitalize on the "British Invasion" of popular music in the 1960s, *American Bandstand* was an important forerunner of the emergent youth culture of that decade. The program helped unite teenagers in all parts of the country, who quickly imitated the latest dance steps and styles of their more urbane, sophisticated cousins who were eager to move to the music as long as it had a "beat." On the other hand, the show was long criticized for including only white teenagers, even though many of the records they danced to were created by African American artists. It was not until 1965 that *American Bandstand* featured its first black dancing partners.

Edward Moran

For More Information

Blitz, Stanley J., as told to John Pritchard. *Bandstand: The Untold Story.* Phoenix: Cornucopia, 1997.

Clark, Dick, and Fred Bronson. *Dick Clark's American Bandstand.* New York: Collins, 1997.

Clark, Dick, and Richard Robinson. *Rock, Roll & Remember.* New York: Thomas Y. Crowell Co., 1976.

Corliss, Richard. "Philly Fifties: Rock 'n Radio." *Time.* http://www.time.com/time/sampler/article/0,8599,167553,00.html (accessed July 28, 2011).

Delmont, Matthew F. *American Bandstand, Rock 'n' Roll, and the Struggle for Civil Rights in 1950s Philadelpha.* Berkeley: University of California Press, 2012.

Jackson, John A. *American Bandstand: Dick Clark and the Making of a Rock 'n' Roll Empire.* New York: Oxford University Press, 1997.

Shore, Michael, with Dick Clark. *The History of American Bandstand.* New York: Ballantine Books, 1985.

Candid Camera

Long before the rise of **reality TV** (see entry under 1990s—TV and Radio in volume 5) shows such as ***Survivor*** (see entry under 2000s—TV and Radio in volume 6) and ***The Real World*** (see entry under 1990s—TV and Radio in volume 5) in the 1990s, *Candid Camera* featured real people reacting to real situations beginning in the late 1940s and continuing off and on for the next forty-five years. *Candid Camera* was the brainchild of Allen Funt (1914–1999), a radio writer and producer. The show's idea was rather simple. Part psychology experiment and part practical joke, Funt would set up an odd situation and then film people's reactions to it. The show was called "candid" camera because it caught people candidly, or off guard.

Funt wanted to show how people would react to new and unusual situations. His guess that their reactions would prove highly entertaining was

Comic great Harpo Marx surprises a soft drink customer from inside a vending machine on this May 1961 Candid Camera *telecast.* © CBS PHOTO ARCHIVE/GETTY IMAGES.

right on target. The show was always good-humored. Funt never humiliated anyone or set up gags designed to hurt anyone's feelings. If he caught people doing things that were too embarrassing he would choose not to show that tape. Often his gags were as simple as putting salt in the sugar container at a restaurant and watching the customer's reactions. In other gags, someone would be hired to work in an office while odd phone calls came their way. Sometimes Funt himself would play a character or hire actors to play small roles in the gags. At the end of the gag, Funt would reveal the setup to the unsuspecting person and say "Smile, you're on candid camera," often pointing out where the hidden camera was located.

Candid Camera ran on **television** (see entry under 1940s—TV and Radio in volume 3) in the late 1940s and early 1950s. It came back to TV from 1960 to 1967, and again as *The New Candid Camera* from 1974 to 1978. The show returned once again in the early 1990s, this time hosted by Dom DeLuise (1933–2009). Another version hosted by Funt's son Peter aired from 1998 through 2004. Reruns aired on the cable network GMC later in the decade. Unlike later reality shows, which often focused on conflict, *Candid Camera* showed that reality TV could be done with humor, grace, and good-natured fun.

Timothy Berg

For More Information

Candid Camera Online! http://www.candidcamera.com/ (accessed July 28, 2011).

Funt, Allen. *Eavesdropping at Large: Adventures in Human Nature with Candid Mike and Candid Camera.* New York: Vanguard Press, 1952.

Funt, Allen, and Philip Reed. *Candidly, Allen Funt: A Million Smiles Later.* New York: Barricade Books, 1994.

McNeil, Alex. *Total Television.* 4th ed. New York: Penguin Books, 1997.

O'Reilly, Finbarr. "Behind the *Candid Camera*: All Smiles." *Globe & Mail* (June 17, 1998).

Perry, Patrick. "Catching Up with *Candid Camera*." *Saturday Evening Post* (May-June 1992): p. 50.

Captain Kangaroo

For more than thirty years, Bob Keeshan (1927–2004), also known as Captain Kangaroo, opened the doors to an imaginative "Treasure House" every weekday morning (and for a few years, on Saturday

mornings as well) on CBS. The gentle children's TV program ran for nearly ten thousand episodes, making it the longest-running children's series in network history. The Captain remains a treasured memory for millions of American children. The show has since been revived in a slightly altered form for a new generation of viewers.

Captain Kangaroo debuted on October 3, 1955. Its host was a one-time ***Howdy Doody Show*** (see entry under 1940s—TV and Radio in volume 3) regular and the creator of Clarabell the Clown. His soft speaking voice, grandfatherly manner, and push-broom moustache instantly endeared him to the show's pint-sized audience. Keeshan was more than just a hired gun, however. He took an active role in shaping the tone and direction of the series—contributing to the scripts, overseeing the production, and even selecting which commercials would air during the program.

Joining the Captain (called Kangaroo because of his bottomless jacket pockets) in the Treasure House were many human and puppet companions. The most prominent was Mr. Green Jeans, a rangy farmer played by children's TV veteran Hugh "Lumpy" Brannum (1910–1987). Mr. Green Jeans was a jack-of-all-trades who occasionally sang songs and played his guitar and introduced viewers to a wide range of animal "guests." In fact, more than two thousand species of animals appeared on

Captain Kangaroo during its run. Puppet characters on *Captain Kangaroo,* animated by puppeteer Gus Allegretti (1927–), included Mr. Moose and Bunny Rabbit. The show also featured numerous celebrity guest stars over the years, including Walter Cronkite (1916–2009), Phyllis Diller (1917–), and even another famous low-key children's host, **Mister Rogers** (1929–2003; see entry under 1960s—TV and Radio in volume 4) himself.

In 1982, CBS moved *Captain Kangaroo* to weekends only, and then cancelled the show in December 1984. Keeshan moved the show to PBS, where it ran until the early 1990s. In 1997, *The All New Captain Kangaroo,* starring character-actor John McDonough, debuted. Longtime viewers of Keeshan's program did not warm easily to the new captain, but the show retained much of the wholesome, family-friendly feel of the original series.

Robert E. Schnakenberg

For More Information

Captain Kangaroo. http://timstvshowcase.com/kangaroo.html (accessed July 28, 2011).
"*Captain Kangaroo.*" *TV.com.* http://www.tv.com/captain-kangaroo/show/8495/summary.html (accessed July 28, 2011).
Keeshan, Robert. *Good Morning, Captain: 50 Wonderful Years with Bob Keeshan, TV's Captain Kangaroo.* Minneapolis: Fairview Press, 1996.

Davy Crockett

There was a real person named David Crockett (1786–1836) who fought with future president Andrew Jackson (1767–1845) against Creek Native Americans, represented Tennessee in the U.S. Congress, and died at the Alamo. But the real life of the man pales when compared with the legends about him that occupy such a prominent place in the nation's popular culture.

Although there had been some accounts of his exploits in the nineteenth century, mostly in the form of **dime novels** (see entry under 1900s—Print Culture in volume 1), it took the **television** (see entry under 1940s—TV and Radio in volume 3) age to make Davy Crockett's name a household word. A new TV show from **Disney** (see entry under 1920s—Film and Theater in volume 2) called *Disneyland* broadcast the first episode of a planned Crockett trilogy on December 15, 1954. "Davy Crockett, Indian Fighter" starred Fess Parker (1925–2010) in the title role. Crockett's friend Georgie Russell was portrayed by Buddy Ebsen (1908–2003), who would later find fame on *The Beverly Hillbillies* (1962–71; see entry under 1960s—TV and Radio in volume 4). The story was introduced with a theme song built around the refrain, "Davy, Davy Crockett, king of the wild frontier."

The episode was a huge success, especially with children, and Crockett's popularity continued to grow as the rest of the trilogy was shown. "Davy Crockett Goes to Congress" was broadcast on January 26, 1955, and "Davy Crockett at the Alamo" followed on February 23, 1955.

A $300 million marketing frenzy quickly followed the Crockett craze. The most popular item was a coonskin (raccoon skin) cap like the one that Parker wore in his role. There was also great demand for such items as toy muskets, action figures, moccasins, and lunch boxes—many of which were pricy collectible items by the twenty-first century. Various recordings of the theme song (one performed by Parker himself) sold over seven million copies in total.

Although the Davy Crockett fad soon faded, the character made other periodic showings in popular culture. The best known of these was in the 1960 film *The Alamo,* in which Crockett was played by **John Wayne** (1907–1979; see entry under 1930s—Film and Theater in volume 2), who also directed and produced the film. However, in the years since Wayne's big-budget extravaganza, most of Crockett's appearances have been in forgettable made-for-TV movies and in cable-channel documentaries.

Justin Gustainis

Actors Buddy Ebsen as Georgie Russell and Fess Parker as Davy Crockett in a still from the Davy Crockett *television trilogy, broadcast 1954–55.* © PARAMOUNT/THE KOBAL COLLECTION/ART RESOURCE, NY.

For More Information

Davis, William C. *Three Roads to the Alamo: The Lives and Fortunes of David Crockett, James Bowie, and William Barret Travis.* New York: HarperPerennial, 1998.

Groneman, Bill. *Death of a Legend: The Myth and Mystery Surrounding the Death of Davy Crockett.* Plano, TX: Republic of Texas Press, 1999.

Johnston, Marianne. *Davy Crockett.* New York: PowerKids Press, 2001.

Stanley, George Edward. *Davy Crockett: Frontier Legend.* New York: Sterling, 2008.

Wallis, Michael. *Davy Crockett: The Lion of the West.* New York: Norton, 2011.

Dobie Gillis

Actors Dwayne Hickman as Dobie Gillis and Bob Denver as Maynard G. Krebs were the stars of the television show The Many Loves of Dobie Gillis, *which aired from 1959 to 1963.* © CBS-TV/THE KOBAL COLLECTION/ART RESOURCE, NY.

The fictional character of Dobie Gillis was an average American teenager with three primary interests: girls, girls, and girls. Actually, Dobie was all in favor of having wads of money and owning spiffy automobiles as well. But mainly he was obsessed with the opposite sex.

Dobie was the creation of writer Max Shulman (1919–1988), who first published Dobie stories in humor magazines in 1945. The character appeared on screen in *The Affairs of Dobie Gillis* (1953), a musical comedy starring Bobby Van (1928–1980) as a college-aged Dobie. The most

fondly remembered Dobie, however, was played by Dwayne Hickman (1934–) on the **television** (see entry under 1940s—TV and Radio in volume 3) **sitcom** (see entry under 1950s—TV and Radio in volume 3) *The Many Loves of Dobie Gillis* (1959–63). In that program, Dobie was a high school student, endlessly falling for attractive young women but seemingly destined to end up with an aggressively determined "Plain Jane" named Zelda Gilroy (Sheila James, 1940–). Other characters rounded out Dobie's family and townspeople, but the most memorable supporting character was Maynard G. Krebs, Dobie's zany **beatnik** (see entry under 1950s—Print Culture in volume 3) pal, played by Bob Denver (1935–2005), who would later star in the sitcom ***Gilligan's Island*** (1964–67; see entry under 1960s—TV and Radio in volume 4).

As the series evolved, Dobie and Maynard enlisted in the army and attended junior college. Years after its last episode aired, two other *Dobie Gillis* TV projects were produced: *Whatever Happened to Dobie Gillis?* (1977) and *Bring*

Me the Head of Dobie Gillis (1988). The question posed in the first title was immediately answered: Dobie—like so many aimless dreamers who are brought down to reality by everyday life—ended up marrying Zelda Gilroy and running his father's business.

Rob Edelman

For More Information

Denver, Bob. *Gilligan, Maynard, & Me.* New York: Carol Pub. Group, 1993.

Hickman, Dwayne, and Joan Roberts Hickman. *Forever Dobie.* New York: Birch Lane Press, 1994.

Shulman, Max. *I Was a Teen-Age Dwarf.* New York: Random House, 1960.

Shulman, Max. *The Many Loves of Dobie Gillis: Eleven Campus Stories.* Garden City, NY: Doubleday, 1951.

Dragnet

Dragnet was one of the most popular police-oriented **television** (see entry under 1940s—TV and Radio in volume 3) series in the 1950s. But it was no slam-bang, action-packed cop show featuring handsome police officer heroes. Instead, its lead character, Los Angeles Police Department sergeant Joe Friday, played by Jack Webb (1920–1982), was notoriously colorless and efficient, so much so that his blandness made him ripe for parody.

Friday—who grimly announced to the viewer, "My name's Friday. I'm a cop"—was the essence of the steadfastly dedicated policeman whose interpretation of the law was strictly "by the book." He had neither a wife nor a personal life. Seemingly, he was a twenty-four-hour-a-day, seven-day-a-week upholder of law and order. He courteously explained to people he questioned during his investigation that all he was concerned with was "just the facts." Predictably, by the end of the show, Friday and his partner nabbed the culprit. As the arrest was made, Friday ordered, "Book him on a 358" or "Book him on a 502." At the very end of the show, mug shots of the culprits appeared on screen with the details of their sentences dutifully reported.

Webb first played Friday on a radio version of *Dragnet* (1949–56). The TV series then originally ran from 1951 to 1959, with a revived version from 1967 to 1970. The success of the first TV show resulted in a feature-film version (1954). In most TV series episodes produced in

Just the facts: actor/director/producer Jack Webb was Sgt. Joe Friday and actor Harry Morgan was Officer Bill Gannon in the revived Dragnet *of the late 1960s.* © PHOTOFEST.

the 1950s, Friday's partner was Officer Frank Smith (Ben Alexander, 1911–1969). When the show returned to the air in the late 1960s, Smith was replaced by Officer Bill Gannon (Harry Morgan, 1915–2011). The latter *Dragnet* (which was respectively titled *Dragnet '67, Dragnet '68,* and so forth) was notorious for depicting Friday and Gannon busting student protesters, hippies, and youthful lawbreakers.

One of the constants on both versions was their famous theme music. Additionally, every *Dragnet* episode reportedly was based on an actual case. At the beginning of each show, an announcer soberly intoned, "The story you are about to see is true. The names have been changed to protect the innocent." Webb produced *Dragnet* through his Mark VII production company and also directed the show. Five years after his death, and decades after *Dragnet*'s demise as a series, a feature-film semi-parody came to movie theaters in 1987. Dan Aykroyd (1952–) starred as Joe Friday's nephew. Tom Hanks (1956–) played his partner and Harry Morgan played Captain Gannon, their supervisor. In 2003, another revival of the television series aired on ABC under the title *Dragnet*. Renamed *L.A. Dragnet* during its short, two-season run, Ed O'Neill (1946–) played Lt. Joe Friday, while Ethan Embry (1978–) played Detective Frank Smith.

Rob Edelman

For More Information

Badge 714: The Dragnet Webb Site. http://www.badge714.com/ (accessed July 28, 2011).

Deming, Richard. *Dragnet: Case Histories From the Popular Television Series.* Racine, WI: Western Pub. Co., 1970.

Hayde, Michael J. *My Name's Friday: The Unauthorized But True Story of Dragnet and the Films of Jack Webb.* Nashville: Cumberland House, 2001.

Moyer, Daniel. *Just the Facts, Ma'am: The Authorized Biography of Jack Webb.* Santa Ana, CA: Seven Locks Press, 2001.

New York Daily News columnist Ed Sullivan hosted a televised variety show that ran from 1948 to 1971.
© CBS-TV/SOFA ENTERTAINMENT/THE KOBAL COLLECTION/ART RESOURCE, NY.

The Ed Sullivan Show

Every Sunday night for almost twenty-three years between 1948 and 1971, millions of Americans tuned in at 8 PM to watch a live variety show on CBS. *The Ed Sullivan Show,* with an assortment of acts ranging from stand-up comics to rock bands to bears riding on bicycles, was the most popular variety show of its time, despite being hosted by a man best known for his awkward behavior in front of the camera.

First called *Toast of the Town,* the show debuted on June 20, 1948, at 9 PM. It later moved to its familiar, earlier time slot so that children could stay up to watch it. Its name was changed to *The Ed Sullivan Show* in 1955.

The show stayed on the air until May 30, 1971, and presented the best-known entertainers of its time. Two of the show's most famous moments featured performances by **Elvis Presley** (1935–1977; see entry under 1950s—Music in volume 3) in 1956 and the **Beatles** (see entry under 1960s—Music in volume 4) in

1964. Presley was shown from the waist up so as to avoid showing his dangerously swiveling hips. The Beatles made their American **television** (see entry under 1940s— TV and Radio in volume 3) debut in the episode that earned the highest ratings ever for the show.

The Ed Sullivan Show was also the place to see opera singers, ballet dancers, ventriloquists, jugglers, circus performers, and a talking mouse called Topo Gigio. The show presented old stars and created new ones. According to singer Connie Francis (1938–), quoted by Nick Tosches in his article, "Mr. Sunday Night": "If you went on *The Ed Sullivan Show,* everybody knew who you were the next day."

The host of the show, Edward Vincent Sullivan (1902–1974), was a New York newspaper columnist. Despite having experience as the master of ceremonies for various stage shows, he was notoriously stiff in front of an audience and was known as "Old Stone Face." He would stand with his arms crossed or with his hands on his hips and mispronounce names. He could not sing, dance, act, or tell jokes, yet the public loved him, perhaps because he seemed so similar to them.

Sullivan was a shrewd judge of talent and very much in tune with middlebrow American tastes of the mid-twentieth century. His show both reflected and shaped those tastes. It offered good clean fun for the whole family, reflecting the innocence of its time, even though some of the performers who appeared on its stage were leading the way toward the less innocent times to come.

Sheldon Goldfarb

For More Information

Barthel, Joan. "After 19 TV Years, Only Ed Sullivan Survives." *New York Times Magazine* (April 30, 1967): pp. 24–25, 100–104, 109–11.

Bowles, Jerry. *A Thousand Sundays: The Story of the Ed Sullivan Show.* New York: Putnam, 1980.

"The Ed Sullivan Show." *The Museum of Broadcast Communications.* http://www. museum.tv/eotvsection.php?entrycode=edsullivans (accessed July 28, 2011).

Ilson, Bernie. *Sundays with Sullivan.* Lanham, MD: Taylor, 2009.

Lear, Martha Weinman. "Let's Really Hear It for Ed Sullivan." *Saturday Evening Post* (April 20, 1968): pp. 84–87.

Leonard, John, et al. *A Really Big Show: A Visual History of the Ed Sullivan Show.* New York: Viking Penguin, 1992.

Maguire, James. *Impresario: The Life and Times of Ed Sullivan.* New York: Billboard Books, 2006.

Nachman, Gerald. *Right Here on Our Stage Tonight!: Ed Sullivan's America.* Berkeley: University of California Press, 2009.

The Official Ed Sullivan Show Site. http://www.edsullivan.com/ (accessed July 28, 2011).
Tosches, Nick. "Mr. Sunday Night." *Vanity Fair* (July 1997): pp. 118–34.

Game Shows

The game show has been a popular entertainment genre, first on **radio** (see entry under 1920s—TV and Radio in volume 2) and later on **television** (see entry under 1940s—TV and Radio in volume 3), since the 1930s. With a mixture of competition, entertainment, celebrities, ordinary citizens, and often outrageous formats, game shows have attracted large audiences, if not always critical appreciation. Jefferson Graham, in *Come on Down!!!: The TV Game Show Book,* quotes a *New York Times* critic who wrote that game shows were the "thorniest, stoniest area in the wasteland of television—infested with the scorpions of greed and strewn with the bones of those who perished pursuing the mirage of a new Cadillac Seville, a trip for two to Tahiti or a bushel basket of cool green cash." Despite such criticism, it has been estimated that one hundred million Americans watch game shows every week.

Although a variety of quizzes had aired on radio since the early 1930s, the first distinctive game show was *Uncle Jim's Question Bee,* which premiered in 1936. *Professor Quiz,* starring Craig Earl, followed this program two years later. Earl's show was broadcast from various movie theaters across the country and soon spawned more than two hundred imitators. Audiences flocked to these programs and their opportunities for fame and fortune.

Television aired its first game show, *Cash and Carry,* hosted by Dennis James (1917–1997), from a grocery store in 1946; TV has shown at least one game show every season since. The popularity of such programs is often credited to the appeal of instant riches and fame offered to the contestants. Home viewers enjoy the display of consumerism and capitalism promoted within these programs. The broadcast networks love the game show format because the programs are both cheap to produce and highly profitable. In general, the budget for an average game show is less than half the amount of other TV programming.

Game shows were especially popular on 1950s television. Notable programs included *Beat the Clock, What's My Line, You Bet Your Life,* **The Price Is Right** (see entry under 1950s—TV and Radio in volume 3),

Queen for a Day, and ***The $64,000 Question*** (see entry under 1950s—TV and Radio in volume 3). In the late 1950s, the nation was shocked to learn that America's most famous game show contestant, Charles Van Doren (1926–), had cheated with the aid of the producers of *Twenty-One.* Van Doren and other contestants on various programs had been coached to increase dramatic tension and promote contestants with strong audience appeal. Van Doren was disgraced and many games were pulled off the air.

Game shows survived the "quiz show scandal" and returned to prominence in the 1960s and 1970s. Among the most popular programs of this era were *The Hollywood Squares, Match Game, Password, To Tell the Truth,* and *The Dating Game.* Talk-show host Merv Griffin (1925–2007) created two of the genre's leading programs—*Wheel of Fortune* and *Jeopardy.* Both shows remained popular in the twenty-first century. Game shows regained some new popularity in 1999 with the enormous success of ***Who Wants to Be a Millionaire?*** (see entry under 1990s—TV and Radio in volume 5), starring Regis Philbin (1933–). Other new primetime game shows successfully introduced in the early twenty-first century included *The Weakest Link* and *Deal or No Deal.* Many classic game shows can still be enjoyed on cable's Game Show Network.

Charles Coletta

For More Information

Anderson, Kent. *Television Fraud: The History and Implications of the Quiz Show Scandals.* Westport, CT: Greenwood Press, 1978.

Blumenthal, Norm. *When Game Shows Ruled Daytime TV.* Albany, GA: BearManor Media, 2010.

DeLong, Thomas. *Quiz Craze: America's Infatuation with Game Shows.* New York: Praeger, 1991.

Graham, Jefferson. *Come on Down!!!: The TV Game Show Book.* New York: Abbeville Press, 1988.

Hall of Game Show Fame. http://www.gameshowfame.com/ (accessed March 8, 2002).

Holbrook, Morris. *Daytime Television Game Shows and the Celebration of Merchandise: The Price Is Right.* Bowling Green, OH: Bowling Green State University Popular Press, 1993.

Ryan, Steve, and Fred Wostbrock. *The Ultimate TV Game Show Book.* Chicago: Bonus Books, 2004.

Schwartz, David, Steve Ryan, and Fred Wostbrock. *The Encyclopedia of TV Game Shows.* 3rd ed. New York: Facts on File, 1999.

Gunsmoke

In the 1950s, TV was populated largely with singing cowboys and their lovable horses, but *Gunsmoke* was different. It was the first "adult" **Western** (see entry under 1930s—Film and Theater in volume 2), with flawed characters and gritty stories that were designed with a degree of realism. The show's popularity kept it on the air for twenty seasons, longer than any other Western, or any other dramatic series, in **television** (see entry under 1940s—TV and Radio in volume 3) history.

The show actually began on **radio** (see entry under 1920s— TV and Radio in volume 2), in 1952. Set in the Old West town of Dodge City, Kansas, it featured the same core group of characters that would form the nucleus of the TV show: Marshal Matt Dillon, Deputy Chester Proudfoot, local physician Doc Adams, and Miss Kitty, beautiful proprietor of the Long Branch Saloon. Matt Dillon was portrayed by William Conrad (1920–1994), who would later star in such TV series as *Cannon* (1971–76) and *Jake and the Fat Man* (1987–92). When the television show premiered in 1955, the radio program stayed on the air until 1961.

Television's Matt Dillon was played by James Arness (1923–2011). Dennis Weaver (1924–2006) was Chester, the limping deputy who was often used for comic relief. Weaver left the series in 1964 and his character was replaced by Deputy Festus Haggen (Ken Curtis, 1916–1991). Milburn Stone (1904–1980) played gruff but kindly Doc Adams, and Miss Kitty (Matt Dillon's love interest) was portrayed by Amanda Blake (1929–1989).

The show was a half-hour long at first but was expanded to a full hour after five years. The half-hour episodes were later repackaged as the series *Matt Dillon*. As with all 1950s television programs, *Gunsmoke* was filmed in black and white. It followed the trend of color broadcasting in 1966.

One of the things that made *Gunsmoke* an "adult" Western was its portrayal of violence. Gunfights, although common, were not portrayed as "fun," as they often were on children's Westerns. Shooting someone, even a villain, was treated as a serious matter. Despite the name of the series, Matt Dillon did not relish the chance to use his gun. Instead, the show honored a person's honesty and integrity.

Justin Gustainis

For More Information

Arness, James, and James E. Wise Jr. *James Arness: An Autobiography.* Jefferson, NC: McFarland, 2001.

Barabas, SuzAnne, and Gabor Barabas. *Gunsmoke: A Complete History and Analysis.* Jefferson, NC: McFarland, 1990.

Costello, Ben. *Gunsmoke: An American Institution.* Chandler, AZ: Five Star, 2005.

Gunsmoke: The Great American Western. http://www.gunsmokenet.com/ (accessed on July 28, 2011).

The Honeymooners

Most every **television** (see entry under 1940s—TV and Radio in volume 3) situation comedy of the 1950s featured characters who were contented members of the middle class. Whether living in a big city, a **suburb** (see entry under 1950s—The Way We Lived in volume 3), or a small town—and whatever the comic situations they found themselves in—these characters inhabited an idyllic mid-twentieth-century America and enjoyed the fruits of the economic boom after World War II (1939–45). One glaring exception was *The Honeymooners.* The quartet of characters featured in this landmark **sitcom** (see entry under 1950s— TV and Radio in volume 3) was anything but middle-class and comfortable. They were strictly of a lower "blue-collar" class and struggled to pay their bills and to realize their modest American dreams.

Ralph Kramden, the primary character on *The Honeymooners,* was a New York City bus driver and grade school drop-out who was forever conjuring up get-rich-quick schemes that never seemed to work. With his practical-minded wife Alice, blustery Ralph resided in a small, sparsely decorated Brooklyn, New York, apartment. Ralph and Alice were no cheery married couple; they were constantly battling, usually over the latest of Ralph's hair-brained projects. As Alice pointed out the illogic or impracticality of Ralph's plan, he would yell and protest and threaten to send Alice "to the moon" in "bang, zoom" fashion. Sometimes he would sarcastically declare, "Har har hardy har har," and tell her, "Oh, you're a riot, Alice." Soon enough, as the idiocy of his scheme became apparent, Ralph would stammer "Haminahaminahamina." Yet, despite these clashes, Ralph and Alice Kramden were united in love and loyalty. At the finale, after Ralph had been humbled yet again into

Jackie Gleason, Audrey Meadows, Art Carney, and Joyce Randolph pose on the set of The Honeymooners *in 1956.* © JACKIE GLEASON ENTERTAINMENT/THE KOBAL COLLECTION/ART RESOURCE, NY.

realizing his silliness, he would take his beloved Alice in his arms and tell her, "Baby, you're the greatest."

Two other characters played key roles on the show: Ed Norton, Ralph's neighbor and best pal, a lovable but dim-witted sewer worker who often would be drafted reluctantly into "Ralphie boy's" latest scheme; and Trixie, Ed's wife.

Comic actor Jackie Gleason (1916–1987) created the character of Ralph Kramden. Art Carney (1918–2003) was perfectly cast as Norton. Both characters are among the most recognizable in all of TV history. Over the years, several actresses played Alice. The first was Pert Kelton (1907–1968), who lost the role after she was **blacklisted** (see entry under 1950s—The Way We Lived in volume 3), that is, put on a "do-not-hire" list of people suspected of being communists or of sympathizing with communists. In later years, Sheila MacRae (1924–) played the part. But easily the most famous Alice Kramden was Audrey Meadows (1922–1996). Some viewers felt that the attractive Meadows was too pretty to play the drab Alice, but Meadows made the character memorable by playing the part with a steely, determined spirit. Joyce Randolph (1925–) was the original Trixie Norton; the character was also played by Jane Kean (1924–).

The Honeymooners started out as a series of sketches that initially appeared in 1951 on the DuMont network's *Cavalcade of Stars* (1950–52), a variety show. They continued when the program moved to CBS and became *The Jackie Gleason Show* (1952–55). Easily the most famous *Honeymooners* episodes are the thirty-nine half-hour-long shows that were produced and aired between 1955 and 1956. These programs were filmed before a live audience and have been rerunning in syndication ever since. The show was revived in 1966 and aired as hour-long episodes of a revamped *Jackie Gleason Show* (1962–1970). Five years later, these programs were rerun as *The Honeymooners*.

Rob Edelman

For More Information

Bacon, James. *How Sweet It Is: The Jackie Gleason Story*. New York: St. Martin's Press, 1985.

Crescenti, Peter, and Bob Columbe. *The Official Honeymooners Treasury*. Rev. ed. New York: Perigee Books, 1990.

Henry, William A. *The Great One: The Life and Legend of Jackie Gleason*. New York: Doubleday, 1992.

The Honeymooners. http://www.honeymooners.net/ (accessed July 28, 2011).

McCrohan, Donna. *The Honeymooners' Companion: The Kramdens and Nortons Revisited*. New York: Workman, 1978.

McCrohan, Donna, and Peter Crescenti. *The Honeymooners Lost Episodes*. New York: Workman, 1986.

Meadows, Audrey, with Joe Daly. *Love, Alice: My Life as a Honeymooner*. New York: Crown, 1994.

Starr, Michael. *Art Carney: A Biography*. New York: Fromm, 1997.

I Love Lucy

I Love Lucy (1951–1957) is considered one of the most popular and influential of all **television** (see entry under 1940s—TV and Radio in volume 3) situation-comedy series. The debut program aired on CBS on

October 15, 1951, and after a few weeks it was the number-one-rated comedy on television. Since 1959, the **sitcom** (see entry under 1950s— TV and Radio in volume 3) has been broadcast in reruns to an international audience and dubbed into many languages.

The basic plotline involves Lucy Ricardo, played by Lucille Ball (1911–1989), a zany redhead who gets involved in unorthodox adventures without the knowledge of her Cuban bandleader husband Ricky, played by Ball's real-life husband, Desi Arnaz (1917–1986). In the early 1950s, the pairing of a Cuban male with a Scottish American female (Lucy Ricardo's maiden name is MacGillicuddy) was considered a risk

Lucille Ball as Lucy Ricardo in a scene from I Love Lucy.
© CBS-TV/THE KOBAL COLLECTION/ART RESOURCE, NY.

among potential advertisers who were worried about the public's acceptance of the mixed marriage. But, as it turned out, the public loved the Ricardos and all their quirks. Lucy was perpetually trying to break into show business, but Ricky was against her being anything but a housewife, and eventually a mother—the broadcast of the birth of their son, Little Ricky, on January 19, 1953, was a national media event.

Lucy is often aided in her exploits by her neighbors and friends, Fred and Ethel Mertz, played by William Frawley (1887–1966) and Vivian Vance (1909–1979). Most frequently it is Ethel who is Lucy's conspirator, and together they cook up all sorts of schemes that land the two of them in trouble with their husbands. Although the general formula of hijinks within a marriage has been used over and over through the years on TV sitcoms, it has never been done with such consistent originality as it was with the Ricardos and Mertzes. Among the best-remembered *I Love Lucy* episodes: Lucy and Ethel get jobs on an assembly line in a candy factory; Lucy does a television commercial for Vitameatavegamin, with unpredictable results; Lucy becomes pregnant and tries to tell Ricky the good news; and a barefoot Lucy stomps on grapes in the vineyards of Italy.

Once the half-hour episodes ceased production after the 1956–57 season, a number of one-hour shows were produced that aired as specials over the next several years. Ball and Arnaz divorced in 1960. Ball went on to do *The Lucy Show* (1962–68), which also featured Vance for three years. Ball then moved on to *Here's Lucy* (1968–1974), and she briefly reappeared in 1986 in the short-lived *Life with Lucy*. In each of her post–*I Love Lucy* shows, veteran character actor Gale Gordon (1906–1995) was her comic foil.

Decades after the show's debut, *I Love Lucy* fan clubs are still flourishing, and memorabilia such as **T-shirts** (see entry under 1910s—Fashion in volume 1), pajamas, lunch boxes, pins, and dolls are sold worldwide.

Audrey Kupferberg

For More Information

Andrews, Bart. *The I Love Lucy Book*. Garden City, NY: Doubleday, 1985.

Ball, Lucille. *Love, Lucy*. New York: Putnam, 1996.

Edelman, Rob, and Audrey Kupferberg. *Meet the Mertzes*. Los Angeles: Renaissance Books, 1999.

Edwards, Elisabeth. *I Love Lucy: A Celebration of All Things Lucy*. Philadelphia: Running Press, 2011.

Edwards, Elisabeth. *I Love Lucy: Celebrating 50 Years of Love and Laughter*. Rev. ed. Philadelphia: Running Press, 2011.

Fidelman, Geoffrey Mark. *The Lucy Book.* Los Angeles: Renaissance Books, 1999.

Krohn, Katherine E. *Lucille Ball: Pioneer of Comedy.* Minneapolis: Lerner, 1992.

Lucille Ball-Desi Arnaz Center. http://www.lucy-desi.com/ (accessed July 28, 2011).

LUCYlibrary.com. http://www.lucylibrary.com/ (accessed July 28, 2011).

McClay, Michael. *I Love Lucy: The Complete Picture History of the Most Popular TV Show Ever.* New York: Warner Books, 1995.

Oppenheimer, Jess. *Laughs, Luck … and Lucy: How I Came to Create the Most Popular Sitcom of All Time.* New York: Syracuse University Press, 1996.

We Love Lucy. http://www.lucyfan.com/ (accessed July 28, 2011).

The Lawrence Welk Show

From 1955 to 1982, bandleader Lawrence Welk (1903–1992) and his Champagne Music Makers presented an hour-long program of easy-listening popular music that appealed to traditional audiences who disliked **rock and roll** (see entry under 1950s—Music in volume 3) and other musical styles of the younger generation. The show was sponsored for many years by Geritol, a tonic medicine for older people, and Sominex, a brand of sleeping pills.

Welk was born in Strasburg, North Dakota, but never lost the accent of his Eastern European parents. He was famous for expressions such as "wunnerful, wunnerful" and for starting his musical selections by waving a baton to the words "ah-one and ah-two." After many years as a struggling bandleader, he got his break in 1951 when KTLA-TV in Santa Monica, California, began to broadcast a show featuring his band. The show went nationwide on ABC-TV four years later. His shows presented a wholesome image of optimism and good cheer offered by performers such as Norma Zimmer (the "Champagne Lady"; 1923–2010), Irish tenor Joe Feeney (1931–2008), accordionist Myron Floren (1919–2005), and the most famous of all, the Lennon Sisters. Each week, Welk thrilled the female members of his studio audience by waltzing with them as his band played romantic standards. He was known for enforcing strict regulations that sometimes made his show seem old-fashioned. In 1959, he fired singer Alice Lon (1926–1981) because her dress was too revealing, and he even scolded the Lennon Sisters for wearing one-piece bathing suits during a poolside segment.

Bandleader Lawrence Welk sings with two of the Lennon Sisters, Dianne and Janet, during his television show in 1955.
© EVERETT COLLECTION.

In 1971, ABC dropped *The Lawrence Welk Show* from its lineup, claiming that it did not appeal to the younger audiences it was trying to attract. After an outpouring of support from loyal listeners, Welk decided to syndicate the show himself. It was soon seen on more than 250 stations from coast to coast. Welk retired in 1982 and last played with his band in 1989, three years before his death.

Edward Moran

For More Information

Drooker, Arthur, producer and director. *Lawrence Welk: A Wunnerful, Wunnerful Life* (video). A&E Home Video, 1997.

"Lawrence Welk." *Space Age Pop Music.* http://www.spaceagepop.com/welk.htm (accessed July 28, 2011).

Sanders, Coyne Steven, and Ginny Weissman. *Champagne Music: The Lawrence Welk Show.* New York: St. Martin's Press, 1985.

Stars of the Lawrence Welk Show. http://www.welkshow.com/ (accessed July 28, 2011).

Welk, Lawrence, with Bernice McGeehan. *Ah-One, Ah-Two!: Life with My Musical Family.* Englewood Cliffs, NJ: Prentice-Hall, 1974.

Welk Musical Family.com. http://www.welkmusicalfamily.com/ (accessed July 28, 2011).

Leave It to Beaver

In the late 1950s and early 1960s, *Leave It to Beaver* (1957–63) was one of a number of TV **sitcoms** (see entry under 1950s—TV and Radio in volume 3) set in an idealized, middle-class suburban-American environment. Along with such sitcom classics of the era as ***The Adventures of Ozzie and Harriet*** (1952–66; see entry under 1950s—TV and Radio in volume 3) and *Father Knows Best* (1954–62), *Leave It to Beaver* portrayed a "typical" American family. In this family, the father dutifully went off to work, the mother never mussed her hair as she maintained the household, and the children experienced the gentle trials of coming of age. What set *Leave It to Beaver* apart from the other shows was that it focused on its title character and youngest family member: Theodore "Beaver" Cleaver, played by Jerry Mathers (1948—).

When the series began, the Beaver was a cute seven-year-old. No matter how hard he tried to be well-behaved, he always found himself neck-deep in mischief. The Beaver was no budding juvenile delinquent. At his core, he was a lovable, obedient child; his comic antics and predicaments provided the show with its plot lines and its punch.

Three other members of the Cleaver family were featured on *Leave It to Beaver*. Wally (Tony Dow, 1945–), the Beaver's older brother, started out as a twelve-year-old who was the ideal all-American youngster. June Cleaver (Barbara Billingsley, 1922–2010), the boys' mother, was a patient and caring housewife. Ward Cleaver (Hugh Beaumont, 1909–1982), Wally and the Beaver's dad, was a wise, devoted parent. June always looked as if she were dressed for an afternoon bridge game; Ward was always neatly dressed in a business suit. The Cleavers lived in a well-kept home surrounded by a white picket fence in the fictional town of Mayfield. They were, indeed, the perfect American family, 1950s-style. One of the show's most notable supporting characters was Eddie Haskell

(Ken Osmond, 1943–), Wally's friend. Eddie was an obnoxious lout who would fake respect while dealing with parents; once the adults were out of sight, he would turn on the Beaver and his friends, treating them poorly.

Leave It to Beaver, first broadcast on CBS and later on ABC, was only mildly successful during its five-year run. Only in retrospect has it been so fondly viewed by **baby boomers** (see entry under 1940s—The Way We Lived in volume 3) who grew up in the late 1950s. The show's protracted popularity resulted in its frequent reappearance in syndication (the selling of shows to independent stations for rebroadcasting). Also produced were a made-for-TV reunion movie, *Still the Beaver* (1983), and a subsequent series with the same name (1985–89), also known as *The New Leave It to Beaver*. In 1997, a feature film based on the series was released. *Leave It to Beaver* featured Christopher McDonald (1955–) as Ward, Janine Turner (1962–) as June, and Cameron Finley (1987–) as the Beaver.

Audrey Kupferberg

For More Information

Applebaum, Irwyn. *The World According to Beaver*. New York: Bantam, 1984.

Leave It to Beaver: Jerry Mathers & Gang. http://www.leaveittobeaver.org/ (accessed July 28, 2011).

Mathers, Jerry, with Herb Fagen. *…And Jerry Mathers as "the Beaver."* New York: Berkeley Boulevard, 1998.

The Mickey Mouse Club

The Mickey Mouse Club, which aired from 1955 until 1959, was one of the most popular childrens' programs in **television** (see entry under 1940s—TV and Radio in volume 3) history and one of the most beloved properties of the **Disney** (see entry under 1920s—Film and Theater in volume 2) empire. The series was seen each weekday afternoon. It presented two dozen happy youngsters between the ages of nine and fourteen participating in musical numbers, comedy routines, and educational features. Many classic Disney cartoons were also showcased. The program offered wholesome family entertainment to the **baby boomer** (see entry under 1940s—The Way We Lived in volume 3) generation.

Before the show began, Walt Disney (1901–1966) conducted a nationwide search for personable children who could sing, dance, perform comedy, and project the Disney image of innocence and enthusiasm. The children selected for the series were known as "Mouseketeers." Among the most talented and charismatic of the Mouseketeers were Sharon Baird (1943–), Darlene Gillespie (1941–), Karen Pendleton (1946–), Cubby O'Brien (1947–), Lonnie Burr (1943–), Bobby Burgess (1941–), Tommy Cole (1942–), Sherry Alberoni (1946–), and Annette Funicello (1942–). Two adults supervised each episode's activities: Jimmy Dodd (1910–1964), an actor and dancer, and Roy Williams (1907–1976), a long-time Disney animator. Although all the children were given the opportunity to shine, Funicello soon became the most

popular and prominent Mouseketeer, and went on to more fame when she starred with Frankie Avalon (1940–) in a series of **beach movies** (see entry under 1960s—Film and Theater in volume 4).

The Mickey Mouse Club followed a consistent weekly pattern, with each day of the week devoted to a specific theme. The series also included other popular features. Jiminy Cricket from *Pinocchio* (1940) hosted an educational segment. Several live-action serials, such as ***The Hardy Boys*** (see entry under 1920s— Print Culture in volume 2) and *The Adventures of Spin and Marty* were popular with viewers. In 1959, the series was unexpectedly canceled despite still being the top-rated children's program of the season. The original Mouseketeers have reunited occasionally for

Disney TV specials. The 1950s series can still be seen on cable's Disney Channel.

In 1977, a new generation of Mouseketeers appeared in an updated version of the series. This program was, however, short-lived. The Disney corporation was more successful with its third incarnation of *The Mickey Mouse Club,* which ran from 1989 to 1994. This version of the series is noted for launching the careers of a number of young, talented performers who later rose to stardom, including Justin Timberlake (1981–; member of the pop band NSYNC, successful solo artist, entrepreneur, and actor), Keri Russell (1976–; star of the TV series *Felicity*), singer Christina Aguilera (1980–), and singer **Britney Spears** (1981–; see entry under 1990s—Music in volume 5).

Charles Coletta

For More Information

Armstrong, Jennifer. *Why? Because We Still Like You: An Oral History of the Mickey Mouse Club.* New York: Grand Central, 2010.

Bowles, Jerry. *Forever Hold Your Banner High: The Story of the Mickey Mouse Club and What Happened to the Mouseketeers.* Garden City, NY: Doubleday, 1976.

Keller, Keith. *The Mickey Mouse Club Scrapbook.* New York: Grosset & Dunlap, 1975.

The Original Mickey Mouse Club Home. http://www.originalmmc.com/ (accessed July 28, 2011).

Santoli, Lorraine. *The Official Mickey Mouse Club Book.* New York: Hyperion, 1995.

The Price Is Right

The Price Is Right (1956–65, 1972–) is a **game show** (see entry under 1950s—TV and Radio in volume 3) with a simple yet clever formula: contestants must guess the cost of various consumer items. Viewers have not tired of this formula for decades. As a result, *The Price Is Right*—created by fabled game show producers Mark Goodson (1915–1992) and Bill Todman (1918–1978)—has the distinction of being the longest-running program of its type in **television** (see entry under 1940s—TV and Radio in volume 3) history.

The host of the first edition of *The Price Is Right,* which aired on NBC, was Bill Cullen (1920–1990), a likable TV personality. Cullen

Host Bill Cullen during the taping of The Price Is Right *television show in 1961.* © EVERETT COLLECTION.

made his mark during TV's early years as a game show master of ceremonies and quiz show panelist. This first edition of the show stuck to a rigid formula in which contestants appeared on camera and competed against one another. The winner was the player who came closest to guessing the value of the item without going over the manufacturer's suggested list price. This version switched networks in 1963, moving to ABC, and was canceled two years later.

The Price Is Right seemed doomed to the unfortunate fate of dozens of other similar TV game shows. However, it resurfaced in 1972 in two versions, both of which briefly were known as *The New Price Is Right*. One version, hosted by dependable veteran master-of-ceremonies Dennis James (1917–1997), was syndicated (sold to independent stations) and aired in the evening. The other version of the show, a more enduring entry, was broadcast on CBS. This version was hosted by Bob Barker (1923–), another experienced host whose outgoing personality helped spark the show's newfound popularity. In addition, the format of *The Price Is Right* was expanded. For instance, various price-guessing games were employed, which added variety. Contestants were selected on camera, right from the audience, with the show's announcers— Johnny Olson (1910–1985), followed by Rod Roddy (1937–2003) and then Rich Fields (1960–)—inviting the chosen few to "Come on down!" Some of the prizes were handed out by "Barker's Beauties," a bevy of attractive models.

The handsome, platinum-haired Barker remained the show's host until his retirement in June 2007. He had the distinction of logging more hours in front of the TV camera than any other individual in history. Barker was replaced by actor/comedian Drew Carey (1958–), who continued to host the show in the second decade of the twenty-first century.

Audrey Kupferberg

For More Information

Barker, Bob, and Digby Diehl. *Priceless Memories.* New York: Center Street, 2009.

Blits, Stan. *Come On Down!: Behind the Big Doors at "The Price Is Right."* New York: Harper Entertainment, 2007.

The Price Is Right. http://www.cbs.com/daytime/the_price_is_right/ (accessed July 28, 2011).

The Price Is Right. http://www.priceisright.com/ (accessed July 28, 2011).

Schwartz, David, Steve Ryan, and Fred Wostbrock. *The Encyclopedia of TV Game Shows.* 3rd ed. New York: Facts on File, 1999.

Sitcoms

The situation comedy (often abbreviated to "sitcom") has been one of TV's most popular and long-lasting programming formats. A sitcom is generally a half-hour comedy program (twenty-two minutes of programming and eight minutes of commercials). Each program features a recurring group of characters who become involved in humorous situations. Episodes are typically self-contained, meaning viewers do not have to possess any previous knowledge of the show to get the jokes. Sitcoms have aired on **television** (see entry under 1940s—TV and Radio in volume 3) since the 1950s.

Although comedy entertainment on the surface, the shows reflected the nation's changing attitudes toward gender, race relations, sex, the population shift to the **suburbs** (see entry under 1950s—The Way We Lived in volume 3), and other social concerns. The format has often been criticized as overly simplistic, artistically bankrupt, and appealing to the lowest common denominator of viewer. Although audiences have witnessed scores of predictable and unfunny sitcoms, TV history is also marked by many sitcoms filled with wit, intelligence, and memorable characters.

The TV sitcom has its roots in network **radio** (see entry under 1920s—TV and Radio in volume 2) programming of the 1930s and 1940s. Among the most popular comedies of this era were ***Amos 'n' Andy*** (1928-60; see entry under 1930s—TV and Radio in volume 2), ***Fibber McGee and Molly*** (1935-59; see entry under 1930s—TV and Radio in volume 2), *The George Burns and Gracie Allen Show,* and ***The Jack Benny Program*** (see entry on Jack Benny under 1940s—TV and Radio in volume 3). With the rise of TV in the 1950s, many radio comedies migrated to the new medium. Audiences could now see the antics of their favorite characters rather than merely listening to them. The most innovative and successful sitcom of the decade was ***I Love Lucy*** (1951-57; see entry under 1950s—TV and Radio in volume 3), which starred Lucille Ball (1911–1989) and her husband, Desi Arnaz (1917–1986). The show depicted the wacky misadventures of a housewife who constantly attempted to enter show business despite her husband's irritation. The show was innovative in that it was filmed (not aired live) in front of an audience using a three-camera process. This technique created high-quality prints that could be broadcast for decades as reruns. The three-camera process is still used in most sitcom production.

During the 1950s, sitcoms like ***Leave It to Beaver*** (1957–63), ***The Adventures of Ozzie and Harriet*** (1952–66; see these entries under 1950s—TV and Radio in volume 3), and *Father Knows Best* (1954–63) depicted perfect nuclear families removed from the harsh realities of modern life. The sitcoms of the 1960s were generally escapist fantasies filled with outrageous

The Father Knows Best *cast in 1955: (clockwise from upper left) Jane Wyatt, Robert Young, Elinor Donahue, Lauren Chapin, and Billy Gray.*
© BETTMANN/CORBIS.

characters in unbelievable plots, such as ***Gilligan's Island*** (1964–67), ***Mr. Ed*** (1961–65), ***Bewitched*** (1964–72; see these three entries under 1960s—TV and Radio in volume 4) and *My Favorite Martian* (1963–66) or rural-based shows that emphasized "hayseed humor," such as ***The Andy Griffith Show*** (1960–68), ***The Beverly Hillbillies*** (1962–71; see these two entries under 1960s—TV and Radio in volume 4), *Green Acres* (1965–71), and *Petticoat Junction* (1963–70). In the 1970s, sitcoms became less outlandish and more focused on relevant social issues. In *All in the Family* (1971–79), producer Norman Lear (1922–) openly used risqué language, crude humor, and racial epithets to discuss contemporary concerns. "Black sitcoms" such as *The Jeffersons* (1975— 85), *Good Times* (1974–79), and *Sanford and Son* (1972–77) debuted in the 1970s. And ***The Mary Tyler Moore Show*** (1970–77; see entry under 1970s—TV and Radio in volume 4) was another of the decade's highlights as it presented a modern portrait of a single, working woman.

Sitcoms remained popular during the 1980s, 1990s, and the early 2000s. In the 1980s and 1990s, many programs were developed around popular stand-up comics like **Bill Cosby** (1937–; see entry under 1980s—TV and Radio in volume 5), **Roseanne** (1952–; see entry under 1980s—TV and Radio in volume 5), and **Jerry Seinfeld** (1954–; see entry under 1990s—TV and Radio in volume 5). In the early 2000s, a number of popular situation comedies focused on interpersonal and work relationships. The long-running ***Will and Grace*** (1998–2006) centered around the close friendship of the titular characters, a gay man and a straight woman and their friends, while *The Office* (2005–) featured distinctive characters who work at the Pennsylvania branch of a paper company and was a mockumentary (that is, it was shot documentary style, but events were fictional). Modern sitcoms may deal with material that was previously taboo, but they continue to present likable characters in wacky predicaments that are solved by each episode's end. The popularity of sitcoms is best demonstrated by the hours of reruns that continue to fill the airwaves.

Charles Coletta

For More Information

Bloom, Ken, and Frank Vlastnik. *Sitcoms: The 101 Greatest TV Comedies of All Time.* New York: Black Dog & Leventhal, 2007.

Brooks, Tim, and Earle Marsh. *The Complete Directory to Prime-Time Network and Cable TV Shows, 1946–Present.* 9th ed. New York: Ballantine, 2009.

Marc, David. *Comic Visions: Television Comedy and American Culture.* 2nd ed. Malden, MA: Blackwell, 1997.

Marc, David, and Robert Thompson. *Prime Time, Prime Movers: From "I Love Lucy" to "L.A. Law"—America's Greatest TV Shows and the People Who Created Them.* Boston: Little, Brown, 1992.

Mitz, Rick. *The Great TV Sitcom Book.* Rev. ed. New York: Perigee, 1988.

Taflinger, Richard. "Sitcom: What It Is, How It Works." *Richard Taflinger's Home Page.* http://public.wsu.edu/~taflinge/sitcom.html (accessed July 28, 2011).

Taylor, Ella. *Prime Time Families: Television Culture in Postwar America.* Berkeley: University of California Press, 1989.

The $64,000 Question

Throughout the history of TV, quiz and **game shows** (see entry under 1950s—TV and Radio in volume 3) have been highly popular among viewers. On them, contestants compete against each other as they play word games, guess the price of items, or display their knowledge of a range of subjects. One of the most fabled of all quiz shows was *The $64,000 Question,* which aired on **television** (see entry under 1940s—TV and Radio in volume 3) from 1955 to 1958. In its prime years, the program was an instant hit, earning the top spot in the ratings. During the notorious game-show scandals of the late 1950s, the show's reputation was tarnished. It was alleged—and, in some cases, proven—that contestants on other quiz shows were given answers to questions before going on the air.

Contestants on *The $64,000 Question* were asked a question relating to their area of expertise. If they responded correctly, they would double their money. Then, they were asked to make a choice. If they wished to, contestants could stop playing and keep their present earnings, or they could return the following week for an additional knowledge test—knowing full well that the questions would become increasingly difficult. Players reaching the show's upper levels were placed in an isolation booth to intensify the suspense. Those going for the $64,000 grand prize could bring with them an expert of their choosing to assist them. If they reached the higher levels and lost, they still received consolation prizes.

The first $64,000 winner was a U.S. Marine captain whose area of knowledge was gastronomy, the study of cooking and eating good food. Among the big-money winners: a preteen boy (for his expertise in science); a police officer (Shakespeare); a jockey (art); a shoemaker (opera);

and a housewife (the Bible). Several celebrities-to-be earned the top prize. Dr. Joyce Brothers (1928–), a psychologist, TV-radio personality, and newspaper columnist, was the second winner. Brothers's subject was boxing. Barbara Feldon (1939–), who played Agent 99 on the TV comedy series *Get Smart* (1965–70), won for her knowledge of Shakespeare. The success of the show resulted in a spin-off series, *The $64,000 Challenge* (1956–58). On this show, contestants who had won at least $8,000 on the first program were invited back to compete for further riches.

In 1958 and 1959, the quiz-show scandals erupted and shook the TV industry. No declarations of cheating by *$64,000 Question* and *$64,000 Challenge* contestants ever were substantiated. Both programs were canceled, however, along with their fellow prime-time quiz shows, in the wake of the uproar surrounding the scandals.

Rob Edelman

For More Information

DeLong, Thomas A. *Quiz Craze: America's Infatuation with Game Shows.* New York: Praeger, 1991.

Holms, John Pynchon, et al. *The TV Game Show Almanac.* New York: Chilton, 1995.

Quiz Show (film). Buena Vista Pictures, 1994.

Stone, Joseph, and Tim Yohn. *Prime Time and Misdemeanors: Investigating the 1950₂ TV Quiz Scandal.* New Brunswick, NJ: Rutgers University Press, 1992.

This Is Your Life

. . . .

This Is Your Life (1952–1961, 1970, 1983) is one of the most excessively sentimental yet fascinating shows in **television** (see entry under 1940s—TV and Radio in volume 3) history. It was one of the first exploitation-oriented TV programs; that is, it used the lives of everyday people for entertainment.

Each week, an unsuspecting individual would be invited to a public place, often in the company of a friend, a relative, or a colleague. While spending what was supposed to be a quiet evening in a restaurant, or making an low-profile appearance at a social function, he or she would be met by *This Is Your Life* host Ralph Edwards (1913–2005). Edwards then announced to the unknowing person and the world, "This is your life!" The surprised person would be hustled off to the show's studio, where childhood pals and acquaintances would be paraded across the stage, along with relatives and present-day friends and colleagues. All would offer reminiscences and anecdotes about the person in the spotlight. Before each guest came on camera, however, the "honoree" would hear a voice and would be asked to guess the person's identity. At the finale, all the participants would appear together on camera with the honoree, who would be presented with a gift: a film of the show and a projector on which to view it, perhaps, or a watch or a charm bracelet. All the while, Edwards would oversee the proceedings and attempt to squeeze the utmost sentiment from subject and guests.

While some of the *This Is Your Life* "honorees" were ordinary citizens or distinguished businesspeople, most were movie stars or TV personalities. Among the more memorable were legendary screen comics Stan Laurel (1890–1965) and Oliver Hardy (1892–1957), making a rare TV appearance. However, not all were delighted to be on the show. One was Lowell Thomas (1892–1981), the famed newscaster, author, and adventurer, who refused to smile during the program and even cracked, "This is a sinister conspiracy." Another was actor William Frawley (1887–1966), of *I Love Lucy* (see entry under 1950s—TV and Radio in volume 3) fame, who was offended that one of the "surprise" guests was his much-despised former wife and vaudeville partner, from whom he had long been divorced.

Occasionally, a subject was informed beforehand about his or her appearance on the show. One was singer and comic actor Eddie Cantor (1892–1964), who suffered from heart disease; Edwards did not want the shock of his appearance to result in a coronary attack. Another was actress-singer Lillian Roth (1910–1980), who had been married and divorced eight times and had battled alcoholism throughout her life. Roth's career peaked in the late 1920s and early 1930s. She had been long forgotten when she appeared on *This Is Your Life* in 1953. Her past had been too burdened by struggle to have it examined on national TV without her permission.

Rob Edelman

For More Information

Brooks, Tim, and Earle Marsh. *The Complete Directory to Prime-Time Network and Cable TV Shows, 1946–Present.* 9th ed. New York: Ballantine, 2009.

McNeil, Alex. *Total Television.* 4th ed. New York: Penguin Books, 1996.

This Is Your Life Official Web Site. http://www.thisisyourlife.com/tiyl.html?id_tiyl=0728TL292574 (accessed July 28, 2011).

Today

An early morning news and entertainment program, NBC's *Today* set the standard that other shows, like *Good Morning America,* would later adopt. Since its 1952 debut, *Today* has run through many different hosts, has gone up and down in the ratings race, but has retained the basic format developed by creator Sylvester "Pat" Weaver (1908–2002). It remains an important part of the morning ritual for millions of American viewers in the twenty-first century.

A pioneer of TV's golden age, Weaver structured *Today* around news, interviews, and lifestyle segments. Viewers could watch bits and pieces of the program on their way out the door to work or school. The first host of *Today* was newsman Dave Garroway (1913–1982). One of his "cohosts" during those early telecasts was J. Fred Muggs, a chimpanzee whose antics helped attract younger viewers. The mischievous ape became something of a cult hero and generated a lot of publicity for the show with live appearances around the country. Muggs "retired" in 1958.

Over the years, the show has utilized other gimmicks to lure in bigger audiences. These included using "Today girls" on features or to report on the weather; such "girls" included Florence Henderson (1934–) and Lee Meriwether (1935–). Jolly weather-man Willard Scott (1934–) has also wished Happy Birthday to centenarians (100-year-olds). Another unique aspect of *Today* was its ground-floor New York City studio, through which ordinary citizens could watch the show and appear on camera. The glass-walled studio was discontinued for many years before returning in 1994.

Hosting duties on *Today* have helped launch the careers of many network news stars, including Tom Brokaw (1940–), Barbara Walters (1931–), and Jane Pauley (1950–). Bryant Gumbel (1948–), an NBC sportscaster who took over as *Today* host in 1982, proved to be one of the show's most durable and controversial personalities. He feuded with his colleagues on the show, especially weatherman Scott, whom he criticized in an infamous 1989 not-meant-to-be-public memo. Nevertheless, Gumbel's tenure saw *Today* achieve some of its highest ratings ever. In the 1990s, the team of perky NBC News correspondent Katie Couric (1957–) and handsome New York City native Matt Lauer (1957–) was successful and maintained *Today's* dominance of the 7:00 to 9:00 AM time slot. A new weatherman, Al Roker (1954–), replaced Scott in 1996. In early 2000s, Couric left to become the host of *CBS Evening News* in 2006, and was replaced by veteran newswoman Meredith Vieira (1953–). When Vieira ended her run in 2011, longtime *Today* news anchor Ann Curry (1956–) took over Vieira's spot on the show. Despite the rotating female co-hosts, the *Today* show remained atop the morning show ratings during this time period.

Robert E. Schnakenberg

For More Information

Battaglio, Stephen. *From Yesterday to Today: Six Decades of America's Favorite Morning Show.* Philadelphia: Running Press, 2011.

Davis, Gerry. *The Today Show: An Anecdotal History.* New York: Morrow, 1987.

Kessler, Judy. *Inside Today: The Battle for the Morning.* New York: Villard, 1992.

Metz, Robert. *The Today Show: An Inside Look At 25 Tumultuous Years … and the Colorful and Controversial People Behind the Scenes.* Chicago: Playboy Press, 1977.

Mink, Eric. *This Is Today: A Window on Our Times.* Kansas City, MO: Andrews McMeel, 2003.

Today.com. http://www.today.com/ (accessed July 28, 2011).

The Tonight Show

• •

NBC's talk program *The Tonight Show* has been entertaining late-night **television** (see entry under 1940s—TV and Radio in volume 3) viewers since 1954. Although the hosts have changed, the show retains the same mix of topical humor, comedy skits, and light-hearted talk that made it successful and inspired numerous imitators.

The focal point of *The Tonight Show* has always been its host. From 1954 into 2002, only four men sat behind the "big desk" on a permanent basis. Steve Allen (1921–2000), the first host of the program, emphasized outrageous comedy stunts like those later seen on the TV shows of comedian **David Letterman** (1947–; see entry under 1980s—TV and Radio in volume 5). Allen departed in 1956 after just four years as host. Jack Paar (1918–2004), a former game-show host, replaced Allen. Paar remade *Tonight* around intelligent interviews with celebrities and world leaders like Richard Nixon (1913–1994) and Robert F. Kennedy (1925–1968). Paar also became famous for walking off the program in the middle of a broadcast in February 1960. He soon returned but lasted only a short period at the helm, from 1956 to 1962.

Vivian Vance (left) and Lucille Ball join host Jack Paar of The Tonight Show. © PHOTOFEST.

To many people, the next host of *The Tonight Show* was the man who truly personified the program. Nebraskan **Johnny Carson** (1925–2005; see entry under 1960s—TV and Radio in volume 4) took over the host's chair in 1962 and remained there until 1992. A former magician, Carson combined some of Allen's comedy showmanship with a bit of Paar's conversational style. He also had a quick wit and offered his take on the events of the day in a monologue (a series of jokes from a comedian) that opened every show. Politicians and other famous figures often gauged their popularity with the public according to how many times they made it into Carson's monologue. Other aspects of Carson's version of the show became equally beloved. Sidekick Ed McMahon

(1923–2009) began each show by bellowing "Heeeeeere's Johnny!"—a line that became so fixed in the public mind that it even made into the movies as the chilling greeting of murderous maniac Jack Nicholson (1937–) in the 1981 horror classic *The Shining*.

Carson opted to step down as host in 1992, opening up a spot for his regular guest host, Jay Leno (1950–). Leno beat out Letterman, whose own NBC program followed *The Tonight Show,* for the hosting position, a snub that forced the sensitive Letterman to move his program to a rival network, CBS. In the 1990s, Leno remained largely true to Carson's formula: a topical monologue followed by celebrity interviews and brief bits of comedy. Although initially beaten by Letterman's program in the ratings, *The Tonight Show* under Leno eventually reasserted its position as America's favorite late-night talk show.

In 2004 it was announced that Leno would retire in 2009 and that his replacement would be the host of NBC's *Late Night with Conan O'Brien.* As soon as **Conan O'Brien** (1963–; see entry 2000s—TV and Radio in volume 6) began hosting *The Tonight Show* in June 2010, ratings dropped to a position much lower than had ever been experienced during Leno's tenure, and they never recovered. The situation was difficult as O'Brien still lived in Leno's shadow because the latter had his own weeknight talk show on NBC, *The Jay Leno Show,* starting in the fall of 2009. NBC essentially forced O'Brien out as host, and Leno returned to *The Tonight Show* in March 2010. O'Brien soon found a late night home on TBS, which began airing *Conan* in the fall of 2010. Though Leno's ratings were initially low as well, *The Tonight Show* soon rebounded and returned to its place as the most popular late night talk show on American television.

Robert E. Schnakenberg

For More Information

Alba, Ben. *Inventing Late Night: Steve Allen and the Original "Tonight Show."* Amherst, NY: Prometheus, 2005.

Carter, Bill. *The Late Shift: Letterman, Leno, and the Network Battle for the Night.* New York: Hyperion, 1993.

Carter, Bill. *The War for Late Night: When Leno Went Early and Television Went Crazy.* New York: Viking, 2011.

Cox, Stephen. *Here's Johnny!: Thirty Years of America's Favorite Late-Night Entertainer.* Rev. ed. Nashville: Cumberland House, 2002.

Here's Johnny! The Official Tonight Show Website. http://www.johnnycarson.com/carson/ (accessed March 11, 2012).

Katz, Jesse. "The Coco Insurrection: He Lost His Job and Became a Hero to the Downtrodden." *New York* (February 1, 2010)

Lafayette, Jon. "Conan's Baaaack … and Right where He Belongs." *Broadcasting & Cable* (November 8, 2010): p.10.

McMahon, Ed. *Here's Johnny!: My Memories of Johnny Carson, the "Tonight Show," and 46 Years of Friendship.* Nashville: Rutledge Hill Press, 2005.

Metz, Robert. *The Tonight Show.* New York: Playboy Press, 1980.

Paar, Jack. *P.S., Jack Paar.* Garden City, NY: Doubleday, 1983.

"The Tonight Show with Jay Leno." *NBC.com.* http://www.nbc.com/The_Tonight_Show_with_Jay_Leno/index.html (accessed March 11, 2002).

Transistor Radios

Small, portable, and convenient, transistor radios did not offer excellence in sound quality, but they did provide another important feature—privacy. American teenagers saw the pocket radios as a way to listen to the driving beat of **rock and roll** (see entry under 1950s—Music in volume 3) music away from the judgment of their parents. The first transistor radio (the Regency TR-1) was produced by Regency Electronics in cooperation with Texas Instruments in 1954.

The magazine *Popular Mechanics* had published instructions for building a do-it-yourself pocket radio, using a wooden glove box for the body, in 1925. The invention of the transistor in the early 1950s paved the way for a mass-produced pocket radio. A transistor is a small device, about the size of a pencil eraser, that generates and amplifies electric signals. It could be used instead of the bulkier vacuum tubes to control the signals that sent **radio** (see entry under 1920s—TV and Radio in volume 2) broadcasts through the air.

Japanese manufacturer Sony exported its TR-63 transistor radio to the United States starting in 1957. Sony quickly became the market leader as American teens fast became eager buyers of the compact radios. In 1957, one hundred thousand transistor radios were shipped to the United States. By 1959, the number had risen to six million, over half of all

The transistor radio allowed the listener to take music anywhere. © COMSTOCK/JUPITERIMAGES/GETTY IMAGES.

the pocket radios manufactured in Japan. By the 1960s, transistor radios were even more popular as people became accustomed to hearing their favorite music, sports, and news wherever they went. By the 1970s and 1980s, the **Walkman** (see entry under 1970s— Music in volume 4) essentially replaced the transistor radio, due to its superior sound quality and ability to play cassette tapes.

Tina Gianoulis

For More Information

Fitch, Richard D. "Portables." *Radio-Electronics* (Vol. 58, January 1987): pp. 74–79.

Lane, David R., and Robert A. Lane. *Transistor Radios: A Collector's Encyclopedia and Price Guide.* Radnor, PA: Wallace-Homestead, 1994.

Schiffer, Michael Brian. *The Portable Radio in American Life.* Tucson: University of Arizona Press, 1991.

Smith, Norman R. *Transistor Radios, 1954–1968.* Atglen, PA: Schiffer, 1998.

Stein, Mark V. *Machine Age to Jet Age: Radiomania's Guide to Tabletop Radios, 1933–1959.* 2nd ed. Baltimore: Radiomania Books, 1998.

"The Transistor." *DigitalAmerica.* http://www.ce.org/Press/CEA_Pubs/945.asp (accessed July 28, 2011).

The Twilight Zone

The Twilight Zone (1959–62, 1963–64) is one of the most distinctive series in all of **television** (see entry under 1940s—TV and Radio in volume 3) history. Part science fiction, part fantasy, and part surreal drama, the show was—quality-wise—far removed from most ordinary TV programming. *The Twilight Zone,* which aired on CBS, was an anthology series; each week, it presented stories that were unrelated to one another, and which featured completely different casts. A typical episode would challenge the viewer, toying with his or her mind and sense of logic and reality. It would portray characters who were struggling for survival in a frightening, confusing, irrational world, and who were victimized by unpredictable plot twists. Many *Twilight Zone* characters were average human beings facing extraordinary dilemmas and situations.

The Twilight Zone was the brainchild of Rod Serling (1924–1975), a former World War II (1939–45) paratrooper and Golden Gloves boxer who began writing radio scripts in the late 1940s and, during the following decade, authored teleplays for top dramatic series. Two of his most famous scripts were "Patterns" (1955), the chronicle of a power struggle

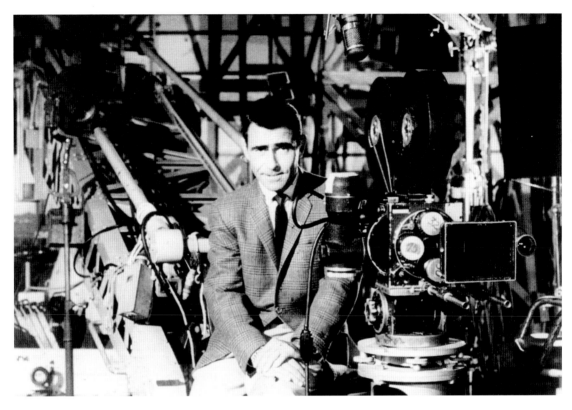

Rod Serling, writer and host of television's The Twilight Zone. © EVERETT COLLECTION.

within the walls of a corporation, broadcast on *Kraft Television Theatre* (1947–58); and "Requiem for a Heavyweight" (1956), the story of a broken-down boxer who is forced to compromise his integrity, which aired on *Playhouse 90* (1956–61).

Serling not only wrote many of the *Twilight Zone* scripts—he penned three-fifths of all the original episodes—but was also the show's host. He introduced each episode by first noting that he would be transporting viewers into the "twilight zone," a "fifth dimension, beyond that which is known to man." He then reappeared at the finale, to add a final note of irony to the story in his characteristic voice. The initial *Twilight Zone* episode, titled "Where Is Everybody," set the tone of what was to follow. It involved a man who desperately attempts to locate the inhabitants of a deserted town. The plot twist is that he is an astronaut, being subjected to an experiment in an isolation booth.

Quite a few *Twilight Zone* episodes are TV classics. "Time Enough at Last" told the story of an introverted bank teller who never could find sufficient time to read. He survives a nuclear attack, and he is delighted that he now is alone and can spend all his hours reading. However, before he can begin, he trips and breaks his glasses, rendering him unable to see the words on the books' pages. In "Escape Clause," a man makes a pact with the Devil, allowing him immortality, but he commits murder and is sentenced to life in prison. In "The Eye of the Beholder," a woman undergoes surgery to rid herself of facial disfigurement. To the viewer the operation is a success, as she emerges a beauty. Only then is it revealed that she lives in a society in which all citizens are horrendously deformed. By their standards, she now is considered a freak.

All *Twilight Zone* episodes were filmed in black and white. The show originally was one half-hour long. It was dropped after three seasons and soon returned to the air, this time expanded to a full hour. For its final season, it reverted to the half-hour format. Additionally, the series is of note for its casting of quite a few movie and TV stars-to-be. Three of the more celebrated were Robert Duvall (1931–), William Shatner (1931–), and Robert Redford (1937–).

Eight years after Serling's death, and nineteen years after the final original series episode aired, *Twilight Zone—The Movie* (1983) came to movie houses. The film consisted of four parts, three of which were remakes of original series' episodes. Two years later, a new *Twilight Zone* (1985–87) returned to TV, filmed in color and presenting a mixture of new stories and reworkings from its predecessor. In 2002, *Twilight Zone* was revived again for television. Hosted by actor Forest Whitaker (1961–), this most recent version aired on UPN for one season.

Rob Edelman

For More Information

Brode, Douglas, and Carol Serling. *Rod Serling and "The Twilight Zone": The 50th Anniversary Tribute.* Fort Lee, NJ: Barricade, 2009.

Grams, Martin. *The Twilight Zone: Unlocking the Door to a Television Classic.* Churchville, MD: OTR, 2008.

Stanyard, Stewart T. *Dimensions Beyond the Twilight Zone.* Chicago: ECW Press, 2007.

The Twilight Zone. http://www.syfy.com/twilightzone/ (accessed July 28, 2011).

Wolfe, Peter. *In the Zone: The Twilight World of Rod Serling.* Bowling Green, OH: Bowling Green State University Popular Press, 1997.

Zicree, Marc Scott. *The Twilight Zone Companion.* 2nd ed. Los Angeles: Silman-James Press, 2004.

1950s

The Way We Lived

The 1950s are sometimes thought of as America's bland decade, a decade when family life was stable and America's cities were safe. The economy was booming and most Americans enjoyed increased prosperity. Americans celebrated this prosperity by having babies in record numbers, continuing a surge in the population known as the "baby boom" that started when veterans returned home after World War II (1939–45). Growing numbers of Americans moved their families to new homes in developments, called suburbs, outside of cities. Sales of cars increased dramatically. Travel was made easier by the development of a national highway system that connected all of America's largest cities.

America celebrated its prosperity in a variety of ways. The energy of youth expanded American culture, as shown by the rise of a variety of toys and amusements for young people, including the Slinky, Silly Putty, the Frisbee, and the hula hoop. Attendance at amusements parks soared. A new form of music called rock and roll emerged as an important expression of youth culture.

This serene picture of progress and prosperity was darkened, however, by storm clouds of suspicion and emerging social trauma. The suspicion was largely the result of the ongoing Cold War (1945–91) with the Soviet Union. Americans built bomb shelters behind their suburban homes. Many worried about the influence of communists in their midst.

U.S. senator Joseph McCarthy (1909–1957) of Wisconsin chaired the Army-McCarthy hearings to investigate communism in the armed forces. His anticommunism crusade touched all areas of American culture. Even Hollywood was tainted by its experience with a "blacklist" that ruined the careers of many liberal writers and filmmakers.

Many of the social disruptions that changed America in the 1960s began in the 1950s. Women became increasingly unhappy with their status as homemakers. Many sought jobs outside the home. African Americans began to protest the systematic discrimination that they faced. People also began to rebel against the conservative sexual ideas of the time. *Playboy* magazine and the invention of the birth control pill were symbols of the coming sexual revolution. The 1950s were a time of change.

Amusement Parks

The pursuit of fun is a most American activity. Amusement parks developed as places where fun is the most important business, available year round, for a price. Since their creation in the late nineteenth century, amusement parks have changed as the culture has changed, but their appeal has remained constant. Amusement parks, with their games, rides, performances, and exotic foods, create a small separate world, away from the cares of everyday life, where having fun and being excited are the only demands impressed upon visitors.

From earliest times, people all over the world brightened their daily work lives with fairs and festivals. Circuses and other traveling shows made their rounds, creating a holiday when they arrived in town. Amusement parks differed from these events because they were permanent. In 1893, the rides and displays at the Chicago **World's Fair** (see entry under 1900s—The Way We Lived in volume 1) dazzled those who attended it. The fair inspired Paul Boyton (1848–1924) to build two permanent amusement parks, Chutes Park in Chicago, Illinois (1884), and Sea Lion Park at **Coney Island** (see entry under 1900s—The Way We Lived in volume 1), near New York City (1885).

Coney Island became the most popular amusement area in the country between the 1890s and the 1950s. There, visitors could experience many different amusement parks side by side, such as Steeplechase Park and Luna Park. In 1887, George C. Tilyou (1862–1914) installed

New York City's famous Coney Island at night. © WILLIAM GOTTLIEB/CORBIS.

the country's first **roller coaster** (see entry under 1900s—The Way We Lived in volume 1) in Steeplechase Park. In the summer of 1947, six million people visited Coney Island over a four-day Fourth of July weekend.

By the 1920s, there were almost two thousand small amusement parks around the country, but the **Great Depression** (1929–41; see entry under 1930s—The Way We Lived in volume 2) and World War II (1939–45) had hurt the industry and reduced the number to several hundred. By the 1950s, amusement parks were no longer the glamorous, dazzling fairylands of the early 1900s but were seen as dirty, seedy places where low-class people gathered. Walt **Disney** (1901–1960; see entry under 1920s—Film and Theater in volume 2) changed all that in 1955, when he opened a new kind of amusement park.

Walt Disney's Magic Kingdom, also known as Disneyland, was a theme park, with several different parks (Tomorrowland, Fantasyland, and Frontierland, for example) within it. Disneyland, located in

Anaheim, California introduced a new, clean-cut image to amusement parks. Theme parks, which reproduce another time or place within the park, remain the most popular type of modern amusement park. Disney has opened other parks, such as Walt Disney World in Orlando, Florida, in 1971; Disneyland Tokyo in Tokyo, Japan, in 1983; and EuroDisney in Paris, France, in 1992. Though Walt Disney World is the most popular amusement park in the world, with over forty million visitors annually, many people criticize the Disney parks as being too artificial and too commercial.

In 2007, attendance at amusement parks in the United States topped 341 million visitors to over 400 parks generating $12 billion in revenue. Although the need for fun may be the same as that of parkgoers at the turn of the last century, the fun itself has gotten more and more extreme, with new and more creative rides added each year to keep attendees coming year after year. Coney Island's first roller coaster went six miles per hour in 1887. Modern roller coasters achieve speeds of at least 128 miles per hour.

Tina Gianoulis

For More Information

Adams, Judith A., and Edwin Perkins. *The American Amusement Park Industry: A History of Technology and Thrills.* Boston: Twayne, 1991.

Greene, Katherine, and Richard Greene. *The Man Behind the Magic: The Story of Walt Disney.* New ed. New York: Viking, 1998.

O'Brien, Tim. *Legends: Pioneers of the Amusement Park Industry.* Orlando, FL: Ripley, 2006.

Samuelson, Dale, and Wendy Yegoiants. *The American Amusement Park Industry.* St. Paul, MN: MBI, 2001.

Van Steenwyk, Elizabeth. *Behind the Scenes at the Amusement Park.* Niles: IL: Albert Whitman &, 1983.

Watson, Bruce. "Three's a Crowd, They Say, But Not at Coney Island!" *Smithsonian* (Vol. 27, no. 9, December 1996): pp. 100–10.

Army-McCarthy Hearings

The end of the anticommunist crusade of U.S. senator Joseph McCarthy (1909–1957) of Wisconsin began in the spring of 1954 during hearings, televised live, of the Senate Permanent Subcommittee on Investigations. The Subcommittee was investigating a series of charges

U.S. senator Joseph McCarthy of Wisconsin with his attorney, Roy Cohn, seated to his left, during the Army-McCarthy hearings in June 1954. © YALE JOEL/TIME LIFE PICTURES/GETTY IMAGES.

and countercharges made between McCarthy and the U.S. Army's top generals, which is why the proceedings became known as the "Army-McCarthy Hearings."

The hostility between the two parties began in November 1953 when a member of McCarthy's staff, G. David Schine (1927–1996), was drafted into the army. Almost immediately, McCarthy and his chief counsel, Roy Cohn (1927–1986), began to lobby the army to get Schine special treatment, such as easy training and assignment to a desirable duty station. When the army did not cooperate with his requests, McCarthy charged that it was using Schine as a hostage to prevent McCarthy's exposure of communists in the military. The army responded with accusations of interference on McCarthy's part. Thus was the stage set for the confrontation.

Up to this time, although most Americans knew who Senator McCarthy was, they had seen little of his manner and tactics as he tried to hunt down suspected communists in government. McCarthy had received much print coverage, but the newspapers and magazines failed to convey a sense of what the man was like and he received little **television** (see entry under 1940s—TV and Radio in volume 3) coverage. The hearings, carried by two TV networks, lasted from April 22 to June 17. The U.S. Army was represented by lawyer Joseph Welch (1890–1960). Throughout the hearings, McCarthy and Cohn often came across as bullies, while Welch was professional and restrained.

The climax to the hearings came on June 9, after McCarthy charged that a young attorney at Welch's firm had communist affiliations. Welch's response was: "Until this moment, Senator, I think I never gauged your cruelty or recklessness…. Have you no sense of decency, sir, at long last? Have you left no sense of decency?" The audience in the visitor's gallery erupted into applause.

Public support for McCarthy and his anticommunist campaign soon shrank. A few months later, the Senate passed a motion censuring McCarthy. McCarthy continued to serve as a senator until his death on May 2, 1957, but his effectiveness all but ended at the hearings. The term "McCarthyism" became a synonym for reckless smear tactics intended to destroy a victim's political standing and public character.

Justin Gustainis

For More Information

"The Army-McCarthy Hearings." *C-SPAN Video Library.* http://www.c-spanvideo.org/program/158934-1 (accessed July 29, 2011).

"The Army-McCarthy Hearings." *The Museum of Broadcast Communications.* http://www.museum.tv/eotvsection.php?entrycode=army-mccarthy (accessed July 29, 2011).

Hirschfeld, Burt. *Freedom in Jeopardy: The Story of the McCarthy Years.* New York: J. Messner, 1969.

Ranville, Michael. *To Strike at a King: The Turning Point in the McCarthy Witch Hunts.* Troy, MI: Momentum Books, 1997.

Sherrow, Victoria. *Joseph McCarthy and the Cold War.* Woodbridge, CT: Blackbirch Press, 1999.

Shogan, Robert. *No Sense of Decency: The Army-McCarthy Hearings.* Chicaog: Ivan R. Dee, 2009.

Blacklisting

During the 1930s, when the United States was economically crippled by the **Great Depression** (1929–41; see entry under 1930s—The Way We Lived in volume 2), some Americans came to believe that the capitalist system (where production and distribution of goods and services are owned by private groups or individuals) had failed. A few who were looking for economic alternatives joined the American Communist Party. Others simply were liberals and humanists; they were concerned about the future of their country and disturbed by the suffering of their fellow citizens. After World War II (1939–45), and at the beginning of the subsequent **Cold War** (1945–91; see entry under 1940s—The Way We Lived in volume 3), which pitted the United States against the Soviet Union, the House Un-American Activities Committee (HUAC), a subcommittee of the U.S. House of Representatives, began investigating alleged influence by communists (who support the control of an economic system by a single government) in the motion picture industry. The result was the **Hollywood** (see entry under 1930s—Film and Theater in volume 2) blacklist.

HUAC eventually called scores of witnesses to testify at its hearings, including motion picture directors, producers, actors, and screenwriters. First, these people were asked if they were then or had ever been members of the Communist Party. They were expected to answer in the positive and express remorse for what HUAC considered to be their immaturity and stupidity. Then, they were to further cleanse and humiliate themselves by "naming names" of other guilty parties. If these witnesses refused to comply in any way with HUAC, they were blacklisted, which meant that they were removed from the payrolls of the Hollywood studios and made unable to find employment in the American motion picture industry.

The first witnesses called before HUAC, in the fall of 1947, were a group of writers, producers, and directors who came to be known as the "Hollywood Ten." They collectively refused to respond to the "Are you now or have you ever been …" question on the grounds that, in the United States, one's political or religious affiliations—whether left, right, or middle-of-the-road—are supposed to be one's own personal affair. Nonetheless, all were cited for contempt of Congress. Not only were they blacklisted, but they received year-long jail sentences and $1,000 fines.

The actual blacklist—a real list of those people who were considered politically dangerous and thus unemployable—was put together by Aware, a self-appointed guardian organization, and published by the American Legion. Present and former Communists were not the lone blacklistees. Individuals with left-of-center politics, who supported such liberal causes as the Loyalist faction of the Spanish Civil War (1936–39), also were victimized. In the wake of the blacklist, careers were altered if not altogether ruined. Directors Joseph Losey (1909–1984) and Jules Dassin (1911–2008) were among those who fled to Europe to continue their careers. Dozens of screenwriters managed to keep working, but in some cases un-blacklisted colleagues agreed to be listed as the authors of their screenplays. Writers also worked under pseudonyms (false names) and were paid a fraction of their prior salaries. "Robert Rich," winner of the Academy Award for Writing (Motion Picture Story) for *The Brave One* (1956), was actually the blacklisted Hollywood Ten screenwriter Dalton Trumbo (1905–1976). Abraham Polonsky (1910–1999) was one of dozens of directors and screenwriters whose then-promising careers were sidetracked by the blacklist. Scores of actors, including former Academy Award winners Gale Sondergaard (1899–1985) and Ann Revere (1903–1990), found themselves unemployed, their careers ruined.

Furthermore, in the wake of the blacklist, friendships were ended and lives were destroyed. The blacklist may have died out in the late 1950s and early 1960s, but the horrors of the period, in which friends ratted out friends and no one was above suspicion, were not soon forgotten.

Esteemed director Elia Kazan (1909–2003) chose to name names when called before HUAC. He claimed that he had done so to expose the evils of communism, while his detractors alleged that he just wished to save his career. Decades later, Kazan remained unforgiven—and unrepentant—in the eyes of his critics, who, in the late 1990s, loudly complained when the Academy of Motion Picture Arts and Sciences chose to honor the filmmaker with a special Oscar. Finally, the tragic deaths of such actors as John Garfield (1913–1952), Mady Christians (1900–1951), J. Edward Bromberg (1903–1951), Canada Lee (1907–1952), and Philip Loeb (1894–1955) may be directly linked to their troubles with HUAC.

Rob Edelman

For More Information

Bernstein, Walter. *Inside Out: A Memoir of the Blacklist.* New York: Alfred A. Knopf, 1996.

Buhle, Paul, and Dave Wagner. *Blacklisted: The Film Lover's Guide to the Hollywood Blacklist.* New York: Palgrave Macmillan, 2003.

Ceplair, Larry, and Steven Englund. *The Inquisition in Hollywood: Politics in the Film Community 1930–1960.* Garden City, NY: Anchor Press/Doubleday, 1980.

Freedland, Michael. *Hollywood on Trial: McCarthyism in Hollywood.* London: Robson, 2007.

The Front (film). Columbia Pictures, 1976.

McGilligan, Patrick, and Paul Buhle. *Tender Comrades: A Backstory of the Blacklist.* New York: St. Martin's Press, 1997.

Navasky, Victor. *Naming Names.* New York: Viking Press, 1980.

Schickel, Richard. "An Oscar for Elia." *Time* (March 8, 1999): pp. 72–74.

Diets

Though weight-loss diets may seem an essential part of American culture, they are a relatively new fad, which only attained widespread popularity during the 1950s. Although many see dieting as a path to greater health and beauty, others claim that weight-loss diets not only do not work, but that they can actually cause weight gain and health problems. Other critics state that women, who are by far the majority of dieters, are often distracted from more positive pursuits by the national focus on thinness.

Thinness has not always been the ideal of beauty or health. In earlier centuries, diets prescribed by doctors were most likely designed to help women gain weight, as thinness was seen as unhealthy and unattractive. It was only in the 1920s, with the arrival of the **flapper** (see entry under 1920s—Fashion in volume 2) style, that slimness began to symbolize lively, energetic youthfulness. Women began to try to lose weight, some going so far as to swallow tapeworms to speed up the process. Even then, only women of the upper classes dieted. During the 1950s, as women were being encouraged to abandon the jobs they had taken over during World War II (1939–45), mass media began to focus on female fashion and beauty, and the modern diet craze began in earnest.

Thousands of magazine articles and books were published, each offering its own "fool-proof" diet. Doctors prescribed amphetamines, a dangerous drug sometimes called "speed," which helped their patients stop eating, but which also increased nervousness, sleeplessness, and depression. Women, and some men, went to psychiatrists, support groups, and hypnotists to lose weight. Fashion models, popular culture's representation of beauty, became dramatically thin, beginning with Twiggy (1949–) in the 1960s and evolving into the "waif" look of **supermodels** (see entry under 1980s—Fashion in volume 5) like Kate Moss (1974–) in the 1990s.

Over the next several decades, Americans' obsession with dieting and thinness increased, and more and more extreme methods were introduced for achieving that thinness. Doctors not only prescribe diets, but also perform various weight-loss surgeries. Eating disorders like anorexia nervosa, where people, often teenage girls, starve themselves, or bulimia (eating large amounts of food, then vomiting or using laxatives to get rid of the food), were once rare, but are now common. The 2002 *Books in Print* catalog lists 1,412 books about diets and dieting and 483 books about eating disorders. Weight loss has become a profitable industry, worth nearly $60 billion a year in 2010.

Some voices have risen to protest this national preoccupation with weight loss. Some overweight people, who feel victimized by the diet industry, have formed a "fat-positive" movement to promote acceptance of different body sizes. **Television** (see entry under 1940s—TV and Radio in volume 3) movies and talk shows have drawn attention to the dangers of anorexia and bulimia. An annual International No-Diet Day occurs each March to highlight the negative side of dieting.

Tina Gianoulis

For More Information

Atrens, Dale. *Don't Diet.* New York: Morrow, 1988.

Chernin, Kim. *The Obsession: Reflections on the Tyranny of Slenderness.* New York: Harper and Row, 1981.

Freedman, Marjorie R. "What Is Really Known about Popular Diets?" *Consumers' Research Magazine* (Vol. 84, iss. 2, February 2001): pp. 24–28.

Hamilton, Cathy. *Dieting and Other Weighty Issues.* Kansas City, MO: Andrews McMeel, 2001.

Kirby, Jane. *Dieting for Dummies.* 2nd ed. New York: Wiley, 2004.

Highway System

As the twentieth century wore on, the automobile increasingly became a critical component of the American way of life. A car allows an individual

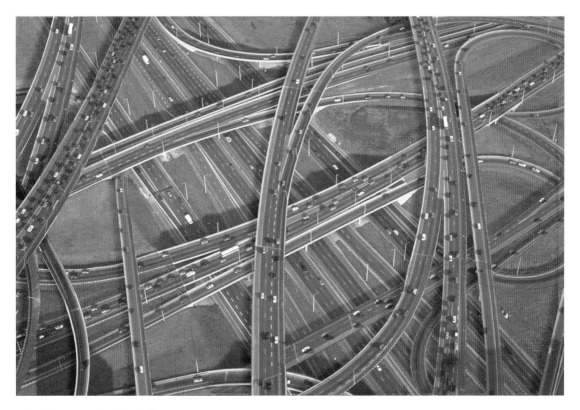

A bird's-eye view of modern highways converging. © OLIVIER MACKAY/CORBIS.

the freedom to travel not just around town but across the country. People often drive from east to west or south to north not only out of necessity—to transport goods, or to move one's belongings and resettle in another section of the country—but also for pleasure and curiosity. America's growing appetite for "hitting the road" parallels the development of the highway system: a series of asphalt and concrete roadways that eventually linked every area of the continental United States.

The construction of America's highway system was a gradual process. The Lincoln Highway, the nation's first coast-to-coast roadway, was completed back in 1915. It linked New York City and San Francisco, California, and came to be known as "America's Main Street." Over the years, other, more local routes were constructed. Among them: the Pennsylvania Turnpike, a four-lane thoroughfare that opened in 1940 and was a predecessor of the interstate highway system.

By the mid-1950s, when automobile manufacturers in Detroit, Michigan, sold 7.92 million cars in one year and 70 percent of all

American families owned a car, the road system connecting the nation remained inadequate. With the exception of toll roads in the East, there were no four-lane highways. Expressways existed only in major cities. Most states were connected only by smaller roads, whose size necessitated lower speed limits (and, thus, longer travel times). These roads often featured sharp curves and steep grades and were ill equipped to handle the demands of increased traffic. Furthermore, during the 1950s, the threat of a nuclear war with the Soviet Union hung over America like a storm cloud. A national highway system would speed military movement or evacuation in the event of a nuclear attack.

In response to this transportation dilemma, President Dwight Eisenhower (1890–1969) authorized construction of a forty-three-thousand-mile-long interstate highway system. It was no easy proposition. Among the obstacles were disputes between federal and state authorities involving the funding of construction; the cost of acquiring land in urban areas; and the decision over whether highways should be built around cities or directly through them.

Nonetheless, the highways were eventually constructed. They made cross-country travel faster and safer; one now could drive coast-to-coast in less than a week. Even more tellingly, they had an enduring and multifaceted impact on American life. The roadside towns that once were travel way-stations no longer could depend upon travelers to eat in their diners, sleep in their motels, and spur their economies. Entire urban neighborhoods ceased to exist, as they were covered over by city freeways. Commuting became quicker. The highway system helped stimulate the mass middle-class flight from the cities, and the development of the **suburbs** (see entry under 1950s—The Way We Lived in volume 3). Its impact is still being felt well into the twenty-first century.

Rob Edelman

For More Information

Karnes, Thomas L. *Asphalt and Politics: a History of the American Highway System.* Jefferson, NC: McFarland, 2009.

Murphy, John. *The Eisenhower Interstate System.* New York: Chelsea House, 2009.

Patton, Phil. *Open Road: A Celebration of the American Highway.* New York: Simon & Schuster, 1986.

Spangenburg, Ray, and Diane K. Moser. *The Story of America's Roads.* New York: Facts on File, 1992.

Swift, Earl. *The Big Roads: The Untold Story of the Engineers, Visionaries, and Trailblazers Who Created the American Superhighways.* Boston: Houghton Mifflin Harcourt, 2011.

Whitman, Sylvia. *Get Up and Go: The History of American Road Travel.* Minneapolis: Lerner, 1996.

Hula Hoop

In the late 1950s, children found much delight in playing with hula hoops. The hoops—lightweight, hollow, brightly colored circular bands that were 4 feet in diameter—were a simple yet clever creation. The object was to spin one around your waist and then wiggle and reel your hips in an attempt to prevent it from falling to the ground.

The origin of the hula hoop dates to ancient Egypt, Greece, and Rome. It also was popular with children and adults in England during the fourteenth century. Back then, the hoops were made of wood, vines, or grasses. The word "hula" became linked to the toy in the early nineteenth century, when British sailors traveled to the Hawaiian Islands and noticed the similarity between hooping and the rhythmic movements of the hips in hula dancing.

Modern-era hula hoops were manufactured and marketed by Wham-O, a toy company. They were made out of a tough, heat-resistant plastic called Marlex. These hoops were introduced in California in 1958. Their price: $1.98. Kids immediately saw the fun in moving like a hula dancer. The toy's popularity quickly spread first across the United States and then to Europe, Japan, and the Middle East. During the first six months of production, Americans bought twenty million hula hoops. By the end of 1958, about one hundred million had been sold worldwide. At the height of the hula hoop craze, Wham-O produced twenty thousand hoops a day. Contests were held to see who could spin a hoop for the longest time and how many hoops could be twirled at the same time. The mass-popularity of hula hoops was short-lived; by the end of 1958, the fad began dying out. However, hula hoops still are produced into the early twenty-first century.

Lori Lynn Lomeli (1958–) began entering hula hoop tournaments as a child. In 1973, she emerged as the World Hula Hoop Champion. She has been cited in the Guinness Book of World Records for spinning

fifteen hoops around various parts of her body at the same time, and for spinning eighty-two hoops, all at once, for three complete turns.

Rob Edelman

For More Information

Asakawa, Gil, and Leland Rucker. *The Toy Book*. New York: Knopf, 1992.

"Hula Hoop." *The Great Idea Finder.* http://www.ideafinder.com/history/inventions/hulahoop.htm (accessed July 29, 2011).

Wulffson, Don L. *The Kid Who Invented the Popsicle: And Other Surprising Stories about Inventions*. New York: Dutton, 1999.

The Pill

Of all the medical advances of the twentieth century, the birth control pill has probably had the most influence on American culture. Until the 1960s, many young women found themselves looking after children when what they really wanted was a career outside the home. By enabling them to choose the number and the timing of their children, the Pill—as it was popularly known—gave women the chance to take control of their lives. In the 1960s, the Pill was partly responsible for what became known as the **sexual revolution** (see entry under 1960s—The Way We Lived in volume 4). Before **AIDS** (see entry under 1980s—The Way We Lived in volume 5) came along, the Pill allowed women and men to be sexually active with only a small risk of unwanted pregnancy.

Social activist Margaret Sanger (1879–1966) argued for better birth control methods in the late nineteenth century. The sixth of eleven children, she blamed her mother's early death on the number of pregnancies she went through. In 1950, when she was over eighty years old, Sanger helped raise money for research on a birth control pill. The technology that made it possible was developed by Carl Djerassi (1923–) in 1951. Early versions of the Pill proved highly dangerous. Blood clots killed many women and left others disabled. Containing 300 micrograms of the hormone estrogen, early birth-control pills were almost ten times as strong as the Pill prescribed in the early 2000s. Although some women do still experience side effects, today's Pill is among the safest of all prescribed drugs. There is even some evidence that it improves bone strength and prevents acne, and helps reduce the risk of certain cancers and rheumatoid arthritis.

At first, feminists saw the Pill as a weapon in the fight for equal rights for women. When men began to assume women would be "on the Pill" and therefore sexually available, feminists turned against it. Some critics hold the Pill responsible for an increase in **sexually transmitted diseases** (see entry under 1970s—The Way We Lived in volume 4) and for destroying family life. Because it is not totally effective, the Pill has been blamed for increasing the number of abortions. Despite religious and ethical concerns, it is estimated that over 80 percent of women in developed countries will take the Pill at some time in their lives.

Chris Routledge

For More Information

Asbell, Bernard. *The Pill: A Biography of the Drug That Changed the World.* New York: Random House, 1996.

Juhn, Greg. *Understanding the Pill: A Consumer's Guide to Oral Contraceptives.* New York: Haworth, 1994.

Marks, Lara. *Sexual Chemistry: A History of the Contraceptive Pill.* New Haven, CT: Yale University Press, 2001.

May, Elaine Tyler. *America and the Pill: A History of Promise, Peril, and Liberation.* New York: Basic Books, 2010.

Satellites

When the Soviet Union launched the first spacecraft in October 1957, it proved that a man-made object could survive in space. The faint, crackling beeps received from the satellite, named *Sputnik,* were used to track it from Earth as it made its solitary orbits. *Sputnik* lasted just ninety-two days before it fell back to Earth and burned up. But the fact that signals could be received from outside Earth's atmosphere marked the beginning of a new age of communications. Within twenty years, satellites would become a billion-dollar link in a global communications chain.

Although it made history by being the first device of its kind, *Sputnik* was a crude machine. Technicians in the United States worked on a more complex satellite that would transform the communications industry. *Telstar,* as their creation was known, was launched into a 3,000-mile-high orbit on July 10, 1962. On July 11, American **television** (see entry under 1940s—TV and Radio in volume 3) viewers had the dubious pleasure of watching French entertainer Yves Montand (1921–1991) singing "La Chansonette," broadcast live from France. *Telstar*'s main disadvantage was that it could only be used as it passed through a certain part of the sky over the Atlantic Ocean. Thus, *Telstar* could relay signals for only 102 minutes in every day. In 1963, *Sycom II* became the first "geosyncronous" satellite, meaning it held a fixed position above a point on the Earth's surface—in this case, 22,235 miles away. This heralded the opening of permanent communication links around the globe.

In 1962, **AT&T** (see entry under 1910s—Commerce in volume 1) ran an **advertising** (see entry under 1920s—Commerce in volume 2) campaign that ensured *Telstar*'s fame for decades to come. Yet satellites are so much a part of everyday life in the twenty-first century that they are almost forgotten. Silently working miles above the Earth, spy satellites gather military information and monitor the decommissioning of nuclear weapons. Weather satellites make long-term weather forecasts more reliable, while TV signals travel around the globe. Hand-held global positioning devices benefit travelers from arctic explorers to car drivers lost in an unfamiliar part of town. Because of satellites, the cost of transatlantic telephone calls has dropped from over ten dollars per minute in 1965 to just a few cents in the early 2000s. Today, the miracle of *Telstar*'s first transatlantic broadcast seems as commonplace as talking to a neighbor across the garden fence.

Chris Routledge

For More Information

Bunch, Bryan H., and Clint Hatchett. *Satellites and Probes.* Danbury, CT: Grolier Educational, 1998.

Gavaghan, Helen. *Something New Under the Sun: Satellites and the Beginning of the Space Age.* New York: Copernicus, 1998.

Herda, D. J. *Communication Satellites.* New York: F. Watts, 1988.

Miller, Ron. *Satellites.* Minneapolis: Twenty-First Century Books, 2007.

Whalen, David. "Communications Satellites: Making the Global Village Possible." *NASA Headquarters.* http://www.hq.nasa.gov/office/pao/History/satcomhistory.html (accessed July 29, 2011).

Suburbs

The development of suburbs—residential communities on the outskirts of cities—was one of the most dominant features of American life in the twentieth century. Far from being merely a way Americans organized their housing and changed their landscape, the suburbs created an entirely new way of ordering American social life and culture. The result was a phenomenon known as "suburbia," a term meaning both a physical place and often a cultural and social mind-set as well.

As a physical place, suburbs first appeared in the nineteenth century as a way for wealthier Americans to move out of crowded, dirty, and often dangerous cities into the calm and quiet of the country. Because most of these Americans still worked in cities, however, they had to stay somewhat close to the *urban* center, thus these new areas were called sub*urbs.* As suburbs developed in the early twentieth century, many cities ran railroad lines out to these new areas, and they became what historian Sam Bass Warner Jr. (1928–) called "streetcar suburbs." Wherever the train lines went, suburban development intensified. These streetcar suburbs can still be seen in places like Brookline, Massachusetts, a one-time suburb of Boston that is now part of the larger metropolitan area in look and feel. This process of suburbanization took place in cities across the country, and in the 1920s, the process intensified as automobiles became more widely used. With the car, people were no longer dependent on railway lines. Now they could live in suburban developments anywhere and drive their cars to work in the cities. Housing developers like J. C. Nichols (1880–1950) in Kansas City, Missouri, took advantage of this trend and built carefully planned housing subdivisions that also included a prototype of what would become shopping **malls** (see entry under 1950s—Commerce in volume 3).

Nichols's subdivisions were meant for the well-to-do. But after World War II (1939–45), suburban living became more accessible to Americans of more modest incomes. That development was largely the work of Long Island, New York, developer William J. Levitt (1907–1994). Levitt pioneered the idea of making small houses affordable to everyone in order to sell more of them. Using mass-production techniques, Levitt kept his costs down by building largely identical houses close together on an old potato field starting in 1946. He called the housing development **Levittown** (see entry under 1940s—The Way We Lived in volume 3). Soldiers just back from the war could purchase a house for as little as $0 down and $53 a month. At prices like these, Levittown became a big hit. Now almost everyone could afford a suburban house, and Levitt set a trend in suburban development that had not slowed down by the end of the twentieth century.

The reasons for the suburbs' success went far beyond affordability, because suburbia represented an idea as much as it did a place. Americans have long had a love/hate relationship with cities, and American culture has long celebrated what is called the "agrarian ideal," an idea that the United States was a nation of farmers known for their simplicity, work ethic, and honesty. The key to keeping up those traits was land. As long as Americans could keep spreading out, the agrarian ideal could be preserved. While few Americans refer to that idea by name, the belief in that idea can be seen throughout the suburbs, where each homeowner does his or her part to care for their lawn, their part of the great mythic garden that is America. The suburban home was also celebrated as an ideal place to raise a family, an idea promoted in many television shows and motion pictures, notably the TV show *Leave It to Beaver* (see entry under 1950s—TV and Radio in volume 3) in the 1950s. As a safe haven from all that was wrong with cities and the world, suburbia became a very powerful idea with immense popularity.

This ideal, however, was not without its problems. As suburbia developed rapidly after 1945, some observers criticized what they viewed as the uniformity and, often, the stifling social conformity of suburbia with its identical homes and rigid social roles that kept women, in particular, in a state of isolation. While that experience was not true for everyone, there was evidence to suggest that the critics were on to something. Another problem involved the racial makeup of suburbs. Through legal and social means, African Americans were largely kept out of suburbs. The dark side of suburbia came in part from the fact that white Americans were fleeing the largely minority-populated inner-city areas in greater and greater numbers, leaving the minority residents in increasingly impoverished urban centers. In addition to these problems, by the 1990s the environmental costs of the suburbs were beginning to be recognized, and these problems were all related to something known as "sprawl." As suburbs sprawled over the landscape, environmental problems followed in their wake: traffic jams, air pollution, waste of water resources as everyone watered their lawns, energy over-consumption, environmental pollution by lawn chemicals, and the destruction of farm land and other open natural space. Although these problems were beginning to be addressed, they were growing, not shrinking, in the late twentieth and early twenty-first century. As solutions were being sought to transform thesea areas by the early 2000s, the suburbs continued to be popular, an enduring testament to the continued belief in the American agrarian ideal as expressed in suburbia.

Timothy Berg

For More Information

Baxandall, Rosalyn Fraad, and Elizabeth Ewen. *Picture Windows: How the Suburbs Happened.* New York: Basic Books, 2001.

Gans, Herbert. *The Levittowners.* New York: Pantheon, 1967.

Garreau, Joel. *Edge City: Life on the New Frontier.* New York: Doubleday, 1991.

Jackson, Kenneth T. *Crabgrass Frontier: The Suburbanization of the United States.* New York: Oxford University Press, 1985.

Jenkins, Virginia Scott. *The Lawn: A History of an American Obsession.* Washington, DC: Smithsonian Institution Press, 1994.

Palen, J. John. *The Suburbs.* New York: McGraw-Hill, 1995.

Teaford, Jon C. *City and Suburb: The Political Fragmentation of Metropolitan America, 1850–1970.* Baltimore: Johns Hopkins University Press, 1979.

Walsh, Tom. "Recycling the Suburbs." *Time.* http://www.time.com/time/specials/packages/article/0,28804,1884779_1884782_1884756,00.html (accessed July 29, 2011).

Where to Learn More

The following list of resources focuses on material appropriate for middle school or high school students. Please note that the Web site addresses were verified prior to publication, but are subject to change.

Books

America A to Z: People, Places, Customs and Culture. Pleasantville, NY: Reader's Digest Association, 1997.

Beetz, Kirk H., ed. *Beacham's Encyclopedia of Popular Fiction.* Osprey, FL: Beacham, 1996.

Berke, Sally. *When TV Began: The First TV Shows.* New York: CPI, 1978.

Blum, Daniel; enlarged by John Willis. *A Pictorial History of the American Theatre, 1860–1985.* 6th ed. New York: Crown, 1986.

Brinkley, Douglas. *The Great Deluge: Hurricane Katrina, New Orleans, and the Mississippi Gulf Coast.* New York: Morrow, 2006.

Brooks, Tim, and Earle Marsh. *The Complete Directory to Prime Time Network and Cable TV Shows, 1946–present.* 9th ed. New York: Ballantine, 2007.

Cashmore, Ellis. *Sports Culture: An A to Z Guide.* New York: Routledge, 2000.

Condon, Judith. *The Nineties (Look at Life In).* Austin, TX: Raintree Steck-Vaughn, 2000.

Craddock, Jim. *VideoHound's Golden Movie Retriever.* Rev. ed. Detroit: Gale, 2011.

Daniel, Clifton, ed. *Chronicle of the Twentieth Century.* Liberty, MO: JL International Pub., 1994.

Dunning, John. *On the Air: The Encyclopedia of Old-Time Radio.* New York: Oxford University Press, 1998.

Dunning, John. *Tune in Yesterday: The Ultimate Encyclopedia of Old-Time Radio 1925–1976.* New York: Oxford University Press, 1998.

Ehrenreich, Barbara. *Nickel and Dimed: On (Not) Getting By in America.* New York: Metropolitan Books, 2001.

Epstein, Dan. *20th Century Pop Culture.* Philadelphia: Chelsea House, 2000.

Finkelstein, Norman H. *Sounds of the Air: The Golden Age of Radio.* New York: Charles Scribner's, 1993.

Flowers, Sarah. *Sports in America.* San Diego: Lucent, 1996.

Friedman, Thomas L. *Hot, Flat, and Crowded: Why We Need a Green Revolution—and How It Can Renew America.* New York: Picador, 2009.

Gilbert, Adrian. *The Eighties (Look at Life In).* Austin, TX: Raintree Steck-Vaughn, 2000.

Godin, Seth. *The Encyclopedia of Fictional People: The Most Important Characters of the 20th Century.* New York: Boulevard Books, 1996.

Gore, Al. *An Inconvenient Truth.* Emmaus, PA: Rodale Press, 2006.

Grant, R. G. *The Seventies (Look at Life In).* Austin, TX: Raintree Steck-Vaughn, 2000.

Grant, R. G. *The Sixties (Look at Life In).* Austin, TX: Raintree Steck-Vaughn, 2000.

Green, Joey. *Joey Green's Encyclopedia of Offbeat Uses for Brand-Name Products.* New York: Hyperion, 1998.

Green, Stanley. *Encyclopedia of the Musical Theatre.* New York: Da Capo Press, 1976.

Hischak, Thomas S. *Film It with Music: An Encyclopedic Guide to the American Movie Musical.* Westport, CT: Greenwood Press, 2001.

Katz, Ephraim. *The Film Encyclopedia.* 6th ed. New York: Collins, 2008.

Kirkpatrick, David. *The Facebook Effect: The Inside Story of the Company That Is Connecting the World.* New York: Simon & Schuster, 2011.

Lackmann, Ron. *The Encyclopedia of American Radio: An A–Z Guide to Radio from Jack Benny to Howard Stern.* New York: Facts on File, 2000.

Lebrecht, Norman. *The Companion to 20th-Century Music.* New York: Simon & Schuster, 1992.

Levitt, Steven D., and Stephen Dubner. *Freakonomics: A Rogue Economist Explores the Hidden Side of Everything.* Rev. ed. New York: Harper, 2009.

Lissauer, Robert. *Lissauer's Encyclopedia of Popular Music in America: 1888 to the Present.* New York: Facts on File, 1996.

Lowe, Denise. *Women and American Television: An Encyclopedia.* ABC-CLIO: Santa Barbara, CA, 1999.

Maltin, Leonard, ed. *Leonard Maltin's Movie Encyclopedia.* New York: Dutton, 1994.

Martin, Frank K. *A Decade of Delusions: From Speculative Contagion to the Great Recession.* Hoboken, NJ: Wiley, 2011.

McNeil, Alex. *Total Television: The Comprehensive Guide to Programming from 1948 to the Present.* 4th ed. New York: Penguin, 1996.

National Commission on Terrorist Attacks. *The 9/11 Commission Report: Final Report of the National Commission on Terrorist Attacks Upon the United States.* New York: Norton, 2004.

Newcomb, Horace, ed. *Encyclopedia of Television.* 2nd ed. Chicago: Fitzroy Dearborn, 2004.

Packer, George. *The Assassins' Gate: America in Iraq.* New York: Farrar, Straus, and Giroux, 2005.

Rosen, Roger, and Patra McSharry Sevastiades, eds. *Coca-Cola Culture: Icons of Pop.* New York: Rosen, 1993.

Schlosser, Eric. *Fast Food Nation.* New York: Houghton Mifflin, 2001.

Schwartz, Herman M. *Subprime Nation: American Power, Global Capital, and the Housing Bubble.* Ithaca, NY: Cornell University Press, 2009.

Schwartz, Richard A. *Cold War Culture: Media and the Arts, 1945–1990.* New York: Facts on File, 1997.

Sennett, Richard. *The Culture of the New Capitalism.* New Haven, CT: Yale University Press, 2007.

Sies, Luther F. *Encyclopedia of American Radio, 1920–1960.* 2nd ed. Jefferson, NC: McFarland, 2008.

Slide, Anthony. *Early American Cinema.* Rev. ed. Metuchen, NJ: Scarecrow Press, 1994.

Tibbetts, John C., and James M. Welsh. *The Encyclopedia of Novels into Film.* 2nd ed. New York: Facts on File, 2005.

Tibbetts, John C., and James M. Welsh. *The Encyclopedia of Stage Plays into Film.* New York: Facts on File, 2001.

Vise, David A. *The Google Story.* Updated ed. New York: Delacorte Press, 2008.

Weisman, Alan. *The World Without Us.* New York: St. Martin's Press, 2007.

Wilson, Charles Reagan, James G. Thomas Jr., and Ann J. Abadie, eds. *The New Encyclopedia of Southern Culture.* Chapel Hill: University of North Carolina Press, 2006.

Woodward, Bob. *Bush at War.* New York: Simon & Schuster, 2002.

Web Sites

Bumpus, Jessica. "The Noughties' Fashion Highlights." *Vogue* (December 22, 2010). http://www.vogue.co.uk/spy/celebrity-photos/2010/12/22/the-noughties (accessed September 23, 2011.)

Markowitz, Robin. *Cultural Studies Central.* http://www.culturalstudies.net/ (accessed August 7, 2011).

"The Noughties: Year by Year." *The Sunday Times,* October 20, 2009. http://women.timesonline.co.uk/tol/life_and_style/women/the_way_we_live/article6881549.ece (accessed September 23, 2011).

"100 Songs That Defined the Noughties." The *Telegraph,* September 18, 2009. http://www.telegraph.co.uk/culture/music/rockandpopfeatures/6198897/100-songs-that-defined-the-Noughties.html (accessed September 23, 2011).

"Pictures of the Decade." *Reuters.* http://www.reuters.com/news/pictures/slideshow?articleId=USRTXRYG2#a=1 (accessed September 23, 2011.)

"A Portrait of the Decade." *BBC News,* December 14, 2009. http://news.bbc.co.uk/2/hi/8409040.stm (accessed September 23, 2011).

Washington State University, American Studies. *Popular Culture: Resources for Critical Analysis.* http://www.wsu.edu/%7Eamerstu/pop/tvrguide.html (accessed August 7, 2011).

Yesterdayland. http://www.yesterdayland.com/ (accessed August 7, 2011).

Zupko, Sarah. *Popcultures.com: Sarah Zupko's Cultural Studies Center.* http://www.popcultures.com/ (accessed August 7, 2011).

Index

Italic type indicates volume number; **boldface** indicates main entries; (ill.) indicates illustrations.

E

Q

R

U

W

X

Y